Gabriele Klein
Pina Bausch's Dance Theater

Critical Dance Studies
Edited by Gabriele Brandstetter and Gabriele Klein | VOLUME 56

Gabriele Klein

Pina Bausch's Dance Theater

Company, Artistic Practices
and Reception

Bibliographic information published by the Deutsche Nationalbibliothek — the Deutsche Nationalbibliothek lists this publication
in the Deutsche Nationalbibliografie; detailed bibliographic data
are available on the Internet at http://dnb.d-nb.de

© 2020 Gabriele Klein

All rights reserved. No part of this book may be reprinted or reproduced or utilized in any form or by any electronic, mechanical,
or other means, now known or hereafter invented, including photo-
copying and recording, or in any information storage or retrieval
system, without permission in writing from the publisher.

COVER DESIGN, LAYOUT AND TYPESETTING Büro Brüggmann
TRANSLATION Elena Polzer
COPY EDITING Lydia J. White
PRINTED BY sieprath GmbH, Aachen
PRINT ISBN 978-3-8376-5055-6
PDF ISBN 978-3-8394-5055-0
https://doi.org/10.14361/9783839450550

Contents

8 Introduction
"PINA": Pioneer, icon, myth, brand · Pina Bausch and the Tanztheater Wuppertal: The dance productions · My research process · The praxeology of translation: A new approach to dance theory · Architecture of this book · Gratitude

20 Pieces
26 ARTISTIC PHASES · 26 1967-1973: Democratic awakening and aesthetic upheaval · 39 1973-1979: Development of a new concept for choreography and stage · 51 1980-1986: Internationalization and stabilization of aesthetic language · 61 1986-2000: Intercultural artistic production and the rediscovery of dance · 73 2001-2009: The love of dance and nature

86 Company
91 Translating hunches: Artistic collaboration · 92 The choreographer: Pina Bausch · 104 The costume and stage designer: Rolf Borzik · 112 The costume designer: Marion Cito · 121 The set designer: Peter Pabst · 137 The musical collaborators: Matthias Burkert and Andreas Eisenschneider · 145 The dancers: Translating experience · 146 How Pina Bausch saw her dancers · 152 How the dancers remember working together · 159 A chosen family – "We are the piece"

164 Work Process
170 Developing pieces · 184 Research trips – artistic research · 197 Artistic practices of (un)certainty · 202 Choreographic development as translation · 205 Passing on choreographies · 212 Practices of passing on · 226 Between identity and difference · 229 Practices of learning: *The Rite of Spring* · 234 Passing on and inheriting

240 Solo Dance
245 Body/dance – writing/text: Positions in dance studies · 248 Translation manual: Feldpartitur · 254 Anne Martin in *Viktor* · 260 Beatrice Libonati in *Masurca Fogo* · 265 Dominique Mercy in *"...como el musguito en la piedra, ay si, si, si..."* · 272 Translating dance into writing: Methodological reflections

278 Reception 282 DANCE CRITICISM · 288 The practice of dance criticism · 292 The Tanztheater Wuppertal and dance criticism · 302 Translating between performance, perception and text • 304 THE AUDIENCE · 309 Investigating audience perception: Methodological approaches · 314 Audience routines · 318 Expectations and knowledge · 321 Remembering what has been perceived · 322 Being affected and speaking about being moved · 328 Audience research as a praxeology of translation

330 Theory and Methodology 335 TRANSLATION AS A NEW APPROACH TO DANCE AND ART THEORY: Toward a praxeology of translation · 336 Translation and its beginnings in media and cultural studies and the social sciences · 350 Translation as practice: Praxeological premises • 361 TRANSLATING AS METHODOLOGY: Praxeological production analysis · 364 Translation as a basic methodological principle · 368 Methodological approaches to dance practice · 368 Performance and movement analysis in dance studies · 371 Academic and artistic approaches to practice research · 377 The logics of artistic and academic practice · 379 The scholar as translator: Reflecting upon one's own actions

382 Conclusion Translating (into) the Present: Doing Contemporaneity · What is contemporaneity? · Contemporary art / contemporary dance · A contemporaneity open to the future

398 Indexes 398 Notes · 412 Literature · 430 Images · 434 Chronology of Works

Introduction

"PINA": Pioneer, icon, myth, brand

When Pina Bausch took over as the ballet director of the municipal Wuppertaler Bühnen theater in 1973, she and her company – who would later go on to become world-famous as the Tanztheater Wuppertal Pina Bausch, so the official name – presented things unlike anything anybody had ever seen before: dancers coughing as they danced; dancing in flip-flops, rubber boots and high heels, with fins on their feet and branches on their heads; jumping, writhing and running through water and soil, over carnations and stones; speaking, shrieking, giggling, yawning, sleeping and smoking cigarettes; hitting, flirting with and screaming at each other; frying eggs on an electric iron, making sandwiches for the audience, offering them tea and showing them family photos; wrapping themselves in rugs, lolling around on pillows, jumping into mountains of flowers and climbing up walls. The Tanztheater Wuppertal broke with a multitude of traditions, a departure from the familiar so bold and astonishing that it divided both audiences and critics alike: they were either fascinated and delighted to witness the emergence of something akin to radical change in more than just the aesthetics of dance, or they were shocked and angered, sometimes loudly venting their rage and storming out of the auditorium.

In many countries, the 1970s were a time of great social tension. In West Germany, the student movement or "Generation 68" set out to radically transform the politics, society and culture of silent, conservative, postwar (West) Germany. While Social Democratic Chancellor Willy Brandt's slogan "Dare More Democracy" attempted to stay abreast of these changes, the activities of the far-left militant organization, the Red Army Fraction (RAF), sent shockwaves through the country. What Pina Bausch and her company brought to the Wuppertal stage amidst this troubled political atmosphere was undoubtedly daring. For their art was an aesthetic revolt, fundamentally rattling the paradigms of both theater and dance: there was no narrative dramaturgy, there were no storylines, no scenes, no conventional choreographic rules or work processes, no orthodox dance techniques, no leotards, no classical scenery, no librettos, no preselected or illustrative music.

These radical innovations were part and parcel of more expansive changes taking place throughout the art world – changes that had been breaking fresh ground since the 1960s in dance and theater: the aesthetic radicalism of Merce Cunningham and Judson Dance Theater in the USA, provocative new performance art aesthetics in Europe, the advent of German dance theater (Tanztheater), which emerged at the same time at the Tanzforum Cologne in the late 1960s, and the radical theater of Peter Stein and Peter Zadek. But Pina Bausch's pieces, developed out of the unwavering perspective of a dancer, broke with established theater conventions, previous understandings of dance and customary viewing habits, in what were yet again different ways: never before had anyone so radically questioned the concepts of both dance and theater, and never before had anyone so unconditionally declared the acts of speaking, singing or screaming, simple gestures and everyday habits and emotions, the movements of animals, plants, materials and objects to be dance and, as such, choreographically transformed them. The dance theater of Pina Bausch appeared to push the boundaries of all previous genres, aesthetic categories and perceptions.

Over the course of her more than 35-year long career, Pina Bausch went on to develop 44 choreographies with the Tanztheater Wuppertal. Some were considered masterpieces of the century, such as *The Rite of Spring* from 1975. In the late 1970s, the company began touring worldwide and, to this day – more than ten years after the death of its choreographer – the company is still almost ritually revered in many cities, countries and cultures. Be it in Japan, Brazil, India, Argentina, Chile, France, Italy or Hungary, Pina Bausch is often considered an important precursor to new and contemporary, national and regional developments in dance. But there is more to the extensive reputation of Pina Bausch and the Tanztheater Wuppertal than their pieces, which feature dancers as distinct individuals, and the company's long history of collective collaboration. What has been imitated and modified worldwide is also and in particular the Tanztheater's open and inquisitive method of asking questions, which it has transformed into an innovative artistic work process. Thanks to the international coproductions, which began with *Viktor* in 1986 and would take the company to 15 different coproducing locations in the following 23 years, this method took on intercultural relevance. The company engaged in comprehensive research trips to examine people's everyday lives, their cultures and customs, their habits and rituals, their dance and music. But the pieces also incorporated the magic and beauty of nature: stones, water, earth, plants, trees and animals were all given their own space on the stage – in an age in which ecological destruction and climate change were already noticeably present. The coproductions themselves were pioneering feats in their own right, for these research trips began long before "artistic research" became a hotly contested topic of artistic and academic discourse in the 1990s.

For Pina Bausch, dance was the medium through which to explore human nature – and her dancers provided her with the material she needed. As an anthropologist of dance, she was a translator. She motivated her dancers to discover gestures, bodily practices and everyday rhythms in different cultures, to find and artistically transform the claviature of the human in everyday life. In her pieces, she took this material and set both the similarities and cultural differences fundamental to it in relation to each other. The success of her cultural-anthropological research was also due to the way in which she deliberately selected the members of her company. Coming from up to 20 different nations, all of her dancers contributed different languages, degrees of experience and artistic habitus; they each dealt differently with what they experienced and discovered on their journeys due to their biographical backgrounds. Pina Bausch's pieces, like her rare interviews and speeches, reveal an artist deeply convinced that there is a *conditio humana* inherent to all people, no matter their skin color, gender, age or class. Her work searches for and reveals not that which separates us, but rather what connects us to each other – as well as to nature, plants and other animals.

On June 30, 2009, Pina Bausch died at the age of 68. By this point, she was already a living legend and had been showered with a range of significant awards. Today's 'Pina' reflects many desires: she is a pioneer, an icon, a myth, a brand. More than ten years after her death, young theater and dance audiences mainly know Pina Bausch and her Tanztheater Wuppertal as historical figures, pioneers of the past, as a bygone, already largely forgotten period of 1970s German dance theater. But Tanztheater Wuppertal performances still sell out worldwide. The company has now become one of the few globally touring dance ensembles that larger audiences, even those that are not very familiar with dance, feel that they need to have seen at least once. There is a desire to marvel at the cultural object, the intangible cultural heritage. Even though this seems like musealization, it also means that Pina Bausch's art lives on: there are many artists, not only in dance but also in theater, film and other artistic fields, who have been influenced by her. To this day, we find fragments of her aesthetics either consciously and purposefully or unconsciously and unwittingly referenced in many works of dance and theater. Much of what she invented in her pieces has unwaveringly found its way directly, albeit in distorted or deconstructed form, into the canon of contemporary aesthetics, which means that it is still topical. The aesthetics and some of the typical movements and scenes from Pina Bausch's pieces are now so taken for granted that their origins are often overlooked or forgotten.

With the death of the choreographer, Pina Bausch and her dance theater entered the annals of dance history. But her work still lives on: in restagings, adaptations and variations of past productions, and in acts of 'passing on' roles to younger dancers and pieces to other companies. It lives on in ways that have been much discussed, applauded and disputed in artistic circles, and that must and should be provided with an institutional framework, funding and security.

**Pina Bausch and the Tanztheater Wuppertal:
The dance productions**

There has already been much published in many languages about Pina Bausch and the Tanztheater Wuppertal: interviews, essays and academic, semi-academic and general interest articles, as well as books, photo collections, films and tv documentaries. As in the artistic works dealing with her oeuvre, many of these publications have and are confronted with the problem that access to materials about Pina Bausch and the Tanztheater Wuppertal has hitherto been almost completely blocked, meaning that authors have been unable to reference primary sources and have had to make do with the few existing secondary sources. It is above all due to this difficult situation that the interpretations of Pina Bausch's art first established in the 1970s and 1980s have been constantly reproduced and 'codified' over decades, although the choreographer herself began changing her aesthetic in the 1990s. Not only has discourse on Pina Bausch's art now established itself accordingly across the globe, but this situation has also created a myth about her early years while simultaneously turning the name 'Pina,' formerly only used by her own inner circle, into a global trademark.

This book proposes taking a different, new perspective, shifting the focus away from the choreographer and specific pieces and instead examining the artistic productions of the Tanztheater Wuppertal Pina Bausch. In this book, the term 'production' is defined as the interplay between the work process (the development of a piece, its restagings, the passing on of material), the piece in question and its performances, as well as its reception. This book explores this interplay by focusing on the 15 international coproductions, which it analyzes together for the first time.

My research process

In 1976, when I was still just a high school student, I saw a piece by Pina Bausch in Wuppertal for the very first time. Like many people of my generation who were excited about dance, it affected me deeply.

During the 1980s, dance theater became an important part of the research for my dissertation *FrauenKörperTanz: Eine Zivilisationsgeschichte des Tanzes*,[1] which discussed the relationship between women's history, the history of the body and the history of dance from the perspectives of both cultural theory and social history. During the 2000s, I explored Pina Bausch's *The Rite of Spring* together with Gabriele Brandstetter. We were looking at how to approach the piece and its performance methodologically while specifically focusing on the company's practices of restaging and passing on material over decades.[2] This book picks up where I left off back then. I began working on it in 2011 with a preliminary study, followed by a four-year research grant provided by the German Research Foundation (DFG) from 2013. It was the first externally funded research project to take place in cooperation with the Pina Bausch Foundation. The project was moreover supported by various branches of the Goethe-Institut and other funding programs in the countries where Tanztheater Wuppertal pieces were coproduced.

Thanks to these collaborations, I was able to draw on extraordinary, new and at that point untouched empirical material, such as recordings of performances and the paratexts of the choreographies, which the Pina Bausch Foundation made available to the project from the archives, which had not yet been cataloged at the time. I analyzed visual and written documentation of rehearsals, some of which I generated myself during my own visits and some of which was given to me by Tanztheater Wuppertal dancers. The research project also gave us the opportunity to collect other empirical material such as audience surveys, which the Tanztheater Wuppertal allowed us to conduct for the very first time. Detailed interviews with dancers, with patrons of the company at the various Goethe-Institut offices and with associated artists, collaborators, friends and partners of Pina Bausch worldwide helped us to gain more insight into how the pieces had been created and received in a way that went beyond what was already known and had been described by others before me. In addition, I read thousands of reviews and hundreds of texts, interviews and speeches by and about Pina Bausch and the Tanztheater Wuppertal.

In order to grasp the work process, the Tanztheater Wuppertal's research trips, the performance conditions in each respective city and country, and audience reactions, I undertook several research trips myself, which led me to India, Japan, Brazil, New York, Paris, Budapest, Lisbon and frequently to Wuppertal. In Kolkata, I heard various accounts of why the Tanztheater Wuppertal's first tour of India had failed, while the second one firmly established the myth of Pina Bausch and her company. In Kochi, I stayed at the same hotel that Pina Bausch had visited. I listened to the gentle sounds of the palm trees and began to understand why the India piece *Bamboo Blues* was so gentle and peaceful – for some disconcertingly so – a heterotopia in a country marked by such incomprehensible suffering and misery. In Budapest, the capital city of the *Wiesenland*, Hungary, I visited the flea markets where the dancers had collected all kinds of bric-a-brac during their research trip there and spoke with many artists and companions on the same weekend that Viktor Orban closed Hungary's borders due to the so-called "refugee crisis," initiating a momentous turning point in the history of the European Union. In Brazil, I was astonished to find that – unlike in Germany – there was a young generation of dancers and dance researchers who saw no contradiction between contemporary dance and dance theater. In Japan, I was fascinated by the passionate, empathetic way that young artists and academics spoke about Pina Bausch and her influence on Japan's nascent dance scene. This motivated me to go beyond these singular conversations and interview the audience after a Tokyo performance of *The Rite of Spring*.

In each of the countries that I visited, I had wonderful encounters with people who provided me and my research with a lot of help and support, as did colleagues in various municipal, state and dance archives, in particular the staff of the Tanztheater Wuppertal und the Pina Bausch Foundation. To them all I owe my thanks. They are mentioned in detail further below.

**The praxeology of translation:
A new approach to dance theory**

The theoretical framework of this book is a theory of translation that I developed into a 'praxeology of translation' during the research process. The term 'translation' is not used here in the usual linguistic sense, but is rather defined as a cultural practice in the same vein as in translation studies and postcolonial studies. The basic proposition is that acts of translation are fundamental to artistic work processes and creations. In this book, translation is presented, firstly, as a central artistic practice (in dance) and, secondly, as a fundamental research concept in the field of dance studies. A dance production is thus a permanent, complex process of translation: between speaking and moving, moving and writing, between different languages and cultures, between various media and materials, between knowledge and perception, between company members developing a piece or passing it on, between performance and audience, between piece and dance review, between artistic and academic practice.

This book outlines a praxeology of translation. It does not inquire into what the translation of or in dance is, but rather demonstrates how processes of translation characterize a dance production.

This *how* focuses on the manner of translation, i.e., on its practices. This praxeological perspective is not only new in discourse on the theory of translation in the fields of cultural and social theory but also in the field of dance research. In this book, I illuminate its historical, cultural, media, aesthetic, interactive and physical aspects.

This volume is based on empirical research. From a methodological standpoint, research that focuses not only on the pieces but on the entire dance production – in other words on the interplay between work processes, collaboration, the piece itself, its performance and its reception – cannot merely rely on conventional analytical tools and methods from theater and dance studies such as performance, dance or choreographic analysis. For this reason, during my research, I developed the methodological approach of what I call 'praxeological production analysis,' which forms the methodological basis of the analyses and whose framework and methodological concept will be elucidated toward the end of this book. 'Praxeological production analysis' describes a method that neither exclusively analyzes the performance or specific staging nor concentrates on the audience, as is often the case in sociological art research. Instead, the focus is on the relationality of work process, piece, performance and reception. The suitability of this perspective becomes particularly evident in the case of a company such as the Tanztheater Wuppertal, as several generations of dancers have restaged its pieces over the course of decades and then presented them to different audiences in different countries and cultures. As a method, praxeological production analysis attempts to do this justice by addressing the entanglement between work process, piece, performance and reception, but by grasping them abstractly using the concept of translation. In doing so, praxeological production analysis makes use of different methodological procedures: empirical social research from the fields of cultural anthropology and sociology (ethnography, quantitative and qualitative interview techniques), analytical methods from theater and dance studies (performance and choreographic analysis), methods from media studies (video analysis), content analysis and hermeneutic methods.

This book brings together the extensive body of material[3] that I generated and examined during my research, while pursuing the reciprocal strategy of embedding the material within the framework of a praxeology of translation while in turn attempting to refine and activate this framework using the empirical material. By making use of the theoretical concept of translation, the methodological approach of praxeological production analysis and a comprehensive corpus of material, this book develops a new reading of the art of Pina Bausch and the Tanztheater Wuppertal. By using this prominent example, it seeks to encourage debate in dance research about the theoretical concepts and methodological considerations that arose during my research process. This scholarly approach is one way of gaining a deeper understanding of what is linguistically 'incomprehensible,' of that which defies translation (not only) in the art of Pina Bausch and the Tanztheater Wuppertal.

This experiential research process not only meant mastering mountains of very different kinds of material, it also required me to constantly question my own position as such and in relation to my field of research. It was important to reflect on the roles of proximity and distance, of empathy and criticism, as well as of art and scholarship, specifically: of practices in the artistic and academic fields. The research process spanned many years and produced social relationships that also included friendships. This took a balancing act: on the one hand, my research was only possible due to my expanding curiosity but, on the other hand, it was vital for me to curb my scholarly interest somewhat when it came to the ethical foundations of research, such as data protection and the privacy of dialogue partners. I wanted the contacts that I established to become mutually rewarding relationships for everyone involved.

Alongside these issues of research ethics, I also had to address the different logics of art and academia. Scholarly research – its theoretical and methodological tools and practices, its specific pace, language and media – generally adheres to a different logic than that of artistic work. Again, I faced the fundamental problem of transfer: how can this material be translated into writing? This book is in itself an attempt at translation, at finding a theoretical language for aesthetic practices. That this attempt at translation will have its limitations and will inevitably fail to bridge the gap between aesthetic practice and discourse is a fact embedded within the foundations of translation itself.

Architecture of this book

This book is designed not to be linear, but rather modular. The individual chapters PIECES, COMPANY, WORK PROCESS, SOLO DANCE and RECEPTION each deal with one aspect of a dance production. The chapter THEORY AND METHODOLOGY explains the book's theoretical and methodological principles. The final chapter discusses Pina Bausch's œuvre in terms of its contemporaneity. All chapters conceptually and stylistically reflect the topic and the material that they deal with. They are translated and structured accordingly: to be essayistic, analytical or theoretical.

Instead of adhering to a chronological concept, the chapter PIECES takes the systematic approach of describing and interpreting select pieces. Pina Bausch's pieces are classified into artistic phases.

These artistic phases are then described and characteristic aspects of the artistic work established, going beyond the specific pieces. Finally, these aspects are placed within their respective historical, social and political contexts. This also provides answers to a question rarely posed in research about the Tanztheater Wuppertal: what is the relationship between various phases in Pina Bausch's work and both specific historical events and contemporaneous artistic developments? In other words: are these events and developments translated into the pieces and, if so, in what ways?

The chapter COMPANY focuses on the Tanztheater Wuppertal as a social figuration. It is the first time that biographies of its members have been presented together. It details Pina Bausch's view of her dancers and vice versa, while also inquiring into forms of collaboration, everyday routines, individual perspectives on shared work and the bonds that have tied and held the group together over so many years and decades.

The chapter WORK PROCESS deals with the company's artistic work processes and presents them as practices of translation. They include rehearsals during the development of pieces, especially as they relate to the "research trips" to coproducing cities and countries, and how the pieces and the different roles have been passed on to young dancers at the Tanztheater Wuppertal and to other dance companies.

The translation of body/dance into writing/text is the main topic of the chapter SOLO DANCE. Three select solos, one by Anne Martin in *Viktor* (PREMIERE 1986), one by Beatrice Libonati in *Masurca Fogo* (PREMIERE 1998) and one by Dominique Mercy in "*...como el musguito en la piedra, ay si, si, si...*" (PREMIERE 2009) are presented with the help of the digital notation software Feldpartitur.

The chapter RECEPTION adopts the perspective of viewers and inquires into the relationship between piece, performance, perception and knowledge. It examines the ways in which dance critics have made reference to Pina Bausch's pieces over the years and decades while also looking at what audiences expect of a piece after 40 years of the Tanztheater Wuppertal, how they perceive the performance and put that perception into words.

The chapter THEORY AND METHODOLOGY provides a theoretical and methodological framework. It introduces the main characteristics of a praxeology of translation as well as the methodological fundamentals of praxeological production analysis. It then uses these theoretical and methodological concepts as a backdrop to once more reflect on the previously described translation processes in dance productions.

The final chapter focuses on the temporalities of translation and examines them in relation to the concept of contemporaneity.

It asks whether the pieces of the Tanztheater Wuppertal should only be regarded as performed historical documents, as is the case for some classical ballet pieces, or whether, with their multiple processes of translation and the accompanying entanglements between different temporalities, they are actually an indication of what can be considered contemporary at all.

Gratitude

This book is my attempt to translate the extraordinary work of Pina Bausch and the Tanztheater Wuppertal into words and to grasp it within a scholarly context. Moreover, by processing this extensive corpus of material, it is also my attempt to introduce 'translation' as a central concept to describe artistic creation and performance in globalized and interconnected societies. It was my academic work on a multicultural and multinational, intergenerational and internationally touring, world-famous dance company that gave rise to this concept of translation. The work of Pina Bausch and her company – their rehearsals, the way they develop pieces and performances, their various forms of collaboration and solidarity – have allowed me to demonstrate this understanding of translation.

All her life, Pina Bausch remained convinced that dance cannot be put into words, that it stands for itself and must be experienced and felt. She still held this opinion when conceptual dance began deconstructing previous contemporary dance forms in the 1990s, resulting in growing academic and theoretical discourse about dance. This skepticism, which Pina Bausch probably would have felt in relation to my endeavor to academically translate her work and which some of her companions still share, accompanied me on every page. The reputed paradox between dance and text was already inherent to my doctoral thesis. But while I largely assumed at the time that the text leads to a loss of the aesthetic, I would like to show in this book that there is also something to be gained by translating art into scholarship, the aesthetic into the discursive, dance into text. It can broaden our understanding and the impact of both by allowing for new forms of perception, new perspectives and interpretations – and by provoking art to live on in the process.

During this research, it was a great and crucial desire of mine to work with the artists about whom I am writing. Since I only came into contact with the Pina Bausch Foundation, which was founded and is now run by her son Salomon Bausch, shortly after Pina Bausch's death, I did not have the chance to directly communicate with Pina Bausch herself for this book. Nevertheless, I had the unforgettable opportunity to accompany the reinvention of the Tanztheater Wuppertal during a precarious and fragile, but important phase, and in my many conversations, I experienced the Tanztheater Wuppertal as a special, unparalleled group of artists. This book is therefore not only about Pina Bausch, the legendary choreographer but also very much about the ensemble, its individual members and their translation achievements.

I therefore express my gratitude first and foremost to the company: to the dancers, collaborators, friends and partners who patiently made time for me and with whom I was able to have long, intense, frank and touching conversations. I am grateful to Marion Cito, Peter Pabst, Matthias Burkert und Andreas Eisenschneider for providing me with insights into their own biographies. Raimund Hoghe helped me to better understand the 1980s, when he was a dramaturge at the Tanztheater Wuppertal, while Norbert Servos provided me with a deeper understanding of his interpretation of Pina Bausch's pieces. I thank Robert Sturm and Ursula Popp for their fantastic support and their many tips and insights into various written and visual documents. I am also grateful to the Tanztheater Wuppertal for allowing me to attend rehearsals and for having enough confidence in me to allow me to conduct the first-ever audience surveys in Wuppertal. I wish to thank the Pina Bausch Foundation for our many excellent years of collaboration, a first careful step on the part of the newly created institution toward collaborating with academia. Finally, above all, I wish to thank Salomon Bausch for placing the necessary trust in me.

On my journeys, I came into contact with many people who tended to and supported the company on tour and during its research trips. In this respect, I would like to thank Anna Lakos and Péter Ertl for their generous support in Budapest. Prasanna Ramaswamy, Nandita Palchoudhuri and Alarmel Valli not only enriched my understanding of how dance theater is perceived in India but also gave me a glimpse into the rich world of Indian dance and theater. For that, I thank them sincerely.

The directors and staff of the various Goethe-Institut offices gave me much assistance while I was preparing for and carrying out my research trips and provided me with valuable information. They include Martin Wälde, Heiko Sievers, Raju Raman and Georg Lechner. I would especially like to thank Robin Mallick for his prudent support, his interest and his general company in India and Brazil.

I am very grateful to the German Research Foundation for the generous financial support it provided to this research project. I also wish to thank my research assistants on this project – Stephanie Schroedter, Elisabeth Leopold and Anna Wieczorek – for the many years of great teamwork during our examinations of the paratexts. I would also like to extend my thanks to the members of the Hamburg Research Group "Translation and Framing: Practices of Medial

Transformation" for the innumerable, enriching theoretical discussions. Stephan Brinkmann, a former dancer at the Tanztheater Wuppertal, and Marc Wagenbach, personal assistant to Pina Bausch, also provided me with many supportive insights thanks to their intimate knowledge of the company, and for this, I am deeply grateful.

Elena Polzer accompanied me as translator on this book's journey into English, and Lydia White was our English copy editor. Christian Weller copyedited the original German edition of this book and also played an important role in the development of this English version, while Andreas Brüggmann was responsible for the layout and cover design. Johann Mai helped me with the final proofreading of this book. Hirohiko Soejima provided me with much support during the audience survey in Tokyo. Dance scholar Susan Foster gave me helpful tips and encouraging comments, and I am very grateful for our many supportive, motivating and helpful conversations. I thank them all for their commitment, patience and diligence.

I am indebted to transcript publishing house for its many years of trust and collaboration. I also wish to thank Gero Wierichs for his excellent professional support and, above all, Karin Werner for her involvement, encouragement and willingness to publish the book in German and English.

Finally, I am deeply indebted to Alexander Schüler for his patient and considerate, yet tireless years of support and companionship. This book is dedicated to him.

Gabriele Klein
HAMBURG, MARCH 2020

1 *Vollmond*
Wuppertal, 2006

Making a piece is no pleasure at all. Up to a certain point, yes, but when it gets serious… Every time, I say that I never want to do another one. Really. For so many years now. Why do I even do it? It's actually quite horrible. And once it's come out, I'm already planning something new.[1]

Pie

ces

What is the real secret to Pina Bausch's art? What is so special about her pieces? These questions have not only been extensively discussed in dance reviews and in the arts sections of newspapers (→ RECEPTION) but also in academic publications worldwide. What is striking about all of these publications is that the central narratives and interpretations of Pina Bausch's oeuvre, which first cropped up and established themselves in the 1970s and 1980s, still prevail to this day. Discourse surrounding her work has always been less influenced by academics and more so by the journalists who followed Pina Bausch's work in Wuppertal from the outset. They had access to the company, sometimes even travelling with it on tour, and then translated their knowledge into text and film. From very early on, the writings and films of Anne Linsel,[2] Eva-Elisabeth Fischer,[3] Chantal Akerman[4] and others made the artistic work of Pina Bausch accessible to a larger, general audience through books,[5] TV coverage and motion pictures such as the documentary *What are Pina Bausch and her Dancers Doing in Wuppertal?* (1982).[6] Most of all, it was the critics writing for Germany's most renowned national newspapers – such as Klaus Geitel and Jochen Schmidt for the *Frankfurter Allgemeine Zeitung* (FAZ) and *Die Welt*, Eva-Elisabeth Fischer for the *Süddeutsche Zeitung* (SZ), Rolf Michaelis for *Die Zeit* and Norbert Servos for *Theater Heute* and the *Tagesspiegel* – who decisively translated the Tanztheater Wuppertal's art into other media, becoming curators of the (inter-)national discourse surrounding it.

It was Norbert Servos who in particular set a significant course together with Hedwig Müller in the very first book published about the Tanztheater Wuppertal.[7] In this book, they describe Pina Bausch as "the permanent nuisance"[8] and explore her work by not only presenting the pieces but also by outlining the work processes and choreographic practices behind them, as well as by discussing various audience reactions. The books subsequently published by Servos and Jochen Schmidt substantially consolidated the discourse on the Tanztheater Wuppertal.[9] Here, they formulated the decisive narratives that many other authors would then adopt and repeat in various forms. Norbert Servos wrote that Pina Bausch's work had "an ability to look at people and their behavior with unswerving honesty and precision without judging them."[10] For him, it showed "not only that dance possesses a unique language for the political and social,"[11] but also that "Pina Bausch's work requestions the fundamental nature of dance and the elementary problems of human interaction as if for the first time."[12]

In the 1980s, theories of the body in cultural and social studies were still nascent, and Servos thus positioned the art of Pina Bausch and the Tanztheater Wuppertal outside of the logic of consciousness and language. For him, her work demonstrated that "defining, determining and deactivating are in fact the arch enemies of everything which lives and moves."[13] He believed that her pieces followed a logic that was not that of consciousness, but rather of the body "following the principle of analogy rather than laws of causality."[14] The subject of dance theater was thus the "moving/moved body,"[15] that which had socially and historically 'inscribed' itself into the body and that reemerges in everyday behavior. Servos ends his introduction with reflections on civilization theory, positing dance as the cultural-critical antithesis to rationality and the logic of consciousness. He presents dance as a place in which to take refuge from a rationalized modernity that is hostile to the body.

In my first book,[16] which also featured a chapter about Pina Bausch, I elaborated further on this critique of civilization. Back then, unlike Servos, I was already defining dance as a medium that is resistant, but also has a conservational function. In its ambivalence, it is both an instrument of corporeal revolution as well as a vehicle for social restoration that affirms social order.[17]

Like many other monographs,[18] Servos' book draws on descriptions of the pieces, sorted in chronological order, to give readers an understanding of Pina Bausch's work. This approach is based on a discourse that focuses on the pieces and interprets them, often implicitly, using the semiotic methods prevalent in theater studies in the 1980s. Translating the observed pieces into text, this approach was based on a paradox understanding: on the one hand, art itself was considered to be linguistically inaccessible, while, on the other hand, the aim was to translate the ostensible meaning of the piece into language and text. The authors/translators here appear as agents of meaning, i.e., as mediators between art and audience/the public.

Describing and interpreting pieces were common practices in the arts sections of newspapers as well as in art and theater studies analysis – and they sometimes still are. This chapter takes a different path: it seeks neither to add further interpretations to existing descriptions of the pieces nor to proceed chronologically along the timeline of Pina Bausch's œuvre.[19] In no way does it consider dance to be a merely corporeal phenomenon that cannot be translated into language. In fact, the translation of dance and choreography into language and text is here understood as a becoming similar, the coming closer of two things as in Walter Benjamin's theory of translation (→ THEORY AND METHODOLOGY),[20] as the brushing together of dance and writing, choreography and text in the process of translation. The productivity and 'surplus' of translation thus lie in its very failure to linguistically determine and explicitly define.

Instead of taking an approach that describes and interprets the individual pieces chronologically, this chapter chooses a systematic approach. It is systematic in that it is the first to ever categorize Pina Bausch's pieces into artistic phases.[21] It then identifies characteristic aspects of Pina Bausch's work, going beyond the content of the individual pieces, and embeds it within its own historical, social and political context. This method also answers a question rarely posed in research about the Tanztheater Wuppertal: what is the relationship between various phases of Pina Bausch's work on the one hand and respective historical events and contemporaneous developments in art on the other? In other words: are these events and developments translated into the pieces and, if so, in what ways?

Artistic phases

Pina Bausch's choreographic œuvre can be divided into five main phases, the last four of which were with the Tanztheater Wuppertal: 1967-1973, 1973-1979, 1980-1986, 1986-2000 and 2001-2009. I will go into further detail below about the characteristics of each of these phases, although I will neither discuss all of the pieces belonging to each phase nor describe their 'content.'[22] Artistic phases are not characterized by one development, by a singular or definitive signum; old and new elements tend to mix within Pina Bausch's individual pieces. The formative origins of what may be characteristic for one phase usually lie much further back, and they often extend into a subsequent phase. These ambivalences may also be one of the reasons that there have not yet been any attempts made to categorize the works of Pina Bausch with the Tanztheater Wuppertal into artistic phases or, moreover, to relate them to global political, cultural or artistic developments.

1967-1973: DEMOCRATIC AWAKENING AND AESTHETIC UPHEAVAL

When Pina Bausch started as the director of the ballet department of the Wuppertaler Bühnen for the 1973/74 season, 'defiant' *(aufmüpfig)* had just been declared Word of the Year in Germany. Arno Wüstenhöfer, the theater's bold and innovative managing director *(Intendant),* had been courting the young dancer and freshly hatched choreographer for some time. After he had commissioned a few visiting choreographies for Wuppertal that Pina Bausch had developed as the head of the Folkwang Tanzstudio in Essen – such as *Aktionen für Tänzer* (PREMIERE 1971), where he pit the young choreographer against Wuppertal's existing ballet director, Ivan Sertic, in kind of choreographic competition; and the *Tannhäuser Bacchanal* (PREMIERE 1972), based on Wagner's opera – she finally accepted. "I never actually wanted to work in a theatre. I didn't have the confidence to do it. I was very frightened. I loved working freely. But he [Arno Wüstenhöfer, GK] wouldn't give up and kept asking me until I finally said: 'I can give it a try.'"[23]

Accepting the position of ballet director after being wooed for years by Wüstenhöfer meant a decisive change for Pina Bausch: moving from a university in the placid, middle-class town of Essen-Werden – the city where she had begun her dance career at the Folkwang Hochschule für Musik, Theater und Tanz and where she was able to develop under the protection of her mentors – to the municipal theater of an urban region beset by a postindustrial crisis, to Wuppertal, the neighboring city of her hometown of Solingen.

Pina Bausch had only just begun choreographing about six years before, in 1967, at the Folkwang Hochschule – the same institution where she had received her training, which had been renamed and had achieved the rank of a tertiary institution in 1963. Just one year later, she took over from Kurt Joss as artistic director of the Folkwang Tanzstudio, which had developed out of the Folkwang Ballet and comprised a small group of Folkwang graduates. She choreographed for this young ensemble for two years and also toured internationally with her dancers. At the same time, she began teaching dance at the Folkwang Hochschule and elsewhere, for example, at the Frankfurter Sommerkurse, a summer school for dancers in Frankfurt am Main in West Germany. After this short but very busy period of gaining experience as a director and choreographer, she was awarded the German state of North Rhine-Westphalia's Förderpreis für junge Künstlerinnen und Künstler (a prize for upcoming young artists) – as the first choreographer to ever receive the prize – after creating only a handful of pieces that did not even fill an evening. This move to Wuppertal was thus a bold venture for both her and the Wuppertaler Bühnen, although it was not an unusual one in this period of democratic upheaval, which motivated some managing directors to experiment and take daring risks.

Experiments were not just taking place in the world of modern dance, but also, e.g., in neo-classical narrative ballet. During his time as ballet director in the southern German city of Stuttgart, John Cranko – a South African choreographer in the tradition of George Balanchine – established this as a new genre, bringing about what was referred to as the "ballet miracle of Stuttgart." In an unusual move for the time, he also relaxed the traditional hierarchies of the ballet company and allowed young dancers to develop choreographies of their own. In doing so, he made a fundamental contribution to the appointment of one of the young dancers in Stuttgart, the American John Neumeier – who was 29 years old at the time – to the position of ballet director in Frankfurt am Main in 1969, despite his lack of experience as a choreographer. Four years later, Neumeier

2 Protest against the
German Emergency Acts
Munich, 1968

3 *Kontakthof*
Wuppertal, 2013

transferred to the Hamburger Staatsoper in the port city of Hamburg, one of Germany's largest cities, where August Everding, another influential managing director, had enough confidence in him to reform what was at the time the provincial Hamburg Ballet. Neumeier, one year older than Pina Bausch, thus not only concurrently developed his first group choreographies in 1968/69 but also, in that same year of 1973, took on a ballet ensemble that would come to bear his aesthetic signature for decades to come and make the company world-famous. Both Pina Bausch and John Neumeier were able to do this because they had internationally renowned mentors in the form of Kurt Jooss and John Cranko on the one hand and the support of recognized, politically influential and brave managing directors such as Arno Wüstenhöfer and August Everding on the other. The first two made it possible for them to take the step from being dancers to becoming choreographers, while the others gave them the necessary backing and the trust required to find their own artistic path during their first creative years as ballet directors.

Pina Bausch's development as a choreographer took place in a climate of social, political, cultural and artistic awakening and upheaval. She was a typical 'war baby' like most of her fellow students at the Folkwangschule (→ COMPANY). This was a generation born during the Nazi regime. They grew up during the war and the postwar years and, as young adults, they rebelled against the older generation's reluctance to discuss the Nazi past in 1960s West Germany. This generation was unwilling to accept the postwar years' hushed, frantic attempts to quickly rebuild and turn back the clock. As a result, they directly confronted their parents' generation with what had happened and with the authoritarian structures of the nuclear family and social institutions. This rebellious stance intensified in the face of the protests against the Vietnam War; the civil rights movement in the US; outrage over the invasion of Hungary and Czechoslovakia by the Soviets and their brutal military suppression of democratic awakening; the aggressive reactions in West Germany against students, culminating in the shots that killed Benno Ohnesorg in 1967 in West Berlin; the subsequent attempt by a right-wing fanatic to assassinate the figurehead of the German student movement, Rudi Dutschke, which was further aggravated by the violent language of a national conservative press; and finally, the anti-democratic emergency laws, passed in 1968 by the first grand coalition of the German Bundestag. All of this stirred up the social climate and opened up deep trenches between the members of West German postwar society.

In theaters, this generation of children born during the war and influenced by the student movement was also submitting the performing arts to a fundamental critique. They rejected the bourgeois manifestations of theater as well as most managing directors' conformist attitudes toward the ruling political system and their exclusive focus on the needs of the educated middle class. By the same measure, they refused to accept authoritarian theater company structures, strict hierarchies, undemocratic decision-making structures, the extreme division of labor, the production restraints that failed to take into account the needs of the arts, the degradation of actors and actresses to service providers and the passive role of the spectator. 'Participation' was not only a demand being made by the trade unions but also the decisive code word for democratic awakening: "We expect all activities of the theater to be discussed in advance with all persons involved, i.e., with the actors and the artistic staff, so that we can decide on the program together."[24] When Jürgen Schitthelm introduced his new model of collective work and joint decision-making at the West Berlin Schaubühne in 1970 – turning it into a place that would play a central role in the new, shifting theater landscape – the exciting process of actors and dancers emancipating themselves from the role of passive executors of instruction and becoming thinking performers had already begun. Austrian choreographer Johann Kresnik, who made a substantial contribution in the late 1960s to the establishment of dance theater as a performing art throughout the German-speaking world, described the changes at the time some years later, saying: "It used to be that no one could ever go to a managing director unsolicited." But now they could "open the doors of management [...] and go in and say: we would also like to voice an opinion."[25]

At the peak of the West German student movement, theater and activism, art and protest merged into one. Theater now also meant activism, happening, agitprop and audience participation. It no longer merely addressed the educated middle class, but also targeted less privileged groups. Some considered the existing theaters incapable of reform, so they developed new organizations outside the institutions. The independent scene *(freie Szene)* emerged, and with it came alternative forms of theater that went beyond those of established literary theater and ballet, disrupting the established German tradition of municipal and state theater, which is organized into three divisions *(Sparten):* opera, text-based theater *(Schauspiel)* and ballet. The theater scene blossomed, especially in the urban metropolises, defining itself as an alternative to the traditional municipal and state theaters. Frustrated theater makers left the institutions and joined forces to establish working groups and artists' collectives, often living together in those communities as well.[26]

The demand for democracy as a principle of institutional organization was accompanied by upheavals in artistic work processes. The younger generation replaced strict hierarchical production methods and authoritarian structures with teamwork, equal rights and artistic collectives and collaborations. In many places, the previously undisputed, sole reigning managing director was replaced by an executive committee. Topics, aesthetics, artistic approaches, venues, audience, art criticism – everything was called into question. The 1968 movement likewise fundamentally motivated aesthetic innovations and movements toward democratization in concert dance. Johann Kresnik – an active member of the communist party in Austria – presented his piece *Paradies?* at the choreography competition of the Sommertanzakademie in Cologne that same year. It was a political dance piece about the assassination of Rudi Dutschke and showed police using clubs to beat people on crutches, while a tenor sung *Ô, Paradis!* In the audience, representatives of the student movement sat with red flags chanting "Ho Chi Minh." This provocative, one-off performance did not prevent Kurt Hübner, the influential managing director of Bremen's municipal theater, from bringing the almost 30-year-old Kresnik to Bremen that same year, where he further developed the aesthetic principles of his choreographic theater and continued to battle imperialism, warmongering and repressive social systems using aesthetic means while also searching for new, adequate forms of theater.

In 1972, the former ballet dancer Gerhard Bohner began experimenting as a choreographer. Like many others at the time, he chose to move from a hierarchically organized institution – in his case, the Berliner Staatsoper – to Darmstadt. Here, he gathered together brilliant soloists – including Silvia Kesselheim and Marion Cito, who had also come from the Berliner Staatsoper and would later join the Tanztheater Wuppertal (→ COMPANY) – into an ensemble that also called itself dance theater. The group publicly declared its goal of leaving old hierarchies and ballet aesthetics behind in favor of democratic participation. However, the experiment soon failed. Its radical approach was one generation ahead of its time. It was not until the 1990s that artists would once again choose to so radically experiment with models of participation, joined by a new generation of spectators that had been gradually schooled in new forms of theater.

Pina Bausch's decision to take over the dance department in Wuppertal was made in the midst of this heated and nerve-wracking atmosphere of upheaval, which also spread through the student body of the Folkwang Hochschule. Hers was also and above all an attempt to activate democratization and modernization in society by utilizing culture and art and their institutions. This step was quite daring in light of the young, 33-year-old choreographer's still limited experience – all the more so considering that women in such positions were still virtually non-existent at the time. Even in 1968, at the height of the student movement, women's rights were only very slowly being asserted.

But Pina Bausch accepted the challenge: her first choreographies had already revealed her desire to break with dance traditions and viewing habits. She also clearly sought to overcome the previous symbolism of dance theater in the tradition of Kurt Jooss: in *Nachnull* (PREMIERE 1970), she distanced herself for the first time from the traditions of expressionist dance *(Ausdruckstanz)* that she had studied at the Folkwangschule, but also from modern dance, which she had explored in depth at the Julliard School during her years in New York (1960-1962). During this intense time, in what was then the center of dance, she had witnessed a broad spectrum of dance forms, e.g., pieces by George Balanchine and Martha Graham, and had worked with pioneering choreographers and dancers such as Antony Tudor, José Limón, Margaret Craske, Alfredo Corvino and Louis Horst. She had danced in Paul Taylor's newly founded New American Ballet and had been hired as a dancer by Antony Tudor, who was ballet director of the Metropolitan Opera at the time. She danced in his choreographies, such as in *Tannhäuser* (PREMIERE 1960) and *Alcestis* (PREMIERE 1960), as well as in pieces *en pointe*, where she discovered her love of opera. It cannot be ascertained, at least not from her own statements, whether Pina Bausch also came into contact in New York with Judson Dance Theater and the young generation of choreographers that included Lucinda Childs, Steve Paxton and Trisha Brown, who envisioned choreography as an emergent order, as something situatively and performatively generated. But the wide spectrum of dance aesthetics that converged on New York undoubtedly had an immense influence on her courage and will to find a new language for dance.

One year after *Nachnull*, in *Aktionen für Tänzer* (PREMIERE 1971), she applied Günter Becker's compositional term *Aktion* (happening/activism) to concert dance – *Aktion* being a term used in German art and theater not only as a political slogan but also as an antithesis to the reigning bourgeois representational model of theater. In her rather associative, satirical choreography, she made it unmistakably clear that the renunciation of traditional forms of dance for the stage was an irreversible process and began to fundamentally call concert dance into question as a theatrical event. In this piece, a woman in a shirt lies motionless on a hospital bed. All of the company members get into bed with her, playing macabre games with her lifeless body. They roll it over the stage and hoist it up on a pulley, letting it dangle from the ceiling.

At the end of this phase Pina Bausch had clearly demonstrated with just a few short, one-act pieces that she was striking out to develop a new aesthetic for dance and the stage that would go beyond that of traditional modern dance.

4 Pina Bausch in
Im Wind der Zeit
Essen, 1969

5 Penelope Slinger
Wedding Invitation
1973

6 *Fritz*
Wuppertal, 1974

7 Prisoner of the
National Front
for the Liberation of
South Vietnam,
Vietnam, 1967

1973-1979: DEVELOPMENT OF A NEW CONCEPT FOR CHOREOGRAPHY AND STAGE

When Pina Bausch moved to Wuppertal for the 1973/74 season, she arrived in a city in the midst of a deep postindustrial crisis. However, like many comparable crisis-ridden regions and cities, it was also a center of new art: since the 1960s and 1970s, Wuppertal had had its own nationally acclaimed jazz music scene, of which Matthias Burkert – Pina Bausch's music collaborator from 1979 onward – was also a member. Moreover, Wuppertal was one of the centers of the Fluxus movement. Along with the action pieces of Joseph Beuys and Wolf Vostell, John Cage's musical performances and Nam June Paik's video experiments, the famous 24-hour happening at Galerie Parnass in 1965 is today still considered one of Fluxus' finest hours. According to a contemporary eyewitness: "Five o'clock in the morning. Professor Beuys is still perching on a crate. Between foot and head cushions made from margarine, he does artistic yoga. A kind of spiritualized abdominal training."[27]

8 Niki de Saint-Phalle
She – A Cathedral
Stockholm, 1966

Things were not as experimental at Wuppertal's municipal theater. Its audience appreciated the classical and modern ballet pieces that Ivan Sertic offered them. "A certain aesthetic was expected," Pina Bausch later remembered, "[that] other forms of beauty [existed aside from that aesthetic was not open to debate]."[28] Upon Pina Bausch's arrival, most of the dancers in the company left the Wuppertaler Bühnen together with Sertic. Pina Bausch immediately and eagerly implemented her efforts at aesthetic reform and democratization, not only insisting on the autonomy of her dance ensemble but also promptly renaming the Wuppertaler Ballet "Tanztheater Wuppertal," thus joining the ranks of a small group of young choreographers who were already bringing extraordinary things to West German theater stages under the label of 'dance theater.' Her initial fears, which she later confessed to dance critic Jochen Schmidt, had turned to resolve: "I didn't think that it was at all possible to do anything individual. I thought of the routine and the whole gamut, thought that the theater had to run as usual; I was very afraid of that."[29] In an interview in the 1973 edition of the annual dance magazine *Ballettjahrbuch,* she made a public pledge to participation and emphasized that she wished to encourage the dancers "to actively participate in the creation of new choreographies by voicing opinions, criticism and advice."[30]

9 *Bluebeard: While Listening to a Taped Recording of Béla Bartók's "Duke Bluebeard's Castle"*
Venice, 1985

However, this was never put into practice, for the dancers of the Tanztheater Wuppertal never really had an equal say in the decision-making process. Still, from 1978 onward, they did begin to develop their own idiosyncratic form of implementing an artistic model of participation (→ COMPANY) in the form of the working method of 'asking questions' (→ WORK PROCESS). These activities and declarations reveal that Pina Bausch shared the desire of many other young choreographers of her generation to eventually expand the municipal theaters' focus for classical ballet to include contemporary dance. Their dedicated work resulted not only in the establishment of a new aesthetics of concert dance that would continue to diversify and grow even more complex in the following decades but also opened up new markets for artistic concert dance. This work also managed to generate new, young audiences that rejected the bourgeois theater of representation and were looking for an adequate aesthetic form capable of reflecting the social upheaval around them, believing that they had found something with which they could identify and an expression of their zeitgeist in contemporary dance forms. In Germany, no other genre was quite like dance theater in this respect and, with her pieces, Pina Bausch provided the crucial aesthetic explosives.

But just as the young choreographer began shaking up concert dance in Wuppertal, a ceasefire was signed between North Vietnam and the US after decades of war, and the US military began withdrawing from the Northern part of a divided Vietnam. In South America, the state of emergency that had gripped Chile since the summer ended in a bloody military coup that would claim thousands of lives in the years to come. In the US, protests against the Vietnam War and the Watergate Affair caused a major domestic and international crisis, climaxing in the resignation of President Richard Nixon in 1974. The second women's movement of the 1970s chose to reject political representation, dismissed the separation between the private and the public, and focused on politicizing the personal and the private. The slogans "The private is political" and "The personal is political" opened up a new political playing field that German feminists used to address large audiences in rallies against anti-abortion laws and to organize campaigns against violence toward women, sexual violence in the media, advertising and pornography, as well as in the domestic sphere. What was referred to in Germany as *Politik der ersten Person* (the 'politics of the first person') also influenced new social movements, the citizen's initiative movement and various grassroots and ecological movements that would later give rise to Germany's Green Party.

In 1970, the US literary academic, writer, sculptor and feminist Kate Millet published her book *Sexual Politics,* which would go on to become a classic of the women's liberation movement: "The word 'politics' is enlisted here when speaking of the sexes primarily because such a word is eminently useful in outlining the real nature of their relative status, historically and at the present. It is opportune, perhaps today even mandatory, that we develop a more relevant psychology and philosophy of power relationships beyond the simple conceptual framework provided by our traditional formal politics."[31] No one at the time could yet imagine that the politicization of the private, which was so important for publicly exposing gender relations, would later help to pave the way for the commodification of the personal and the private by new markets in the wake of 1980s hedonism and the German literary movements of *Neue Innerlichkeit* (New Inwardness) and *Neue Subjektivität* (New Subjectivity).

As is more or less common knowledge, highlighting and dissecting the power structures of gender relations would become a central topic of Pina Bausch's work, at least in the first work phases. In this respect, she was once again a child of her time: by the early 1960s, the new artistic genre of feminist performance art had begun examining the politics of the personal, shining a spotlight on the private and the personal, on that which relates to the female body. Only through performance art, happenings and body art did debate over gender theory enter the world of art and art theory. These new intermedial art forms largely derived from the visual arts and provided predominantly female artists with a new radical platform of expression. They broke open the concept of the artwork in favor of a process of artistic creation. They addressed the relationships between art and life, between artists and their 'works of art.' They shifted the focus of artistic production to artists and their bodies and confronted the 'finished work of art' with the situationality of exhibiting it. Finally, they questioned the relationship between performativity and representation, demonstration and performance, presentation and fabrication.

Second-wave feminism developed parallel to these upheavals in modern art. In the late 1960s, the feminist art movement emerged in the US as more and more female artists started making work that portrayed feminist content. Feminist art included all female artists actively working to expose patriarchal structures in the art world. It addressed such topics as traditional images of femininity, corporeality, sexuality, sexual violence, pornography and prostitution, while sometimes also actively participating in the women's rights movement. Protagonists included Louise Bourgeois, Valie Export, Helke Sander, Lynn Hershman, Orlan, Yoko Ono, Gina Pane, Ulrike Rosenbach, Cindy Sherman, Katharina Sieverding and Rosemarie Trockel. Even before the rise of gender studies, which began discussing the body in the 1970s, these female artists demonstrated that gender was directly tied to, symbolized and represented by the body in which it materializes, and that it is the body that is charged with heteronormative phantasies and popular imagination.[32] Their works not only directly linked body and gender but also body and image.³³ These female artists explored their own bodies, paraded them, exhibited them, staged them – and in doing so, they practiced acts of both "doing gender"³⁴ and "performing gender."³⁵ This art form reached its climax in the public eye in the 1970s, although for some, such as Jeremy Strick, Director of the Museum for Contemporary Art in Los Angeles, it is still "the most influential international movement of any during the postwar period"³⁶ decades later.

Nonetheless, it would be wrong to label all female artists examining gender roles, images of femininity or gender-specific power structures as feminist artists. For example, like Pina Bausch, the performance artist Marina Abramović and the painter and sculptor Niki de Saint Phalle did not and do not consider themselves to be feminist artists. In an interview Bausch said: "Feminism – perhaps because it has become such a fashionable word – always makes me retreat into my shell. Perhaps this is also because it so often means a strange separation that I dislike. It sometimes sounds like it's about being against instead of with one another."³⁷

Still, her artistic work did aesthetically link life and art, much in the same way as intended in the second-wave-feminist slogan "The private is political." Her pieces addressed existential situations, especially during her first three artistic phases. They showed personal, private, everyday relationships and interactions between the sexes. Her first calling card as director of the new Tanztheater Wuppertal was the piece *Fritz*, which premiered in January 1974. It is loosely based on the Brothers Grimm fairytale *The Story of the Boy Who Went Forth to Learn Fear*.³⁸ The piece was embedded within a three-part program, which Pina Bausch used to make reference to her own artistic development by placing her first piece within a framework of choreographic masterpieces. As she would do in subsequent pieces, she thus took gender equality into account. First came the world-famous anti-war piece *The Green Table* (PREMIERE 1932) by her mentor Kurt Jooss, in which she had once danced herself. The piece portrays the First World War as a dance of death, initiated and negotiated at the "green table" while claiming the lives of millions of people. As the other piece, she chose *Rodeo* (PREMIERE 1942) by the American choreographer Agnes de Mille. It was Mille's most well-known ballet and cemented her career and worldwide reputation as a choreographer, with Mille herself dancing the main role – an entertaining piece, robust, simultaneously delicate and full of optimism.

It was within this polarizing framework that Pina Bausch positioned *Fritz*. Like many of her later pieces, such as *1980 – A Piece by Pina Bausch*³⁹ (PREMIERE 1980) or *For the Children of yesterday, today and tomorrow* (PREMIERE 2002), it explores the subject of childhood. The main character is a boy who encounters his familiar surroundings with great intensity, exaggerated movements and gestures, as the dancers move through a nightmarishly surreal environment. Dominique Mercy wore an undershirt at the premiere, coughing as he danced, beginning a movement, then abandoning it again and again. The significance of this introductory piece was clearly formulated in the evening's program: "Within the scope of this evening's program, *Fritz* plays a key role in the work of Pina Bausch and her troupe. Dance is understood as a language that articulates itself corporeally without formalizing itself into the corset of a normative classical ballet style. One could also say formulaically: Pina Bausch understands dance as an 'open' form of 'ballet' dictated by the conceptual and the playful."[40]

Unlike the other two accompanying pieces, which had brought their choreographers worldwide acclaim, the reactions from newspaper critics and Wuppertal audiences were disastrous. Somebody called it a "half-hour of vileness that depicts the antisocial milieu and the insane asylum as a child's realm of experience." The audience also clearly thought that the young choreographer was struggling and called for managing director Arno Wüstenhöfer to protect them from her work. But occasionally there were other voices. Renowned German novelist Judith Kuckert, born in 1959, remembers the groundbreaking importance that the piece had for her as a teenager: *"Fritz's* radicalism, for which Pina Bausch was attacked and ridiculed at the time, catapulted me beyond the confines of my girlhood. From then on, the movement and visual language infected me with a hunger for meaning, which even took over my dreams. Just like the performers up there onstage in Wuppertal, I wanted to look life in the eye from now on – not just in the theater."[41]

Pina Bausch was undaunted by the vehemence and bluntness of the criticism, although she did later mention it in her acceptance speech for the Kyoto Prize in 2007: "The first years were very difficult. Again and again spectators would leave the auditorium slamming doors, while others whistled or booed. Sometimes we had telephone calls in the rehearsal room with bad wishes. During one piece I went into the auditorium with four people to protect me. I was scared. One newspaper wrote in its review: 'The music is very beautiful. You can simply shut your eyes.'"[42]

Pina Bausch returned to opera and modern dance for a while in the following three pieces. A mere three months after *Fritz*, she staged *Iphigenie auf Tauris* (PREMIERE 1974) and, one year later, *Orpheus und Eurydike* (PREMIERE 1975), both early classical operas by the German composer Christoph Willibald Gluck. In these pieces, she reinvented the genre of dance opera *(Tanzoper)* by assigning dance a role equal to that of music. This was in stark contrast to the predominantly entertaining, less dramaturgically important function that dance usually plays in opera, especially in the still prevalent German municipal theater system, which hierarchically favors the genres of opera and theater over that of dance. "I only chose works that gave me the freedom to relate to it in my own way. In *Iphigenie* and *Orpheus und Eurydike,* for example, Gluck gave me a great deal of space to link his works to something of my own, something that I had to say. In these works, I found exactly what I needed to speak about. And that led to a new form: the dance opera."[43] She cast the three leading roles of Orpheus, Eurydice and Amor with both a singer and a dancer and did so not only for conceptual reasons but also because the choir and the orchestra of the Wuppertaler Bühnen refused to collaborate: "The orchestra and [the choir] also made things very difficult for me. I wanted so much to develop something with the [choir]. They turned down every idea."[44]

Gluck himself had sought to reform the opera and, in 1774, 200 years before the Bausch premiere, during the rehearsals for the premiere of *Orfeo ed Euridice* in Paris, he likewise encouraged his singers to do more than just sing: "Don't think about the music or about the [choir], but at that point scream with pain as if someone is cutting your leg off! And if you can, express this pain as if it comes from within you, from your very soul and heart."[45] Dominique Mercy, who danced the role of Orpheus in the original cast, repeatedly doubled up, waved his arms about, writhed and flailed – and yet, in spite of his apparent ecstasy and eccentricity, played a rather still, self-absorbed mourner and sufferer. In the same way that Gluck sought to keep his singers from merely singing, Pina Bausch withheld dance in her dance opera. During a central, very well-known aria at the end of the opera, when Orpheus laments, "Che faro senza Euridice" ("I have lost my Eurydice"), there was no dancing at all for several minutes. Where the audience might have expected a translation of the scene into dance, Orpheus merely knelt in the furthermost back left corner with his back to his spectators, a heap of misery that just as soon disappeared from the stage.

Pina Bausch's choreographic masterpiece *The Rite of Spring* (PREMIERE 1975) also falls within this phase. It is based on the music of Igor Stravinsky, which, due to its unusual rhythmic and tonal structures, is considered a key composition of 20th-century music. Stravinsky's original *Le Sacre du Printemps* premiered one year before the outbreak of the First World War, with the Ballets Russes in Paris dancing the brilliant and scandalous choreography of Vaslav Nijinsky. Since then, the piece has been considered one of the most important, challenging and difficult dance pieces of the 20th century.[46] It has been rechoreographed several hundred times, e.g., by Maurice Béjart (PREMIERE 1959) and John Neumeier (PREMIERE 1972), who both interpreted the sacrificial victim in the same way as Nijinsky, as the suppression of eroticism and sexuality. Pina Bausch recontextualized the gender roles of the sacrificial myth: in her version, it is a woman who is both the sacrificial victim and the chosen one. She is sacrificed by men and women watching the sacrifice. This sacrificial scene was one that developed during rehearsals: Pina Bausch rehearsed the role of the sacrificial victim separately with Marlies Alt and then showed the solo to the group. What she then used in the choreography was precisely the other dancers' initial reactions, their bewilderment, helplessness and dismay. In an essay about the piece, art historian Michael Diers has drawn parallels between Pina Bausch's interpretation of the sacrificial victim and contemporaneous West German discourse about victims and perpetrators,[47] prompted by debate about the relationship between the militant Red Army Fraction (RAF) and state power.

For Pina Bausch, this groundbreaking choreography was also a farewell: never again would she develop a choreography completely composed of her own movements, and only once more would she solely concentrate on a single piece of classical music, namely in *Bluebeard: While Listening to a Taped Recording of Béla Bartók's "Duke Bluebeard's Castle"* (PREMIERE 1977).[48] In the years that followed, the choreographer premiered a whole host of pieces, which transformed conventional theater and dance aesthetics and, at the same time, spectators' viewing habits. One of the first steps in this process was her next piece, the two-part "Brecht/Weill Evening" *The Seven Deadly Sins* (PREMIERE 1976),[49] in which she introduced the new choreographic method of montage, where 'parts' or actions are layered on top of and interwoven with one another associatively and convolutedly. With this piece, Pina Bausch proved that she was already working conceptually[50] – i.e., fundamentally reflecting on traditional theater concepts – 20 years before the advent of 'conceptual dance,' which claims to have first invented the term in the 1990s. As in the dance operas that came before it, she dismantled Brecht's socio-critical text, only to reinterpret it by focusing on the female perspectives (Anna I and II). Instead of representing the social conditions that, according to the Marxist Brecht, were what made humans who they were, she highlighted the individual fates of women. Rather than focusing on the Protestant work ethic, she showed the sacrifices that women make for family, replaced capitalist exploitation with patriarchal exploitation and equated the grueling monotony of work with the selling of one's body to paying customers. Brecht's idea that in capitalism the good is always based on exploitation was here transformed into a tension between autonomy and the desire to fit in with the normative order, which Pina Bausch believed affected women just as much as men. She staged this tension using the genre of the revue from the musical theater tradition and presented it as a hopelessly broken world, as she would in subsequent pieces such as *Renate Emigrates* (PREMIERE 1977).

She continued to radically pursue the conceptual basis of the "Brecht/Weill Evening" in *Bluebeard*. This piece not only dismantles the opera's libretto – Bluebeard leads the charming Judith into his fairytale castle and shows her seven rooms before finally reaching the resting place of the Duke's murdered, royally dressed former wives – but also translates it into the everyday world of gender relations. In this piece, Pina Bausch also potentiated the characters of Bluebeard and Judith by transposing their individual actions onto the group and presenting the couple's relationship as a structural pattern of gender relations. Women and men are shown to be mutually lacking in understanding, thus once again also revealing the choreographer's position on this subject – the woman is not just a victim, but also uses her body as a weapon; the man, on the other hand, is not just a patriarch, but also his own prisoner – clearly illustrating the hegemonic differences in the ambivalences of each gender.

While it is important to mention the ways in which *Bluebeard* thematically tied into previous pieces and, like the "Brecht/Weill Evening," dramaturgically deconstructed the libretto, the truly innovative aspect of this piece was its set design. *Bluebeard* is the piece that can be used to demonstrate the intermediality and interdisciplinarity of dance theater, as it completely intertwines dance, opera, acting and film. Even the performativity of things plays a decisive role: the stage, Bluebeard's castle, is an empty, spacious, somewhat run-down old building with withered leaves strewn across the floor, emanating a distinct scent (like the peat in *The Rite of Spring*) as they are crushed underfoot, rustling and leaving traces as the dancers move around. The performativity of things is especially striking in the way that music is used. Not only does it come from offstage in recorded form, but it also emanates from a tape recorder visibly positioned on the stage, virtually the only prop in the entire piece. This tape recorder is attached to a moving table, which is connected to a cable that runs along the ceiling, thus turning the tape recorder into a dancing protagonist when pushed back and forth. This very specific handling of the music symbolizes the piece's reluctance to follow any form of linear dramaturgy – as already evident in Pina Bausch's renunciation of classical three-act narrative dramaturgy in favor of the montage: the tape recorder – and with it the narrative – is rewound over and over again.

But once again, this innovative approach to music – as unusual as it was even for the theatrical genre of dance theater – was actually a make-shift solution: "In *Bluebeard* I was unable to put my idea into practice at all because they provided me with a singer who, although I liked him very much in all other respects, was not a Bluebeard at all. In my desperation I thought up a completely different idea with Rolf Borzik. We designed a sort of carriage with a tape recorder [...]. Bluebeard could now push this carriage and run along with it wherever he wanted. He was able to rewind the music and repeat individual sentences. In this way he was able to wind forwards and backwards to examine his life."[51]

In order to circumvent her problems working with the choir and the orchestra, she based the next piece *Come dance with me* (PREMIERE 1977) on folk songs that the dancers sung themselves. In *Renate Emigrates,* she used prerecorded music and occasionally – as in this piece, and, e.g., in *1980* (PREMIERE 1980) and *Palermo Palermo* (PREMIERE 1989) – also invited individual musicians to play.

Today, some critics consider the "Macbeth Piece" *He Takes Her By The Hand And Leads Her Into The Castle, The Others Follow,* which premiered one year later, to be one of Pina Bausch's seminal pieces,[52] marking her transition to a radically new aesthetic. She created it on the invitation of Peter Zadek. Zadek was born in 1926 to a progressive bourgeois Jewish family in Berlin and emigrated to London with his family in 1933. In 1958, he returned to (West) Germany for the first time at the invitation of a theater in Cologne. He worked at theaters in Ulm and Bremen before assuming his first post as the managing director of the Schauspielhaus Bochum in 1972. It was here that he produced his spectacular Shakespeare productions. His work split audiences, meeting with both ecstatic approval and vehement rejection. It was experimental, challenged theater conventions and thus also the viewing habits of spectators. Inviting Pina Bausch to stage Macbeth in Bochum fit in perfectly with his desire to develop other forms of dramatic theater.

The "Macbeth Piece" was the first time that Pina Bausch used her new method of 'asking questions' (→ WORK PROCESS) to develop a piece – and she explained this approach in the program booklet and in some subsequent programs.[53] It was the radical continuation of a conceptual approach similar to that of 'director's theater' *(Regietheater),* a term introduced into German-language theater research in the 1970s to describe a production that was less true to the written work, in which the director's concepts take precedence over the ideas of the author, the performers, the composer, the singers and the conductor. In this sense, Pina Bausch pared down the original Shakespearean piece to its core scenes and motifs and translated the topics of power, greed, sin and guilt into everyday behavior. Fragmentary citations and set parts of the Shakespearean text establish a connection to the original piece in a dense, circularly constructed montage, which refutes all linear narrative dramaturgy. The absence, the denial of the familiar and the expected characterize the piece: classical roles are dissolved and evenly distributed among all performers. The four participating actors and actresses of Bochum's Schauspielhaus did not speak, the four dancers from Wuppertal acted, and the singer did not sing, but spoke instead. The result was an (inevitable) collision with the viewing habits and expectations of the theater audience. All of the action took place on a stage reminiscent of a dilapidated late 19th-century mansion, whose furnishings were not just there to complete the representative look. Instead, the piece presented the performativity of objects: the chair compelled the sitter to sit with a straight back; the glass cabinet not only exhibited bourgeois wealth but also the dancer's body.

Later that same year, *Kontakthof* (PREMIERE 1978) stylistically followed in the footsteps of the "Macbeth Piece" when Pina Bausch tied together different levels by condensing them into a question about the relationship between theater and reality. Again, she linked men and women's compulsion to display themselves, to show themselves off in search of intimacy and security to a critique of bourgeois representative theater, of playing pretend, while also dealing with the spaces that dance provides in order to practice exhibiting one's body. In this piece, the scene is a ballroom, once again in turn-of-the-century style, presented as a place where people seek out happiness, where everyday gestures of joy, fear, shame, vanity, affection, pleasure and desire collide. That the ballroom can be a microcosm of human desire for people of all ages would later become more visible in alternative translations of the piece: in 2000, the piece was performed by seniors (men and women over the age of 65), in 2008 by teenagers aged 14 and older.[54] People who were neither professional performers nor dancers took over the roles of the dancers after rehearsing together for one year. In this respect, these translations also ask how a piece changes with different ensembles and what it means to perform it.

In between the "Macbeth Piece" and *Kontakthof,* Pina Bausch premiered a piece that would come to play a special role within her œuvre with the Tanztheater Wuppertal: *Café Müller* (PREMIERE 1978). Named after a café not far from Pina Bausch's childhood home (→ COMPANY), it was – with the exception of a short dance sequence in *Danzón* (PREMIERE 1995) – the only piece that Pina Bausch developed with the Tanztheater Wuppertal in which she herself would dance for many years. It was also an exception to the extent that *Café Müller* was initially the title of a four-piece evening to which Pina Bausch invited three guest choreographers – namely Gerhard Bohner, Gigi-Gheorghe Caciuleanu and Hans Pop – to develop pieces of their own. Again, she took a conceptual approach. All that connected the four pieces was a few key parameters: the stage was a café; there were four performers and no bright stage lights. Out of this four-part evening, Pina Bausch's piece was the only one to stay on in the repertoire and be shown for years on a double bill together with *The Rite of Spring.* It is, by virtue of Henry Purcell's arias alone, a melancholy piece, addressing a range of difficult issues, from feeling lost, isolated, and lonely to feelings of intimacy, security, and being abandoned, as well as mindfulness and attentiveness to others. Once again, the dancers stand in a dilapidated hall, chairs everywhere; there is no space to dance. The dancers move through the space as if sleepwalking, aimlessly wandering, self-engrossed, with their eyes closed. Rolf Borzik, set designer and Pina Bausch's partner at the time, literally cleared the stage for them: he created space to move, snatching away the chairs so that the dancers could make their way without stumbling or injuring themselves.

After the first five years of intense work in Wuppertal and the excitement caused by the production (→ WORK PROCESS) and reception (→ RECEPTION) of the "Macbeth Piece," *Café Müller* seemed like a pause, like a reflection in choreography and dance upon the work shared so far, especially that of Pina Bausch and Rolf Borzik, in response to the question: where is the space of dance? Where and how can dance evolve?

The new aesthetics developed during the second artistic phase were ultimately condensed into the piece *Arien* (PREMIERE 1979), simultaneously marking the end of this phase of creation. It was the last piece that Pina Bausch completely developed with her partner and artistic companion Rolf Borzik (→ COMPANY). Schmidt describes *Arien* as "a kind of requiem for the set designer during his lifetime."[55] In this piece, Rolf Borzik has spectacularly stripped the stage right down to its firewalls and submerged it in water, while additionally integrating a small swimming pool, in which some of the dancers move around, but which above all houses a remarkably realistic looking hippopotamus. "Animals and flowers, all things that we use onstage, are actually things that we are familiar with. But at the same time, due to the way they are used onstage, they tell a completely different story [...]. You can use the hippo in *Arien* to tell a beautiful, sad love story. At the same time, you can show something of the loneliness, the need, the tenderness. Everything is directly visible. Without explanations and without clues."[56]

What is not visible are the people inside the papier-mâché hippo, crawling across the stage while its little hippo feet move with the help of a small windshield wiper battery. *Arien* is a condensed culmination of all aesthetic stylistic devices, material and motifs of this phase into one fundamental theme: the struggle between life and death, the fight against the passing of time, desperation in the face of impermanence – yet once again, there are glimmers of hope in the darkness, which take the form of children's games and jokes.

Legend of Chastity (PREMIERE 1979) was the last piece for which Rolf Borzik would design the stage and whose premiere he and Pina Bausch would experience together. A few weeks later, he died at the age of 35. It was the piece that he imagined. During the rehearsals for *Legend of Chastity,* the company "had known for some time that he didn't have much longer to live. Yet this *Legend of Chastity* is not a tragic, sad piece. Rolf Borzik wanted it like it was: with a feeling of wanting to live and to love."[57] The piece was sexually provocative like no other piece before it, razor-sharp in its analysis of contradictions and contrasts, satirical, brazen, bitter, critical, but also dreamy, gentle, tacky, hectic, bustling, cheerful and loud, as well as calm, lonely, sad and quiet.

Almost 30 years later, Pina Bausch would say: "I never intended to invent a particular style or a new form of theater. The form emerged entirely by itself: from the questions that I had."[58] Yet at the end of this first phase in Wuppertal, the full complexity of Pina Bausch's artistic signature style with the Tanztheater Wuppertal had already taken shape, in the interplay between dance/choreography, theater, music, materials, stage and audience. Much had been experimented with: various stage formats, theatrical forms from the operetta (e.g., in *Renate Emigrates)* and dance operas *(Iphigenie auf Tauris, Orpheus und Eurydike)* to modern dance pieces *(The Rite of Spring)*. Productions had worked with formats such as the revue (as in the "Brecht/Weill Evening") and experimental forms (e.g., *Café Müller)*, theatrical scenes (e.g., the "Macbeth Piece"), unprecedented set designs, unusual theatrical spaces and scenography, unexpected costumes (e.g., second-hand clothing, bathing suits, queer costumes) and materials (the entire props collection), with the participation of real and artificial animals, with innovative choices of music and a collage-like compilation of music from different genres and cultures. The work had opened up and entered into dialogue with the audience and altered conceptions about dancers (the dancer as performer), and provided a new understanding of what a 'work' (the 'piece') and choreography (a collage and montage-like conflation of individual 'parts' into a 'piece' based on spatial and temporal principles, and rhythm) could be.

By the end of this phase, Pina Bausch had produced more than ten full-length pieces[59] in addition to a handful of one-act choreographies, usually managing to produce two new pieces a year. She had developed a signature style, which would not just lead to a paradigm shift in concert dance worldwide, but would also radically call theater into question as an institution of bourgeois representation and as a site of bourgeois affirmation. In this phase, Pina Bausch created something radically new, which translated many of the ideas with which theater and dance were experimenting at the time into a very specific concept of theater and the stage, of choreography and dance. Her new concepts transposed the idea of 'director's theater' onto dance. Dance shifted from being a representative art form to being a performative one, guided by action and experience rather than script and drama, focusing on dancers as subjects and not as characters, thus allowing them to appear as performers performing themselves, and not only dancing but also speaking and singing. Behind all this lay her new work process of 'asking questions,' which she also integrated into the pieces themselves.

Moreover, these new concepts yielded a new idea of choreography that refuted linear dramaturgy and narrative structures, dissolving the perspective of centralized action onstage in favor of multiple simultaneous centers. This also meant a radical reflection on what dance could be beyond beautiful, conventional virtuosity, thus additionally redefining its significance in the artistic canon of the three-genre theater. Pina Bausch translated democratic ideas of participation and a critique of hierarchically organized theater institutions into her artistic work through new forms of collaboration with dancers in the development of the pieces as well as through institutional attempts at autonomy (occupying the Lichtburg, a former cinema, as her exclusive rehearsal space → WORK PROCESS). Ultimately, this special form of collaboration with her dancers came to establish a microcosm of multicultural society.

It was apparent at the time that Pina Bausch and her aesthetics had irrevocably initiated a paradigm shift in concert dance, one that would not only influence and change concert dance but also theater and film worldwide. However, the extent and sustainability of this shift as we recognize it today was not yet clear. The next artistic phase would help to further develop that which what had just emerged and to make it known worldwide as a specific national genre of concert dance: German dance theater. Pina Bausch would come to represent this genre like no other for the rest of her life. This was also largely due to the support of the Goethe-Institut, the Federal Republic of Germany's cultural association, which promotes the study of German abroad and encourages international cultural exchange. It was this institution that turned the Tanztheater Wuppertal into a top export item. For Pina Bausch and her dance theater were, together with their themes of searching and longing for understanding and reconciliation, ideal representatives of the cultural politics of a young democratic Federal Republic of Germany finding its place among the invisible trenches of a raging Cold War.

1980-1986: INTERNATIONALIZATION AND STABILIZATION OF AESTHETIC LANGUAGE

The 1980s were a decade floating between the rearmament debate in the wake of the NATO Double-Track Decision and the collapse of the "real socialist" countries – with international skirmishes aggravating conflicts between East and West. The East-West arms race caused Germany to debate its role in helping the West to stockpile and station weapons against the Soviets. In the year 1979/80, a new hot spot, which would lose nothing of its explosivity in the decades to come, emerged in the Middle East: the Republic of Iran. After Shah Mohammad Reza Pahlavi fled the country and Shiite religious leader Khomeini returned to power, the Islamic Revolution led to international conflict, especially with the US. In neighboring Iraq, Saddam Hussein solidified his power base. Ideological antagonisms between the two countries became more acute. After the détente politics of the 1970s, the subsequent First Gulf War and the Soviet Union's invasion of Afghanistan further exacerbated the East-West conflict, once again seriously endangering world peace.

While the 1980s saw the climax of the postwar arms race, the mood in West Germany oscillated between hedonism and anxiety about the future. The Green Party was founded in 1980 and was soon voted into the Parliament of Baden-Württemberg, one of Germany's southern states, for the first time. In 1983, right-wing opponents of Franz Josef Strauß, a powerful leader of the Christian Social Union in Bavaria, founded the Republican Party. This led to an expansion of the right-wing of politics that continues to this day in the form of new

parties like the AfD – an expansion that has consistently undermined Germany's process of coming to terms with its Nazi past while eroding democratic debate. In 1986, a reactor catastrophe at the Chernobyl power plant in the Ukraine caused radioactive fall-out all across Europe. That same year, a commando of the Red Army Fraction

(RAF) killed the German Siemens manager Karl Heinz Beckurts. Parallel to these various political crises, the 1980s heralded in radical social transformation, causing major anxiety about the future. The industrial age gave way to the advent of information technology. The world was introduced to computers and to the New Economy. Post-Fordism, global trade and neoliberal politics changed the way people did business. In post-industrial European countries, the welfare state began its slow demise.

However, the 1980s were also an age of hedonism, of the "adventure society,"[60] of the first generation in Germany to grow up during a time of prosperity – a generation that German author Florian Illies would later call "Generation Golf."[61] These were the years of flamboyant blow-dry hairstyles, drainpipe jeans and shoulder pads; the Walkman, ghetto blasters and disco kids; Michael Jackson fans, cult TV series such as *Dallas, Dynasty* and – on German TV – *Lindenstraße;* casting shows, Saturday night game shows such as *Wetten, dass…?* and cruise ship series such as *Das Traumschiff.* In pop culture, it was the decade that rediscovered dance in clubs. Thanks to disco, hip hop and punk,

10 "Oh my God, it's raining!"
Graffiti after the nuclear disaster of
Chernobyl, Eppertshausen, 1986

11 *Ahnen*
Wuppertal, 2014

urban dances such as breakdancing, pogo and the robot conquered the dancefloor. At the same time, Teddy Boys and, in Germany, consumerist Popper culture experienced a revival, and Yuppie culture began to spread. Environmental issues and political voices for peace gained ground and consolidated into their own distinct movements and subcultures. Last but not least, it was also the decade in which AIDS ended the candor and carelessness of permissive sex.

As the East-West conflict grew, the art world of the 1980s was (still) primarily concentrated in (Western) Europe and North America. Much of that which still holds true today was established during this floating decade. A veritable art market, even for contemporary art, emerged. Minimal art, conceptual art and pop art were transformed in subtle strategies that attempted to resituate art within a society increasingly dominated by the mass media. In concert dance, work done with the physicality of the body and its boundaries returned alongside disco and club dance; groups such as the English DV8 Physical Theatre, young Belgian choreographers such as Anne Teresa de Keersmaker and Wim Vandekeybus, and the Canadian group LaLaLa Human Steps introduced new dynamic aesthetics and a passion for movement that bordered on total physical exhaustion. They birthed a new genre, one that would go down in dance history as 'contemporary dance' and would henceforth historically and aesthetically push on to differentiate itself from the genre of dance theater.

Pina Bausch's second artistic phase with the Tanztheater Wuppertal fell in the midst of this floating, dance-loving decade. It was a phase characterized by internationalization on the one hand and aesthetic differentiation on the other. The troupe expanded its international touring activities and created pieces that added new flavors to what had come before.[62]

The beginning of this phase was marked by a deep personal and artistic turning point as Pina Bausch surrounded herself with a new team: after the death of Rolf Borzik, she worked with set designer Peter Pabst for the first time on the piece *1980,* who she had met during rehearsals for the "Macbeth Piece" in Bochum. For costumes, she chose Marion Cito, who had previously been employed as a dancer and then as her assistant (→ COMPANY). However, these personnel changes did not result in aesthetic upheaval. On the contrary: this phase of creation was one of stabilization and aesthetic differentiation. Unlike some other forms of theater and dance theater such as that of Johann Kresnik, her dance theater did not seek to refer to anything outside of what was visible onstage, nor did it intend to mean anything more than that which was occurring onstage in a process of constant transformation, mutation, repetition, variation and recontextualization. The elements of Pina Bausch's dance theater (sound, lighting, music, color, movement, language, materials) were

12 Wuppertaler Bühnen poster, 1989

13 *Ahnen* Wuppertal, 1987

not a vehicle for any other content outside of themselves. They did not present something; they created something distinctly new in every individual scene of every single performance. Pina Bausch's pieces renounced representation; they were performative. In every show, the dancers and the spectators directly experienced the many little worlds of everyday human existence. Over the years and through the wealth of pieces, these worlds painted a colorful picture of universal humanity, but also of gender-specific and culturally differentiated realms of experience: an accumulated cultural archive of human practices, attitudes and habits. Pina Bausch's art has often been described as a theater of emotions, but it was more than that: it was an approach that demonstrated in visible and physical 'doings' and 'sayings' the many ways in which these practices are sustained by feelings and emotions and in which they are constitutive for social situations.

Like the previous phase, the second phase in Wuppertal also began with a piece about childhood. *1980* – which would later go on to become one of the choreographer's most successful pieces, touring over 40 times (until 2019), with 30 performances before 1994 – tied into much of what had been aesthetically developed during the previous phase, while adding further layers to it. It is a choreographic piece with guiding melodies ("Jeden Tag fährt ein Schiff über den Ozean" ["Every Day a Ship Sails Across the Ocean"]), leitmotifs (birthdays), themes and counter-themes (childhood, joy, fun, passion/loneliness, grief, fear, loss), repetitions and variations (including interwoven scenes from previous pieces), group formations in circles, lines, and spirals. The piece works with *Verfremdungseffekte* or alien-nation effects ("Happy Birthday" sung in different constellations), exaggeration and recontextualization (the repeated spooning of soup in various contexts), and the layering of 'parts'/scenes. Overall, the piece presents little dance. One exception is a solo danced under a sprinkler, originally by Anne Martin. Most of the dancing is done by the entire ensemble in revue formation with dancers, e.g., moving about the auditorium. In addition, there are fast-paced, twitching figurations of movement, following one after another in breathtaking choreographic arrangements, beginning with a solo that resembles the disco dance 'the robot.' The music is a mixed collage of 'serious' and popular music by John Dowland, the Comedian Harmonists, Benny Goodman, Francis Lai, Edward Elgar, Johannes Brahms, Claude Debussy, Ludwig van Beethoven and John Wilson. The kind of scratchy old records still sold until the early 1960s underline the childhood theme of the piece as well as memories of the choreographer's childhood in the 1940s.

The set designed by Peter Pabst, a green roll of turf, underpins the rather cheerful overall impression made by the piece. Once again, the stage is an *Aktionsraum* (action space) as it had been in many past set designs. Like the peat in *The Rite of Spring* and the water in the "Macbeth Piece" and *Arien* (–› COMPANY), it not only influences the movement but also adds an olfactory dimension to the performance: during the course of the piece, the smell of the lawn spreads, humid and fresh.

1980 is danced theater, i.e., theater that tells stories through and with bodies, as Norbert Servos has repeatedly and convincingly described,[63] with more of a choreographic and musical structure rather than a theatrical one. This aspect has often been neglected in reviews of the piece. Moreover, unlike in dramatic plays, the performers are not just acting something out for the audience, but playing with the audience. As in earlier pieces, the speech acts are directed at the spectators, not at other performers as in classical theater. Here, the spectator is the performers' real partner, as is also apparent in the way that the dancers repeatedly break through the fourth wall between stage and auditorium.

As in the case of earlier pieces, *1980* draws attention to the recurring tension between human emotion and action, but even when dealing with grief, it does so in a somewhat lighter way than before, with much irony and wit. The fact that the subtitle *A Piece by Pina Bausch* is always mentioned, unlike in the case of other pieces, may not be accidental, but rather an indication that this piece is actually also a piece that tells part of the story of Pina Bausch in the year 1980.

One central, new theme in this piece was interculturality, which was performed through the internationality of the dancers, their languages, gestures and national icons (for example the cue: "Use three words to describe your own country," to which the dancers variously responded: "Adenauer, Beckenbauer, Schopenhauer," "Flamenco, Torreros, Picasso," and "Geisha, Honda, Harakiri," etc.). However, it also shows this in more fundamental ways: the relationships between individuals and the group shifts toward interactions between culturally marked individuality and transnational society. Interculturality, migration and cultural gestures are themes that would become central topics in the international coproductions of Pina Bausch's next artistic phase with the Tanztheater Wuppertal. In *1980,* this future still seems uncertain: in the final scene, one person stands facing the group. It is a scene that appears once before in the first part and that ends with the performers individually uttering set farewell phrases, emphasizing them in different ways using culturally specific gestures. However, in this final scene, nothing is resolved; the individual faces of the group are speechless and motionless. Could Pina Bausch continue working as a choreographer with this group after such a personal and artistic turning point?

Yes, she would continue. But it was the last time that there would be two new pieces in one year. The second piece of the year was *Bandoneon* (PREMIERE 1980). Pina Bausch probably found the inspiration for it during the company's South American tour of summer 1980, which also led them to Argentina. Scratched up records playing tangos by Carlos Gardel, an Argentinian icon from the first half of the 20th century, establishes the musical mood. The piece deals with dancers' personal histories. The dances are grotesque, deformed parodies – Pina Bausch was not looking to mimetically present the tango on stage. Raimund Hoghe cites Pina Bausch during rehearsals: "We'll just use the music – without anyone dancing a tango. During a tango the man only goes forwards or to the side, the woman backwards. Maybe the man can try to do the thing with the fire and to stroke the woman – or maybe something with a trick. I'd just like to see what it looks like. And do it over the music, very slowly."[64] This piece was thus already addressing a question that would characterize later coproductions above all: how is it possible to translate everyday dances and the dances of other cultures – the cultural gestures of everyday life on the one hand and folk dances, popular dances and ethnic dances on the other – into dances for the stage?

Bandoneon also deconstructed the stage, which was designed by Gralf Edzard Habben, who one year later would go on to cofound the independent Theater an der Ruhr in the city of Mülheim, close to Wuppertal and the river Ruhr, which he would direct until his death. For *Bandoneon,* he created a space reminiscent of the milonga dance halls in the suburbs of Buenos Aires: little old gyms with photos of boxers hanging on the walls, small tables and old, cheap chairs scattered all around. But over the course of the piece, the set is gradually dismantled by stagehands: furniture, pictures, clothing and lights are removed, the dance floor ripped out. This was not intended as a theatrical reference to the fact that milonga spaces also occasionally serve other purposes and can transform back into gyms; it was, like the method of 'asking questions' in the "Macbeth Piece" and the use of prerecorded music in *Bluebeard,* the result of a rehearsal situation: due to a belated general rehearsal one day before the premiere, the artistic director of the opera house lost his patience and demanded that the stagehands dismantle the set to make room for the opera performance planned that night. But the company continued to rehearse – and so this confrontation between the demands of the art establishment and the choreographer's need for time and space in order to continue creating made its way into the piece as an invasion of the real into the space of the theatrical. It translates the institutional demands and necessities of theater into an aesthetic concept, while simultaneously calling them into question

– in a way that conceptual dance would later claim for itself in the 1990s. Not only do the performers perform authenticity, but their actions also reveal the uncertainty of real and fake, of play and seriousness, of work process and piece.

What followed was the longest artistic hiatus in Pina Bausch's entire career. The year 1981 passed without any new creations. The next piece was *Walzer* (PREMIERE 1982), which the choreographer developed in September 1981 after the birth of her son Rolf Salomon Bausch. As in previous pieces, Pina Bausch once again addressed the subject of interwoven opposites: "The opposites are important [...]. They're the only way that we can get any idea of the age that we are living in today."[65]

The piece dramaturgically unfolds along the fault lines of kitsch, melancholy and joy: its subject matter is being born and dying, giving birth and killing, arrival and departure, travel and crossing borders, war and peace, grief and survival. The focus is on both the battlegrounds of world politics and inner struggles: relationships with family and memories. Here, dance only exists as social dance and polonaises, which worm their way across the stage.

In this piece, Pina Bausch continued to inquire into the ways in which artistic work processes could aesthetically be translated onto the stage. She laid bare the rehearsal process and the relationships between choreographer and dancers by letting the dancers say, "And then Pina asked..." before showing what they had developed. When asked about peace symbols, for example, Jan Minařík, answered by putting on an evening gown, throwing flowers from his skirt and hopping like a pigeon. The piece was a renewed affirmation and confirmation of the ensemble's views – and it was also a reflection of current political and social events, such as the virulent discussions provoked by a reinvigorated peace movement.

Tune and timbre soon changed with *Nelken* (PREMIERE 1982). This piece presents both a dream of modest happiness and the im-/possibility of this dream becoming a reality. After having not been involved in the last two pieces, Peter Pabst resumed responsibility for the stage design, producing a sea of flowers probably inspired by a field of carnations that Pina Bausch had seen in an Andean valley during the South America tour of 1980.[66] Peter Pabst built it out of hundreds of faux fabric blossoms, produced in Asia under inhuman working conditions – a fact that was not addressed in the piece. Many of the flowers tore during the performance.

In this piece, wardens with German shepherd dogs patrol the field of carnations. This scene is a materialization of the piece's thematic conflict between utopia and reality, between hope and fear, in the dream-like imagery of a flowery landscape scarred by the simultaneous presence of police control and violence. Although it was not the first time that live animals were used onstage – the original version of *Bandoneon* included Beatrice Libonati's hamster – they were now active, participating performers. Once again, Pina Bausch revealed herself to be a pioneer of new performance aesthetics: what is a performer? What constitutes the situation of performance? In what ways are the animals' movements different from those of human beings? The last question appears particularly vividly in a scene in which the dancers hop through the carnations like frightened rabbits. One of the central topics of the piece is migration and the harassment that travelers suffer at the borders of different nation states. How closely are dance and the military related? Answering the question of why they became dancers, a question to which all dancers reply facing the audience, the last dancer says: "[...] because I did not want to become a soldier." War – a reoccurring motif of the wartime generation – reappears in *Two Cigarettes in the Dark* (PREMIERE 1985), as well as in its predecessor *On the Mountain a Cry was Heard* (PREMIERE 1984). The former is a colder, more bitter piece, which began with Mechthild Großmann in the original cast sweeping toward the audience in a white evening gown with outstretched arms, saying: "Do come in; my husband is at war."

One striking aspect of *Nelken* in terms of its dancing is not only the sign language into which Lutz Förster translated George and Ira Gershwin's ballad "The Man I Love" but also the ensemble sequence in which the dancers depict the seasons in gestures. Since Pina Bausch's death, this dance has been popularized as "The *Nelken* Line," danced worldwide as a participatory community event. The website of the Pina Bausch Foundation states: "Many people from all over the world have danced with us and are sharing videos of their personal *Nelken* lines here. They dance in unusual places, in costume or in everyday clothes. With family, friends and pets. In winter, in spring, sometimes sad or rather funny. Together, alone or in almost never-ending lines. The variations are already as diverse as life itself."[67]

By the end of this artistic phase, various themes that had been carried over from the previous phases, such as men and women, childhood and loneliness, love and sex, home and flight, life and death had been developed with new images. Some motifs were revisited, such as the song "Mamatschi, schenk mir ein Pferdchen, ein Pferdchen wär' mein Paradies..." (Mummy, Give me a Little Horse, a Little Horse would be my Paradise...) from the piece *1980* in the new piece *Two Cigarettes in the Dark*. The song is reminiscent of a childhood spent during the war. It was one of the most popular Christmas songs in 1942 (→ COMPANY).

This revisiting of motifs occurred during an introspective phase of what had now become an internationally acclaimed company. It was also a phase that not only fundamentally questioned concert dance and its conventions and norms but actually ripped apart and literally stripped the dispositif of theater itself and of theater as a site of bourgeois representation down to the naked bricks of the firewalls. At the same time, this phase set the course for changes to come: the company's extensive touring activities in the 1980s had created a strong international focus that led to a growing emphasis on questions of interculturality, migration, cultural difference and similarity. This also marked the beginning of a phase in which Pina Bausch would no longer develop new pieces with the entire ensemble.

1986-2000: INTERCULTURAL ARTISTIC PRODUCTION
AND THE REDISCOVERY OF DANCE

If defined as a phase of increased coproduction, then Pina Bausch and the Tanztheater Wuppertal's third artistic phase started with the piece *Viktor* (PREMIERE 1986; → WORK PROCESS). "The idea from the Teatro Argentina in Rome of working with us on a piece that was to come about through experiences gained in Rome was of decisive, I could even say fateful, significance for my development and way of working."[68]

The coproductions were frequently supported by local branches of the Goethe-Institut and highlighted the Institut's new policy of a more locally embedded cultural politics of cooperation. The aim was to encourage more German artists to work abroad. However, in doing so, it also furthered the expansion of a globalized cultural industry. Once again, the Tanztheater Wuppertal led the way. Its collaborations strengthened the company's international focus and fed its growing interest in expanding its danced, staged archive of human practices, attitudes and habits via the direct experience and artistic exploration of other cultures (→ WORK PROCESS). Accessing this wealth of human existence and bringing it to the stage would remain, with a total of 15 coproductions, one of Pina Bausch's most central activities. It was during this phase that she became what I refer to as a 'cultural anthropologist of dance,' practicing an ethnography of everyday life using artistic means. In his speech at the memorial service marking her death in September 2009 at the Opernhaus Wuppertal, filmmaker Wim Wenders said: "[...] Pina was a scientist, a researcher, a pioneer of the uncharted territories of the human soul."[69] Two years earlier, she had described her own work as follows: "Getting to know completely foreign customs, types of music, habits has led to things that are unknown to us, but which still belong to us, all being translated into dance. [...]. And so everything that influences us in our coproductions and flows into the pieces also belongs to the dance theatre forever. We take it with us everywhere. It's a little bit like marrying and then becoming related to one another."[70]

This artistic phase comprised a total of eleven pieces.[71] Eight of them were coproductions.[72] In addition, Pina Bausch shot her first and only film during this period, *The Plaint of the Empress*, from October 1987 until April 1988.[73] She was probably motivated to do so by her role as the silent countess in Federico Fellini's film *E la nave va* (And the Ship Sails On; 1983). Her own film was an experience that would continue to influence her work.

Aside from artistically focusing on the interculturality of everyday gestures, attitudes and habits, as well as on the universality of the emotions that guide them, this work phase was characterized by a generational shift in the company. After *Viktor*, the company took in new dancers (→ COMPANY) such as Barbara Hampel (later known by her married name, Kaufmann), Julie Stanzak and Julie Shanahan, who became some of the best-known performers of the Tanztheater Wuppertal.[74] At the end of this phase, the company had assembled most of the members with whom Pina Bausch would continue to work until her death. These changes in the ensemble fundamentally altered the aesthetics of the pieces. The young and energetic dancers brought dance back onto the stage; the pieces featured more, longer solos danced individually in succession at the expense of group dances and 'theatrical' spoken scenes.

Pina Bausch's (re)discovery of dance, of its beauty, its lightness and perfection of form and her simultaneous departure from themes such as power, violence and destruction also need to be regarded in this new light. For this aesthetic transformation within the Tanztheater Wuppertal ran contrary to the paradigm shift in contemporary dance at the time, i.e., the rise of 'conceptual dance,' a dance form that chose to almost entirely abstain from any dancing whatsoever. Most notably, this artistic phase occurred during a period of radical sociopolitical and global economic upheaval: a century and a millennium were coming to an end – and with them established mentalities and ways of life, ideas, ideologies and technologies. A new economic, political and social world order was emerging. The media extensively covered political scientist Francis Fukuyama's prophesy of the "end of history,"[75] and it was not just at the beginning of the piece *Palermo Palermo*, which premiered on December 17, 1989, that walls surprisingly came tumbling down (→ COMPANY).

The "peaceful revolution" in East Germany, which euphorically began in late 1989 with the fall of the Berlin Wall and led to the reunification of a country that had been separated for 40 years, soon transformed into an atmosphere of lethargy, disappointment, anger and hate. In many ways, the 1990s were the opposite of the 1960s – that decade of democratic awakening. Back then, the general desire for democratization had led to a profound change in values, with people freeing themselves from traditional contexts, norms, milieus and communities and demanding individual freedom and autonomy, while placing value on individual self-expression over order and discipline. The 1990s, by contrast, were a decade of stagnation and paralysis, of resignation and disappointment – in spite of the democratic upheavals in Eastern Europe and even in spite of apartheid ending in South Africa in 1994. In the early 1990s, war and civil war returned to Europe, namely to the region of former Yugoslavia. The wars were accompanied by a resurgence of nationalism and new confrontations that to this day fuel inner-political strife in many places across Europe, as well as tensions between the national interests of individual countries and those of the European Community. Religion, which had lost meaning in Western Europe in the wake of secularization, became a new source of identity, confidence and meaning in many parts of the world, as well as an ideological engine for political action and a strategy for justifying crime and assassinations.

In Germany, reality overtook the promised future of the "flourishing landscapes" that former "Chancellor of Unity" Helmut Kohl had so euphorically promised to the East Germans. The former East German states increasingly suffered from rising unemployment numbers and brain drain. The loss of all that had previously been so certain and the breakdown of institutional order, the educational backlog and a politics of stalemate took their toll. Moreover, civil war in the Balkans kindled a new wave of migration, and the growing numbers of refugees were reason enough for many to incite a fear and hate of immigrants. In the early 1990s, there was a return of what was thought to have been pushed back during the 1960s and 1980s: distrust, rejection, stigmatization, persecution. Attacks on homes for asylum seekers became a symbol of the decade. Nationalist, right-wing radicalism, Islamic terror, speculative stock exchange trading, filter bubbles, the pressures of self-optimization, the digitalization of communication on the Internet and mobile phones, as well as the transformation of vast sections of journalism into tabloids – all of it was already part and parcel of the decade's bourgeoning globalization and digitalization.

This wave of profound change was accompanied by a media culture in love with naiveté. The 1990s produced *Baywatch*, *Seinfeld and Friends*, *Pulp Fiction* and *Forrest Gump*, cast boy bands like Take That and the Backstreet Boys and girl groups such as the Spice Girls and All Saints, but it also spawned grunge and gangsta rap, Nirvana and Oasis. In Germany, techno was born in the same year that the wall fell, soon leading to huge mass events such as the Love Parade in Berlin, which took place annually from 1989 until 2010, with as

14 After the fall of the wall
    Berlin, 1989

15 Love-Parade
    Berlin, 1995

16 *The Window Washer*
Wuppertal, 1997

17 »*..como el musguito en la piedra, ay si, si, si...*«
Sankt Pölten, 2015

many as 1.5 million people dancing in the streets in 1999. Rebecca Casati – very much a child of the hip, 'zeitgeist journalism' of the time – called the 1990s "an overall presentable, but latently self-pitying era completely without secrets."[76] She based this assessment on the body modifications of the time: "tramp stamps, neck or tribal tattoos, pierced eyebrows, tongues, noses or bellybuttons, nose jobs done a bit too small and slipped implants, today, they all say: yes. It didn't matter. But I was there."[77] The 1990s were also the first decade that never really ended, because before they were over, they had already been revived in the form of media hype. New digital media began to play a major role in this era: the 1990s were the decade in which we not only learned that everything can be reproduced by the media but also that it would always be accessible and that – with the introduction of mobile phones – anyone can be reached anywhere and at any time.

In art, this decade experienced the unfolding of a global art market, accompanied by an expansion of festival and event culture in the arts. The global art market, in which (Western) curators quickly established themselves as the new ruling elite, found its match in artists' rejectionist attitudes and an absence of the spectacle. The fall of the Berlin Wall and the collapse of the Eastern Bloc together with consumer culture, globalization and digitalization played decisive roles in this process: art shifted its attention from the production of things to the processing of symbols, data, words, images and sounds. Art had begun examining its own dispositif, the aim being, as some said, not only to produce but to "renegotiate" art. Producing nothing, but creating symbolic references and exhibiting work processes and materials was typical of 1990s art.

Conceptual dance likewise pursued parallel developments during the 1990s. It distanced itself from its 'object,' from dance itself. Contrary to the developments made by the Tanztheater Wuppertal, conceptual dance began staging the disappearance of the dancing subject. In doing so, it radicalized dance's process of reflexivity up to the point of not dancing at all. After dance theater had questioned dance's role as a form of 'beautiful appearance' *(schöner Schein),* and after the 1980s had drawn attention to the physicality of the body, conceptual dance in the 1990s caused dance as a physical, performative event to disappear altogether. In the same way that conceptual art in the 1960s had valued the idea over its presentation and the concept over the piece itself, conceptual dance replaced the performative act of dancing and the execution of movements with the introspection of choreography. Unlike dance theater, conceptual dance directly addressed the separation of concept and visible piece, of choreography and dance, of representation and performance, of dancers and dance. This transformed perceptions: the perception of dance as a physical aesthetic event was overshadowed by reflections on the conceptual topic of the piece. Unlike in dance theater, the audience was no longer invited to empathize with the piece, but rather challenged to actively participate in the process and reflect on the conceptual idea. While Pina Bausch opened her pieces up to the audience, conceptual dance even more fundamentally questioned the role of the spectator. Conceptual dance's contribution to dance history has been the realization that spectators are coproducers of choreography.

In this phase, the aesthetic development of the Tanztheater Wuppertal formed a counterpart to this aesthetic paradigm shift. For decades, Pina Bausch's dance theater had refused to dance in the classical sense and had staged dance in broken, distorted, lampooned and satirized form. Thus, it could certainly be seen in this respect as a precursor to conceptual dance. But while conceptual dance increasingly dominated dance discourse, the Tanztheater Wuppertal rediscovered its joy of dancing – in a sociopolitical period of paralysis and uncertainty, but also of geopolitical transformation.

Pina Bausch had always integrated the impressions, experiences, materials and music collected on tour into her pieces. With the advent of the coproductions, this method became the aesthetic hallmark of her work. The 'familiar' and the 'foreign,' central topics of discourse in cultural studies and the social sciences during the 1990s, now formed the core of her art: the foreign appeared within the familiar, making the perception of the familiar seem foreign, making it felt as a narrow horizon.

This process simultaneously opened up new horizons in the distance, new ways of seeing the familiar. The interplay between the familiar and foreign was an intrinsic part of the international company's work from the start, but it gained new intensity with Pina Bausch's method of 'asking questions' and even more so with their research trips to coproducing cities and countries (→ WORK PROCESS). In her search for the familiar in the foreign and the foreign in the familiar, Pina Bausch shifted her attention to a key cultural-anthropological question: are there similarities that all people share in spite of their cultural differences? The coproductions were therefore not about translating the influences of a country into dance as Marion Meyer titled one chapter of the German version of her book about Pina Bausch,[78] but rather about tapping into a giant mosaic of human existence and actions by experiencing other cultural spaces, cultural differences and similarities.

The coproductions of the Tanztheater Wuppertal were informed by an "ethos of respecting and disrespecting boundaries,"[79] as formulated by German philosopher Bernhard Waldenfels. They did not exhibit the 'foreign,' i.e., did not make a display of people, present themselves as supposed tour guides or exhibit folklore, as some critics expected them to. Many viewers were disappointed when they were unable to discover anything of the coproducing country in the pieces. For example, it is easy to discern the author's disappointment after the premiere of *Viktor* in the following lines: "They say the piece was developed in Rome. There is not much Italianità in it, although the observation of other social customs in another country would undoubtedly have provided new impulses."[80] A critic in the *Westfälische Anzeiger* argued similarly after the premiere of *Masurca Fogo* in 1998: "It is almost impossible to recognize what is typically Portuguese about this piece. Except the music of course, which, aside from fado, also includes some melancholy songs from Cabo Verde and Brazilian Samba, in other words the former colonial regions of Portugal's erstwhile global empire."[81] And even novelist Judith Kuckart, who fell in love with Pina Bausch's art at the early age of 15, dejectedly wrote after the premiere of *Viktor:* "Rome, meant to be the actual theme of the piece, is only hinted at, as a citation of what are often typical tourist impressions."[82]

The pieces are not accusatory – not even in cases of known human rights violations in the coproducing countries. They do not try to elevate themselves or claim any cultural authority. The translation of what the company had observed and perceived during its research trips occasionally produced scenes that reflect the everyday culture of the cities and countries that they had visited – such as the funeral rites in *Palermo Palermo,* the chants of college students in *Only You* (PREMIERE 1996), which was coproduced in Los Angeles with various universities, and the enthusiastic "Good morning – Thank you" opening scene in *The Window Washer* (PREMIERE 1997), a coproduction with Hong Kong. This was also the case in the next artistic phase: the massage rituals in the Turkish bath of *Nefés* (PREMIERE 2003), coproduced in Istanbul, or the bath scenes in *Água* (PREMIERE 2001), a coproduction with São Paulo. However, these experiences are more subtly reflected in the choreographies themselves: in the abrupt transitions of *Rough Cut* (PREMIERE 2005), a coproduction with Seoul in which the daily rhythms of the South Korean metropolis are translated into the theatrical and musical dramaturgy of the piece; in the meditative undertone of *Ten Chi* (PREMIERE 2004), the Japanese coproduction, which ends in an ecstatic dance by all; and in the fabric blowing gently in the wind in *Bamboo Blues* (PREMIERE 2007), the coproduction with India.

Thus, translating here does not mean transposing typical gestures of a cultural site (coproduction location) into a piece. It allows the everyday as a lifestyle pattern, as a horizon of meaning and as a cultural form to pass through a number of interwoven steps and practices of translation throughout the work process: what the dancers perceived during their research is transposed into their own horizons of experience and then into individual scenes or dance solos, i.e., into aesthetic form, to finally be reframed in the choreography, the set design, the music and the costumes, which are in turn perceived in different ways by various audiences in different temporalities and in various cultural contexts. Central metaphors for this work are travel, movement, migration, the fluid and the transitory, which are given a performative setting through the stage designs (e.g., ships, quickly raised barracks), materials (flowing dresses, video projections), music (a mix of music from different cultures) and above all through the dancing.

"I have had so much luck in my life, above all through our journeys and friendships. This I wish for a lot of people: that they should get to know other cultures and ways of life. There would be much less fear of others, and one could see much clearer what joins us all. I think it is important to know the world one lives in. The fantastic possibility we have onstage is that we might be able to do things that one is not allowed to do or cannot do in normal life. Sometimes, we can only clarify something by confronting ourselves, with what we don't know. And sometimes the questions we have bring us back to experiences which are much older, which not only come from our culture and not only deal with the here and now. It is, as if a certain knowledge returns to us, which we indeed always had, but which is not conscious and present. It reminds us of something, which we all have in common. This gives us great strength."[83]

Pina Bausch considered life to be a journey.[84] Dance is also a journey – a journey through one's own body. In her pieces, this journey takes place on volatile ground in a constant back and forth between the poles of home/flight, security/fear, love/hate, joy/grief, intimacy/distance and life/death. The coproductions present and perform these tensions in all their cultural differences. In doing so, the work of the Tanztheater Wuppertal emphasizes travel as a philosophy and as a principle of life in the age of globalization, migration, flight and (re)invigorated xenophobia and segregation. It thus also addresses the same question posed by Walter Benjamin in his famous essay "The Task of the Translator"[85]: what is the relationship between the similarities shared by human beings in something akin to "suprahistorical kinship"[86] and their many undeniable cultural differences? In the work of the Tanztheater Wuppertal, what connects humanity is not only the struggle for love, security and happiness but seemingly also nature, its beauty and grandeur, its role as a protector, a place of refuge and utopia, as well as the threat of its destruction. The pieces feature, for example, bird and animal calls, rainforests, sand dunes in *The Piece with the Ship* (PREMIERE 1993), islands of water in *Ein Trauerspiel* (PREMIERE 1994), rocky landscapes in *Masurca Fogo* (PREMIERE 1998) and reoccurring video projections of natural landscapes, travelers, palm trees and underwater worlds.

Together with *Ahnen* (PREMIERE 1987), which was not a coproduction, it is possible to see *Viktor* and *Palermo Palermo* as a trilogy. They all have a more aggressive, rather than melancholy, baseline. They were aesthetically developed under the influence of Pina Bausch's first artistic phase and thus mainly feature ensemble dances. In the early 1990s – during a period of social paralysis, of disorientation and new segregation – much of this changed, as dance in Pina Bausch's pieces increasingly became a place of refuge: a utopian space and a place to experience the Other in an otherwise inhospitable society. Ultimately, all of Pina Bausch's pieces reference what dance has meant to her since childhood: a peaceful place of hope and happiness, playfulness and complacency, longing and affection, but also a world of strife and loneliness, inner struggles and battlegrounds – and a physical way to experience the extra-ordinary.

This new orientation in her work revealed itself in the next three pieces – *Tanzabend II* (PREMIERE 1991), *The Piece with the Ship* and *Ein Trauerspiel* – which Pina Bausch herself also considered to be a trilogy, as she explained in an interview in 1995: "The kind of questions I ask are a little different than before, when I was looking for gestures and other things. *Tanzabend II*, *The Piece with the Ship* and *Ein Trauerspiel* belong together for me."[87] The piece *Tanzabend II*, a coproduction with Madrid, was created in 1990/91 amidst the impressions of the second Gulf War and is actually a piece about dance itself. Solos, duets and ensemble dances are the primary medium used to make rage and grief tangible. At the same time, dance is a medium of the imaginary and the dreamlike, where desires and hopes can be experienced. One year later, in *The Piece with the Ship*, it was the dances that presented the subjects' inner strife, torn between grief and despair, longing and hoping. Next, *Ein Trauerspiel* once again set out in search of dance, a search that went beyond all of the forms and figurations that had already been shown and broken, and had now become ineffectual. Here, dance is used as a physical medium of personal affirmation. In the piece, a dancer yells into the audience, "What do you think it all means? – Nothing!" Not only does this question/statement pay homage to Jacques Derrida's deconstructionist philosophy of language, which was being hotly debated at the time, it also reveals what dance means to Pina Bausch's dance theater, as something that is momentary and present in perception – as a movement, form, trace, sound and rhythm. Dance allows the dancers' subjectivity to emerge, but it does not represent it. Dance is a performative practice – and as such, it is translated.

Danzón, which was not a coproduction, is similar in this respect: dance returns to the stage in an exploration of ethnic and colonial dance cultures. Danzón is a partner dance popular in Cuba and also much loved in Mexico. It developed out of French contredanse, popular in aristocratic circles of the 17th century, as well as out of English country dancing. It then made its way to Haiti and Cuba in the 18th and 19th centuries with French immigrants. In Cuba, it evolved into danza in the mid-19th century – elegant salon music played by charangas, classical ensembles resembling European orchestras. In the late 19th century, danzón emerged as a rhythmic variation of the danza. The movements of this partner dance are calm, elegant and expressive, quite different from the dance madness or mania described by Servos.[88] At first, the Cuban partner dance danzón was only danced by the white upper class and in the most exclusive clubs of Havana, until gradually the Black population adopted it in the late 1920s and developed it into a new syncopated style.

Danzón explores everything that dance can be: it is wild, sudden, angular, accentuated, driven, as in the dances of the men, but also desperate, abandoned, crouching and writhing, as in some of the female solos, or sad, melancholy, self-absorbed, lonely but also devoted, as in the solo danced by Pina Bausch herself. For this piece, she once again took to the stage for the first and last time since *Café Müller*, dancing to the sound of three fados against a video backdrop of colorful fish, which filled the entire stage. In the end, she waved to the audience as she left the stage.

In the following pieces – the coproductions *Only You, The Window Washer, Masurca Fogo, O Dido* (PREMIERE 1999) and *Wiesenland* (PREMIERE 2000) – dance took up more and more space, especially in the form of solos. Partner dances and duets in all kinds of variations – e.g., as seated dances or group formations – were always an integral part of Pina Bausch's pieces, because they allowed her to explicitly exhibit the unity and insularity of the couple and its intimacy. But now, her focus was increasingly shifting toward solos: individual dancers increasingly assumed the task of revealing sources of tension and the simultaneous presence of contradictions.

As the choreographer said: "When you watch a person dancing alone, you have time to pay special attention to them: what they emanate, how vulnerable they are, how sensitive. Sometimes it's the tiny little things that make someone special. […]. How do we deal with our helplessness in the present age, how can we express our distress [?]"[89]

Dance had become a medium of self-affirmation, of finding one's place in turbulent times, a means of translation, able to communicate something that went beyond the mere representation of acquired skill, beyond a presentation of virtuosity. It manifested in risky, exhaustingly dynamic solos and in delicate and joyful movements of resistance and courage, of desperation, intimacy and sincerity, exhaustion and introspection, of strength and solace, meditation and joie de vivre, happiness and eroticism, desire and courtship, of shimmers of hope and as a utopian medium for the affirmation of existence. "Dance, dance – otherwise we are lost," is what a Roma girl once said to Pina Bausch, and this statement was to become the leitmotif of Wim Wender's film *pina* (2011).

Dancing also brought humor and wit back into the pieces. It was not the garish, wild humor of earlier artistic phases, but something lighter. As in the 1970s and 1980s, when Pina Bausch's bitter, piercing, harsh pieces formed a counterpart to the cultural complacency and ostensibly secure social security net of West German society, these pieces were her answer to the world's growing brutality and propensity for violence, as well as to the increasing disenfranchisement of political institutions in globalized societies. "When times are good, I think I have a tendency to talk about things that are kind of harsh, or serious, or violent. At the moment I think it's rather the opposite. And the pieces aren't just cheerful, I don't think so at all. For example, in the case of the Hong Kong piece, if there wasn't something for me to laugh about at the moment, I wouldn't know how to go on. And I think that what comes out of it has something to do with a balance that I'm looking for, I don't know exactly. All my pieces came into being in a certain time."[90]

This reaction to the time was a "homage to life,"[91] to beauty, love, intimacy, devotion, pleasure, community, to life's dreams and to vitality. But once again, there was a hidden downside, as Pina Bausch explained: "There is no cheerfulness without the other thing, humor is a certain form of coping. Perhaps I'm trying to find something in that sense: how can we laugh at something together or be snarky? It's an agreement, and it's good for us to find this point, it makes things easier, but doesn't take away any of the hardship or the like, but perhaps it's a way of dealing with it."[92]

This fourth artistic phase ended with a special kind of translation: *Kontakthof with Seniors* (PREMIERE 2000) transposed the material produced by professional dancers onto a group of senior citizens with little to no stage experience. "From very early on, I wanted to see this piece once the dancers were old, but I didn't want to wait that long, and they always look so young [...]. I wanted it because there's life experience there and because tenderness plays such a big role in all my pieces. [...]. And at the same time, of course, it was also my gesture toward the region here in Wuppertal [...]. Of course, I had no idea what a huge influence it would have on all the people who participated and on their families. The grandmothers are no longer the grandmothers of before. So, it was lovely, the right thing to do."[93]

Other pieces such as *Viktor* and *Only You* had also already included some semi-professionals. But now, the roles of professional dancers were passed on to completely different people for the very first time. This translation also constituted a first step toward popularizing the company's own pieces – something that the Pina Bausch Foundation continues to do to this day, e.g., with workshop series and participatory events such as "The Nelken Line." In *Kontakthof with Seniors,* Pina Bausch allowed a different age group, that of Wuppertal's core audience, i.e., the spectators who had aged with the company, to experience the piece with their own bodies.

2001-2009: THE LOVE OF DANCE AND NATURE

Pina Bausch's last artistic phase with the Tanztheater Wuppertal was during the first decade of the 21st century. The 2000s are considered to be the years in which "the world switched into turbo gear."[94] In 2009, *Time* called this decade of crisis a "decade from hell."[95] 'Digital,' 'global,' 'catastrophic,' 'contradictory' and 'rapid' were the catchwords of a short decade that more or less began on September 11, 2001, sparking a war based on the false statements of the US government, and then prematurely ended in 2008 with the financial crisis and the election of the first Black American president. It was at this time that the Internet had its breakthrough: from now on, communication would be exceedingly fast and ubiquitous in new types of communities, with email, chat, text, Skype, links, blogs and Twitter. Ever since, we have been learning to do it all at the same time from any digitally connected place on earth. Multitasking, which was once a psychological term, became the hallmark of everyday life. iPods and iPhones became the epitomes of a latent feeling of being 'already there.' We began drinking 'to go' and eating 'slow.' We celebrated peaking stock markets and discussed new social security policies. The decade's global challenges took on new political poignancy with the publication of the report of the Intergovernmental Panel on Climate Change in 2007. Now, the world had substantiated findings to prove that humanity's activities were truly responsible for global warming. The German Federal Government's 2008 Report on Poverty and Wealth unmistakably showed that, even in Germany, the social divide had dramatically increased during the 20 years since reunification.

However, this decade was not only one of political and social crisis and catastrophe, it was also a decade in which social isolation resulted in new forms of solidarity. When the Elbe River flooded Saxony in 2002, crowds of volunteers provided hands-on support, and when a tsunami killed 230,000 people from East Africa to Indonesia at Christmas 2004, people worldwide donated a total of USD 14 billion. In 2006, Germany hosted the FIFA World Cup and garnered international respect and sympathy for not only organizing the massive event well but also for being an excellent host and for presenting itself as a generous, soccer-loving nation.

This was Pina Bausch's last work phase and, after celebrating the first "Fest in Wuppertal" in 1998 to mark the 25th anniversary of the company, she too assumed the role of international hostess

18 *Wiesenland*
Wuppertal, 2012

19 Pina Bausch
in *Danzón*
Wuppertal, 1995

in her own country. In spite of the company's lively touring activities and despite new productions and restagings, she chose to act as artistic director for the new International Dance Festival in 2004 and 2008 in the German state of North Rhine-Westphalia. In this role, she invited young choreographers such as Anne Teresa de Keersmaker, Sasha Waltz and Sidi Larbi Cherkaoui, as well as a large number of internationally acclaimed artists, to a three-week long celebration, showcasing 50 different performances from 20 countries at 13 different venues in 2008 alone. The pieces developed by the Tanztheater Wuppertal in this phase had a different aesthetic than before. As noted two years earlier, in a 1999 review in *The Guardian:* "Bausch's closest fans feel that her recent work has become more dancerly in tone – reflecting the more precocious technique of a younger generation of dancers – and this trend may please critics, who complained of the lack of choreography in earlier works."[96] In this phase, the trend toward a more 'dancerly' style increased. The pieces of this decade are mainly composed of solos,[97] strung together like pearls in a necklace. Pina Bausch compared their dramaturgy to a rosary: "Yes, the dances are like rosaries in that respect (laughs). It's something incessant, something that goes on and on. There's always someone new. But I could also repeat it and start all over again. There's an arc, a circle in it."[98]

Interestingly enough, both authors and a large number of critics describing the pieces from this phase tended to simply list scene after scene and action after action.[99] They were mere chronological retellings of what had happened onstage and, unlike in the case of earlier works, rarely grasped the thematic, conceptual or dramaturgical heart of the pieces. It is also striking that the solos, which played such a major role in these pieces, were mentioned, but not described in depth. What was the reason for this? Was it a lack of expertise in describing dance or was it a failed attempt to translate dance into text? (→ SOLO DANCE)

Servos, a profound authority on Pina Bausch's work and long-standing companion of the Tanztheater Wuppertal, tried hard to thematically grasp the pieces from this phase. In the end, he narrowed them down to the subject of 'love.' He described *Masurca Fogo* as "a testimony to the self-renewing power of life," and *Água* – which premiered approximately four months before 9/11 and represented the (tentative) end of the company's complete overhaul of its ensemble – as "a plea for beauty and pleasure," a call "to enjoy life here and now – without any reservations."[100] *Nefés* was "an almost seamless sequence of images depicting love,"[101] an "advocation for sensuality and pleasure,"[102] and *Rough Cut* an indication that "the desire for love is existential and should not be denied."[103] Was the reason behind these generalized, only slightly varying descriptions that a lover of Pina Bausch's art could no longer grasp the pieces properly, because solos were harder to translate? Or was it because the pieces had distanced themselves from acute and current social issues and showed dance as an antithesis to everyday crises and the stage as a world of utopian spaces?

Questions like these arise above all if we take global events, but also the specific social and political backdrop of the coproducing countries into account: the piece *Nefés,* for example, premiered the same year that the US military invaded Iraq. This was a military maneuver that George W. Bush's government justified with false information, drawing in the support of Great Britain and the so-called Coalition of the Willing, thus leading to the outbreak of the Iraq War (Second Gulf War). In Turkey, a parliamentary election in November 2002 shook up Turkey's political system.[104] One year later, in 2004, Pina Bausch took up, as in *Nefés,* an antithetical position to the tense global situation: while terrorist attacks became almost daily news worldwide, she produced *Ten Chi* – a piece that is pensive, quiet, introverted and meditative, but also flirtatious and ecstatic. That same year, the company also premiered *Bamboo Blues* at the onset of the financial crisis, while the effects of climate change made themselves noticeable in heat waves, severe thunderstorms, earthquakes, forest fires and flash floods. In contrast, the coproduction with India was reminiscent of the gentle sound of palm trees and light breezes in Kochi, Kerala, where both the company and Pina Bausch herself had traveled several times during their research. The piece explores forms of intimacy in duets and trios. Like all other coproductions in this phase, the piece does not deal with social evils as everyday conflicts. There is no mention of the inhumane conditions in India, the poverty, the subordinate role of women, the rigid caste system or the enormous production of garbage – although the research journey had been closely coordinated by the Indian offices of the Goethe-Institut in order to actually show the company all these things. It therefore disappointed not only some critics[105] but above all some members of the Indian audience, especially in light of the Tanztheater Wuppertal's frenetic

20 US-soldiers and Iraqi demonstrators Iraq, 2004

welcome in Mumbai, Chennai, Kolkata and New Delhi during the last tour of *Nelken* in 1994, after the first tour with *The Rite of Spring* had ended in a veritable scandal in 1979, when the performance in Kolkata had to be cancelled (→ RECEPTION).

However, in *Bamboo Blues,* Pina Bausch continued to pursue an idea originally initiated by the offices of India's Goethe-Institut and its dynamic director of the time, Georg Lechner, although in other ways. During the 1994 tour of India, both the Tanztheater Wuppertal and Chandralekha – a women's and human rights activist and former star of classical Bharatanatyam dance, now pioneer and grande dame of modern Indian dance – presented their work to an audience on a double bill entitled East-West Encounter. Many years later, Pina Bausch transformed this idea for her own company. '*Sweet Mambo*' (PREMIERE 2008) experiments with the multiple facets of aesthetic and cultural translation already apparent in Pina Bausch's work. While the coproductions explored the relationship between the familiar and the foreign in various different cultural contexts, '*Sweet Mambo,*' which was not a coproduction, attempts a kind of artistic comparative study. It is a companion piece to *Bamboo Blues,* using other dancers, but taking place on the same set and asking the same questions. Rehearsals for the premiere only took place in Wuppertal. There was no research trip. In other words: the piece shifted the cultural framework, repatriating the foreign into the familiar, intending to explore "how two different pieces can be created using different dancers but the same starting point."[106] In 'Sweet Mambo,' Pina Bausch reverses the practice of cultural translation as established in the coproductions while simultaneously demonstrating the impossibility of repetition and the difference in variation.

But were the pieces in this last phase of her work really so apolitical, so disinterested in social events as critics suggest? Did they not in fact concentrate on individual, situative encounters with threats and violence, dangers and boundaries – while simultaneously searching for ways to escape into a politics of the personal, of the everyday? No, they were not apolitical and yes, they did in fact offer an alternative path. The full title of Pina Bausch's last piece "...*como el musguito en la piedra, ay si, si si*..." (Like Moss On the Stone) (PREMIERE 2009) was provided by her long-term partner, German-Chilean poet Ronald Kay. The title is a line from the song *Volver a los diecisiete* (To Be Seventeen Again) by Violeta Parra, a Chilean folk musician (1917-1967). Parra began composing music as a child. In the 1950s, she started collecting and recording rural folk music. In doing so, she encouraged the rediscovery of the poetic dimensions of Chilean folk songs and of the culture surrounding them. Her work in the 1960s and 1970s formed the basis for La Nueva Canción Chilena, a song movement that combined elements of folk music with religious forms, parts of the 1960s protest movement and social criticism. After the Chilean military coup in 1973, she became an icon of the people, who were suffering under the military dictatorship and fighting for a return to democracy. The lyrics of her song celebrate childhood and tenderness, the innocence and purity of love, like many of Pina Bausch's own pieces, and it also features the number 17. Pinochet's military junta was in power in Chile for 17 years, from 1973 until 1990, inflicting suffering upon thousands. The song explains the need to face challenges in order to overcome suffering.

Like Violeta Parra's lyrics, this last piece by Pina Bausch is all about loving – and about its fragility, especially in the face of death. "When I was offered the coproduction, I was more afraid than interested," Pina Bausch admitted during one of her press talks in Chile, "[...] it's a great responsibility toward the country. The countries have very different stories. [...]. But the people have a lot in common: feelings, love. I'm looking for the great will that moves them. It's always life, the things in life, that belong to them."[108]

*To be seventeen again
after a century of living
is like deciphering signs without wisdom or competence,
to be all of a sudden
as fragile as a second,
to once again feel
like a child facing God,
that is what I feel
in this fecund instant.*

*My steps going backwards
while yours go forward,
the arch of alliances
has got inside my nest,
with all of its wide palette
it has ambled through my veins
and even the hard chains
with which destiny binds us
are like a blessed day
that brightens my calmed soul*

*What feelings can grasp
knowledge cannot understand,
not even the clearest behaviour
not even the broadest thought,
the brimming, condescending
moment
changes everything
sweetly removes us
from rancour and from violence,
only love with its science
makes us so innocent*

*Love is a whirlwind
of primeval purity,
even the fierce animal
whispers its sweet trill,
it stops pilgrims,
it liberates prisoners,
love with its solicitude
turns the elderly into a child
as to the bad person
only affection makes him pure
and sincere*

*The window opened wide
as under a spell
love entered with its blanket
like a warm morning,
and the sound of its beautiful
reveille
prompted the jasmine to flower
flying like a seraph
put earrings on the sky
and the cherub turned my years
into seventeen.*

*Entangling, entangling it moves
like ivy on the wall,
and so it sprouts up, and keeps
sprouting,
like tiny moss on the stone.
Oh yes oh yes*[107]

Before making this piece, Pina Bausch had already toured Chile twice with the Tanztheater Wuppertal in 1980 and 2007. Now, the company took a research trip to the desert in Northern Chile, to the Andes and traditional villages, where they experienced an Atacamian ritual. They flew 3,000 kilometers south to the island of Chiloé, which is famed for its natural beauty, participated in a curanto (a cooking ritual in which food is heated in the ground), took dance classes in the form of a Chilote waltz typical of the island, roamed the harbors of Valparaiso and Santiago at night, visited Villa Grimaldi, General Pinochet's torture center, met with members of a proletarian enclave, a hub of resistance against the dictatorship, and visited *cafés con piernas* (cafés with legs), where women in suggestive dress sell coffee.

These impressions were later made directly available to the audience in the form of landscape portrait photos printed in the program booklet. But they also reveal themselves in individual scenes, with dancers performing the *café con piernas,* and they are evident in Peter Pabst's set, which resembles a desert landscape with fissures, like an earthquake zone. The dancers have to traverse these gaps – and they do. In this piece, it is the female dancers who are especially powerful and self-confident. The piece bubbles over with life and vitality. Moreover, although the male dancers are less prominent, the solo originally danced by Dominique Mercy plays a major role, acting as a dramaturgical parenthesis, a light, permeable and flexible dance that also searches inwardly, torn and lost (→ SOLO DANCE) – like shattered love.

Like this piece, all other pieces in this last phase were aesthetically quite different from the work developed by the Tanztheater Wuppertal in the 1970s and 1980s, which continued to be the hallmark of the company well into the late 1980s. The new pieces no longer angrily, furiously or confrontationally draw attention to social conventions, but rather calmly and amusingly comment on them. The pieces from this phase use fewer 'theatrical' scenes than before to dramaturgically convey contrast, countermovement and tension. Critics called the pieces 'more dancerly,' describing the last piece "*…como el musguito en la piedra, ay si, si si…*", for example, in the following way: "There is much dance onstage, wonderful, precise, powerful and highly expressive solos all strung together,"[109] or "there is more dancing in this piece than there has been in a long time."[110]

And yet there was more than just an increase in the number of solos. The choreographic and dramaturgical structure of the pieces also changed: there is no convoluted dramaturgy of simultaneous or merging scenes. Instead, the choreography is built on the principles of rhythm, time and duration. The pieces demonstrate a passion for dance, not only for dance of the highest quality but for dance that combines movement with a sense of being moved. These are dances that move the viewer, because they come from the dancers themselves and say something about them and their situative perceptions.

In her first artistic phase with the Tanztheater Wuppertal, Pina Bausch's famous statement, "I am not interested in how people move, but in what moves them," led her to deny dance and to develop her method of 'asking questions.' Now, the many solos, but also the duos and trios, showed what was actually moving individual dancers. The ways that the movements were danced revealed each dancer's affiliation with a specific generation, their cultural and technical dance backgrounds. Upon accepting the Kyoto Prize in November 2007, Pina Bausch explained her understanding of dance: "There must be a reason for dancing other than mere technique and routine. Technique is important, but it is only one foundation. Certain things can be said with words and others with movements. [...]. It's about finding a language – using words, images, movements, moods – that makes something of what is always there already [...]. It's very precise knowledge that we all have, and dance, music, etc. are a precise language that we can use to divine this knowledge."[111]

In this respect, her pieces are multiple, varied declarations of her love for dance – from powerful inner struggles and wild turmoil to gentle movements. It is a love for the dances of different cultures, for dancing as the physical sensation of being with oneself, for dance as a medium of affirmation that can be taken everywhere and, finally, for dance as a physical aesthetic utopia. They are a clear plea to enjoy life in the here and now, to take pleasure without any reservations – through dance, as a medium of presence. The theme of the work is no longer that which hinders people's happiness, what makes them fall back on their routines over and over again, but rather what could be possible. Dance is the tool on this journey. The musical collages form a counterpoint: they support the atmospheric tapestry that unfolds through the movements being danced. Moreover, it is the specific 'dancerly' quality of the dramaturgy, the rhythm of the pieces that make reference to each coproducing country and to the ways in which its atmosphere has been perceived.

This celebration of dance is simultaneously a celebration of nature in an age of climate change and environmental disaster, as indicated by the set designs or rather by the environments created onstage: coastlines, snow (or cherry blossoms) falling from above, a whale fin at centerstage *(Ten Chi)*, a white wall of ice, conquered by mountain climbers *(Rough Cut)*, video projections of palm trees and ocean *(Bamboo Blues)*, or the wide ditch of water in *Vollmond* (PREMIERE 2006), reminiscent of *Arien* and the "Macbeth Piece."

21 *Orpheus und Eurydike*
    Wuppertal, 1975

22 *Água*
    Wuppertal, 2004

But are the pieces really, as Servos states, about 'love' – here proffered as an answer, as a counterpart, as an escape, as a source of refuge in the face of crisis? Can the choreographies, especially those from the last phase, be considered a choreographic encyclopedia of gestures of love? Pina Bausch did in fact 'ask questions' on the subject of 'love' during the development of the coproductions; some of the questions she had also used before, albeit in slightly different form. Examples of the 'questions' include: *Love's woes · Wanting to fall in love · Not loving yourself six times · Love love love · Lovemaking from a distance · Ritualize something about love · Loving creatures · Loving details · Special love for a body part · What do you do, in order to be loved? · Oh love.* She also asked the dancers to write the word 'love' in movements. But the word itself rarely appears in the actual pieces. There are a few scenes in which love is spoken of. In one scene, a man asks, "Do you love me?" and a woman answers, "Maybe." In another, a dancer shrieks, "You don't love me!" Both scenes illustrate what Pina Bausch intended: to show just what speaking about love can do, that it all ends in misunderstanding, that it fails, misses the mark, creates uncertainty, fear and blame, provokes jealousy, power games and violence.

"Love is just a word" – this saying is mirrored in the work of the Tanztheater Wuppertal in that it translates the richly metaphorical, highly symbolic and sometimes tacky and commercialized discourse of love into love's physical, individual and intersubjective practices with all its public gestures. For Pina Bausch, the work was thus always less about longing for love than it was about how love concretely expresses itself in actions. The dancers in the pieces mainly stage the subject of love as a performative act. Love is an invocation demonstrated by the body, which – according to the philosophy of Louis Althusser's [112] – is what foremost constitutes the subject. It is less about an inner feeling and more about a form of 'doing' – a tender touch, using passionate, sensual, erotic or vulnerable gestures. Loving is not choreographed here as an 'inner world' of longing, but as an intersubjective, interactive, atmospheric phenomenon, as an act that succeeds, but can also always fail. For gestures of love can quickly turn into gestures of violence – like when stroking becomes hitting. The audience is able to observe what this performative act means: that a change of movement is not only influenced by intent or by a subjective motive but that it unfolds its social effectiveness due to changes in temporal relationships and the balance of strength – a slow, soft, flowing, tender movement becomes a fast, vigorous, whipping one. As we see here, the flipside of the longing for love is always hate and violence. These last pieces by the Tanztheater Wuppertal transport this knowledge less through 'theatrical' scenes and more through the dance itself. In the more 'dancerly' pieces of this last phase, these performatively staged gestures of love are contained in the dramaturgy of the dances themselves and in their choreographic arrangements of conflict associated with the subject of love: hate, grief, despair, suffering and anger, but also longing, passion, emotional turmoil, hope, joy, lust and sex, eroticism and ecstasy. Both *Vollmond* and *Ten Chi* end, for example, in ecstatic, orgiastic dancing.

And so, these pieces show that the desire for love takes social effect in the many ways that people treat each other, in their practices of loving. They also show that it takes courage to overcome limits and leave previous securities behind while simultaneously respecting each other's boundaries. The balancing act between respecting and violating boundaries was central to Pina Bausch's work with the Tanztheater Wuppertal. Loving is staged as a permanent performative act, the negotiations of which repeatedly fail, because loving is based on reciprocal actions that must be negotiated, and these negotiations take people through all kinds of emotional landscapes. In his essay "The Task of the Translator,"[113] Walter Benjamin emphasizes the tension between "suprahistorical kinship," as he calls it, and cultural difference. Pina Bausch likewise showed us that all people share fundamental affects and emotions, but that they are negotiated in different ways culturally and socially, and that this is what leads to misunderstandings and sometimes to defeat.

Pina Bausch's pieces reply to the philosophical idea of love as the desire to become one or the psychological concept of a psychodynamics of love as a "battle between two opposing powers [...]: the desire for unity and the fear of merging into one,"[114] by offering an idea gleaned from cultural sociology: they show the game and battle of giving and receiving love and of experiencing failure in all its facets as a set of culturally framed, social and physical practices, as a deeply human struggle for recognition and respect.

1 Rehearsals for *He Takes Her By The Hand And Leads Her Into The Castle, The Others Follow* Bochum, 1978

We play ourselves,
we are the piece.[1]

pany

Not only does the Tanztheater Wuppertal enjoy a unique status in the dance world due to its global artistic significance – what makes it a truly remarkable ensemble is the fact that its members have worked together for years and even decades. Other large companies – such as the New York-based Alvin Ailey Dance Theater or, in Germany, the Hamburg Ballett, which has been run by John Neumeier since 1972 – also demonstrate high levels of continuity, but there is often fast dancer turnover, in part because ballet dancers' stage careers normally end at an early age after a fairly short amount of time, much like those of competitive athletes. However, in the case of the Tanztheater Wuppertal, dancers remain members for decades, even if some do leave the company for short periods in between. Each generation of dancers has generated its own specific material for the stage (→ WORK PROCESS) and, over many years, has exclusively brought this material to life in performance, before passing the pieces on to other companies (→ PIECES). For audiences and critics alike, it is the dancers who are the public face of the Tanztheater Wuppertal. However, they are not the only ones who have shaped its image. Behind the scenes, set designers, costume designers, music directors, assistants, technical, management and office staff – many of whom have also been working for the Tanztheater Wuppertal for decades – have also contributed in many different ways to its global success. The company is a group comprising a total of approx. 60 people. As is evident from the interviews that I conducted, many of them consider the Tanztheater Wuppertal to be a "family" – even those who at some point took their leave.

In many respects, the Tanztheater Wuppertal is a unique ensemble. Composed of an equal number of men and women from different continents and various generations, it is a social and cultural model of reality. At the same time, the ensemble is utopian – both as a modern company that has rejected classical hierarchies from the outset, but also as the guardian of an important legacy of the transitory, contemporary art form of dance. Moreover, the company is ultimately a historical model, one that now, under the neoliberal conditions of artistic production at the beginning of the 21st century, would no longer be able to establish itself or endure for as long as it has. The Tanztheater Wuppertal is also the result of German cultural policies of the 1970s, when culture was considered an important factor in the development of democracy and emerging art forms found the appropriate patrons and niches to develop that democracy. Since the 1990s, the media-driven battle for attention in the age of global digitalization, the struggle for innovation and sensation, competition in the global art market and cuts to national and local government cultural funding have significantly increased the pressure on theater and festival directors to publicly legitimize their venues by optimizing the number of seats sold, etc. Institutionalized theaters have not been spared from these developments, leaving little to no room for young artists to develop. Neither the 'independent scene' *(freie Szene)* nor these large institutions can provide them with safe havens from the kind of immense criticism and resistance that Pina Bausch faced during her early years. The company is thus also a reflection of a historical moment in time, as it could not have worked the way that it did without the years of incomparable, generous support that it received from various branches of the Goethe-Institut worldwide, which the Goethe-Institut has long since ceased to grant to individual artists for such long periods of time. Finally and most importantly, the Tanztheater Wuppertal is a historical model in the sense that it fundamentally differs from today's network-based modes of working on single productions for short, clearly delimited periods of time in hasty partnerships of necessity, with collaborators often involved in multiple projects at the same time. Today, there are rarely long-term, ongoing artistic working relationships within a dance ensemble of this scale that would allow for the development of a shared 'artistic signature.'

This chapter therefore focuses on the long-standing structures of collaboration within the Tanztheater Wuppertal. It inquires into forms of collaboration, daily routines, personal views on the work shared, and the bonds that have tied and held the group together for so many years and decades.

Translating hunches: Artistic collaboration

Pina Bausch and her long-term artistic collaborators at the Tanztheater Wuppertal, but also the dancers involved in the company from the beginning, were all members of the same generation. They were 'war babies,' born between 1930 and 1945. While many publications about Pina Bausch mention her childhood,[2] most only roughly describe her family background. Very little attention has been paid to the fact that Pina Bausch and her colleagues Rolf Borzik, Peter Pabst and Marion Cito were children of the war and that the Second World War and the postwar era fundamentally influenced how they experienced everyday life. This deficit in the literature corresponds to a surprising general lack of historical research on childhood during WWII,[3] especially in terms of what kind of effect growing up during the war had on later artistic production. What were these childhoods like and how are they remembered? How did the daily experiences of war and of rebuilding after the war influence personal identity and each person's approach to their work? How did this translate into forms of collaboration? This section takes a closer look at these questions.

Based on memories shared by individual members of the company in public talks and discussions or in interviews with me, it outlines the lives and working methods of longtime artistic collaborators at the Tanztheater Wuppertal and asks what it was that allowed their collaboration to continue for years and even decades.

THE CHOREOGRAPHER: PINA BAUSCH

Pina Bausch was born Philippine Bausch on July 27, 1940, in Solingen. After her siblings Anita and Roland, she was August and Anita Bausch's third and youngest child. Her parents ran a tavern attached to a guesthouse, Hotel Diegel, located in a neighborhood called Zentral.[4] Her father came from a humble background in the Taunus, a mountain range in Hessen. He worked as a truck driver before taking over the tavern.

Today, Zentral in Solingen is a rather unattractive place to live – a traffic hub where different streets cross and then radiate outward toward Essen, Wuppertal, Solingen, Wald and Hilden. One of them is Focherstraße, on which Pina Bausch grew up in a house with the number 10, close to a large intersection. Today, this is an area of overgrown vacant lots and plain, unsightly postwar housing, with little to no stores, public institutions or other urban infrastructure. The only striking exception is the Bergisches Haus beside the intersection at the end of Focherstraße, an old half-timbered building with slate facades and green window shutters, which now houses a pharmacy. It is all that is left of Zentral's once radiant past. This same building was once home to Café Müller – the same café that gave its name to one of Pina Bausch's most famous pieces. A few years ago, the city installed a sign on the wall outside to commemorate this fact.

Nonetheless, Zentral and Solingen in general boast a proud history, which stretches as far back as the 13th century. For centuries, its inhabitants owed much of their prosperity to the knife-making industry. The First World War led to a collapse of the export-based knife-making trade and plunged hitherto wealthy, prosperous Solingen into a deep crisis. Unemployment and homelessness increased at alarming rates, especially after the Great Depression of 1929. In the two years following the Nazis' "rise to power" in 1933, their political opponents in the city – which was also the birthplace of Adolf Eichmann, the bureaucratic administrator of the Holocaust about whose trial in Israel Hannah Arendt wrote her famous book, in which she described his bureaucratic

2 Pina Bausch during the filming of *The Plaint of the Empress,* Wuppertal, 1988

3 Former Café Müller building, Solingen

reign as the "banality of evil"[5] – were arrested, accused of high treason, tortured, sent to concentration camps and killed. Even before the war began, Solingen had already deported three-quarters of the approx. 200 Jews who had lived there before 1933. More were sent to concentration camps during the war.

At midnight on June 5, 1940 – about seven weeks before the birth of Philippine Bausch – the first bombs fell on the city of Solingen. Nights were often filled with the wailing of sirens after the Allies decided to begin their strategic carpet bombing in 1942. In August of that year, the US joined in on the aerial warfare and, together with the British, concentrated on bombing major cities and key areas of the German arms industry. What followed from May to July 1943 went down in history as the Battle of the Ruhr. Heavy air raids laid waste to the industrial Ruhr region, but also to cities neighboring Solingen such as Wuppertal-Barmen, which would later become Pina Bausch's workplace and home to the Tanztheater Wuppertal. From 1944 onward, the Allies achieved complete dominance over Germany's skies, with bombers now attacking during the day as well. On November 4 and 5, 1944, Solingen was extensively bombarded and the Old Town completely destroyed. Further attacks followed in short succession in the subsequent days and weeks.[6] On the evening of November 5, British radio finally proclaimed: "Solingen, the heart of the German steel goods industry, has been destroyed. It is a dead city."[7] Pina Bausch was four years old at the time. On April 16 and 17, 1945, two weeks prior to Hitler's suicide and three weeks before Germany's unconditional surrender, the war ended in Solingen when American troops marched into town. "Pina," as family and friends called her, was not even five years old. She and her family had survived.

After the end of the war, the British and American occupying forces concentrated on bringing about a swift return to normalcy. Classes in Solingen's primary schools resumed as early as in August. Just one year after the end of the war, the city's municipal theater was rebuilt and, in its first season, already boasted more than 4,500 season-ticket holders. One year later, this number had tripled. On average, 10 percent of Solingen's population of approx. 140,000 people were attending the theater. In 1948, the destroyed city of Solingen was almost undisputedly the leading city in the western occupied sectors when it came to theater and cinema. With over 2,700 theater seats, it was the second-largest theater city after Hamburg and also took second place in film, with ten cinemas hosting over two million visitors on more than 4,200 seats. Even ballet schools reopened right after the war. Like her sister Anita, who was two years her senior, Pina Bausch benefited from this development: at the age of five, shortly after the end of the war, she enrolled in Jutta Jutter's ballet school.

"[Some] of what I experienced as a child [resurfaced] again much later on the stage,"[8] is the opening sentence of Pina's Bausch's acceptance speech for the Kyoto Prize in 2007, in which she spoke extensively about her childhood, describing it as a time of fear and hardship, but also of joy, discovery and happiness. This speech, which was very important to her and on which she worked for a long time with various people, is a testament to her work of remembrance, a reconstruction of her own war and postwar history. It is also a document that reveals some of her own ideas about translating her early childhood experiences into her artistic work, as indicated by what she presents in the speech and when and how she mentions it.[9]

In Pina Bausch's words: "The war experiences are unforgettable. Solingen suffered a tremendous amount of destruction. When the air raid sirens went off, we had to go into the small shelter in our garden. Once a bomb fell on part of the house as well. However, we all remained unharmed. For a time, my parents sent me to my aunt's in Wuppertal because they had a larger shelter. She thought I would be safer there. I had a small black rucksack with white polka dots, with a doll peering out of it. It was always there packed ready so that I could take it with me when the air raid siren sounded.

I remember too our courtyard behind the house. There was a water pump there, the only one in our area. People were always lining up there to fetch water. This was because people had nothing to eat; they had to go bartering for food. They would swap goods for something to eat. My father, for example, swapped two quilts, a radio, and a pair of boots for a sheep so we would have milk. This sheep was then covered – and my parents called the baby lamb 'Pina.' Sweet little Pina. One day[,] it must have been Easter[,] 'Pina.' lay on the table as a roast. The little lamb had been slaughtered. It was a shock for me. Since then I haven't eaten any lamb.

My parents had a small hotel with a restaurant in Solingen. Just like my brothers and sisters, I had to help out there. I used to spend hours peeling potatoes, cleaning the stairs, tidying rooms – all the jobs that you have to do in a hotel. But, above all, as a small child I used to be hopping and dancing around in these rooms. The guests would see that too. Members of the [choir] from the nearby theater regularly came to eat in our restaurant. They always used to say: 'Pina really must go to children's ballet group.' And then one day they took me along to the children's ballet in the theatre."[10]

In spite of the war, Pina Bausch describes life with her immediate family as sheltered, safe and affectionate. After the war ended, she began dancing. "Dance, dance, otherwise we are lost" – this sentence that a young girl called out to her many years later in Greece aptly describes how she experienced her childhood: when the need is greatest, dance is a physical, sensory medium of self-affirmation. From her early childhood, the world of dance was a utopian space. The ballroom, which her parents did not build as planned, only existed as a ruin, as a hope for another, more carefree life. Pina Bausch depicts this overgrown dancefloor as a paradise, a place of childlike dreaming and longing, as a refuge from the daily lives of the adults and as a space to experiment with putting on her first small performances. Perhaps it was a protected place, much like what the Lichtburg, the Tanztheater Wuppertal's rehearsal space, would later become for her.

"There was a garden behind our house, not very large. That's where the family shelter was and a long building – the skittle alley. Behind it was what used to be a gardening center. My parents had bought this plot of land in order to open up a garden restaurant. They started off with a round dance floor made of concrete. Unfortunately nothing came of the rest. But for me and all the children in the neighborhood it was a paradise. Everything grew wild there, between grasses and weeds there were suddenly beautiful flowers. In summer we were able to sit on the hot, tarred roof of the skittle alley and eat the dark sour cherries that hung over the roof. Old couches on which we were able to jump up and down as if on a trampoline. There was a rusty old greenhouse; perhaps that's where my first productions began."[11]

Some aspects of these memories appeared in later pieces – such as dancers jumping on an array of old couches in the "Macbeth Piece" *He Takes Her By the Hand And Leads Her Into The Castle, The Others Follow* (PREMIERE 1978). Back then, in the postwar period, the children pretended that they were famous actors and actresses, one of them Marika Rökk, a former star of the German Cinema (UFA), who openly sympathized with the Nazis and was also able to successfully continue her career after the war. "I was usually Marika Rökk,"[12] says Pina Bausch, and here we see how little self-reflection there was – no one found it strange that children after the war continued to admire and imitate the film stars of the Nazi era.

Pina Bausch thus grew up in a theater-loving city. According to her own stories, members of the choir from the nearby theater visited the tavern on a regular basis, even during the war. Eavesdropping on guests' conversations as a small child, learning to listen and stay silent, gave her an early understanding of theater and led her straight into ballet once the war had ended. For Pina Bausch, dance and theater therefore belonged together from an early age: later, having anything to do with the theater, wanting to do nothing else but dance, to be on the stage, would be like fulfilling the childhood dreams and fantasies she had had during the war. But in the early postwar years, as a member of the children's ballet at Leonore Humburg's Solinger Theater, she initially mainly came into contact with works of a lighter nature, like operettas.

Compared to other children born in industrial and urban environments during the war in Germany, Pina Bausch led a relatively privileged life. Her parents were comparatively well off. They had a large plot of land and a house that had suffered only little damage during the war. They had their own "family bunker" in the yard and, because they owned a water pump, they had access to fresh water, even during water shortages. But by listening in on guests' conversations, Pina Bausch learned more than other children about adult fears, worries and troubles, and about anger, disappointment, hardship, desires, dreams and longing, as well as about hate and violence during and after the war. Sometimes, she sat beneath the tables, kept quiet and listened. She observed and fantasized, took in smells, regarded chairs and table legs, trousers and high-heeled shoes. Herein lies one of the sources of her love for observing everyday life, which would later – magnified by aesthetic means as if under a microscope – characterize her choreographic work. "Compared to reality, none of it means anything. People often say: it's incredible the way the people perform in my pieces, how they laugh, how they do the things they do. But if you just take a look at the way that people cross the street – if you let the same things happen on the stage, completely mundane things, nothing absurd, if you just let the whole sequence take place – the audience wouldn't believe it. It's completely unbelievable. In contrast, what we do is nothing,"[13] she would later explain in a 1998 interview about her pieces. Pina Bausch must have seen, experienced or suspected much of how men and women interact when it comes to love and hate, affection and violence. Her early pieces clearly demonstrate as much. About these early pieces, she said: "It's not about violence; it's about the opposite. I don't show violence to make people want it, I show it to make them not want it. And: I try to understand the origins of that violence. Like in *Bluebeard*. And in *Kontakthof*."[14]

Her first piece as ballet director in Wuppertal was *Fritz* (PREMIERE 1974). The male character Fritz was played by a woman (Hiltrud Blanck). The piece also included a mother (Malou Airaudo), a father (Jan Minařík) and a grandmother (Charlotte Butler). For Pina Bausch, it was the piece that most clearly related to her own childhood, although the subject of childhood featured prominently in many of her other pieces as well (→ PIECES). Fritz, "[…] he was a little boy. But only on the outside. That piece probably had the most to do with my childhood. It was about parents and a grandmother, from the perspective of a child that has strange fantasies. Enlargements, like looking through a magnifying glass."[15]

War and childhood played a role in a number of Pina Bausch's pieces. Motifs were often reused, such as the early 1940s Christmas song "Mamatschi, schenk' mir ein Pferdchen, ein Pferdchen wär' mein Paradies…" (Mummy, Give Me a Little Horse, a Little Horse would be my Paradise…), which appeared for the first time in the piece *1980* (PREMIERE 1980) and then once more in *Two Cigarettes in the Dark* (PREMIERE 1985) – a piece whose title was taken from a song sung for the first time by American actress and singer Gloria Grafton in 1934. The German writer, filmmaker and philosopher Alexander Kluge characterized the situation in which this song was embedded in Germany in 1942 as follows: "The date is December 24, 1942. This is Christmas radio. The propagandists in Narvik are calling their colleagues in Africa, where Rommel's tankers are celebrating 'Christmas in the desert' with palm branches. The shouts ringing out across Europe end in the Stalingrad pocket. All of the melancholy hits since 1936, the year of the Olympics, like 'Hirten auf dem Feld,' are being mobilized. Propaganda, kitsch, but also real fear and anxiety are coming together on this Christmas Eve of crisis: adversity binds people together. One of the songs played most this Christmas, the no. 1 request, is 'Mamatschi, schenk mir ein Pferdchen.' It's about a children's toy, a horse fitted out in military gear, that was once given to the oldest son. And now the news has arrived that the child who received that toy back then has fallen in the war. This war was already lost when it began. At the latest in December 1941, when the German Reich declared war against the US. But only now, on this propaganda-bedecked, oppressive Christmas Eve of 1942 is this state of affairs being acknowledged."[16] In *Two Cigarettes in the Dark,* Jan Minařík, who danced in the original cast, held an axe – a key object in the piece – in his hand as the music played – leaving no doubt about what he would do to the horse.

Pina Bausch remembers her wartime childhood as "not horrible. It was very imaginative though."[17] This is a description of the worlds of childhood in which she lived during that horrific time. "She was allowed to turn everything upside down,"[18] said her mother. Her parents had little time for their children and a disregard for strict discipline. Pina Bausch described her father, who continued to call her "my little monkey"[19] well into adulthood, as a cheerful, patient and reliable man, who told the children stories about his former tours as a truck driver, sang and whistled a lot, was fond of his children, never scolded them, often showed physical affection, trusted them and never made them feel guilty. Her mother was, like many *Trümmerfrauen* (the women who cleared away the rubble after the Second World War), a practically minded person. Pina Bausch describes her as "quiet and withdrawn,"[20] but also as an almost childlike playmate: she walked barefoot in the snow, engaged in snowball fights with the children, climbed trees, had crazy ideas and dreamed of traveling to unusual places. After the war, she tried to give the children special, unusual presents. Pina received a fur coat, tartan trousers and green shoes. Maybe the gifts were intended to make her forget, to hide the wounds and the grief caused by the war.

But Pina Bausch was embarrassed by these peculiarities, these expressions of petty bourgeois luxury in postwar Germany. Perhaps she was also ashamed of the usual strategies of collective suppression. Even as a twelve year old, she wanted neither tartan trousers nor green shoes: "[…] I didn't want to wear any of this. I wanted to be inconspicuous."[21] Nor did she like the hand-sewn dresses with cap sleeves that her grandmother, a refugee from Poland, made for her from leftover, preferably red, flag fabric. "It was a nightmare for me," Pina Bausch later remembered. But fur coats, colorful postwar dresses, the aprons of the 1940s and 1950s, lavish evening gowns and traditional double-breasted men's blazers would later become hallmarks of her pieces. All her life, the choreographer herself, who clothed her female dancers in every variety of feminine sensuality, preferred to wear inconspicuous clothes. Her signature style comprised long, wide-legged black pants, broad blazers, comfortable shoes, quickly pulled-back hair and a face with little to no makeup, except maybe lipstick. "I like dresses. I just feel really strange wearing them: like a decorated Christmas tree."[22] She probably never learned that it could be any other way. During her childhood, people only ever wore pretty dresses or 'dolled themselves up' for the holidays. "Christmas trees" were what the German population – and Marion Cito during our conversation – called the red and green lights that the scout planes used to mark the targets of the Allied bombers during the air raids.

Like many other children growing up during the war, Pina Bausch learned to take responsibility for her own actions. Her childhood taught her great self-confidence and discipline, a willingness to take risks and the courage to do so. "I can't do that" was a statement that not only Pina Bausch eliminated from her vocabulary. The children were left to themselves. Even when in the greatest doubt, they simply tried things out and did them – and this was the attitude that allowed Pina Bausch to manage her parents' restaurant alone at the age of twelve during their absence and one that stayed with her for life. "I can give it a try,"[23] was what she said upon accepting the offer to become ballet director in Wuppertal, after giving it much thought. During our interview, Marion Cito remembered thinking the same thing when Pina Bausch surprised her by asking her to take charge of the costumes. Not taking oneself too seriously was considered a virtue by many, as well as by Pina Bausch – and this required a certain degree of rigor toward oneself, a certain tenacity and resilience, in spite of the doubts that accompanied her through life, as they did many wartime children. She and the others took for granted that they could function and adapt to situations, be pragmatic on the one hand, but also have the courage, strength and will to live and be true to themselves on the other. These qualities corresponded to those that her teacher "Papa Jooss," as she called him, expected of the dancers at the Folkwang Schule when she studied dance there: "As dancers and choreographers, we are challenged to find genuine, meaningful gestures or movements to reflect specific content and use these in new compositions, while practicing rigorous self-criticism and uncompromising discipline. This brief opens up a narrow path, an unforgiving route toward the intrinsic, the essence of meaning,"[24] as Kurt Jooss' credo went.

Pina Bausch acquired these qualities at an early age. Moreover, the constant observing, watching and looking closely that she practiced under the tables of the restaurant became the guiding principles of her artistic work. Not knowing what she was looking for, but having a hunch about what it could be and being certain that she would eventually find it, was how Pina Bausch described her process.

In her Kyoto speech, she remembers a situation onstage where the pianist had not shown up, and she, the dancer, patiently waited and posed onstage with increasing self-confidence: "By that time I had already realized that in extremely difficult situations a great calm overcame me, and I could draw power from the difficulties. An ability in which I have learnt to trust."[25] Mechthild Großmann admired her composure and patience. "Her eyes were fantastic. She could look at you with patience, as only the Japanese can. For hours, without moving [...] and she would reply to everything with: 'Hm, hm....'"[26] Her desire to observe in silence and to keep her observations to herself led her to distrust words. Pina Bausch did not talk about her pieces – neither with the dancers ("No. I cannot talk with any of them. Maybe about certain scenes, about details... but about the piece... no, that's not possible"[27]) nor with her closest collaborators or staff, and not with the audience either. Pina Bausch did not speak about the meaning of her pieces, about explanations or interpretations, but she did talk – with a few people – about their development. The core members of the team, especially during the first artistic phase in Wuppertal, became a tight-knit group, perhaps prompted by the considerable criticism of and resistance to their work. They spent long nights in bars exchanging ideas – and this sitting around in bars was one of Pina Bausch's penchants, perhaps conveying a sense of familiarity that reminded her of her childhood, when her parent's tavern was a place where she was not alone: "I grew up fairly isolated. Everyone was always horribly preoccupied and had to work a lot. I usually hung around the bar, always with people. I still like to go to restaurants. It's where I can think best: isolated among people."[28]

One of her closest discussion partners at the time was undoubtedly Rolf Borzik, with whom she worked closely during the first phase in Wuppertal (→ PIECES). After his death, the birth of her son Salomon and the appearance of a steadily growing age gap between the choreographer and her dancers, Raimund Hoghe and Peter Pabst became her most important dialogue partners.

A letter from January 16, 1959, documents the courage, self-confidence and determination that characterized the young dancer at the time. Eighteen-year old Pina Bausch writes a request to the Cultural Department of her hometown Solingen. One year before, she had been awarded the inaugural Folkwang Prize. She mentions it in her letter as one of the reasons that she wants to continue her dance studies – and states that she wishes to do so in New York, which at the time is the mecca of modern ballet, home to the New York City Ballet under George Balanchine, to modern dance and the companies of people like Martha Graham, José Limon and Anthony Tudor, as well as to protagonists of postmodern dance such as Merce Cunningham and representatives of the Judson Dance Theater. In her handwritten letter, which is stored in the Stadtarchiv Solingen (the city's municipal archives), Pina Bausch asks for financial support and explains: "Studying in New York for nine months would cost about DM 9,000."[29] She says that she is willing to contribute her prize money of DM 1,500, which she was the first to receive at the Folkwang Schule. This letter is both an interesting historical document demonstrating the cultural policies at the time and a testament to the young applicant's determination. Pina Bausch encloses "a few press reviews" with her application and, before ending with respectful salutations, requests that the newspaper clippings be returned to her after they have been read. Also included is an assessment by her "main expert instructor," Kurt Jooss, who attests to her "highly remarkable qualities," "extraordinary and rare talent," "exemplary diligence" and "utter devotion," and describes her as the "phenomenon of a dance artist, of the kind only rarely encountered."[30] According to Kurt Jooss, there is no other young person who "more sincerely and honestly" deserves support than "Fräulein Bausch." He also points out just how much Germany has to gain from her international experience, for the young artist, he says, is very determined to return to Germany after finishing her studies in New York. In this respect, providing her with funding would make a "vital contribution to cultural life." But the city was only willing to make a small contribution, and Pina Bausch therefore applied to the German Academic Exchange Service (DAAD), which provided her with DM 8,500. Together with the prize money, this was now more than what she had originally asked for, and the city considered the case closed until Pina Bausch's father again asked for money, saying that it had now come to their attention that even a modest life in NYC would cost at least DM 1,000 a month. It was a renewed commitment by Pina Bausch's parents to their daughter's career, although they would never see a single one of her pieces. Their opinions were once more validated by the DAAD, which also pointed out that it would applaud any decision by the city of Solingen to provide support to the young dancer. However, once again, the city referred the request back to her father, who contributed DM 500 until the city of Solingen finally agreed to a one- off grant of DM 2,000.

Pina Bausch took the money and set out on her journey by boat to the "land of the free," to the urban metropolis of New York City, without knowing a single world of English. She stayed there for not one, but two years. She had to make the money last, subsisting on buttermilk and ice cream, but she got to know the American dance avant-garde of the 1960s. Two years later, in 1962, she returned "with a heavy heart" at the request of Kurt Jooss and helped him to establish the Folkwang Ballett, here developing her first choreographies and experiencing the burgeoning revolution of the 1960s (→ PIECES). She choreographed her first one-act pieces, came into contact with students from other departments at the Folkwang Schule and made the acquaintance of the student Rolf Borzik, before moving to Wuppertal in 1973. She was accompanied by a small group that she had met during her Folkwang days. They had collaborated with her there for years, and it was with them that she then established the core of the "Tanztheater Wuppertal family," which continued to grow in size over the years. This group included the dancers Marlies Alt and Jan Minařík and, aside from Rolf Borzik, three other main, male artistic collaborators, Hans Züllig, Jean Cébron and Hans Pop, who all continued to accompany and support the work of the Tanztheater Wuppertal in different ways for many years to come. As Pina Bausch once said: "Almost everything that I learned, I learned from men."[31]

The dancer Hans Pop was the first to assume and fulfill the role of artistic collaborator for many years. He was not a dramaturge, a role carried out by Raimund Hoghe from 1980 until 1990, nor was he the kind of assistant that former dancers such as Jo Ann Endicott, Bénédicte Billiet and Barbara Kaufmann would later become in various roles. His role was not comparable with that of Robert Sturm either, who Pina Bausch called her "anyway assistant"[32] and who joined the Tanztheater Wuppertal in 1999, sitting beside Pina Bausch during all rehearsals for new pieces and taking on responsibility within the overall process for a wide range of tasks that had previously been separate, such as filming and organizing rehearsals, taking notes during feedback after the performances and helping to plan research trips. Hans Pop's task was simply described as "collaboration" – which is how it is also officially credited on the website of the Tanztheater Wuppertal. He performed his duties consistently for every new production, from *Iphigenie auf Tauris* (PREMIERE 1974) to *Walzer* (PREMIERE 1982) and then once more for *Ahnen* (PREMIERE 1987). In addition, he was in charge of the company's training in the first few years, supervised all of the rehearsals for *The Rite of Spring* (PREMIERE 1975) into the new century and organized tours.

Hans Züllig (1914-1992) came from Switzerland and had also studied at the Folkwang Schule under Kurt Jooss and Sigurd Leeder in the early 1930s. In 1933, Kurt Jooss and Sigurd Leeder immigrated to England after Kurt Jooss refused to dismiss the Jewish members of his staff. One year later, Hans Züllig followed Kurt Jooss to Devon, where he was teaching dance at the progressive Dartington Hall School. In 1949, he returned with Kurt Jooss to Essen. Hans Züllig danced in ballet pieces by Kurt Jooss during the early 1930s and again with the Folkwang Ballett during the early 1950s. After working in Zurich, Düsseldorf and Santiago de Chile, he was appointed professor at the Folkwang Hochschule in 1968 and followed in Kurt Jooss' footsteps as director of the dance department in 1969. From 1973, when Pina Bausch took over as ballet director in Wuppertal, he also taught dance classes at the Tanztheater Wuppertal until his death in 1992. Pina Bausch describes him as, a "wonderful dancer and teacher. Thanks to his support and his faith in me, I have been able to endure a lot and make a lot possible. He was my teacher, later the teacher of my company, and always my friend."[33]

Jean-Maurice Cébron (1927-2019) was a sophisticated Frenchman. Starting in 1945, he received private ballet lessons from his mother Mauricette Cébron, a soloist at the Opéra national de Paris. In addition, he was taught South-Asian dance, studied in London with Sigurd Leeder, danced as a soloist in the National Ballet of Santiago de Chile, was invited to the US by Ted Shawn and studied the Cecchetti method with Margaret Craske and Alfredo Corvino – who would also become important to Pina Bausch and the Tanztheater – at the New York Metropolitan Ballet Opera School in the late 1950s, shortly before Pina Bausch arrived in the city. He also taught at the legendary School at Jacob's Pillow. In the early 1960s, he moved to Essen like Pina Bausch, worked as a choreographer for the Folkwang Ballett and danced with Pina Bausch in several pieces from 1966 onward. After jobs in Stockholm and Rome, where he held positions as a dance professor, he returned to the Folkwang Hochschule in 1976 as a professor of modern dance, where he also trained the Tanztheater Wuppertal. Pina Bausch considered him to be an important teacher: "Working with dancer and choreographer Jean Cébron was particularly intensive [...]. He is one of the people from whom I learned the most about movement. To become aware of every tiny detail of a movement and what and how everything happens in the body at the same time, and so much more [...]. You have to think so much. You feel like you'll never be able to dance again, a hard lesson to learn – but! Many give up. Unfortunately."[34] Nazareth Panadero, a longtime member of the ensemble, also remembers how important not wanting to give up was to Pina Bausch and recalls her exclaiming: "Oh, dear. You give up too quickly!!!"[35]

For Pina Bausch, as well as for many of her collaborators and friends during the first phase, giving up was inconceivable. They were staggering through a traumatized society, in search of a path to another, more free and democratic community, without knowing how to get there. *Café Müller* (PREMIERE 1978) is undoubtedly one of Pina Bausch's most personal and intimate pieces (→ PIECES). It can be read as a translation of the wartime and postwar generation's lack of orientation, but also as a search for community and a sense of being there for one another. In a disturbing and very personal way, the piece shows a group of people all of the same age, their random wanderings, their careful fumblings into the unknown, the mutual support that they give one another and, at the same time, their desolation, grief, distress and longing. It is one of the few pieces in which Pina Bausch actually appeared (in the original cast). She was joined onstage by her first Wuppertal "family": her partner, stage and costume designer Rolf Borzik and the dancers Dominique Mercy, Malou Airaudo and Meryl Tankard. Pina Bausch moved around, barefoot, shivering, searching with her eyes closed and arms open wide in a small, almost transparent nightgown, stumbling along the walls and through the space filled with black coffeehouse chairs that were randomly and chaotically scattered around – Café Müller after an air raid (→ PIECES). Dominique Mercy ran around, raging against himself, against the wall, against the others, and Tankard wandered lost, decked out in fancy dress, the quintessence of overflowing, trashy femininity in high heels and a wig of red curls, while Rolf Borzik attempted to curb in the chaos, destruction and loneliness – in vain.

THE COSTUME AND STAGE DESIGNER: ROLF BORZIK

Rolf Borzik was what some might call an artistic all-rounder and others would simply consider an explorative artist. His friends described him as fearless, imperturbable, brave and inquisitive. In spite of receiving all kinds of training, he was essentially a self-taught man. Rolf Borzik was born on July 29, 1944, in German-occupied Poznań to Margaretha Fabian and Richard Borzik. Poznań, known in German as 'Posen,' is located in a region that was suffering from long-standing ethnic tensions between the resident German and Polish communities at the time. In its various partitionings, Poznań had repeatedly been ceded to Prussia, and the Polish majority had been marginalized. After the First World War, the Greater Poland uprising began here in late December 1918, bringing the region back under Polish control. With the signing of the Treaty of Versailles, the German government ceded Poznań back to the newly founded territory of Poland. Many Germans fled. During the Invasion of Poland in September 1939, the German Wehrmacht occupied Poznań and the city became the capital of the newly created Reichsgau Wartheland administrative subdivision. Under the Nazis, the Polish population was subjected to systematic terror. By 1945, approx. 20,000 of Poznań's inhabitants had been murdered and 100,000 members of the Polish population had been displaced or deported to camps. A number of concentration and labor camps were built around Poznań. At the same time, Poznań's Imperial Castle was declared the first and only "residency of the Führer" in the German Reich – and it was here that ss commandants, *Reichsleiter* and *Gauleiter* met in 1943 under the leadership of *Reichsführer*-ss Heinrich Himmler to openly discuss the Holocaust and their program to exterminate the Jewish population.

The city remained under Nazi rule until the winter of 1944/45. It was designated a stronghold *(Fester Platz)* in Hitler's defense strategy, intended to help halt the advancing Soviet troops. From a military point of view, it was clear that this strategy was doomed to fail, and so the outcome of the Battle of Poznań in January and February 1945 came as no surprise. The continuously advancing Soviet Army led to a massive exodus of refugees. More than 12,000 people fell during the struggle to defend the city, and a considerable portion of Poznań's architecture was laid to waste.

Rolf Borzik's father died the year that the war ended. His mother emigrated west with her nearly one-year-old infant to the town of Detmold in North Rhine-Westphalia, where Rolf Borzik attended primary school from 1951 until 1956, followed by high school. In 1957, the family moved to Aerdenhout in the Netherlands, between Haarlem and Zandvoort, one of the wealthiest cities in Holland. Rolf Borzik continued his school career in Bloemendaal. In 1960, he returned to Germany, first to study at a high school in Paderborn, before switching to another one in Rahden. For a while, he commuted between Germany and the Netherlands. After completing high school, he interned with a graphic design studio in Detmold, then learned to draw and paint portraits in Haarlem. In 1963, he enrolled in art school, first studying painting in Haarlem then at the Amsterdam Academy of Fine Arts, followed by the Academy in Paris. He roamed between the Netherlands, Germany and France – countries that were still hostile toward one another under the lasting effects of the Nazi regime and the experiences of the war, countries only slowly beginning to reconcile. After studying for three years, he decided to switch from painting to graphics and design, and signed up, at the peak of the student movement, for a corresponding spot at the Folkwang Hochschule in Essen, where he remained for five years until 1972. It was here that he met Pina Bausch, who was four years older and already famous among her students, since she had just won the first Folkwang Prize, lived and danced in New York and was now an outstanding dancer at the Folkwang Studio. He did not seem to find any of this intimidating. He moved in with her in 1970 and, in 1973, when she relocated to Wuppertal as the new ballet director, he followed (→ PIECES).

Rolf Borzik is often only mentioned as the costume and stage designer of the Tanztheater Wuppertal. In many publications about Pina Bausch, he is only noted in passing, if at all. This is a shortsighted and, in its shortsightedness, distorted understanding of his role, for he was Pina Bausch's primary artistic partner during her first artistic phase in Wuppertal. "Without Rolf Borzik, there would have been no Pina Bausch,"[36] as Marion Cito stated plainly in 2015. Even while he was still studying at the Folkwang Hochschule, Rolf

Borzik was already considered a sophisticated, free spirit and an unconventional thinker: someone who unwaveringly followed his own interests, even when they did not conform with the zeitgeist of the late 1960s, especially in politically sensitive and 'artsy' student circles. He drew meticulous pictures of vehicles, including torpedoes, airplanes, tanks and aircraft carriers with heavy artillery, and he also set up an air pistol firing range in the atelier that he shared with fellow student Manfred Vogel. He remembers Rolf Borzik's willingness to engage in constant discussions over whether this was an appropriate and socially relevant task for a student of graphic design.[37] Together, they discussed the role of art in global affairs for nights on end. Rolf Borzik built a sailboat, which sank in the Ruhr and which he then quickly sold. But before its sinking, he had researched detailed sea routes to India and Brazil.

Fellow students saw Rolf Borzik as an artistic researcher. He was someone who loved experimenting, designing and meticulously taking all of the necessary technical details into account, wandering between genres. In her Kyoto speech, Pina Bausch remembers how the two of them began at the Folkwang Hochschule: "During that time I met Rolf Borzik. He painted, photographed, drew incessantly, made sketches, was always inventing something – he was interested in all technical things [...]. He had so much knowledge and was persistently interested in things for which the form was decisive. At the same time, he had an infinite imagination, humor and a very precise sense of style, plus knowledge. But he didn't know what to do with them, with all his abilities and talents. That's how we met."[38]

Rolf Borzik contributed all his skill and talent to the task of establishing the Tanztheater Wuppertal. During the first artistic phase in Wuppertal, both his and Pina Bausch's talents entered into a congenial relationship. The passionate dancer gave up dancing rather reluctantly to become a choreographer, and Rolf Borzik more or less accidentally became a costume and stage designer. Together, they managed to develop an aesthetic far different to that which had been previously been considered dance theater. While Kurt Jooss still defined it as a form of theater,[39] a form that combined "absolute dance" and "dance drama," dance theater was now *Aktion* (happening/activism) and performance (→ PIECES). Pina Bausch and Rolf Borzik's work questioned the basic principles of concert dance and simultaneously caused a paradigm shift in the dispositif of theater.

The costumes and the stage designs expedited this shift. They did not represent, but rather established situations, connecting reality and theatricality, nature and art, by bringing the real into the theater and removing the representative dimension from the theatrical. This meant that costumes were both mundane garments and simultaneously "dance dress" *(Tanzkleider)* – and here Rolf Borzik served up a wild mix: secondhand dresses, evening gowns, cross dressing, bathing suits and diving fins. This meant opening up the stage to the performative and allowing it to take on agency, to join in the performance, be mobile and transform. Rolf Borzik called the stage a "free action space" *(freier Aktionsraum)* and defined it less as a setting and more as a playing field that "[...] turns us into happy and cruel children."⁴⁰ The stage was not a limitation and certainly not decoration. It was literally a playroom, a space for all kinds of action, a place of obstacles and resistance, where situational performance was more important than executing preselected choreographies. The spatial elements entered into dialogue with the performers, their movements changing with the design of the space, just as the room transformed itself in line with their movements and the traces that they made and left behind. It was a paradigm shift in the way that both theatrical and dance space were understood, transforming a representative concept of space into a performative one, into a space where acting 'as if' would have been impossible and pointless. In this respect, one crucial factor in the design was the stage floor, the most important spatial element for dancers. As the first stage designer to do so, Rolf Borzik covered it with natural elements – soil, water, sand, trees – which left a mark on both the dancers and their dancing. In 2007, Pina Bausch described the interactions between dancers and these natural elements as follows: "Earth, water, leaves or stones onstage create a very specific sensory experience. They change the movements, they record traces of movements, they create certain smells. Earth sticks to the skin, water is absorbed into the dresses, makes them heavy and produces sounds."⁴¹

The spaces built by Rolf Borzik often housed the same tensions and contradictions that characterized the aesthetics of the Tanztheater Wuppertal, or they conflicted with the action onstage: a lifeless tree in the ground in *Orpheus und Eurydike* (PREMIERE 1975), an exact copy of a Wuppertal street for the "Brecht/Weill Evening" *The Seven Deadly Sins* (PREMIERE 1976), an empty apartment with a floor covered in autumn leaves in *Bluebeard: While Listening to a Taped Recording of Béla Bartók's "Duke Bluebeard's Castle"*⁴² (PREMIERE 1977), an iceberg invading a residential area in *Come dance with me* (PREMIERE 1977), a children's slide in *Renate Emigrates* (PREMIERE 1977) onto which two massive trees fall, and a soirée in the water with splendid evening gowns in *Arien* (PREMIERE 1979), accompanied by an onlooking hippopotamus. He also loved including details: in *Bluebeard,* there is a little bird rustling around in the leaves, and the artificial crocodile in *Legend of Chastity* (PREMIERE 1979) has a single red painted toenail. The set designs were technically complex, and Rolf Borzik applied himself with passion to solving their technical difficulties. To do so, he often had to be persuasive and was not always successful. He was quickly banned from the costume department at the Wuppertaler Bühnen. The stage technicians had a low opinion of dance, which took on a subordinate role in the theater's hierarchy of genres, and therefore refused to even consider his eccentric designs. Submerge the stage in water? Technically impossible! Too much weight. There would be problems with the electricity, and so on. Pina Bausch once described the challenges posed by the communication: "No matter what it is was, they said: that's impossible! But Rolf always knew how to do it. He sat down with the workshop managers, somehow they then also got interested and became inspired to make it become reality."[43]

Not only did Rolf Borzik symbolically clear a path for the blindly searching Pina Bausch in *Café Müller*, sweeping away the chairs in her path, he also built the spaces that her dance theater required. They were not purist, abstract spaces, but rather spaces both ordinary and extraordinary, familiar and confusing. While this concept varied over the course of different pieces, it never completely changed, although Pina Bausch and Rolf Borzik dealt with a wide range of genres in the development of the distinct aesthetics of the Tanztheater Wuppertal: some pieces were purely dance, others dance opera, operetta or revue. Rolf Borzik's stages were always open spaces with a range of different playing fields, within which dancers could create flexible micro-spaces with the help of materials and objects (tables, chairs, pillows, etc.). These micro-spaces existed side by side, were variable and kept the shifting space onstage in motion. In the 1970s, Rolf Borzik's spaces and Pina Bausch's choreographies even opened up the fourth wall facing the audience, making the boundary between stage and auditorium permeable: the choreography extended outward into the auditorium, with dancers repeatedly moving along its boundaries, the apron and onto the ramp, directly addressing the audience or going down to move among the seats. Stage design, costumes and choreography merged with the music in order to call all of these elements into question. Pina Bausch and Rolf Borzik were close, intimate and constant dialogue partners: "I could talk to him about anything. We fantasized together, came up with better solutions."[44] Other artistic collaborators for set design, costumes and music have described working with Pina Bausch as a largely taciturn and sometimes even non-verbal relationship, as a "silent understanding," in which communication dissolved into action, and as a hierarchical relationship, in which she alone decided everything and the others hardly dared to ask. But in Rolf Borzik's case, Pina Bausch described moments of mutual inspiration, the shared development of ideas and designs, and mutual doubts, but also the support and protection that she experienced with him.[45] Marion Cito, who was still working as Pina Bausch's assistant at the time, remembers: "Rolf was always at Pina's side, and when problems arose, he got up onstage and said to the managing director: 'Now look here, you've made Frau Bausch cry!' He did everything for Pina. Everything. Borzik was amazing."[46]

Pina Bausch and Rolf Borzik were seen as a unit. The young actress Mechthild Großmann, who met them both in 1975 while auditioning to sing in the "Brecht/Weill Evening," admired them: "They seemed so certain of what they wanted."[47] Moreover, although she had been invited by Pina Bausch to come sing, she felt as if "Pina and Rolf" had hired her. Rolf Borzik attended all rehearsals and had an unerring eye. Mechthild Großmann and the dancer Meryl Tankard remember him nodding encouragingly, expressing amusement and dismissing fake posturing by grinning, mocking and even becoming cynical. He was always willing to have a conversation, no matter how abstruse the subject. Mechthild Großmann considered him more than just a set and costume designer: "[...] no, Rolf was interested in everything. Be it movement, language, music. Even the tiniest prop. He wanted to reinvent the moment onstage, to seize a bit of truth, so that it would truly become theater. Everything was important! He gave us wings to fly, made the impossible possible. That's why I trusted him more than others."[48] For the last piece to which he contributed before his death, *Legend of Chastity*, he designed crocodiles and painted the first one himself. He worked in the scene shop with theater sculptor Herbert Rettich until late in the night, tinkering around with technical solutions with childlike abandon, trying to find out, for example, "[...] how to get the crocodile to open its mouth, wag its tail and turn its head,"[49] all the while documenting the process in photos. Whether it was Mechthild Großmann, Meryl Tankard or Marion Cito – everyone who worked with him and experienced him as part of the Tanztheater Wuppertal agrees that his death left an enormous void in the company. Meryl Tankard summarizes: "I felt really close to Rolf. I could speak really easily to Rolf. I was devastated when Rolf died. It was never the same after he was no longer there."[50] Rolf Borzik died on January 27, 1980, at the age of 36 after a long period of illness. His death plunged Pina Bausch into both a deeply personal crisis and an artistic one with the Tanztheater Wuppertal: "After the death of Rolf Borzik in 1980, it was very difficult for me. I thought I would never make another piece or that I had to do something straight away. Rolf had tried everything to live. For me, it was impossible that he could die while I lived and gave up [...]."[51] But she did not give up. Her dancers, colleagues and friends supported her. Together, they created the piece *1980*. Tankard remembers: "[...] somehow we had to give Pina the strength to create a beautiful piece dedicated to Rolf [...] and we created *1980* for him."[52] *1980* changed everything: with Marion Cito, who had previously helped

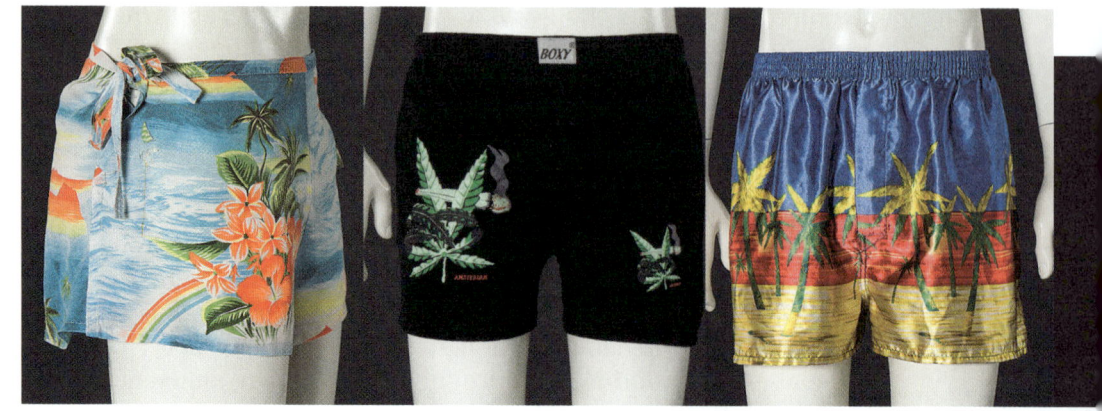

6 Costumes made by
Marion Cito for
Two Cigarettes in the Dark

4 & 5 Costumes made by Marion Cito for *Água*

Rolf Borzik with costumes, taking on full responsibility for costume design and Peter Pabst designing the stage, it heralded in a new phase in the Tanztheater Wuppertal's history – and with it also came a shift in aesthetics. During the next ten years, this shift was supported and accompanied by the Wuppertal critic and journalist Raimund Hoghe, who was also the first to assume the position of dance dramaturge in 1980. However, by this time, Pina Bausch had already developed the artistic cornerstones of the Tanztheater Wuppertal together with Rolf Borzik.

THE COSTUME DESIGNER: MARION CITO

"Pina influenced us all. Pina absorbed everything. She was inspired by everything,"[53] said Marion Cito, looking back on the choreographer and her influence on the company in 2015. When Marion Cito met Pina Bausch, the former was already a well-known ballet dancer who would go on to work closely with the choreographer for over 30 years.

Marion Cito was born in Berlin in 1938. In March of that year, the Nazi regime annexed Austria, marking a turning point in Nazi policies toward Jews, shifting from the discrimination against the Jewish population that had been continuously practiced since 1933 toward its systematic persecution and annihilation – and this was particularly evident in the capital of the "Third Reich," Berlin. Jews were no longer allowed to enter the government district, Jewish lawyers were banned from practicing their profession, streets with Jewish names were renamed, and 10,000 Polish Jews were violently deported from Berlin. All of this not only served to stir up the hatred of the Jews latent among the population but also climaxed in the state-sanctioned violence of the November Pogroms, which culminated in the night of November 9 to 10, 1938, throughout the entire German Reich in a wave of criminal acts ordered by the Nazi leadership and brutally carried out by the SA and SS. Over 1,400 synagogues and prayer rooms were destroyed, of which approx. 100 were in Berlin. Havoc was wreaked on around 7,500 Jewish businesses and homes, Jewish cemeteries and other community institutions. The Gestapo arrested around 30,000 Jewish people and deported them to concentration camps, where hundreds had been murdered or starved to death within a matter of days.

It was into this atmosphere of insecurity, despair, fear, hatred, violence and blatant displays of force and power that Marion Cito was born Marion Schnelle to a bourgeois Berlin family. She was an only child. Her father was a chemist and pharmacist. Marion Cito describes him as suffering from a heart condition. He therefore avoided being drafted into the Wehrmacht and was only later, as she calls it,[54] "conscripted" into keeping the pharmacy running. During an air raid on Berlin, the Schnelle's family home was destroyed. Her father remained in Berlin and sent his wife and his daughter to Thuringia. They did not experience the heavy bombardment of Berlin at the end of the war. Six months before the war ended, her father took his own life – "and no one knows why,"[55] his daughter says, not even 60 years later.

After the war, eight-year-old Marion returned with her mother to a devastated Berlin. After Germany's unconditional surrender, the city was at the center of the Soviet occupation zone, but it had been divided into four sectors and politically placed under the administrative control of the four Allied powers. In 1948, this complicated arrangement, agreed upon by the Allies in 1944, sparked the first deep crisis between East and West: in reaction to the introduction of the Deutsche Mark (DM) by the Western Allies as the new official currency of the western occupied sectors, the Soviet Union reacted with the Berlin Blockade of West Berlin, making it essentially impossible to access the western part of the city by land or water. The Western Allies countered with the Berlin Airlift and supplied West Berlin's population with necessities via airplane for 15 months. In the same year of this "first battle of the Cold War,"[56] Marion Cito's mother was doing everything she could to get her daughter to learn to dance. Perhaps it was the desire for a normal bourgeois life or simply that she and others saw her daughter's talent. But Marion Cito's mother could not afford the classes. Nevertheless, she found solutions, as did many *Trümmerfrauen*.

In 1948, Marion Cito began taking ballet lessons. First, ten-year-old Marion attended a ballet school in West Berlin, located on the once splendid Kurfürstendamm, before switching to the school of Tatjana Gsovsky. Marion Cito remembers her mother choosing Tatjana Gsovsky's school for her daughter, not because she knew that Tatjana Gsovsky was one of the most important personalities of postwar ballet in Germany – she had not even heard her famous name. Her reasons were more pragmatic. Tatjana, as everyone called her, was willing to teach her daughter even though she had no money and could not pay for classes. Tatjana Gsovsky had done the same with other students during the war as well. Marion Cito's mother returned the favor, taking care of the paperwork and bringing homemade cake to the school. Marion Cito remembers this as the kind of reciprocal support that was typical of the times and provided as a matter of course, which would shape her later life.

Tatjana Gsovsky (1901-1993) was one of the most illustrious figures of 20th-century German dance. She danced her way through several political systems, first studying art history and dance in Moscow, later at the studio of her mother, an actress and dancer, and then at the school of the pioneer of American modern dance Isadora Duncan. Only later did she learn Russian ballet, and it was after emigrating, that she began studying rhythmics in the Garden City of Hellerau near Dresden. In 1924, she emigrated from the Soviet Union to Berlin. It was the same year as Josef Stalin's ascent to power. Four years later, she opened a ballet school in Berlin with her husband, the dancer Victor Gsovsky. The school, located on what is the now fashionable Fasanenstraße, soon became the elite training school for ballet in Berlin, although ballet aesthetics had gone out of style and stood at odds with the new dance avant-garde: the 1920s were the golden age of *Ausdruckstanz* (expressionist dance) in Germany; 'balletic' was considered an insult.

However, soon after, during the Nazi regime and the war, many expressionist dancers were unable to continue working. Their art was considered "degenerate" and their schools were closed. In comparison, Tatjana Gsovsky was not only able to continue her artistic work in Berlin until 1940 and at the Oper Leipzig, the Semperoper in Dresden and the Bayerische Staatsoper in Munich until the end of the war, she also managed to keep teaching classes during the air raids, her students paying her in firewood and candles.

Tatjana Gsovsky remembered those days in a 1985 radio show: "We heard the radio: Attention! Planes over Hanover, Braunschweig. Gosh, where did you leave your ballet slippers? That was the only thing you had to hide. The ballet slippers were ready. But we continued. We told ourselves: well, they're coming from Hanover, so we have a good 25 minutes. That should be enough for the ronde de jambes. And when the ronde de jambes came, you could already hear the drone of the planes overhead. So, we quickly grabbed the pointe shoes, the rest of them, the valuable ones, and down to the cellar we went. There was a crash and a bang. [...]. I don't have to explain what war is. Those children, they were children, they weren't scared. They were Berlin children. It was clear as day to them that the house could be hit. And their parents knew that too – and yet they came and studied ballet."[57]

Her knowledge of various dance traditions allowed Tatjana Gsovsky to redefine ballet and combine it with elements of expressionist dance into a new dramatic art form. By dint of her own training in this new dance form, one element typical of her style was the expressive, sculptural shapes made by the upper body and arms; her trademark was the elaborately defined lines of upper body and arm movements, which would later also be characteristic of Pina Bausch. Tatjana Gsovsky's choreographies, for which she collaborated with renowned, groundbreaking experimental composers such as Luigi Nono and Hans Werner Henze, left their mark on the German postwar dance scene until late into the 1960s, when a new generation, some of its members trained by Tatjana

Gsovsky herself, began to break new ground in the wake of social upheaval (→ PIECES) – among them Marion Cito.

Although the school was in the western part of the city, Tatjana Gsovsky developed her choreographic pieces straight after the Second World War at the Staatsoper in East Berlin. As its ballet director until 1951, she completely reestablished the Staatsballett Berlin. However, her hopes for a new beginning were thwarted by growing tensions with the cultural functionaries of the reigning Socialist Unity Party (SED). So, in 1951, Gsovsky relocated to the west side of the city with a large number of her dancers, to the Städtische Oper Berlin (renamed Deutsche Oper Berlin in 1961), where she worked as its ballet director from 1953 to 1966. In 1955, she founded the Berliner Ballett, a modern ensemble based on classical technique, with which she toured across Europe. During this same period, Marion Schnelle became a professional ballet dancer and the lead soloist at the Deutsche Oper. She performed in Leipzig, Dresden and Berlin, where she danced with Constanze Vernon, Silvia Kesselheim, Gerhard Bohner and other famous ballet dancers, not only in Gsovsky's choreographies but also in guest choreographies by George Balanchine, Kenneth McMillan, Serge Lifar, John Cranko and Antony Tudor. During this time, she changed her last name to its Latin form, from then on going by the name of Marion Cito (cito: Latin for 'fast' or, in German, *schnell).*

Like Silvia Kesselheim and Gerhard Bohner, she belonged to the 1960s generation of dancers, who – in the wake of a general climate of social upheaval (→ PIECES) – began searching for a new aesthetics and methods of working beyond the classical ballet repertoire and the traditional performing role of the dancer. At the time, the Akademie der Künste on Hanseatenweg in West Berlin provided a platform for these new forms of dance. But Marion Cito bravely broke with her successful Berlin dance career and followed Gerhard Bohner in 1972 to Darmstadt – with her mother in tow – where she worked with him for three years and participated in his search for new forms of collective collaboration, integrating the audience and the aesthetics of what he called dance theater (→ PIECES).

At the end of this experiment, Gerhard Bohner and Marion Cito gave a joint interview in the German weekly *Die Zeit,* in which they emphasized that more time was needed to establish dance theater, its new aesthetics, collective methods and ways of accessing the audience as an artistic genre. They also said that the time had not yet come for this art form. It was the same year that Pina Bausch premiered both *Orpheus und Eurydike* and a choreography that would go on to be considered one of the century's seminal works: *The Rite of Spring.* In the interview, Marion Cito said, "I have nothing against classical ballet; I did it for too long and was sometimes very happy to do so. But how is it practiced so often in opera houses today? With ready-made productions. It's important to me that I experience the creation of a ballet with someone else and don't just deliver ready-made material like a robot." But change, she said, would not be possible "[...] in such a short space of time if dancers – like myself – come from a different school, a different organization, where a different type of training prevails."⁵⁸ At the Tanztheater Wuppertal, she later had the chance to work with the company on the development of precisely such pieces.

At the end of her time in Darmstadt, Marion Cito returned to Berlin to look for work. During her career, she had not yet come into contact with the developments in dance that had been made at the Folkwang Hochschule in Essen – "that was very far off."⁵⁹ She went to see Pina Bausch's first piece, *Fritz,* on a triple bill (→ PIECES) while still working with Gerhard Bohner and thought that some of it, as she remembers in retrospect, was "whacky," but "great."⁶⁰ In 1976, Malou Airaudo and Dominique Mercy decided to leave the Tanztheater Wuppertal, so the company placed a call for a replacement for Malou Airaudo. Marion Cito heard about it and applied for the position. She did not know Pina Bausch personally. She considered herself a ballet dancer, who "may have done a few crazy things," but what was happening in Wuppertal was something different for her altogether, a completely different aesthetic. Upon introducing herself to the choreographer, Pina Bausch said to Marion Cito: "I know you. I saw you onstage."⁶¹

Marion Cito joined the Tanztheater Wuppertal at a time when the ensemble was going through a difficult phase after the premiere of the "Brecht/Weill Evening." Many dancers were unhappy, turnover was high, and some left the company. Pina Bausch continued working with only a small group on a new piece that would later be called *Bluebeard.* Marion Cito was part of this group, although to her – the ballet dancer – this new method of 'asking questions' that Pina Bausch had adopted seemed disconcerting. She was no longer really able to dance, especially not en pointe. Her knee hurt too much. Pina Bausch also realized that "others [could] do it better," and so – with small exceptions such as her dance role in *Bluebeard* and in other pieces such as *Come dance with me, Renate Emigrates* and *Arien* (→ PIECES) – Marion Cito slipped into the role of assistant to the young choreographer, who wanted Marion Cito to be around her all the time, from morning to night, so that she could best learn about her new working method. "And she made that happen, too,"⁶² Marion Cito, recalls, laughing, 40 years later, 33 years of which she faithfully spent by Pina Bausch's side. She thus witnessed and contributed to decades of ensemble work, in which she participated, almost always and everywhere. Marion Cito attended every rehearsal, initially taking notes for the choreographer and helping Rolf Borzik to look for and sort out the costumes. With him, she rummaged through secondhand shops looking for clothes, altered them, upcycled old items, looked for cheap deals, learned to make do when the fabric tore – and in the process, utilized what she had observed and learned from her mother growing up during the war and in the postwar period.

After Rolf Borzik's death, Marion Cito took on sole responsibility for the costumes for the piece *1980*. The choreographer told her to do so more or less in passing. After the great misfortune of Rolf Borzik's death, Pina Bausch mustered all her energy and set about making a new piece. The strength of this confidence in the face of deep despair also affected Marion Cito. Pina Bausch had no other choice but to ask Marion Cito. But Pina Bausch also had confidence in Marion Cito's ability to take care of the costumes, even though she had neither the training nor enough experience and therefore greatly doubted her abilities herself. This interplay between doubt, fear, confidence, courage, trust in the other and a willingness to take risks generated a productive artistic energy that came to characterize how the company worked not only with the dancers but also with collaborators and staff, as well as the Tanztheater Wuppertal's aesthetics as a whole.

Marion Cito pored over books, conducted research – and henceforth independently and responsibly designed the costumes – or "dance dress" *(Tanzkleider)*, as it is referred to by the Tanztheater Wuppertal – for every piece. The company sought to bring everyday life to the stage, and this also meant that dancers did not appear in leotards or ballet slippers. The costumes were meant to be mundane; however, unlike in contemporary dance, mundane did not mean T-shirts, jeans and sneakers, but rather that they were suitable for the performance practices of the dancers onstage. The costumes were intended to support the use of form in the dance and underline the characters of the dancers. "When the movement begins, the dress comes alive,"[63] says Marion Cito. Particularly in the case of the women, she translated the body aesthetics of Pina Bausch, who wanted to see bare backs while covering the dancers' legs. The form, function and color of Pina Bausch's movement aesthetics (long swinging arms, flowing forms) materialized in Marion Cito's dance dress, as did the way that the choreographer saw the dancers' subjectivities and individualities as different colors. But while Rolf Borzik had dressed the dancers in a wider range of clothes, from secondhand to festive evening gowns, Marion Cito – while initially continuing in the same vein – gradually began to design costumes that were increasingly elegant. They became more stylized and more extraordinary, and there were more and more evening gowns.

Marion Cito took a literal approach to the word 'dance dress.' Like her colleagues in charge of the music, she did not attempt to find, e.g., 'Indian' or 'Hungarian' fabric or motifs to represent the coproducing countries during the research trips for the coproductions, nor was she interested in reproduction: she did not seek to remake Japanese kimonos, Turkish robes or colorful flamenco dresses. Instead, she chose brilliant colors, floral patterns and delicate fabrics that beautifully danced, moved and draped themselves around the body, with patterns that revealed, flattered and joined in with the movement. The ambivalence between freedom and restriction, constriction and expansion, airy and bulky, fragile and hard, which otherwise characterized the Tanztheater Wuppertal, did not materialize in these costumes. They thus primarily helped to underline the shift toward dance that took place in later pieces. This revealed itself in the costumes' shapes, colors and above all materials. In her dance dress, Marion Cito translated her dedication to dance into "daring beauty,"[64] as she titled her own book about the costumes that she had made for the Tanztheater Wuppertal. Her own taste and sense of style provided her with orientation; her benchmarks were color and form, and she adapted them to each dancer, to his or her physique and skin type. If the result resembled a kimono, then that was more coincidence than intention. In the dresses, too, suggestion and interpretative freedom were crucial.

At first, Marion Cito carried out her new role as defined by the framework provided by Rolf Borzik: she "just had to travel with a suitcase to Berlin"[65] to buy secondhand clothes and set up a pool of costumes that the dancers could choose from during rehearsals to queer themselves on the stage – the men in scanty Lurex miniskirts, evening gowns, tutus or wearing ladies' fur coats and chic hats. Later, she remained very price-conscious and usually bought good value for money: always little more than one to two meters of extra fabric to mend the dresses if necessary and to "make do." Ordering two dresses simply was not in the budget during those first years and also felt wasteful to her. Wuppertal was once the heart of the German textile industry – the textile manufacturer Friedrich Engels, one of the cofounders of Marxism, grew up in Wuppertal-Barmen, near the opera house. Marion Cito generally sought advice at one of Wuppertal's oldest traditional textile stores, Buddeberg & Weck, where she was always kept up to date about residual stock for use at the Tanztheater Wuppertal, or she went shopping at the Marché Saint-Pierre in Montmartre, Paris, the one city that the company returned to every year. Over the years, she came to know the dancers well – their bodies, how they moved, their characters. This became her yardstick: she created the clothes for the dancers; for every piece, she designed a maximum of three to four dresses for each performer, which gradually developed into increasingly opulent evening gowns, revealing her love of unusual patterns. But not even these dresses were made for representation, for presenting femininity; instead, they were treated like everyday clothes: in which to butter bread, sit on swings, sleep, run, cook spaghetti, haul buckets of water, run up and down cliffs, jump over crevices, dance across lawns, through fields of carnations and water, and to climb mountains.

Marion Cito produced on a hunch. The choreographer let her do what she wanted and did not ask to know about her ideas and suggestions so early on, for she felt it would restrict the openness of the choreographic process. She wanted to be surprised. Pina Bausch made no suggestions of her own regarding costumes, but six weeks before the premiere, she wanted to see them. That was the "ultimate test" for Marion Cito: the dancers, who occasionally also brought unusual costumes to rehearsals, now tried on the costumes covered in sweat and without makeup. Only rarely did Pina Bausch see a finished dress and ask: "Are you serious?" – which would lead to a sleepless night for Marion Cito. But Marion Cito, as she emphasized in our conversations together, still would have immediately changed it, even if she had meant it seriously, for Pina Bausch "was the boss." Essentially, however, in spite of her "racing heart," she was fairly certain that the costumes would meet the choreographer's expectations. Anything else would have been reckless, for the costume designer began designing very early on in the process, without knowing what the new piece would become. Moreover, when making the dresses, she had to integrate herself into the processes of the dressmaking shop at the Wuppertaler Bühnen, which was also responsible for the opera and the drama departments. In the early years, there was much resistance here: as in the case of the set design shops, collaboration with the dressmakers was complicated and humiliating during that initial period, with the dressmakers acting as if the Tanztheater Wuppertal was ruining everything. Rolf Borzik experienced the same thing until he was effectively banned from entering the dressmaking shop. He therefore sent in Marion Cito during the rehearsals for *Kontakthof* (PREMIERE 1978), and the first thing that the head of dressmaking did was to ask her for her credentials. But that, too, died off over the years – with the worldwide success of the company. "The credentials – they forgot about them eventually,"[66] Marion Cito remembered in 2014.

She began making the dance dress half a year before the premiere, once the cast was fixed and one to two rehearsal phases had already taken place, but at a point when the piece was not even close to being finished. Stage designs where dancers, e.g., danced in water and clothes got wet required other types of fabric. This was something that she only learned quite late when she was forced, as in the case of *Vollmond* (PREMIERE 2006), to more or less react at the last minute and organize the appropriate fabric. The dance dress was usually only added to the production at a very late point in time, even after the music had already been selected. She thus had to demonstrate flexibility, spontaneity and speed. Occasionally, she was asked to change the costumes because the choreographer had rearranged the scenes at the very last minute and, suddenly, several dancers were onstage dressed in the same color. At the premiere of the piece *Nelken* (1982), Pina Bausch decided during the intermission to include a scene with Anne Martin that had previously been removed. Marion Cito quickly had to run to the costume pool and find something for Anne Martin to wear.

Marion Cito's expertise was also required when roles were passed on or recast. Departing dancers were replaced based on their size and proportions in addition to their movement qualities and expressiveness, and this made reassigning costumes somewhat easier. Sometimes, new costumes were required – "additional dress" *(Zusatzkleider)* as the company called it, which resembled the original costumes in style and in color. However, when pieces were passed on to other companies, the situation was different, such as when *For the Children of yesterday, today and tomorrow* (PREMIERE 2002) was passed on to the dancers of the Bayerisches Staatsballett (PREMIERE 2016). One example was when Nazareth Panadero's role was passed on to the dancers Marta Navarrete and Mia Rudic: they had different bodies, heights, shapes and proportions, a different habitus as dancers and different identities as ballerinas. The color and shape of the dance dress therefore had to be readjusted – and by then, this was without the possibility of consulting with Pina Bausch herself on a final decision.

Marion Cito may well have been the first ballerina to become a world-famous costume designer. She developed costumes based on the idea of the dancing body and designed with the eyes of Pina Bausch. She worked independently, but always saw herself as an assistant. She abided by the hierarchical order and always remained insecure, afraid of making mistakes and not satisfying requirements right up to the very end of her time working with Pina Bausch, although she was on very good terms with her "boss." She did in fact work for the Tanztheater Wuppertal day after day and became one of its most intimate insiders. For years, she not only attended rehearsals but also all performances. Her place was beside the choreographer; she spent years summarizing Pina Bausch's critiques, which were then discussed with the company the next day on the basis of her notes. She therefore noticed everything that Pina Bausch said about her dancers in those moments. Together with many others, such as the long-serving organizational team of Claudia Irman, Ursula Popp and Sabine Hesseling, she contributed to ensuring the cohesion of company. Her costumes helped to decisively shape the unmistakable aesthetic of the Tanztheater Wuppertal from the 1980s onward.

THE SET DESIGNER: PETER PABST

Peter Pabst met Pina Bausch for the first time in 1978 while working under Peter Zadek at the Schauspielhaus Bochum. *1980* was the first Pina Bausch piece for which he designed the stage, which consisted of actual turf. It was her first piece after Rolf Borzik's death, and it was a piece of her, a piece of life. A new decade of collaboration thus began with Marion Cito and Peter Pabst, and he, too, would continue to work with Pina Bausch until her death.

Peter Pabst was born in the town of Grodzisk Wielkopolski, known in German as Grätz. The city is located in a region with an unstable history. Like Poznań, Rolf Borzik's birthplace, Grodzisk Wielkopolski was also repeatedly claimed by various powers and was finally handed over to Poland at the signing of the Treaty of Versailles after the First World War. Peter Pabst's father, a lawyer, was a soldier during the Second World War. He was not present at the birth of his son, his third child. At the end of the war, in 1945, Peter Pabst's mother moved to Berlin-Karlshorst with her three children and her mother-in-law. By the beginning of the 20th century, Berlin-Karlshorst had developed into one of the city's most popular suburbs, well-connected to Berlin by train and in close proximity to the Müggelsee lake. The residential suburb there was considered to be a very fashionable part of the city and, in the 1910s and 1920s, a model settlement was built among the trees along the Spree River. It was this settlement to which the Pabst family moved and into this bourgeois environment that the Wehrmacht built its Pioneer School I (Pionierschule I) for the training of officers in the 1930s. In 1942, when a turning point in the war seemed imminent after the Battle of Stalingrad, it was given the somewhat grim new name of Fortress Pioneer School (Festungspionierschule). In April 1945, the Red Army made its headquarters there during the Battle of Berlin, with the Red Army and a few Polish troops participating in a battle that cost approx. 170,000 soldiers their lives, wounded another 500,000 and killed tens of thousands of civilians. Finally, on May 8/9, 1945, it was in Berlin-Karlshorst that German field marshal Wilhelm Keitel signed Germany's unconditional surrender. That was the same year that the Pabst family relocated to Berlin.

After the war, the Soviet Military Administration in Germany (SMAD) took up residence in Karlshorst. It was the highest-ranking occupation authority and thus the actual governing body of the Soviet

Occupation Zone (SBZ) from June 1945 until 1949, when administrative sovereignty was handed over to the government of the East German state, the German Democratic Republic (GDR). From then until 1953, the Soviet Control Commission in East Germany governed the GDR as the Soviet institution of surveillance and control. Right up until 1994, the main building of the former Pioneer School continued to house the world's largest headquarters of the Russian Committee for State Security (KGB) outside of the Soviet Union. Reflecting this military and political infrastructure of the Soviet occupying forces, Karlhorst had *Russenmagazine* (Russian warehouses), shops where things could be bought at moderate prices without food stamps.

Peter Pabst spent the next nine years in this neighborhood growing up without a father. His mother was a seamstress. She quickly established a dressmaking business in Karlshorst and sewed clothes for the wives of high-ranking Soviet officers. She also made costumes for Berlin's theaters, collectively referred to as the "Berliner Bühnen," for she had good connections to their costume director. Thanks to this income and her ties to Russian officers, some of whom paid for room and board in the Pabst family home, the family was well off in spite of having fled from Poland and despite the 'lean years.' His mother's industriousness helped the family to settle in Karlshorst and ensured that they always had enough to eat. The children had toys, and the adults had cigarettes. "The Russians" liked children, or at least that is how Peter Pabst experienced it. He remembers having a good, easygoing childhood. In our conversations, he described it as the basis for his *joie de vivre* and his life-long optimism.[67]

Peter Pabst had close-knit relationships with his family and friends. He was surrounded by a large number of children who, like him, were growing up without fathers. He remembers his mother being a loving person. Her dressmaking shop was a wonderful, warm place, where there was always something going on. But she was busy around the clock, and so the children were left to themselves. Peter Pabst sees it this way: because he was left to his own devices as a child, he was able to develop. He became independent and self-sufficient. He spent time outdoors in a beautiful neighborhood, did not complain and only reluctantly returned home at nightfall. Although he grew up in the Soviet Occupation Zone, he does not remember the political situation playing any role for him as a child. Peter Pabst was ten years old when father and son met for the first time. His father returned from Russian captivity in 1954, and he was not willing to settle down in a city that was under the military command of the power that had incarcerated him as a prisoner of war for so long under such harsh conditions. He went west, to Frankfurt am

Main, at first alone, but the family soon followed. Peter Pabst's mother gave up everything that she had achieved in Karlshorst and moved with her children to be with her husband. At the time, it was still possible to relocate without much bureaucracy: they simply boarded a train to Frankfurt. From there, Peter Pabst's mother informed the authorities that they should forward her emigration papers. Peter Pabst did not experience this move as a transition from East to West, from communism to capitalism, because, in East Berlin, communism had been less noticeable to him in everyday life than Prussian culture. In fact, what did remain was a Prussian sense of duty. In the West, he now encountered something that he had not known in Karlshort: the large-scale project of postwar rebuilding.

Until this point, Peter Pabst had barely missed his father at all. It was not easy to recalibrate family life, which had previously functioned so well. Having himself been raised in authoritarian structures, both personally and politically, Peter Pabst's father found it difficult to adapt, after years of absence, to a family that had got along fine so far without any patriarchal influence. He was not in the best of health, and his desire for a lawyer's upper-class lifestyle, to which he had been used, did not at first correspond to his actual situation. His son was bewildered at his father's sudden attempts to raise him in old authoritarian structures. This did not help to improve their relationship, but it did prepare Peter Pabst for an upper-class lifestyle. Peter Pabst refused to follow in his father's footsteps and rejected the idea of an academic career. He dropped out of school and began an apprenticeship as a tailor. From then on, he appeared to always be in exactly the right place at the right time in his career, and he himself believes that he was just very lucky.

As this luck would have it, his mother secured him a position in the haute-couture fashion house Elise Topell in Wiesbaden, one of the most well-known and prestigious German fashion designers at the time. In the 1930s, when "Berlin chic" had become all the rage, Elise Topell founded a fashion house in Berlin selling ready-to-wear collections. After the Second World War, she left Berlin and relocated to Wiesbaden, whose thermals baths made it one of the oldest spa cities in Europe. A number of millionaires and large corporations had settled here since the early 20th century, turning Wiesbaden into the city with the most millionaires in Germany at the time. This was just the right place for Elise Topell's exclusive fashion – much better than the destroyed Berlin, where exclusive, chic designs no longer really fit the picture. She took up lodgings at the prestigious Biebrich Palace, where she managed her renowned label, which still successfully exists in Wiesbaden to this day. Wealthy women knew Elise Topell. In the 1950s, an haute-couture dress by Elise Topell cost approx. DM 3,000. The apprentice tailor Peter Pabst earned less than DM 300 a month. Nevertheless, he socialized in the chic fashion industry, where he encountered a new dimension of wealth and a world seemingly untouched by the war. He remembers some women spending DM 30,000 to 40,000 on clothes in a single afternoon. Elise Topell also presented her designs at the major international fashion shows in Paris. Peter Pabst experienced the international magnitude of the rich and beautiful – and learned to love their opulent lifestyles. In spite of his own meager income, he rented an apartment on Wilhelmstraße, the stately boulevard of the Hessian capital.

Elise Topell ran a tight ship. Peter Pabst learned discipline and how important accuracy and precision were for top-quality products. It was here that he developed his own sense of quality in connection with his craft. He also learned that mistakes were not allowed, especially not repeated mistakes. In the 1960s, he switched from the world of fashion in Wiesbaden to opera, and once again chose not just any institution, but Richard Wagner's Festspielhaus. He traded the rich, glamorous world of fashion for the wealthy, upper-class world of Bayreuth. Before that, he had shown little interest in opera or theater. By his own admission, the Festspielhaus was the first theater that he became acquainted with after his school theater days. He had had no experience in the world of theater, nor did he know what working at a theater really meant. His entry into this world could not have been less challenging. Once more, he had chosen a global reputation and top-quality artists to measure up to.

In Bayreuth, Peter Pabst switched from fashion to costume design and worked for Kurt Palm, who was the theater's costume director at the time. He, too, was a stickler for quality. Peter Pabst was able to supplement his skill as a craftsman with the specific creativity required in the theater. He found it fascinating to develop costumes that were not just beautiful, but also helped a character to take shape onstage. However, he still had but little contact to the theater itself, for at the time it was more than unusual for a costume or set designer to attend rehearsals. Workplaces were kept strictly separate, and there were no dress rehearsals where the different art forms could be coordinated with one another. Peter Pabst therefore spent most of his time in Bayreuth in the costume workshop.

In 1969, at the peak of the student movement, Peter Pabst decided to leave the upper-class world behind. Having dropped out of school shortly before finishing, he now wished to study. He successfully applied to study costume design at the renowned Kölner Werkschulen (the Cologne Academy of Fine and Applied Arts) and moved to the city of Cologne, which had been heavily destroyed by the war but was now teeming with upcoming art. It was the city where, some years before, Tanzforum Köln under the leadership of Jochen Ullrich had caused quite a stir and where Johann Kresnik had also shown his first pieces in the late 1960s (→ PIECES). Cologne was the city that Peter Pabst would call home for quite some time – which he continues to do to this day. The Kölner Werkschulen, which became his new place of study, were founded in 1926 under Konrad Adenauer, former Mayor of Cologne and the first Chancellor of the Federal Republic of Germany after the Second World War. The concept was developed along the lines of Bauhaus and dedicated to the ideas of the Werkbund, the German association of artists, architects, designers, and industrialists established in 1907. The Nazis tried to coopt and convert the school into an institute for traditionally crafted, anti-Semitic *Heimatkunst* (regional German art), but after the war, teaching resumed as originally intended. In the 1960s, the Kölner Werkschulen were the largest art institute in North Rhine-Westphalia and, alongside Hamburg, Berlin and Munich, one of the biggest in Germany.

Joining in with the wave of student protest, Peter Pabst became politically active in his new home, but he did not consider himself part of "Generation 68." He was a student member of the faculty board, spent nights discussing politics – and all for nothing, as he later said. But he did successfully advocate for the reinstatement of a professorial chair of costume and stage design, which had long been lacking at the school. Max Bignens, an internationally renowned Swiss costume and stage designer, who, aside from many other things, also worked with choreographers such as Wazlaw Orlikowsky, Anthony Tudor and John Cranko, assumed the position in 1972. He became Peter Pabst's teacher, and Peter Pabst thought that he was wonderful.

Once again, Peter Pabst did not complete his education, but rather transferred upon the recommendation of his teacher to Bochum, to the Schauspielhaus, where he became an assistant stage designer. This was another opportunity that was said by his teacher to only come once in a lifetime. Peter Pabst had no stage design sketches to show anyone. Aside from Peter Stein, who was working at the Schaubühne in Berlin at the time, Peter Zadek was the theater director of the hour, but Peter Pabst was not aware of him yet – despite his work in Bayreuth, he had not become a theatergoer. But he never actually worked as an assistant to the stage designer. Peter Zadek had decided to focus on Shakespearean productions. He wanted open work processes, which included having costume and stage designers attend rehearsals for *King Lear*. Peter Pabst was happy to comply. The encounter with Peter Zadek sparked immediate mutual sympathy – and led to a life-long friendship.

In Bochum, Peter Pabst got to know the art and industry of theater and learned that theater is fundamentally about partnerships. He came to believe that it was impossible to work in the theater if one was not able to wholeheartedly apply oneself, if one was unable

7 Set design for
The Window Washer
Wuppertal, 2006

8 Bukhansan National Park
Research trip for *Rough Cut*
Korea, 2004

10 *Rough Cut*
Wuppertal, 2005

9 Stage for *1980*
Wuppertal, 1980

to enter into a kind of love affair over and over again with the piece and with the people involved. This, above all, required patience, trust, curiosity – and the courage to quarrel. These partnerships were often difficult, but when they did succeed, they were an immense joy. Peter Pabst was lucky. He was an employee of the Schauspielhaus Bochum from 1973 until 1979, when Peter Zadek transferred to the Schauspielhaus in Hamburg. From that point on, he continued working as a freelancer with people like Peter Zadek, who died only one month after Pina Bausch, on July 30, 2009. That year, Peter Pabst lost his two most important artistic partners at nearly the same time. With Zadek, he learned to live with doubt and to endure not knowing, to be inquisitive, and he saw Zadek develop an almost unlimited love for his actors and actresses in the same way that he experienced Pina Bausch with her dancers. This love created trust and was a prerequisite for making open rehearsal processes possible at all, for allowing things to happen. Peter Pabst recognized that, aside from curiosity, it takes patience: patience with those with whom you are working, but above all patience with oneself. For him, being able to wait, to endure the fact that nothing, little or only the irrelevant or useless might occur, was vital to retaining the freedom to watch, to not miss anything. He saw this in both Peter Zadek and Pina Bausch.

  Over the years, Peter Pabst worked on a total of around 120 productions, mainly at major German theaters, but also in cities such as Salzburg, Vienna, Paris, London, Geneva, Copenhagen, Amsterdam, Naples, Turin, Trieste and San Francisco. The 26 spaces that he designed for Pina Bausch's pieces during his 29 years of collaborating with the Tanztheater Wuppertal make up only one part of his oeuvre. He first got to know Pina Bausch's work through Peter Zadek, initially because Peter Zadek wanted to travel from Bochum to Wuppertal just to see what was going on there, and then when Peter Zadek invited Pina Bausch to Bochum to stage *Macbeth* (→ PIECES). After Rolf Borzik's death, Pina Bausch asked Peter Pabst whether he would design the stage for her new piece, which would later be called *1980*. He also worked as an independent freelancer for Pina Bausch and was the only one at the Tanztheater Wuppertal to keep that independence.

  From the 1980s onward, Peter Pabst's stage designs became a hallmark and identifying factor of the Tanztheater Wuppertal. Some pieces were even named after the design of the stage, such as *Nelken* (PREMIERE 1982), *Wiesenland* (PREMIERE 2002) and *The Piece with the Ship* (PREMIERE 1993). They are elaborate, meticulously developed, complex spaces built with a great attention to detail. Peter Pabst called them "atmospheric spaces," unlike Rolf Borzik, who referred to them as *Aktionsräume* (action spaces).

And yet, the concept of the action space, which had characterized Rolf Borzik's stage designs, is still visible here. Although he claims to understand nothing of dance, even after almost 30 years of working with Pina Bausch, Peter Pabst built spaces that take bodies, movement and space into consideration together. These spaces, like Pina Bausch's choreographies, do not seek to exhibit something decorative, not even in the coproductions. They have a function, they show familiar, everyday life while also alienating it. This was especially challenging in the case of the coproductions, which were not intended as mere reflections of or as television reports or documentaries about the hosting countries. What Peter Pabst wanted was to find a translation for his stage designs.

His spaces are not sculptural images. Peter Pabst sees them as spaces for people. They are spaces of wellbeing and of obstacles, spaces that translate the tensions of a piece into a concept of stage space: they are spaces of both nature and art, real habitats and poetic, fairy-tale, imaginary landscapes, places of origin and mythical, fantastic spaces. He often transported 'nature' onto the stage, which he believed to be the opposite of the artificial. Natural materials are soft and sensual, bulky and hard, and they are rebellious in the sense that they defy theater as a site of representation. These are the ambivalences that Peter Pabst worked with. He used all kinds of natural materials to lend spaces the semblance of geographical landscapes of the soul, while also simultaneously being places of heavenly surrealism and literal naturalism. He worked with, for instance, grass *(1980* and *Wiesenland)*, stones as walls *(Palermo Palermo)* and stone-like structures that functioned as cliffs *(Masurca Fogo, O Dido, Wiesenland, Rough Cut)*, soil *(On the Mountain a Cry was Heard, Viktor)*, sand *(Only You, The Piece with the Ship)*, salt and paper that looked like snow *(Tanzabend II, Ten Chi)*, water *(Ein Trauerspiel, Wiesenland, Vollmond)*, trees *(Only You)*, plants *(Two Cigarettes in the Dark, Ahnen)*, flowers *(Nelken, The Window Washer, O Dido)*, ashes and shrapnel *(Ein Trauerspiel)*. As in Rolf Borzik's action spaces, animals also appear onstage: a deer in *1980*, a walrus in *Ahnen*, a polar bear in *Tanzabend II*, a whale's fin in *Ten Chi* and even living animals such as German shepherds in *Nelken* and lapdogs in *Viktor*. Moreover, natural materials are either carried on- or offstage – for example, the trunks of spruce trees *(On the Mountain a Cry was Heard)* and a birch grove *(Tanzabend II)* – or lowered down from above – like the treetops in *Palermo Palermo*.

However, these spaces consist of more than just the materials of which they are made. Atmosphere is also created acoustically or olfactorily: they are spaces for listening to the roar of the wind and crashing waves, to chirping birds and the sounds of the jungle *(The Piece with the Ship)*, spaces where you can smell the grass or the soil, where the humidity of water fills the air. In the 1990s, Peter Pabst increasingly began to integrate video projections of natural landscapes and free roaming animals, but also of urban landscapes *(Tanzabend II, The Window Washer, Masurca Fogo, Água, Rough Cut, Bamboo Blues, 'Sweet Mambo')*. Sometimes, he filmed these images himself during the research trips to the international coproduction sites. In *Danzón* (PREMIERE 1995), Pina Bausch danced in front of a large-scale video projection of exotic fish (→ PIECES). Peter Pabst's spaces are not static; they are spaces in motion. This is not just the case in pieces such as *Água* or *Rough Cut*, where the video projections produce projection spaces, i.e., translate that which is distant into the theatrical space, or where moving images enter into dialogue with the dancers onstage. Instead, they are flexible, transformative spaces that sometimes even have moving floors that split open *("... como el musguito en la piedra, ay si, si, si...")*; where water rises and then falls again *(Nefés,* PREMIERE 2003); where walls fall that the dancers have to jump over *(Palermo Palermo);* or where water trickles down a mossy cliff, which tips over to become a climbable boulder landscape *(Wiesenland)*.

These elaborately designed stages rely on a high level of technical finesse. The craftsmanship behind them is complex and requires great attention to detail. "Because I was of the opinion that saying 'no' was not in my job description, I always promised her the moon, without knowing how to actually give it to her,"[68] Peter Pabst reminisced in 2019. Peter Pabst never spoke about how the sets were technically designed, not even with the choreographer. They were his secret. He loathed backstage tours. Like the choreographer, he delivered no explanation for why he made a set the way it was. They were meant to remain associative playgrounds, for he intended his stage designs to evoke surprise, to develop a magic and poetry of their own. The dance floors in particular convey the idea of stage space as a space of action. They are treacherous, filled with obstacles and surprises – and yet they are built so that dancers can safely move around on them, sometimes at high speeds, without hurting themselves. They are surfaces that do not simply allow you to dance beautifully. They always have to be explored anew, are always uncertain. They challenge dance, make it difficult for dancers to rely on familiarity, skill or training, and thus prevent them from falling into a routine. Moving around in these spaces becomes an existential task. It requires the protagonists to dance on insecure terrain, to dance with a heightened awareness of the moment and to understand the surface and materials underfoot as interactive partners. The surfaces provoke staggering, swaying, stumbling, jumping and tumbling movements, i.e., movements that do not belong to the canon of what even today is generally considered concert dance. Peter Pabst's stage designs prompt both dancers and viewers to question and expand their concept of dance, things that Pina Bausch also strived for – even when the dance onstage merged with the video projections and, in the eyes of the audience, changed to appear more dynamic or meditative. In spite of these constantly new and difficult challenges, the dancers know that the stage will never be built in a way that will damage their art, their dancing. However, these stage designs also make it impossible for the dancers to simply and comfortably perform their repertoire or to bask in their own abilities.

Peter Pabst's stage sets require precise, meticulous, minute and long-term preparation. The Wuppertaler Bühnen scene shops often faced enormous challenges, but Peter Pabst was well-prepared and persuasive, and made suggestions. The stage manager and long-standing technical director of the Tanztheater Wuppertal, Manfred Marczewski, who, like Peter Pabst, first joined the company for *1980*, remembers: "It was hell for the scene shops sometimes, to build such a large set in such a short space of time."[69] His task was to supervise full technical operations during a show. He toured with the company, inspected the venues in advance, checked whether the designs met safety and fire regulations, and took care of loading and shipping. Transport was literally (a) heavy duty. Shipping the stage sets as cargo or loading them onto trucks, sending them on the road, sometimes for weeks at a time, and rebuilding them onsite in different theaters under different conditions is more than just a logistical task: turf; thousands of pink carnations made of fabric and wire, tightly arranged on wooden boards with holes on top of a kind of fibrous insulating material, which have to be replaced before every show; a substance that has to be applied to the floor so that it is not too slippery when covered in water; a space, framed by earthen walls, built out of prefabricated building units, which has to be splattered with glue and fresh soil before each performance; a desert landscape made from four- to six-meter-high cactuses, around 50 to 60 of them, with spines made of nylon that have to be blow-dried once they have been stuck in; a wall made out of hollow blocks, constructed so that no sharp edges or corners form when the wall falls; snow made from ten metric tons of salt; a mossy cliff weighing five metric tons, only suspended at four points, so that it can tip over to become a climbable surface; four metric tons of water in total, approx. 4,000 liters per minute, which have to be carted from one side of the stage to the other and needs to remain at a specific temperature so that the dancers can splash about in it; or – and in comparison seemingly simple – 6,400 square meters of fabric hanging in banners from the fly space, set in motion by wind machines. Marczewski did this work for almost 30 years

– with countless hours of overtime for which he was never compensated. Nor did he want the money, for he consciously decided in favor of working with the Tanztheater Wuppertal, for which almost no technicians wanted to work at the time. But he found it exciting, and that was his incentive: "It's a wonderful experience to work for a company that's so successful. And: Pina showed me the whole world. I wouldn't have done it alone [...], and I got to know the world in a different way, experienced things that a normal tourist wouldn't see."[70]

When Peter Pabst began working on a design, the 'piece' was still a very long way off, not even clearly formed in the choreographer's mind. Occasionally, he watched rehearsals, but he did not attend on a regular basis. Once in a while, he asked the choreographer: what kind of piece will it be? But he had to bide his time and wait for the right moment, and he knew that he would not get a full answer. Like his colleagues responsible for the costumes and music, he nevertheless began designing the stage very early on and built four to six models. "Especially because the empty, black box would stare at me and would want to know something that I myself didn't know yet,"[71] as he explained in a 2008 interview.

Occasionally, he would ask Pina Bausch to take a quick look at the mock-ups and then infer from her expression what appealed to her and what did not. Then he would quietly put it aside. His motto was: you have to be generous with your own ideas, not petty. They would think about how certain scenes, which she believed would make it into the piece, could work in one or the other design. Sometimes, she would ask him to attend a rehearsal when she had assembled part of the new piece. They would briefly talk about it, but not much more than that. There were no discussions. The pieces were hers. He was her stage designer. What they had to say to each other, they showed by doing, and over the years, they came to know each other well. They would pass each other the ball and open up new avenues of thought for one another. The hierarchy remained intact, even though he became her most important confidante over the years.

Peter Pabst had to begin preparing the set for a new piece early on. Sets could not be improvised spontaneously. But unlike in his work for the opera and theater, he would be left groping around in the dark for quite some time, for Pina Bausch was hesitant and late to make decisions, even about the design of the stage – sometimes very late, no more than four to six weeks before the premiere. The dancers would know nothing about the stage designs; sometimes, they would only see them four days before the premiere once they had been set up in the theater. Then they would become their playground. They danced in the stage design, but the stage design also danced around and with them.

Peter Pabst portrays himself as a chronically optimistic, fun-loving person. He describes himself as lazy, but he is in fact very industrious; says that he was apolitical in his youth, although he was actually very active. He has repeatedly depicted himself as insecure and careful when it came to his work, but he also had to be certain that his designs complied with what Pina Bausch wanted, and he was always very determined to implement them. He needed patience, but also had to be able to make very quick decisions about what, how, where and when something was made and done. Moreover, he had to reconcile the desires of Pina Bausch, who was often very late in communicating them, but who trusted him to make possible what he had promised, with the technical, material and manual needs and demands of the scene shops. Like the choreographer, Peter Pabst practiced so-called "Prussian values": a sense of responsibility and duty, discipline and an appreciation for professionalism and quality. 'Self-praise stinks' – for him, this motto, which was still being taught to his generation, was a cornerstone of art. In this respect, he resembled the choreographer, with whom he shared a range of other firm principles and who made him one of her most important artistic collaborators: they surprised each other, endured each other's respective vulnerabilities, maintained respect for one another and did not burden the other with their own worries. He described to me how, like her, he lived with insecurity and doubts about whether his work was really any good or not – even after years of collaboration. These doubts were his productive driving force. *Peter für Pina* (Peter for Pina) is the title of his book.[72] It bears testimony to a very unusual, trusting, close and creative collaborative relationship between two people who were very different, but who shared many things, such as courage and doubt.

THE MUSICAL COLLABORATORS:
MATTHIAS BURKERT AND ANDREAS EISENSCHNEIDER

During the early years of the Tanztheater Wuppertal, Pina Bausch worked with an orchestra and a choir, but it was rather difficult and she met with much resistance. Musicians and singers refused to accept the choreographer's unconventional ideas. It was still rare to see women in such theater positions, and she was considered too young and too inexperienced. During the "Brecht/Weill Evening" *The Seven Deadly Sins* (PREMIERE 1974), she was told that it was not music. And yet, the young choreographer still managed to conceptually open up the stage for the audience by using choir music in new ways, such as in *Iphigenie auf Tauris*, in which the choir sang from the balconies and the boxes, and in *Come Dance with Me*, where the dancers sang the folk songs themselves. Pina Bausch also decided to use prerecorded music. In *The Rite of Spring,* the orchestra pit was too small, so she selected a taped version by Pierre Boulez. In *Bluebeard,* the use of the tape recorder and the technical possibilities that it provided, such as fast-forwarding and rewinding, and its mobility onstage, were part and parcel of the aesthetic concept – but this was also a necessity, for the singer with whom Pina Bausch had been provided was no Bluebeard in her opinion. At first, the choice to use recorded music was an attempt at conflict resolution.

Pina Bausch herself summarized: "To avoid the problems with [the choir] and orchestra, in the next piece, Come Dance With Me, I exclusively used beautiful old folk songs, which each dancer sang [...] – accompanied only by a lute. In the next piece, Renate Emigrates, there was only music from tape, and only one scene in which our old pianist played in the background. In this way a completely different new world of music opened up. Since then, the entire wealth of different types of music from so many different countries and cultures has become a fixed component of our work."[73]

The decision not to collaborate with an orchestra or choir brought with it a need for someone to collect and archive music – someone who could pull the rabbit out of the hat at the right point in time. From 1979 onward, Matthias Burkert took on this monumental task. In 1995, he was joined by Andreas Eisenschneider, and they remained responsible for the music of the Tanztheater Wuppertal together until the death of the choreographer.

Matthias Burkert was born in 1953 in Duisburg, a city near Wuppertal in the Ruhr region. He grew up in a musical household. His father was a pastor and played the violin; his mother played piano, Baroque music. Their son learned to play piano from a very early age. He received his first lessons at the age of six, after the family moved to Wuppertal. However, by that time, he had already discovered the piano to be an "adventure playground,"[74] as he calls it. He disliked having to play the usual recitals on special occasions, instead enjoying lifting the lid of the piano and discovering the strings inside, revealing a world of sound beyond the mere major and minor keys. His piano teacher in Wuppertal encouraged his interest. Instead of teaching him in what was the usual way at the time – octaves, playing with two hands and a limited number of keys – he motivated him to improvise, e.g., to develop a melody that reflected the license plate of the new family car. Going beyond analytically listening to intervals and individual notes, Matthias Burkert learned to recognize tone quality and to connect sound to the materiality of his instrument, the piano, to its wood and metal. Having dropped out of the Kunstakademie Düsseldorf after two years, he went on to study piano and graduated from the Hochschule für Musik Köln with a thesis on the antiquatedness of the musical and piano pedagogy of the time.

In Wuppertal, Matthias Burkert, with his passion for piano improvisation, fit right in. Here, he encountered the world of jazz. "Sounds like Whoopataal"[75] – Wuppertal is a city of jazz. Its jazz affinities go back to the legendary Thalia Theater, where Louis Armstrong, Josephine Baker and Stan Kenton all gave spectacular guest performances. In 1926, the Elberfeld radio station began broadcasting its first jazz program into German living rooms and, in the 1960s, Wuppertal became one of the most important European centers for musical improvisation. The names of jazz musicians playing in Wuppertal at the time reads like a 'who's who' of jazz. Wuppertal residents like the "German Benny Goodman" Ernst Höllerhagen, singer and pianist Wolfgang Sauer, saxophonist Peter Brötzmann, bassist Peter Kowald and guitarist and violinist Hans Reichel became outstanding protagonists of jazz, playing to worldwide acclaim. It was in this climate that Matthias Burkert developed his distinct musical style. His own experiences played into his work as the musical director of the Wuppertaler Kinder- und Jugendtheater, (the children's and youth theater), a position that he assumed in 1976 and held until 2011, in spite of his intense work commitments with the Tanztheater Wuppertal. He also taught piano didactics at the Universität zu Köln and had a few private piano students.

Matthias Burkert was very busy when Pina Bausch asked him in 1979 whether he would like to take over from the retiring repetiteur and start working as a pianist for the Tanztheater Wuppertal. The company suffered high turnover among its artistic members that year. Matthias Burkert wanted to present himself in a good light and told the choreographer about all the things that he was doing during their first conversation. Her initial reaction was: "Well, then you don't have any time for me."[76] Nonetheless, he came for a trial, attended by the seriously ill Rolf Borzik, and they hired him. It was a "leap of faith,"[77] as Matthias Burkert recalls, and he wanted to prove himself worthy. At first, he replaced the repetiteur and provided the musical accompaniment to the company's daily training, but he did it differently – without piles of sheet music on the piano. He improvised to the dancers' exercise routines, following certain repetitive phrases. He saw his piano playing as a dialogue with the forms of movement, the buildup of tension, pauses for breath, the figurations of movement. It was a musical translation, situative and momentary, a speechless dialogue capturing the atmosphere of the moment, and that moment was always different. His medium of communication was the gaze: while playing, he watched the dancers, observing the head of that day's training and forging a connection. In this way, he developed an extensive repertoire for piano improvisation over the years and decades. His guiding principle was the moment, the unforeseeable: "I always have to surprise myself.

That's what I enjoy doing. Listening to myself. I know all the exercises that the dancers do, I know what comes next, but I don't really know what I myself will do until I begin playing."[78]

After training, there were other tasks waiting for him: Pina Bausch and the dancers brought heavy suitcases filled with shellac and vinyl records back from their tour to South America (→ PIECES). These records were the inspiration for the piece *Bandoneon* (PREMIERE 1980). Matthias Burkert was entrusted with sorting them all, recording them on tape, editing the tapes and preparing the music for rehearsals – a daunting task under the technical conditions of the time. He had already watched rehearsals for *Legend of Chastity* and *1980* from the back of the auditorium, where he had witnessed the daily developments during an important period of artistic upheaval. Now, he actively participated in them. Matthias Burkert had a mountain of tapes with him, which he carted to rehearsals in suitcases. More and more frequently, Pina Bausch asked him to play a certain tape, but most importantly, he began to collect material. He wanted to have enough at his fingertips to play when the right moment came. Over the years, he collected everything that he deemed musically strong enough, rummaging through record stores, secondhand shops and archives. He selected the music without giving any particular thought to actual dances, not thinking concretely of specific movements.

From 1986 onward, the coproductions made collecting a more extensive task. Matthias Burkert traveled for research to the coproducing cities, first alone and then, from 1996 onward, with Andreas Eisenschneider, together with whom he established contact with local musicians, archives, music schools and radio stations. Matthias Burkert was searching for "the soul of the country"[79] and he found it in ethnic music, especially in choral music, in particular in the mourning songs of the elderly. However, in some countries, the music was too strong, too explicit in form and context, like Spanish flamenco, or would have to be played live, as in the case of Indian music. He knew that the choreographer would not want to touch it out of respect – for the finished form. Moreover, she wanted the music to enter into dialogue with the piece, with the dance. It was not allowed to dominate or be too loud. It was important to her that the dancers be heard: their breathing, their battles. She wanted the music to have its own character in interaction with the stage and the dancing. It had to, as Matthias Burkert says, "open up another window of empathy and understanding"[80] and not simply depict, accentuate or amplify the dancing, just as much as, vice versa, the dancing should not illustrate the music. Over the years, the search for music changed in the coproducing countries: it became easier and at the same time more difficult. The Tanztheater Wuppertal was now world famous; people everywhere were eager to lend their support, to help;

they wanted to be a part of it – and offers of music virtually fell at the two musical collaborators' feet. However, this also made the local search more difficult, as they could no longer randomly roam about as much, and finding something unexpectedly or by chance became increasingly complicated. Sometimes, they no longer even knew where and what they still had to collect.

Aside from listening, one central practice in Matthias Burkert's work was observation. He watched the dancers while they trained to the sound of his improvisations, but he also took careful glances behind the mirrors that hid the dancers while they developed their solos in the Lichtburg rehearsal space (→ WORK PROCESS). He attempted to guess in which direction the dances would develop into in order to collect the right music in advance and have it ready when the choreographer needed it. She decided what music was chosen for individual dances – not the dancers or her musical collaborators. In this respect, the two men did not offer the dancers music for the development of their dances, nor did the dancers in turn ask them for it. The rehearsals also provided Matthias Burkert with an opportunity to observe, where he learned to wait and be patient. He sat at a distance from the choreographer, looking over at her and only going to her table when she beckoned. Occasionally, she would come over and listen to a piece of music. Sometimes he would make careful suggestions, for he was afraid that they would meet with disapproval, that they would be insufficient or would not be the right fit. Now and then, the choreographer would try out countless pieces of music for a single dance, for a scene or a tableau of scenes, which was an exhausting and lengthy process. Scenes were often tested in all possible combinations – and this also called for changes in the music and the musical transitions between scenes. However, there was always a point when everything fell into place and felt right to the choreographer: "I can't tell you how I know when it's right here either," says Pina Bausch. "But among the many, many pieces of music that I listen to for every production, there is always one for every scene that really fits."[81] It took patience from everyone involved to find the one piece of music among hundreds of possibilities. Matthias Burkert and Andreas Eisenscheider would make suggestions and observe Pina Bausch's reactions; they were pleased when she reacted positively and would immediately stop the music when that was not the case. There was not a lot of talking, and her reactions were minimal and highly encoded. In Matthias Burkert's words: "Her eyebrows would go up or down slightly like a thumb signaling yes or no... if she sat back impatiently, changing her usual posture of leaning forwards full of curiosity, we would know that this was not what she had hoped for... lighting a cigarette, blowing the smoke upwards in silent but obvious frustration, was the worst judgement... no, there was nothing more to fear, there were never any harsh words... but still, it made you ashamed to have even suggested such a thing... simply out of respect for a newly discovered connection, something so fragile that nobody wanted to destroy it yet... just glad that there was now a hint of structure, and aware that it was not yet strong enough to support too many mistakes. A cobweb is difficult to repair."[82]

Andreas Eisenschneider reacted more calmly to rejection. He joined the company later, when there was already a sizable musical portfolio but, with his arrival, that portfolio once again expanded enormously. Matthias Burkert described to me in an interview how, in his younger years, he experienced Pina Bausch's dismissive gestures as the world coming to an end, but over the years – and thanks to his overflowing collection of music – he now had countless alternatives at his beck and call. Neither man ever disagreed with the choreographer's decisions, even when they would have enjoyed using the music that she rejected for a scene or dance. In the 30 years that Matthias Burkert and the 15 years that Andreas Eisenschneider spent collaborating with Pina Bausch, they experienced her as someone who called everything – absolutely everything – into question, who measured what she saw by her own reactions as the first spectator, so to speak, and as somebody who had a clear sensibility for form. Matthias Burkert remembers: "When she started getting bored of a sequence that she had already watched ten times, she cut it out."[83] When Pina Bausch spoke with individual dancers about their solos using videos, Matthias Burkert sat in the background, observed and listened. He was fascinated by her unperturbed, confident work on the compositional structure of the solos. "It was not about whether someone felt comfortable or whether a movement looked good. The work was solely determined by a search for form."[84] This search for form was an entirely practical affair, not something done merely conceptually or on paper. Although Pina Bausch did bring notes to rehearsals with her thoughts about what she wanted a sequence to look like, everything had to be tried out again, shown, seen, changed and listened to multiple times – everything was called into question again and again.

Andreas Eisenschneider joined the Tanztheater Wuppertal in 1995. Matthias Burkert remembers, that "everything relaxed a bit"[85] after his arrival. Andreas Eisenschneider, born in Lüneburg and raised in Celle, applied to the Tanztheater Wuppertal as a certified theater sound technician for the position of *Tonmeister* (head sound technician). He was 33 years old at the time and already had a remarkable career to look back on – from the Schosstheater Celle, via the Ruhrfestspiele and the Theater Heilbronn, to the Aalto-Theater and the Grillo-Theater, both located in Essen. He had worked with some of the major players in German *Regietheater* (director's theater), such as Hansgünter Heyme and Jürgen Bosse – the latter making his debut as a director in Rainer Werner Fassbinder's *Katzelmacher* at the Schauspielhaus Wuppertal under Arno Wüstenhöfer in 1970. These collaborations already show how Andreas Eisenschneider was freeing himself from the classical role of the sound technician. His motivator and mentor on this journey was composer and pianist Alfons Nowacki, who was still working with Hansgünter Heyme as the musical director for drama at the Grillo-Theater Essen back then. Andreas Eisenschneider accompanied Alfons Nowacki, one of the most requested repetiteurs in Germany at the time, to his many guest performances. Andreas Eisenschneider also actively contributed, as Alfons Nowacki trusted him and gave him various tasks to do. "That was an opportunity for me to earn a great reputation – aside from the fact that I was able to give him everything he needed and wanted from me."[86] Andreas Eisenschneider was confident; he knew what he was capable of. He had technical expertise, a good feeling for scenes, a sensory approach to technical musical equipment – all of which he had learned since 1979 – and it was with this self-confidence that he applied for a position with the Tanztheater Wuppertal, convinced that he would be hired. "Based on my experience and my credentials, they couldn't really pass me up. I thought to myself: they'd be stupid not to take me."[87]

    He was interested in dance because he hoped to be able to apply more of his skills and knowledge there than in text-heavy plays. It was more or less a coincidence that he had chosen Pina Bausch's company. He was also interested in other choreographers. At first, he met the classical job description of a sound technician: providing sound, but also video support for rehearsals and performances, maintaining equipment, assembling it for tours, etc. But he soon attracted the attention of the choreographer after filling in for Matthias Burkert during a rehearsal. She was curious, for the Tanztheater had not had the best experiences with sound technicians in its early years. It appears that he did well, as he was quickly given additional responsibilities alongside his tasks as a sound technician and became Matthias Burkert's partner. Andreas Eisenschneider had a different taste in music, which meant that the musical repertoire expanded immensely. Both were constantly collecting music. All this was taking place in the 1990s, during a time when a new generation of dancers was beginning at the Tanztheater Wuppertal (→ PIECES) and analog technology was becoming digital. The Tanztheater Wuppertal therefore had to find new ways of organizing the constantly growing collection of thousands of pieces of music. The suitcases full of cassettes – their cases labeled with keywords such as "Armenia," "Slow," "Fast Jazz," "Beethoven," "Arabic," "Judgement Day," "Schubert song," "Harpsichord," "Female voice," "Renaissance," "Jewish dances," "Trombone," "Small melody (piano)," "Sicily," "Death and The Maiden," "Leningrader," "Organ/timpani" and "Timpani without organ"[88] – became collections on CD and then digital files on a computer. This made it easier to archive the music and play it back, while simultaneously making it more difficult to communicate with the choreographer during rehearsals, as she was no longer able to simply rummage around in the suitcases or look at covers. Andreas Eisenschneider remembers: "Pina sometimes complained that she couldn't look into the computer. But ultimately, she found a way to deal with it, because she trusted us."[89] Matthias Burkert and Andreas Eisenschneider produced CDs that they gave the choreographer to listen to during rehearsal breaks, because "[...] she never went home anyway when developing a new production. She slept and ate in the auditorium."[90]

During the years they spent working with Pina Bausch, Andreas Eisenschneider and Matthias Burkert sat in the same row as the choreographer during onstage rehearsals, but always at a safe distance of at least ten seats – a distance that they only rarely traversed of their own accord, except for quick consultations. They were both always well prepared and quickly agreed about when to suggest music for scenes. In spite of this kind of collaboration at a distance, there was a sense of closeness, especially during the late afternoon hours. Matthias Burkert remembers: "The best times were actually in the afternoon, when the building was empty. We sat in the work row. She wrote on slips of paper and sorted the scenes, fastening them together with paper clips. I went through our archive for the nth time. We did this all afternoon. Everything in preparation for the evening rehearsals."[91] During performances, Matthias Burkert sat in the auditorium beside Pina Bausch and managed the communication between the stage manager and the sound desk run by Andreas Eisenschneider. Once again, it was the distance that produced intimacy. "You were never allowed to make the mistake of overstepping a certain boundary. For Pina, it was an important part of building trust, letting it grow, to not be overly familiar."[92] By this time, Andreas Eisenschneider had become an important part of the performativity of each show: the music collages were not prerecorded. He controlled the tracks individually, sometimes keeping tabs of cues for up to 40 different pieces of music in a single performance. In every performance, the scenes and timing changed onstage, and Andreas Eisenschneider had to react in the moment. Pina Bausch's collage-like pieces did not allow for any relationship of dominance between music and dance: the music did not dominate the scenes or vice versa. It was a dialogue, and Matthias Burkert and Andreas Eisenschneider worked to keep it in balance during the show.

Matthias Burkert considered the Tanztheater to be his family and, even years after the choreographer's death, Andreas Eisenschneider still says: "My mission is to be there for Pina."[93] That was what he had promised her, and it is a promise that he intends to keep, for she made things possible: she enabled him to travel, but above all, to develop his musical knowledge and skills, and to experiment – and that is what he wants to give back to her.

Pina Bausch imagined her pieces in colors: the color of a movement, the color of the costumes, the color of the music. There was only little interaction and next to no prior agreement between the individual fields of music, costume and stage design. There were no conceptual meetings, no bilateral or multilateral discussions. Pieces came together thanks to Pina Bausch's sense of what was right for each individual element, and the choreographer saw and felt this form: "Ultimately, everything has to come together, has to merge in such a way that it becomes a indissoluble unit."[94] But crucial responsibility for developing the individual elements and breathing life into them, for turning them into a tangible unit onstage, rests with the dancers.

The dancers: Translating experience

When Pina Bausch began in Wuppertal in 1973/74, the ensemble there went through a radical change. A majority of the dancers followed their former ballet director Ivan Sertic and left. For the young choreographer, this was both a burden and an opportunity: a burden, because this turmoil clearly demonstrated to the public that the previous dancers were unwilling to adapt to what was to come. This frightened the spectators who had been quite satisfied with what had come before. However, it was also a chance for a new beginning, for now Pina Bausch could choose her own dancers. Right from the outset, she took little interest in outward appearances, in factors such as measurements or weight, and she took it for granted that they would be "good dancers": "For me, hiring someone new is something very difficult. I don't exactly know how I do it. Except that I want them to be good dancers."[95] Instead of ideal proportions and brilliant technique, she wanted "people that dance."[96] They should not be nameless dancers, but personalities, not objects under the rule of a choreographer, but subjects whose character would become visible onstage. She thus focused not only on individual but also on cultural differences, on the dancers' internationality. She wanted the company to be a microcosm, where distinct qualities of movement revealed people's cultural differences. Later, she summarized the early years of the company as follows: "One of the few who stayed in Wuppertal was Jan Minařík: he became a very important performer and collaborator for the Tanztheater. I met Dominique Mercy and Malou Airaudo in America. I met Jo Ann Endicott in a studio in London. She was quite fat, but she could move beautifully [...]. I knew some of them, like Marlies Alt, Monika Sagon and others, from my time at Folkwang. They all had a strong influence on the Tanztheater. It was a very mixed group with different qualities; something about each one of them touched me. I was curious about something I didn't know yet."[97]

HOW PINA BAUSCH SAW HER DANCERS

This first group of dancers from the 1970s would largely determine the style of the Tanztheater Wuppertal for years to come while laying the groundwork for what the public would soon call the "Bausch-dancer," i.e., the typical Tanztheater Wuppertal dancer. The dancers formed an unusual ensemble for a municipal theater of the 1970s. It was one of many experiments also being attempted elsewhere at the time, as in Darmstadt (→ PIECES): a group without soloists and without any lead roles to dominate the group. However, what made this group different to other dance company experiments was that the dancers were not the neutral performers of various roles. Instead, the public soon perceived them as subjects; dance critics quickly began to identify individuals by name in published reviews. In public talks and speeches, Pina Bausch characterized her dancers as people "who are eager to give a lot,"[98] as people who love people, who wish to express themselves, who are curious, who have desires but also inhibitions, who hesitate, who do not wish to readily reveal themselves, but nevertheless have the courage to test their limits.[99] The pieces did not allow the performers to simply present something with which they felt comfortable or to dance the pretty movements that they had learned. It was truly about them being themselves, about showing what was real and allowing their own uniqueness to emerge. Pina Bausch wanted the spectator to become familiar with each individual during the performance, to feel close to them, to sense that it was not just a show, but real. As the choreographer saw it: "[...] we play ourselves, we are the piece."[100] This did not mean personal intimacy or gaining insights into a person's private life. What Pina Bausch was really interested in was the phenomenology of the individual subject, in "recognizing something, a bit of their nature, their manner, their quality,"[101] and then generalizing these individual traits as anthropological phenomena. But her statement also reveals something else: it was not just about singularities, but about a 'we,' about what a 'mixed bag' the group truly was and what they could create together.

In order for the dancers to open themselves up, Pina Bausch provided trust, patience and a safe space. In Wuppertal, the company's home was the Lichtburg, a rehearsal space (→ PIECES) where the dancers initially had their own "corners" where they "lived" and stored their personal things. This changed with new productions using smaller ensembles and the introduction of new roles: spots were switched around and exchanged, personal "corners" gradually disappeared and, with them, a certain atmosphere of familiarity. The company kept to itself during rehearsals; only rarely were outsiders invited to attend. Rehearsals were intimate and confidential so that everybody would feel comfortable enough to be able to show themselves. "The dancers should be allowed to engage in any kind of nonsense. And they also have to feel loved. At the same time, I have to be able to try out all my stupid ideas,"[102] said Pina Bausch. And they did not just do this for the choreographer, but also under the watchful eyes of their colleagues. For some, this was motivating, for others it was intimidating and inhibiting, and in some it incited a sense of competition. This rehearsal situation encouraged a gamut of human emotions, all condensed into a singular social fabric: courage, risk, fear, competition, boredom, fun, wit and humor. It was a situation in which the dancers not only had to trust each other and their choreographer but also had to believe in the work process as a whole, for new pieces were based on nothing more than what the dancers brought to rehearsals. It was always a new adventure, a journey into the unknown, and from a certain point in history onward, the dancers also undoubtedly felt privileged to develop pieces with this international icon of dance theater and not be reduced to merely dancing 'repertoire.'

Stephan Brinkmann, who joined the company in 1995, saw this work process as a form of recognition and appreciation, and as a sign of respect for the dancers. "We were not told what to do, but were asked."[103] However, others tired of this process over the years; they had no more ideas and just hung around during rehearsals. They presented no answers to the 'questions' or at least nothing useful, and the choreographer waited – sometimes for long periods and sometimes in vain. But she remained patient – some thought unusually patient: "Pina was very, very considerate. She made a lot of allowances for the personal affairs of individuals, in a way that didn't usually exist in theater."[104] Consideration for others is a very humane approach, but in this context it was more than that: in a production process geared toward individual creativity, it was a necessity for the social fabric and mood of the group. The choreographer knew that, ultimately, all dancers had to play their own part in the piece in order to be content. In developing the pieces, she therefore also had to compensate and balance group dynamics. She was thus not only dependent on dancers contributing to the development of the piece but also had to have alternatives ready when they did not.

The dancers carefully approached possible topics using the open-ended method of 'asking questions.' And because everything was tried out until it "felt right" to Pina Bausch, rehearsals could be exciting, funny and amusing, but sometimes lengthy and occasionally even grueling when multiple variations of scenes were tried out again and again. Over the years, the dancers learned to prepare themselves for her method of 'answering questions,' which they had now grown familiar with. Barbara Kaufmann, who joined the company in 1987, admits: "I often collected certain things with the idea that I might be able to use them to answer a certain question or prompt. After all, she did also repeat some of the questions."[105] Mechthild Großmann, who first met Pina Bausch in 1975 and was a member of the company around the time that the method of 'asking questions' was introduced, would formulate what she had prepared more boldly, almost like a child trying to outsmart its teacher: "Often, I had already prepared something in advance – and then simply took whatever prompt she gave me to present it. Like when she said, 'full moon' or 'longing' or 'apple tree' – those prompts came up every time."[106]

Sometimes, Pina Bausch hired dancers who only opened up after years of being members of the company. Again, the choreographer had to be patient, and her colleagues had to have the right understanding. Pina Bausch explains: "Well, sometimes the group didn't understand why I hired someone. Couldn't understand what I saw in that person. And then... two years later, they saw it."[107] It comes as no surprise that these processes did not always go smoothly. The dancers did not always agree with what Pina Bausch made out of their material: "Sometimes I succeeded in creating scenes where I was happy that there were images like this. But some dancers were shocked. The shouted and moaned at me. Saying what I was doing was impossible."[108] As choreographer, she considered it her task to "to help each individual to find what I'm seeking for themselves."[109] In the work processes (→ WORK PROCESS), the aim of the search was therefore not for the dancers to find themselves, but rather for them to find something within themselves that the choreographer then recognized as that which she had been looking for. For the choreographer, the dancers' search for and creation of material took place within a framework that she provided with her questions and her own underlying search. "What's important is that I'm curious, that I can learn from them. Sometimes just because of their mere presence when I notice myself feeling the same way they do. There are many things that you only become conscious of through collaboration."[110]

Aside from the development of new pieces, dancers also adopt the roles of past dancers. This is just as exciting because, unlike in other companies, where the roles are rehearsed with a ballet master, at the Tanztheater Wuppertal, they are passed on directly from dancer to dancer, in some cases even by those who originally developed the role. Video recordings or descriptions left by dancers are also used to this end, but the main method of passing material on is face-to-face interaction (→ WORK PROCESS). It is important to the overall coherence of the piece that the quality, i.e., the color that individual dancers contribute to the piece, remains visible even after the material has been passed on. Pina Bausch had to find dancers who were capable of this. Stephan Brinkmann describes it as follows: "Pina Bausch chose very much based on type, depending on who had left."[111] Even so, people are rarely perfect copies, and the act of passing on material thus becomes an act of translation. Stephan Brinkmann and dancer Kenji Takagi, who took on his contract and some of his roles in 2001, shared, for example, a history of having studied at the Folkwang Universität. But they were very different dancers, both in terms of their physiognomy and how they moved – and this transformed the color and the roles. Kenji Takagi emphasized this difference to me: "I liked Stephan's dances a lot, and I also felt that they gave me the chance to find certain things in myself, to express them. The dances are different to the ones that I have created, more lyrical, poetic and slow. There are movements that only Stephan can perform. Why? That is the secret. But I feel like I've done them justice, even if I did them differently in the end and gave the dance a different color and character."[112]

For many years, all of the dancers were involved in every production, even in the first coproductions. There were only few exceptions, such as *Café Müller*. This did not change until the repertoire grew so large that touring and restagings required the introduction of new roles and responsibilities, and new pieces simply became too expensive to perform with the entire ensemble. The introduction of these new roles and responsibilities, which were actually initiated as a functional differentiation nevertheless had an effect on the cohesiveness of the company – and not only in terms of its work schedule but also in the minds of the participants. Up to this point, everyone had been seeing each other constantly. Together they had developed, rehearsed and performed pieces, traveled and even taken along their children – it was a kind of traveling circus, binding the group together, especially in the face of their immense workload of over 100 shows per year. The company had high standards when traveling, i.e., did so in comfort, thanks also to the generous support of the Goethe-Institut, and for Pina Bausch, this travel was the substance that held the international group together. The group was stationed in Wuppertal, a city that the choreographer had known since childhood. She associated it with security, because she had occasionally been sent to stay there with relatives during the final years of the war and because it was only ten minutes by car from Wuppertal to her hometown of Solingen. For her, Wuppertal was familiar terrain. It was the city of everyday life, not what she called a "Sunday town"[113] – and traveling provided balance. In interviews, in response to the question of why she never left the city in spite of receiving other offers, she often emphasized: "Well, what's good about Wuppertal is that it really leaves its mark on your consciousness [...]. You just have to bring the sun and everything else into the room and your imagination"[114]; and "I actually really like that Wuppertal is so commonplace, so plain; and because we travel so much, I have that contrast."[115] Living in both Wuppertal and the world was just another facet of Pina Bausch's productive universe of polar opposites. However, for most of the international dancers, Wuppertal was a foreign place and needed getting used to. They were often unable to properly communicate, at least not at first, and even within the Tanztheater Wuppertal, it was difficult for those who did not speak English.

Moreover, Pina Bausch only signed contracts for one year – even for herself at first, for she was skeptical and did not want to feel bound to Wuppertal. She was also afraid that the dancers would leave her without anyone else with whom to continue working. Even after ten years in Wuppertal, she said: "I have lived here in Wuppertal so far as if I were moving out tomorrow."[116] She continued this habit with her dancers, who only ever received annual contracts. As Mechthild Großmann remembers, they worked around the clock for what was at the time DM 2,600 a month. The contracts were automatically renewed every year unless the dancers themselves announced in October that they wished to leave. Then replacements had to be found.

In the company's 35 years of existence under Pina Bausch, there were but few dismissals, no more than a handful in total (→ WORK PROCESS). But when someone did ultimately leave the company, it was not uncommon for emotional ties to be completely severed. It was like being separated from a mother who does not want her children to leave. Raimund Hoghe, who joined the company in 1980 as a dramaturge during an important phase, experienced this after working with the company for ten years: "Pina probably couldn't accept that I was trying to find my own way without her. If you left her Tanztheater, you were dead to her. It was like withdrawing love from her. She couldn't deal with it. She always wanted to be loved by everyone in her vicinity. To say it nicely: those who distanced themselves got to know a very cold and hostile side of the usually kind Pina. Or to say it with a title of a Fassbinder film: Love is Colder than Death."[117] When Raimund Hoghe began his own international career as a choreographer and dancer, Pina Bausch did not come see his pieces, nor did she go see those of other former dancers. This might also have been due to a lack of time. Only few dancers returned and were reinstated as full members of the company after having left. They were mainly dancers of the first generation, such as Jo Ann Endicott, Dominique Mercy, Lutz Förster and Héléna Pikon. Jo Ann Endicott processed her experiences in a book,[118] and in an homage to the choreographer, she writes, "[...] in spite multiple attempts to leave the Tanztheater, [...] I never properly managed to emotionally detach myself."[119] Lutz Förster dealt with his return in the solo *Lutz Förster: Portrait of a Dancer* (PREMIERE 2009), in which he described how he approached Pina Bausch to ask whether he could return to the company after a long period spent living in the US. He presented it in the form of a short conversation between "Pinchen" and "Lützchen," as the two born-and-bred Solingers called each other thanks to Pina Bausch's love of the diminutive, who reach an agreement without much talking. Interestingly, it was these 'returnees' in particular who assumed important, leading roles, not only in the pieces but also – and especially after Pina Bausch's death – in other positions: Jo Ann Endicott and Héléna Pikon as assistants and rehearsal directors, Dominique Mercy as a rehearsal director and an important, long-term dancer in the company (→ SOLO DANCE), Lutz Förster as the long-serving director of the Folkwang dance department, and both Dominique Mercy and Lutz Förster as the subsequent artistic directors of the company.

During Pina Bausch's time in Wuppertal, a total of 210 dancers participated in the development of her work and appeared as members of the original cast in individual pieces. The company was, as Pina Bausch herself ambiguously formulated it: "a world of our own."[120] Around 30 dancers were usually employed per year, joined by numerous guest dancers: for example, members of the Folkwang Tanzstudio, who danced *The Rite of Spring* for years, and former members of the company who continued to dance for the company as guests in certain pieces.

Even later on in the company's history, castings were often informal affairs, although there would sometimes be large auditions as well. Pina Bausch approached many candidates personally, after having met them somewhere, having seen them onstage or having gotten to know them through the Folkwang Universität or the Folkwang Tanzstudio. Some dancers responded to open calls, but even they were communicated through personal and informal channels in the early years and not through extensive application processes. Jean Laurent Sasportes recalls how he went looking for Pina Bausch in the canteen of the opera house when he arrived from Casablanca for his job interview. He did not know who she was, asking Marion Cito, who was also sitting at the same table: "Are you Pina Bausch?"[121]

Until after her death, only few select ensemble members spoke publicly about the Tanztheater Wuppertal in interviews, which were subject to strict rules, required the choreographer's prior consent and were actually something that she frowned upon. The statements of those who did give interviews during those years, together with the things that Pina Bausch herself said, shaped the public image of the "Bausch dancer," of the company and of the collaborative relationship between dancers and choreographer. This public image, like other narratives about the Tanztheater Wuppertal, gradually solidified and became entrenched over decades and was often associated with particular individual dancers of the first generation. They were also the ones to whom audiences and dance critics referred when making comparisons with younger dancers or newer pieces (→ RECEPTION). However, it was not just the public image, but also the framework that affected the dancers within the company, establishing practices and routines that provided guidance to future dancers – which was not always easy, for the makeup of dancers on the payroll was always very diverse, no matter the artistic phase. Not only were they individuals from various cultures with different dance backgrounds – they were above all members of different generations as well, who had grown up in different political contexts and dance scenes. Pina Bausch's focus was on individuals and she did not consider a dancer's age to be relevant to her work. She thus made a significant contribution to questioning the idea of the ideal dancer's body and making the physical aging of dancers visible on the stage at all, sparking debates about stage presence. But while many dancers, especially the experienced ones, emphasized in conversations with me that age was insignificant in their collaborations with Pina Bausch, the specific experiences and attitudes of different generations of dancers did play an important role in the social fabric of the company and continues to do so to this day.

  In spite of all the overlaps, we can identify a total of three generations of dancers during Pina Bausch's lifetime: 1) the dancers of the first phase, 2) the generation of dancers who joined the company from the late 1980s onward and 3) the group of dancers who arrived in the early 2000s. Since the choreographer's death, there has been a fourth generation of dancers who have never directly worked with Pina Bausch or met her in person. These different dancer generations have drawn on different experiences and various types of dance knowledge – and when they joined the company, they did so under different conditions. Over the years, the number of dance schools and institutions of higher learning has grown and grown, gradually adding contemporary dance to their curricula as well. Local dance scenes have become more differentiated, larger international networks between the various scenes have developed, and there has been increased representation of dance in the media, especially in visual and digital media.

When the first generation began in Wuppertal, there were – not just in Germany – virtually no role models for a different, modern type of company that could replace the ballet companies at the state-subsidized German theater houses, which were and largely still are organized into the three genres of opera, drama and dance. There were also almost no venues for the 'independent scene,' which was just gradually beginning to develop. Opportunities to see and experience international (post-)modern dance were extremely rare. Even the Tanztheater Wuppertal only began to increase its number of guest performances in 1977; until then, it had only been possible to see a few of Pina Bausch's pieces outside of Wuppertal, especially as they had not been available as video or television recordings. At the time, the Tanztheater Wuppertal was still an insider's tip in the international dance scene. "Pina an unknown planet,"[122] is how French dancer Anne Martin, who joined the company in 1977, remembers it.

This situation changed in the late 1970s. With the establishment of various independent venues and institutions across Germany – such as the Tanzfabrik Berlin and the Tanzwerkstatt in Düsseldorf, which provided new spaces to train and perform – and with the establishment of independent groups, the conversion of former industrial sites into cultural institutions and the proliferation of dance festivals, greater diversity emerged within the dance and performing arts scenes in general. The following generation of dancers had even more opportunities to discover contemporary dance aesthetics onstage, in courses and in educational programs. In this phase, Pina Bausch and the Tanztheater Wuppertal had also begun to tour extensively across various continents. Dancers of the first generation had either been classically trained or strictly speaking had no real dance education. By choosing to go to Wuppertal and set foot in unknown territory, they had changed their identities as dancers. However, now the Tanztheater Wuppertal was no longer just an insider's tip, but was in the midst of becoming Germany's number one cultural export item. The dancers joining the company from the late 1980s onward knew some of the pieces, had already taken classes with "Bausch dancers" and were also motivated by and aware of the company's international reputation. They knew that being part of the company also meant performing on large stages in front of sold-out audiences with what was now one of the most sought-after dance ensembles worldwide.

This applies even more to the third generation of dancers, who joined in the late 1990s. In the wake of the globalization of

11 Protagonists at the
Next Wave Festival
New York, 1997

12 Pina Bausch
at her desk, 1987

the art market, the deindustrialization and festivalization of cities – something that concert dance also benefited from (for example, the founding of North Rhine-Westphalia's own internationally acclaimed dance festival in the 1990s) – and the institutionalization of former industrial buildings, which were occupied and used by the 'independent' dance community, this generation had seen the international world of dance turn into a global village, accompanied by an increase in the opportunities to see international dance. Moreover, institutions for dance education were still multiplying and further diversifying their programs, allowing these dancers to draw on a wider range of more differentiated training programs. Finally, the development of technical media such as CD, DVDS, software and social media led to contemporary dance using media in increasingly professional ways, which also made a significant contribution to its global distribution.

In this phase, the Tanztheater Wuppertal became a German cultural export hit, partially thanks to the coproductions, which were often commissioned pieces for special occasions, festivals and events – such as *Masurca Fogo* for Expo '98, *The Window Washer* for the Hong Kong Arts Festival and *Nefés* for the international Istanbul Theater Festival. Twelve international coproductions were shown as part of the cultural program at the 2012 Olympic Games in London, a concept that Pina Bausch had originally developed herself. In the 1960s, Pina Bausch had been known as an optimistic, passionate and exceptional dancer. In the 1970s, she came to be seen as a revolutionary, determined choreographer, and in the 1980s, she developed into the new star of the international dance scene, only to become a global icon in the 1990s and a legend in her own lifetime. However, after the paradigm shift in contemporary dance, her art was increasingly considered historical. It now represented a genre, 'German Dance Theater,' that was associated with the prestigious choreographers of the 1970s and 1980s. Among the young choreographers of the 1990s, there were only a few who – even when referencing Pina Bausch's art – would describe their own work as 'dance theater.'

The different generations of dancers have therefore been confronted with different cultural, political, artistic and media contexts and situations. Over the years, the training and habitus of the younger dancers of the Tanztheater Wuppertal have become much more 'dancerly' than those of earlier generations. It has often been assumed that the dance department at the Folkwang Universität serves as a training ground for the company, but only a handful of dancers have actually come from there. The younger generations are "good dancers," but in a different way. However, that does not mean that all of them necessarily learned dance from an early age. In fact, there have been some "good dancers" with rather unusual professional careers in every generation: Barbara Kaufman, for example, was a rhythmic gymnast before discovering dance at the age of 17 and joining the company in 1987/88; Pascal Merighi, who joined the Tanztheater Wuppertal in 1999/2000, originally came from an acrobatics and rock-and-roll background and only began dancing at the age of 18; and Kenji Takagi, who joined the company one season later, first started dancing at the age of 20.

The new dancers work in the same way as before, but the results are different. The new pieces have fewer 'theatrical' parts; there is more dance, particularly solo dance, and a somewhat additive compositional structure. The singular within the multitude, which was once shown simultaneously, has now been replaced by singular succession. The dancers have also encountered different group situations within the company: the first generation lived with the choreographer and her partner as members of a kind of artistic family, in which life and art were closely intertwined. After evening rehearsals or shows, the inner circle would go to the pub for "just one more quick glass of wine and a quick cigarette," as a scene developed for the piece *Walzer* (PREMIERE 1982) was entitled, in which Mechthild Großmann legendarily portrayed Pina Bausch's desire to stay for just a little bit longer. Dancers stayed overnight at the home of Pina Bausch and Rolf Borzik, who occasionally also repaired household appliances for some of them. This intimacy no longer existed in the second generation. Only occasionally were individual dancers allowed to join the 'elders' of the inner circle; you no longer 'simply joined in.' Anne Martin remembers Pina Bausch being very close to her dancers in the beginning: "We were around Pina a lot during that period. She was constantly in some café or restaurant between rehearsals. You could always go sit with her, just be there and talk to her."[123] And former dramaturge Raimund Hoghe remembered in 2015: "I stayed with Pina for ten years, and she was a bit like a sister to me. We both came from a working-class background and both only had a basic school education. That was a different Pina Bausch from the women that newspaper critics venerate like some kind of saint. Pina was no Mother Theresa, nor was she a far-removed, enraptured divinity. She was sensitive and extremely vulnerable. And she spoke about love like no other choreographer or director at the time. I find today's veneration of her quite strange... In my opinion, the silence eventually just became an attitude. She was quite articulate when she wanted to be."[124]

Distance to the choreographer – the star, the icon, the director, the myth – grew with every generation. Absorbed by and drowning in her work, she had to protect and shield herself. She increasingly drew her entourage around her in public – and there were but few who dared to break through this wall. The company continued to cultivate the myth. We see this, for instance, in the many 'moving stories' surrounding her. Almost everyone who ever worked with her has one that they can tell: stories of a deep gaze, a casual sentence, a small compliment, an anecdote. Wim Wenders captured impressions of this in his film *PINA* (2011). Many of the dancers – and the choreographer as well – still occasionally spoke of trust and love in the later phases. But it was the tension between love, intimacy and familiarity on the one hand and distance, respect and authority on the other that subsequently characterized the relationship.

When new dancers joined the Tanztheater Wuppertal, they took on roles and had to find their place in the company's day-to-day operations. The Tanztheater Wuppertal's daily routines were established early on and hardly changed over the years: training at 10:00 a.m., then rehearsals until about 2:00 p.m., then a break, and more rehearsals in the evening, usually until 10:00 p.m., often longer, as Anne Martin remembers.[125] If there was a show the night before, "critique" was dealt out the next day after training. However, this did not primarily comprise the correction of individual solo dances, but rather focused on the *how:* how the individuals walked, did things, said things, how to better produce the intended atmosphere and how to reach agreements, achieve a shared rhythm and solve issues of timing. For the choreographic concept of the pieces was based on rhythm – the rhythmic convergence of individual 'parts' – not on narratives or linear storylines. For this to succeed, it was fundamental that dancers and their scenes and transitions were well coordinated, also in connection with lights and sound, and this listening and reacting to each other had to happen in the moment, in the actual situation itself.

Usually, daily routines provide orientation and a sense of order, but they also encourage unspoken hierarchies and give certain individuals the power to influence internal discourse. This is also the case within the Tanztheater Wuppertal, although, officially, there are still no differences in status, which could be objectively reflected in solos or leading roles. Mechthild Großmann coolly sums it up when she says: "Well, of course, we weren't entirely without tensions within the group. We didn't choose each other. Individual dancers didn't decide who was hired, only Pina. So, we simply had to get along somehow."[126] It is not uncommon in large dance companies for the director to choose company members, but the members of the group assembled here were much more dependent on each other. The dancers knew that it was not just their skills and abilities that allowed them to become members of the famous troupe – it was also their characters. Being a "Bausch dancer" meant being willing to commit to and live for the Tanztheater Wuppertal. The intense work and extensive touring barely allowed for anything else. So, naturally, many couples got together within the company over the years.

"Of course, if you're working all day, maybe if you even came to Wuppertal as a foreigner, then the company is the only place to find a partner. And at some point, it became a kind of couples' party. Pina didn't like that at all. For if you criticize one of them, then the other is immediately offended, too," as Mechthild Großmann sees it. She stayed out of it in every respect. "I think I was one of the few who never fooled around with another member of the company (laughs)."[127]

The extensive traveling supported the self-referentiality and interdependence within the company. But the traveling also changed over the years, especially the research trips. Not only because not all the dancers were involved in every piece anymore, but also because it no longer meant aimlessly roaming about. The company's growing popularity and prominence meant that stays on location became increasingly organized and that the group now had a tight schedule, with buses driving them to each place, appointment and visit. While this provided the group with certain experiences that they would not have had as normal tourists, the research trips from the mid-1990s onward were nevertheless perceived as far more touristy than those of earlier years. The participants themselves also contributed to this development, for they had developed a touristic gaze of their own: video and photo cameras had become constant companions. Here, we once more see how radical innovation turned into guiding routines over the years and how routines became standardized, unquestioned convention.

A chosen family – "We are the piece"

During Pina Bausch's lifetime, the Tanztheater Wuppertal was, in its own understanding, a family. It was a chosen family, one that its members decided to join. Unlike conventional families, people did not involuntarily belong; no one was born into it. It is a figuration of community that has grown fragile – since the death of Pina Bausch, in the absence of previous production routines, since the departure of longtime members, the restructuring of its members and attempts to steer the company aesthetically into a new direction with rotating artistic directors. For longtime members, staff and collaborators, this process has not only been painful, but has also generated a certain degree of social insecurity, which continues even to this day, more than ten years after the choreographer's death.

Pina Bausch and her company shared a distinct attitude toward their work: whether costume design, stage design or music, everyone kept to their own material, attaching great value to providing good, high quality craftsmanship. They focused on that one line of work. Stamina, loyalty, trust, allegiance, courage and the acceptance of hierarchies were the unifying threads of their social

13 *Nefés*
Wuppertal, 2011

14 Research trip for
"...*como el musguito en la piedra, ay si, si, si...*"
Chile, 2009

interactions. This applies in particular to the organizational team, which has grown over the years, but whose long-serving staff members Claudia Irman, Ursula Popp, Sabine Hesseling and Robert Sturm unquestioningly navigate the complex organizational needs of the company behind the scenes.

Pina Bausch's description of her relationship with her dancers is much like that of a mother talking about her children: "I love my dancers, each in a different way."[128] She saw it as a kind of romantic relationship, which was different with every one of them. She explained that she helped them to open up, to develop, and that this not only demanded much of her but also gave her much back. But she also took and expected devotion and unconditional loyalty, especially from her artistic collaborators, for her insecurities remained substantial, even after she had long since become a global icon.

Matthias Burkert remembers: "somehow we were stuck again in this dead end... she quietly called us all together to share her despair... fighting back tears. Indeed, none of us could imagine how this hopelessly confusing collection of fragments, short scenes, images, movement ideas, dances that were only just coming together, a few group dances even, small gestures, unfinished improvised dialogues, texts, musical ideas... how all this might be organized into arcs of tension and form resembling a 'piece' that could be, no, would have to be performed in just a few short days... because of course the date of the premiere was fixed and had long been announced as a yet untitled 'New Piece' in the season brochure."[129]

Her group was a motley crew from various cultures and, over the years, from different age groups too, with distinct backgrounds and dance histories – although it is important to once again note that the difference between the generations was less important to her than cultural differences.[130] "I think it's nice that we have so many different people. Small people, fat people, tall people, elderly people and the many different nationalities bring a lot of different things to the table."[131] In 2007, Pina Bausch characterized the company as "a great big family,"[132] as a family distinguished by trust, mutual respect, emotional attachment, shared feeling – where she was the "venerated elder."[133] She had the final and decisive say in all things. It was a family in which, as in so many families, not much was said, in which plans as to what is done where and how were not made together. Every member kept the experiences that they had during the process to themselves and dealt with them on their own. It was a multicultural family of choice, stretching beyond cultural and political boundaries, while moreover being globally (inter-) connected – a family that also included audiences that had in some cases followed the company for decades, be it in Wuppertal, Tokyo, New York or Paris.

The Tanztheater Wuppertal does not objectively, rationally or pragmatically define itself through shared work or a shared profession, as some large dance ensembles do. Nor does it consider itself to be a group of artists, a community of equals or a collective. The Tanztheater Wuppertal obtained its identity from the figuration of the chosen family, initiated by a choreographer whose own life was characterized by a blurring of boundaries between art and life, between the professional and the private, the personal and the public, and who wanted to live this way with her chosen family as well. Unlike conventional families, chosen families are not related by blood; instead, their kinship is built on shared guiding principles, values and habits. And unlike artistic associations, which primarily consider themselves to be communities formed for the distinct purpose of working together, fully aware that collaboration is only possible by establishing certain forms of communication and attitudes, the identity of the Tanztheater Wuppertal revolves around putting people first. Not only is this humanistic value the necessary basis for good collaboration, but they are also perceived as goals in themselves. The company's identity demonstrates the typical markers of chosen families: it offers support and security; its members are committed to one another in a special way and feel that they can absolutely rely on one another. In spite of their age differences, specific experiences and strengths are encouraged, and individuals are appreciated for their special qualities and quirks. The company manages to successfully validate this identity on a daily basis with the help of routines that have gradually been established over the years, into which new dancers can be integrated. Friction arises when these routines are undermined or simply cease to be common knowledge.

 The emotional bond creates cohesion in groups whose ideological and everyday ties are sustained by emotions and shared attitudes, maintained by blind understanding, a shared ethos and unifying will, whose language depends on trust and intimacy, and which, especially in the context of dance, are based on direct corporeal relationships between members. Such groups are thus uniquely confronted both with the subject of trust – of love, intimacy and loyalty – and its often unexpressed opposites – rivalry, jealousy, envy, defiance and gossip. It is the entire claviature of human affect that leaves its mark on the dynamics of the social figuration – and this is exactly what the works of Pina Bausch, this anthropologist of dance, deal with. Not only are they translations of individual experience, they are also the aesthetic translation of a concrete social configuration, namely that of the company – "We are the piece."

164

1 Tsukiji fish market in Tokyo
   Research trip for *Ten Chi*
   Japan, 2003

With every piece the search begins anew, and every time I'm afraid that it might not succeed this time. There's no plan, no script, no music. There's no stage design. [...] But there's a set date and little time. I think that's enough to scare anyone.[1]

Work P

rocess

Today, it is not unusual for the rehearsals of a full-length contemporary dance piece to take about six to eight weeks, especially in the German 'independent scene' *(freie Szene)*, which relies heavily on project-based funding and rented rehearsal space. Independent artists have to apply for funding from various institutions and funding bodies for each new production. Thus, the amount of time available for rehearsals is, above all, a question of money, as are a range of other factors, such as the number and 'prominence' of team members, the cost of costumes and set designs, the noncommittal, network-like structures of the dance scene and the sometimes parallel collaborations that constantly fluctuate as a result, etc. Most productions therefore only have a small window of max. two months in which to rehearse.

This was very different for the Tanztheater Wuppertal under Pina Bausch. From the outset, rehearsals were structured into two- to three-week phases, which stretched over the course of at least four months, sometimes even an entire year. However, unlike other large companies bound to venues and entirely financed by their institutions, theaters or foundations, the Tanztheater Wuppertal had been forced since the mid-1980s to find additional funding for most of its new productions. Cofinancing for the total of 15 coproductions, from *Viktor* (PREMIERE 1986) right up to the last piece *"...como el musguito en la piedra, ay si, si, si..."* (PREMIERE 2009), allowed the company to continue working on and designing its pieces at the same level that they had established in the period 1973-1986 while simultaneously continuing to perform older pieces as well.

This chapter deals with the company's artistic work processes, i.e., the rehearsals during which the pieces were developed, paying special interest to the question of how these rehearsals related to the "research trips"[2] that the company took to coproducing cities and countries. It also focuses on how the company passed on pieces to younger dancers within the Tanztheater Wuppertal and to other dance companies. The term 'passing on' is presented here as a practice of translation, describing an important artistic dance practice (→ THEORY AND METHODOLOGY). The chapter emphasizes the practices and the sociality of artistic work.

The following analysis is mainly based on the ethnographic material that I collected during performance rehearsals and rehearsals for passing on pieces and individual roles. Other material came from conversations that I had with individual dancers, artistic staff and collaborators about passing on pieces and the analysis of videotaped rehearsals. By taking this approach based on qualitative social research – and thus a sociology of art perspective – I am presenting an analysis of an artistic work process. My method of praxeological

2 Rehearsals for *I'll Do You In* Wuppertal, 1974

production analysis (→ THEORY AND METHODOLOGY) focuses on the relationships between process and product, working methods and piece. This standpoint proposes that the artistic work process is more than a mere preliminary act of developing a piece with the ultimate aim of attaining a finished product. In fact, the aesthetics of the piece are inherent to the work process itself. At the same time, these processes give us an indication of the company's identity as a group and as a community. As I am suggesting here, the questions of *how, when, where* and *what* the company collaborates (on) are therefore central to the production of the aesthetic.

Developing pieces

The extensive literature about Pina Bausch repeatedly describes the way that she asked her dancers 'questions.' The first time she systematically applied this 'working method'[3] was during the making of the "Macbeth Piece" *He Takes Her By The Hand And Leads Her Into The Castle, The Others Follow*[4] (PREMIERE 1978). However, the beginnings of this working method[5] surfaced as early as in 1976 during rehearsals for a piece that would later be entitled *Bluebeard: While Listening to a Taped Recording of Béla Bartók's "Duke Bluebeard's Castle"*[6] (PREMIERE 1977). As dance critic Jochen Schmidt describes it,[7] this method was the result of a crisis. The two-part evening featuring the only ballet for which Bertolt Brecht ever wrote a libretto – *The Seven Deadly Sins*[8] (with music by Kurt Weill and premiered by George Balanchine in 1933 with Lotte Lenya and Tilly Losch in Paris) – and the revue *Fear Not* with songs by Bertolt Brecht and Kurt Weill had not only exacerbated the conflict between Pina Bausch and the Wuppertal orchestra, which did not want to play Kurt Weill's music, but had also driven a wedge between Pina Bausch and some members of the company. All of this also led to a turning point in the choreographer's work. While Pina Bausch's major successes *Iphigenie auf Tauris* (PREMIERE 1974) and *The Rite of Spring* (PREMIERE 1975) still owed a large debt to modern dance and were 'written' solely using her own body, as she described it,[9] the conflict after the "Brecht/Weill Evening" (PREMIERE 1976) birthed a new working method that elicited a new, special relationship between the dancers themselves and between the dancers and their choreographer, while simultaneously encouraging the emergence of the dancers' own identities as artists. Ultimately, it led to a new dance aesthetic, which had a fundamental influence on the development of dance and theater in the late 20th century – that which is now known throughout the world as the dance theater of Pina Bausch, German Dance Theater or as the epitome of dance theater itself.

As a result of the crisis, Pina Bausch began working on the new piece *Bluebeard* with only a couple of dancers – namely Marlies Alt and Jan Minařík. Although the angry dancers who were initially excluded gradually came back, Pina Bausch nevertheless changed the way she worked with them. She asked the dancers questions, at first simply in order to learn more about them rather than to analyze the material for the piece. When Peter Zadek, artistic director of the Schauspielhaus Bochum at the time and well-known for his radical and experimental style of Shakespearean production, invited Pina Bausch to develop a "Macbeth Piece," this working method became a key aspect of the production process while also forming the basis of the development of all future pieces. Rehearsing both with a heterogenous group – consisting of dancers from Wuppertal, actors from Bochum and singer Soňa Červená – and with Shakespearean texts was new to Pina Bausch, who had so far only developed her pieces through bodies, movement and dance. She thus asked questions inspired by the text, by shared situations, experiences and attitudes. The resulting piece, *He Takes Her By The Hand And Leads Her Into The Castle, The Others Follow,* a title taken from Shakespeare's stage directions, was the result of a new working method that got the group and individual dancers considerably more involved in the development of the piece than had been the case before. However, this new working method was not the result of conceptual considerations, but rather something that she developed out of necessity, as Pina Bausch remembers in retrospect:

"Quite simply, because there were actors, dancers, a singer […] in this piece. I couldn't turn up with a movement phrase; I had to start differently. So, I asked them questions that I had been asking myself. The questions are a way to very carefully approach a topic. It's a very open working method, but also very precise. Because I always know exactly what I'm looking for, but I know it in my heart and not in my mind. That's why you can never ask directly. That would be too crude, and the answers would be too banal. Instead, I have to leave what I'm looking for alone with the words, while nevertheless bringing it to light with a lot of patience."[10]

The premiere caused a major theater scandal. The audience was in such a tumult that the performance was on the verge of being shut down, until Jo Ann Endicott, one of the dancers from Wuppertal, pleaded with the audience to be fair after initially insulting its members herself (→ RECEPTION). This was not only an unintentional, novel and provocative act of performatively engaging in dialogue with the audience but also a real-life example of what Austrian poet Peter Handke had intended with his own piece *Offending the Audience,* staged by Claus Peymann (PREMIERE 1966): to encourage the audience to think about theater itself – that which in his opinion primarily consisted of the interactions between performers and the audience during a theater performance.

You will see no spectacle.
Your curiosity will not be satisfied.
You will see no play.
There will be no playing here tonight [...].[11]

These are the first lines of Handke's *Offending the Audience,* and this is probably also what the audience felt like at the premiere of Pina Bausch's piece: they saw neither dance nor Shakespeare's *Macbeth,* merely a surreal succession of images. Although these images were somehow related to Shakespeare's topics of betrayal, insanity and death, they had been translated into Pina Bausch's themes of gender relationships and childhood, quirks and vanities, desires and fears. The new working method had produced a series of single images and individual actions, which were accompanied for the first time by a group dance on the diagonal.

After Bochum, Pina Bausch not only returned to Wuppertal with a new piece, which she would later perform there with a new cast, but also with a reputation for having caused an uproar and a theatrical scandal in the long-established German Shakespeare Society and in the theater landscape in general. Above all, she came back with a new working method – which would become one of the most famous hallmarks of the Tanztheater Wuppertal and has since been frequently copied in choreographic and other artistic work processes, but also in education and outreach contexts, where it has sometimes been misunderstood as an improvisation technique. This is a misunderstanding insofar as improvisation was not characteristic of the rehearsal situations of the Tanztheater Wuppertal. There was no vague improvising; it was about seriously attempting to try things out, as Pina Bausch tirelessly pointed out. Her work had nothing to do with what improvisation usually means: presenting or creating something without preparation, something impromptu, in the moment. On the contrary, Pina Bausch's work was very precise: asking 'questions' that the dancers embraced and whose answers were meant to set something in motion. Only then were they transposed into choreographic form. In an interview with the magazine *Ballett International* in 1983, Pina Bausch placed the development of movement and dance in the context of the 'questions': "The steps have always come from somewhere else. They have never come from the legs. And working on the movements – we're always doing that in between. And then we're always creating little dance phrases that we keep in mind. In earlier days, I might have started with a movement made out of worry or panic and dodged the questions. Now I start with the questions."[12]

The beginning of this new working method of 'asking questions' changed the mediality of developing pieces. From this point on, dancers, assistants and Pina Bausch herself jotted down notes about what happened during rehearsals. However, what really changed with the advent of the 'questions' was the relationship between choreographer and dancers during the rehearsal process. Developing the piece and the rehearsal situation itself became a process of searching and asking questions for everybody involved in the piece, where all dancers were called upon to seek answers. This process not only called into question the traditional role of the dancer, i.e., being asked to simply to study and learn the material that they have been given, but also laid the foundation for long-term, trusting, but also interdependent collaboration between the members of the ensemble – which could also be difficult, tedious and frustrating. During the rehearsals for *Nelken* (PREMIERE 1982), Pina Bausch herself admitted: "Of course, I've posed hundreds of questions. The dancers have answered them, done something. [...]. But the problem is that many of the questions lead to nothing at all, nothing comes out at all. It's not just that I think maybe I'm the only one who isn't capable. Sometimes we're all incapable; it isn't just because of me." [13]

The questions were sometimes intimate and their answers often personal. They produced material that Pina Bausch then used to choreograph. What we know of her 'questions' are sometimes words, sayings, single sentences or thematic triggers. [14] Pina Bausch did not, as many have alleged, [15] simply provide rehearsal stimuli relating to emotional states. In fact, the 'questions' cover a whole range of both existential and profane, everyday topics. They are research questions based on day-to-day observations, touching on physical experiences, attitudes and emotions, everyday and cultural-anthropological, but also geographical and geopolitical topics. The dancers provided their answers in the form of scenes or movements. Pina Bausch then aesthetically and choreographically translated a selection of these 'answers' into the pieces.

About 100 'questions' were usually asked during the rehearsals leading up to a new piece, and Pina Bausch's life's work with the Tanztheater Wuppertal encompasses 44 choreographies as well as two new editions of *Kontakthof:* one with senior citizens aged 65 and older (PREMIERE 2000) and another with teenagers aged 14 and older (PREMIERE 2008). Some of the of the cues listed on the following pages are general 'questions.' Some are what the company called 'movement questions,' which were meant to be answered with a movement phrase, such as movements for gestures like the positioning of the hands or mouth, actions such as lifting, gestures for emotional states like crying or abandoning oneself to something, or movements related to nature. Pina Bausch also frequently asked 'questions' aimed at writing words with movements – a method that she used often, for example in the piece *The Window Washer* (PREMIERE 1997) for the Chinese words *fu* (happiness), *hé* (harmony), *ai* (life) [16] and *mei* (beauty).

THE RIGHT AND THE LEFT HAND · EARTHY · ELEPHANT · HUGGING SOMEONE AND STAYING HUGGE[D] THING THAT RELATES TO FOOD · UNREAL · DANCE AS A WEAPON · EXPRESSING THE WORD 'YUMM[Y'] LIVING FOR · KITA TAKA TARE KITA TOM · CONTINUE CHANGE MOVEMENT · HYGIENE ON THE STREE[T] TO MOUNTAINS RIVERS FORESTS · LIKE MUSIC · IN AWE OF LIGHT BULBS · HUMAN · PEOPLE IN ANIM[AL] LEGS THE WAY DOWN BELOW · PROFOUND JOY · INJUSTICE · TIERRA DEL FUEGO · VISION OF THE FUTUR[E] PALM TREES · BEAUTY · SO SAD AND SO LONELY · A MAN A WOMAN · FLIRT · HIGH SOCIETY · SECR[ET] EXPERIENCED · ABOUT THE BEAUTY OF NATURE · LOVESICKNESS · SPREADING OPTIMISM · POTAT[O] PLAYING WITH FIRE · SOMETHING LIKE THAT · REBELLIOUS MOVEMENT · SOMETHING THAT YOU OTHERW[ISE] DAZZLED · HUMAN AND ANIMAL · SHADOWS · KITSCH · HOT CHOCOLATE · ENCHANTING · DREAMS ARE B[?] REALLY WANT · TEACHING SOMETHING ESSENTIAL · OPTIMISM · ADJUST · LOVING ONE BODY PART LOVE LOVE · CREATING A PARADISE FOR YOURSELF · GREAT DESPAIR · AT A SMALL CREEK · GENTLE RA[IN] DROWN · BREAK THE ICE · SOMETHING NICE IN RELATION TO SOMETHING NATURAL · WARMTH IN T[HE] FOREVER · YOU ARE A MAN · GLIDING · EXTREMELY ELONGATED MOVEMENT · SOMETHING FROM YO[U] AND YOU · DEALING WITH FEAR · SOMETHING THAT MOVES YOU A LOT · POSITIVE POWERFUL ENERG[Y] YELLOW · SOMETHING ABOUT THE COLOR BLUE · FRAGILITY · OLD AND NEW TOGETHER · ATTEMPTS OF EVERYTHING · YOUR MOVEMENTS HAVE TO SHOUT FOR JOY · SOMETHING FRAGILE · EXTREME · BE[ING] SING THE SENSES · DISARMING · SOMETHING REAL · SAVING SOMETHING · RAISING UP TO A MOVEMEN[T] ONE TO GLIDE · WORKING ON HAPPINESS · THE SMALLEST · MOTHERLAND · INFLUENCED MOVEMENT · WH[?] OUT · WANTING TO REALLY FEEL A BODY PART · OPPORTUNITY TO MAKE SOMETHING BETTER · SLIDI[NG] LONELY · MOVEMENT LIKE SWAYING · BRIDGES · SAFEGUARDING · WESTERN ATMOSPHERE · DAMMED · LIKE FRESH WATER · WAKING UP BEFORE SOMETHING · BOAT · GAINING TRUST · HO HARMONY · PULLI[NG] CARESSES YOU · YOU ARE A WOMAN · SOMETHING WITH A FACE AT THE VERY TOP · A SMALL WORLD PATENTED · IN FRONT AND BEHIND · MOVEMENT HEAD LEADS · MAKING MONEY · KEEPING UP APPEARANC[ES] · IGNORING SOMETHING IMPORTANT · TRY TO MAKE THE BEST OUT OF IT · ALL HOPE RESTS ON Y[OU] SINKING INTO A MAGIC SLEEP · HOSPITALITY POOR · LEARN TO BE TOGETHER · STINGY · SHARP TONGU[E] FANTASTIC · A PARODY OF SOMETHING · BEING BOWLED OVER · SOMETHING NICE IN THE MEAD[OW] HEAVY LIGHTLY · MACABRE · A LITTLE BIT CRAZY · ABSURD ORDER · FRIEND · JUDAS · WANTING TO F[?] DOWN FROM AN EMERGENCY · OBJECTS WHERE THEY COME FROM · SOMETHING HEARTFELT · SOMETHI[NG] AND OTHER SPOTS · PURE · TWO CUPS OF COFFEE · OH HOW FUNNY IT WAS · DESCRIBING JOY · IT'S A[?] PROPER BEHAVIOR · TWO CULTURES · HITTING FOR FUN · NEW BEGINNING · HORIZONTAL VERTICAL · DIRE[CT] NECESSITY · SHOWING NO FEAR · TURNING SOMEONE ON · CHEERING SOMEONE UP · DEMON · RICH PO[?] LOVING DETAILS · KINDS OF FISH · BEING BOWLED OVER · MAKING SOMETHING TRIVIAL IMPORTANT · PEACE · FINDING A SOLUTION · LETTING IN A BREATH OF FRESH AIR · NICE MIXTURE · BIG SIGH · COFF[EE] SENDING WISHES · SLEEPING WITH SOMETHING · ALL IN · BIRD OSTRICH · BLACK AND RED · SHOWING SQUEEZING LEMONS BEFORE SUNRISE · SPOILING FOR A FIGHT · QUICK MERMAID · AUCTIONING · CLU[?] AN ACT · CORRECTING · FOLK DANCE · WELCOME · COVERING THE FACE · FACE IN THE DIRT · TWO WRI[STS] BODY CULTURE · STARTING SOMETHING NOT DOING IT · APPEARANCES ARE DECEPTIVE · WITH T[HE] BRAVO · JUMPING DOWN FROM SOMETHING SMALL · LETTERS · CAREFUL · WHERE THE WINGS GRO[W] · A PROBLEM · WITH STONE HOUSE BROKEN · DETERMINED BY THE WEATHER · A SHEET OF WHITE PA[PER] MALE PROFESSION · GETTING YOUR HOPES UP · KITSCH AND REALITY · PROTECT[?] KING FROM AFAR · POISONOUS · BIG-BREASTED · RITUALIZING SOMETHING ABOUT L[?] WELL-DRESSED OPPOSITE PROP · THE LAST RAY OF SUNSHINE · GIANT BALANC[E] LORS AND SAD · VENERATING GODS EXAMPLES · MELODY TRANCE · SOMETHING SMALL FROM A DREA[M] RETREAT · FLYING · PLAYING BALL WITH HANDS AND FEET · MERMAID · COMBING YOUR HAIR AND PUTT[ING] ARM THAT NEVER ENDS · DOING SOMETHING WITH A LIFELESS BODY · SAYING VERY NICE THINGS ANSWER[?]

3 Examples of 'questions' posed by Pina Bausch

…METHING STRANGE FOR YOUR WELL-BEING · TEARS · INSPIRED BY SWAYING PLANTS IN THE RIVER · FOR ISABELLE · SOME-
…FOUND JOY · IN THE MORNING AT THE RIVER · NOT LETTING ANYONE STOP YOU · THE GODS' DELIGHT · SOMETHING WORTH
…METHING THAT MAKES EVERYONE THE SAME · NIGHTS AT LAS RAMBLAS · WANTING TO ALWAYS STAY YOUNG · WHAT HAPPENS
…SKS · SUPPLE LIKE BIG CATS · LIKE CRYING · SENSUALLY EROTIC · FEELINGS OF GUILT · HOLDING A POSE ON TOP SEARCHING FOR
…UTIFUL PAIN · A COLOR · MOVEMENT WITH LARGE STEPS · DREAMS NOWADAYS · A BEAUTIFUL SMILE · TICK STOP · KOLKATA
…ASURE · GIVING POWER · SMALL BUT NICE WITH HEAD AND HANDS · DOING SOMETHING UNEXPECTED WITH A PARTNER · IN-
…ERISHLY AWAITING SOMETHING · IS NOT TRUE BUT TRUE · WISDOM · FULL MOON · GANGES · EVERYDAY LIFE · FRAGILE
…ULDN'T DARE · DESPERATION · MOONLIT NIGHT · BODIES THAT COMPLETE EACH OTHER · MODERNIZING SOMETHING
…ADOWS · THE WORLD · RISKY · WONDER AS TOPIC · SOMETHING ABOUT THE MOON · LARGE MOVEMENT IN SPACE · WHAT YOU
…RTICULAR · PLUCKING UP COURAGE · CHENNAI · BRILLIANT · REALISM SIMULTANEOUSLY FIGMENT OF IMAGINATION · LOVE
… · STORM · YIN · BOUNDARY · KIM CHI · BEAR · YANG · WE ARE SCARED FOR YOU · LIKE SOMEONE WHO DOES NOT WANT TO
…ART · BUNRAKU · ABSURDITIES · PRECISELY PRACTICAL · CHEATING HOW TO ORGANIZE IT · A SMALL WORLD OF YOUR OWN
…EAMS · GLIDING IN PAIRS · SOMETHING CONCERNING MOUNTAINS · PERSEVERING · HIBISCUS · OPTIMISTIC · GRANDMOTHER
…OURING EDUCATION WITH A SMILE · HEALTHY · ONCE I CRIED · RISK · WHAT SHOULD I DO · LONGING IN PAIRS · FRIENDSHIP
…RTING · ARM · INVENTING SOMETHING FOR SOS · EVERYTHING HAS TO GO QUICKLY · MAKING SOMETHING WONDERFUL OUT
…LE TO ENDURE A LOT · CALIFORNIAN LONGING · BEING VERY WELL ORGANIZED · VERY PRACTICAL · JOIE DE VIVRE · ADDRES-
…OND CLASS · SWAPPING · WELL MAINTAINED · WILL TO LIVE · CORRUPTION · WORRY ABOUT THE FUTURE · HELPING SOME-
…J ARE WORRIED ABOUT · EVERYDAY WORK · MAKING SOMETHING POSSIBLE · YOU HAVE TO BE BRAVE · FEELING LOCKED-
…VEMENT · IT WAS MEANT WITH THE BEST INTENTIONS · SIGN OF LIFE · CATCHING · SO BEAUTIFULLY AND SO DESPERATELY
…UTIFUL SOLITUDE · ELBOW PHRASE · SUPER CRITICAL · FEAT OF JOY · IDEALLY BEING AT HOME EVERYWHERE · SAVING FACE
…JR OWN LEG · FEAR OF NOT BEING BEAUTIFUL · MAKING YOURSELF COMFORTABLE · BEING HAPPY TO BE ALIVE · THE WIND
…JR OWN · ABSURD AND VERY SLOW WALTZ · MOVEMENTS THAT TRAVERSE THE SPACE · THE WIND CARESSES YOU · NOT YET
…AVING TRUST · BLUFFING · BOGEYMEN · SOMETHING COZY · HUMILIATING · BETRAYING DEFENSE MECHANISMS SIX TIMES
…ESTURES IN THE HOUSE · A MOVEMENT THAT YOU WOULD LIKE TO DO FOR AN HOUR · FIRST CLASS · DISPELLING FEAR
… IT YOURSELF SITTING · HOPPING LIFT · LOVING DETAILS · I AM A NOTHING · EXPOSING SOMEONE · AT THE WATER · FEELING
…ALLING SOMEONE · ABOUT THE STAGE · FOREIGN · LUCKY CHARM · MOVEMENT SUN SHINING ON IT · TAKING SOMETHING
…LOVE · FEELING SOMEBODY'S PULSE · NOT LOVING EACH OTHER SIX TIMES · OH LOVE · SURPRISINGLY PRACTICAL · CALMING
…TICULOUS · CLOSING A MOVEMENT · OVERSIZED MOVEMENT · ONLY FEELING DESIRE · ALONE WITH YOURSELF · THE NOSE
…BBISH · DISTRACTING · FUNERAL MARCH · PROTECTING SOMEONE · BEING ABLE TO FORGIVE · INTO THE HEART · ALL THERE
… A BAD SPANIARD A BETTER BROTHER THAN A GOOD CHINESE PERSON · A BREATH · OLIVES · KNEE · EXTREME OUT OF
…GETHER · ALL OR NOTHING · FEAR OF MISSING OUT · SOMETHING VERY SENSUAL · STRANGE LOVEMAKING · SORROWS GONE
…RUBBERY · ENJOYING DOING SOMETHING UNOBSERVED · SUDDENLY HIDING SOMETHING ON YOUR BODY · BRIDGING · PLAYING
…USE · STICKY KISS · CREAM · DISTRACTING · WHAT YOU ONLY DO ALONE · PARTNER DANCE HANDS IN UNUSUAL PLACES
…AR · STRANGE HEALING · GIVING YOURSELF UP · IMAGINARY SOCIETY · HOT DUSTY · FEAR EXHAUSTS ME · BETTER LIVING
…TSIDE AT NIGHT TIRED · TULLE DRESS · SQUIRREL · TEACHING SOMETHING · AGREEING ON A PRICE · FLYING · PUTTING ON
…TCHES · CELEBRATING BODIES · THE HEART IS HEAVY · KING KONG IS A HUMAN · SIGNS OF FRIENDSHIP · SIGNS OF HOPE
…GERS · VENERATING NATURE · RAIN · PRAYING WITH THE COWS · BEAUTY FROM A FOREIGN COUNTRY · FEELING BEAUTIFUL
…SHA GAME · LOVING LIVING BEINGS · ANGEL · ON TOP OF SOMETHING · KISS NOT ON THE BODY · SOMETHING WITH THE DEVIL
…OWING THAT YOU ARE INJURED · ON THE CARPET · FLYING CARPET · TRAIN STATION · MALE PROFESSION · SHOCKING · FE-
…ASURE · DESTROYING YOURSELF WITH SOMETHING · SOMETHING BY CRAFTSMEN · DOUBLE-CROSSING SOMEONE · LOVEMA-
…GN HEALTH · UNBELIEVABLY GREAT MESSAGE · ALLOWING SOMETHING POSITIVE TO GROW · ENJOYING WORKING HARD
…VELATION · JUMP WITHOUT JUMPING · CELEBRATION OF NATURE · UNEXPECTED SMALL IMPUDENCE · WITH HEADSCARF · CO-
…ENDING SOMETHING ABOUT DANCE · A KISS · A FORM OF GRATITUDE · WITH YOUR BREATH · YOU AND THE ELEMENTS · KISS
… MAKEUP IN A ROW · CATS · WE WERE LUCKY IT COULD HAVE BEEN WORSE · LIKE SOMETHING STRANGE IN A DREAM · AN
…IOUSLY · BEFRIENDING AN ANIMAL · NOT ALLOWING SOMETHING TO PENETRATE YOU · SOMEONE WHO REBUFFED YOU

Video material

Hands

1) Why not	Capoeira
2) Also nice, also works	Push head
3) Comes up where static	Pendulum
4) Not necessary	Atti
5) Hm Hm	Cutting heart
6) Hm Hm	Sacre Flex
7) Trying	Pulling shirt
8) End? with or end	Little animal
9) Just try	Knee
10) Also just try	Hitting head
11) Yes, could be worse	Stretching and nodding
12) Observe rhythm on the move + faster	Danube
13) Strange foot sequence sloppy	Passe right from the ear
Pas de bourree	

4 Notes by Stephan Brinkmann written while reviewing video recordings of his solo for *Wiesenland* with Pina Bausch. In the left-hand column, he noted what Pina Bausch said about the movement material while they watched the video together. In the right-hand column, he assigned keywords to the short movement phrases in order to better remember them.

Videomaterial

Heinck

1) warten nicht
2) auch schön, geht auch
3) kommt drauf an wo
   Statisch
4) muß nicht sein
5) hinten ...
6) hinten ... Sack flex
7) probieren
8) Ende? mit oder Ende
9) probier mal
10) auch probier ...
11) ja so lala
12) Rhythmus beibehalten
    unterwegs + schneller
13) Luanische Fußsatz
    unsaubere

e capoeira
e Kopf schüttel
e Pendel
e Atti
e Herz Schneiden
Hemd ziehen
Tierchen
Knie
Kopf schlagen
Hosezieher + ...
Donau
um ans paste
rechts
pas de bourrée

NOVEMBER '99

(48) Selbstironie

Nayoung Schlitzaugen

Fernando große Augen

⎡ NY Gina sehen,
⎢ in einer bauen und Nayoung
⎣ umarmen

Aida + Julie versuchen Eddie
anzumachen. Ihn für sie zu
interessieren.

Micha tanzt Walzer und lässt
Frauen Verliebtheiren fest.

Raphi + Rudi. Er mit Hut will
sie küssen, verlangt sein Hut fällt.
Sie hebt ihn auf, setzt den Hut
ihm auf Kopf usw.

Helena malt Gesicht um Titte

NOVEMBER 99

(48) Self-irony

Nayong narrow eyes
Fernando big eyes

> *Give NY bucket,*
> *throw into bucket and hug*
> *Nayong*

Aida + Julie attempt to chat
up Eddie. Make him interested
in them.

Micha dances a waltz and holds
women the wrong way round.

Daphnis + Ruth. He with hat
wants to kiss her, bows, hat falls.
She picks it up, puts the hat
on his head, etc.

Helene paints face around tit

5 Excerpt from Stephan Brinkmann's notebook for *Wiesenland*

Pina Bausch usually asked her 'questions' in German, sometimes in English. In 2013, for example, the company was made up of 32 dancers (18 women and 14 men) from 18 different nations; it was therefore in itself a microcosm of different cultures and different 'mother tongues' – and thus led to a real-life, constant practice of translation. This was also reflected in the making of new pieces: dancers who only understood a little German had to ask someone to translate for them what exactly was being asked. No matter what they understood, they searched for answers using their bodies, their voices, through movement, alone or with others, with the help of materials, costumes and props lying around in heaps in the Tanztheater Wuppertal's rehearsal space, the Lichtburg. The fact that the Lichtburg had become the Tanztheater Wuppertal's exclusive rehearsal space was the result of negotiations between Pina Bausch and the Wuppertaler Bühnen in the late 1970s. The former cinema in Wuppertal-Barmen is located beside a MacDonalds and a sex shop, near the offices of the Tanztheater Wuppertal and within walking distance of the Opernhaus Wuppertal. It has been at the sole disposal of the company since the 1970s, regardless of the larger theater's institutional and contractual requirements. Since then, the company has been able to rehearse there whenever it wants – company members operate the lights and sound themselves. The dancers have their own regular "corners" where they can settle down.

During rehearsals in the Lichtburg, Pina Bausch sat at a large table with coffee and cigarettes spread out before her as well as a large pile of paper and pencils: she wrote everything down by hand. For every 'answer' from each dancer, she used a new piece of paper. Every dancer had their own compartment in a folder, into which the notes disappeared. Assuming that she asked approx. 100 questions per piece and that she worked with around 20 dancers for one piece alone, she probably received around 2,000 answers during the development of a new production. We can thus imagine the page count of these notes for just one piece and the sum of pages for her total of more than 40 choreographies. "First, the questions produce a collection of material. We just do all kinds of things, and much of them are nonsense. We laugh a lot [...]. But there's always something serious to it as well: what do I actually want? What do I really want to say? Now, in this age in which we're living."[17]

Although Pina Bausch asked her questions in German and sometimes in English, she wrote her notes in German, in her own shorthand with abbreviations. Sometimes she gave names to what she saw in rehearsals. In other words: these were her personal notes, and they were written accordingly. She never gave them to anyone to read, but hid them away in her bag during the production process like treasure. After that, they disappeared into her private archive.

"There were now small sequences of moments, dances and scenes, each of them labelled with a single keyword. It was almost like a secret language that all of us could understand or were learning, for we had now been trying for many weeks to connect one with the other, rehearse transitions, discard apparent solutions, try the exact opposite, let things run in parallel without one diminishing – or even drowning out – the other... and by now everything had been reduced to short code words, so that one keyword could refer to a previously rehearsed scene or even a whole sequence of scenes.

She carefully pencilled, almost painted, the keywords along the top of several A4 sheets of paper, which she then pinned together on the left-hand side using paperclips. You could only see the uppermost section that had been written on, then beneath it the top of the next sheet and so on... this is how she made connections, at first in her own mind, in long thinking sessions during the afternoon (between rehearsals) and at night (after rehearsals). Thanks to the paperclips, the A4 sheets could be easily separated, reconfigured and laid out on the table in new thought patterns."

6 Description of the work process by Matthias Burkert, 2019

Even if the Pina Bausch Foundation does ever provide access to this material, decoding and understanding these subjective writings, which were never intersubjectively examined for comprehensibility and were probably meant to be the opposite – that is, encrypted – would be a difficult task indeed. One possible method would be to compare them with the video documentation of rehearsals, although not everything in rehearsals was videotaped. Another potential method would be to compare her notes with those of the assistants and dancers involved.

Since the rehearsal period spanned several rehearsal phases, and because it was uncertain for quite some time what exactly Pina Bausch would want to see again and possibly use in the piece, the dancers also kept notebooks to jog their memories and to take notes during the rehearsal process. Sometimes they wrote in German, sometimes in English, occasionally in their own native languages as well, for example in Spanish, French, Italian, Japanese or Korean. When looking at the dancers' notebooks, a problem reveals itself concerning the ways in which individuals pass on choreography. The problem lies in the unresolvable paradox between identity and difference inherent to the relationship between the piece and these writings. Evidently, none of the dancers took systematic notes, probably because – unlike in academic research processes – working that way usually played and plays next to no role in the rehearsal process. But with Pina Bausch's new method, rehearsals became an artistic research process for the whole company. The notes not only differ in terms of their completeness and language but also document the fact that the dancers understood and interpreted the 'questions' differently, subjectively attaching differing levels of importance and their own meaning to them, perhaps translating them into fitting words from their own languages or into sketches, drawings, verses or poems. Furthermore, some of the dancers did not save their notebooks, which are now lost. Some of the other dancers who were originally involved in the development of older pieces left the company decades ago, so their material would be difficult to access, if it still exists at all.

These notebooks are an interesting yet complicated source of material for the reconstruction of the rehearsal process, because the dancers were so individual when it came to translating what they were asked and shown into writing. Some wrote down all the 'questions' and 'answers', what others had shown and what they liked. Some only noted down the 'questions' that appeared important to them or what they thought were interesting answers. Some only wrote notes about what they themselves had presented – sometimes including the 'questions', sometimes not – or when they had been involved in the ideas of other dancers. Together with the videos, these notes occasionally served as mnemonic aids and helped the dancers when it came time for repetitions, namely when Pina Bausch had decided and told the dancers what she wanted to see again out of all the material that they had shown her. As she said: "Out of ten things that everybody does, I am ultimately maybe only interested in two."[18] In the early 1980s, she emphasized that sometimes "a small gesture, a remark on the side interests me more than a big show."[19] It was moreover very important to her that what she was shown felt like part of what she was looking for but could not describe in words: "Only a small part feels to me as if it is part of what I'm looking for. Suddenly, I find all the puzzle pieces for the image that actually already exists, but with which I am not yet familiar."[20]

After Pina Bausch had selected some of what she had been shown – and she alone made these choices, usually only after weeks and months of rehearsals, without consulting her assistants, other staff or the dancers – the dancers received a list of movements or 'scenes' that she wanted them to reconstruct and show her again. Now came the time to consult the videos and notes made for that very purpose.

Independently, the dancers then began working on their solos, especially from the 1990s onward, as the pieces developed from this point in time included more solos than before. They individually reviewed with the choreographer what they had developed and recorded on video in answer to her 'movement questions.' She occasionally suggested changes, which then had to be implemented, but normally sections were merely cut or shortened. Only rarely did a movement that Pina Bausch would rather not have make it into a solo. Stephan Brinkmann, who was a member of the Tanztheater Wuppertal from 1995 until 2010 and is now Professor of Contemporary Dance at Folkwang Universität, remembers: "She once told me that it would be better not to use the movement that I had developed for the solo. I did so all the same; it stayed in the dance, but it was a real exception. Normally, I took out the movement when she said: 'better not.' It wasn't discussed."[21] The dancers rehearsed their dances in the Lichtburg, in their 'corners' or occasionally hidden behind a mirror, in a familiar framework, fuelled by hope and fear about whether their own solos would find their way into the piece. Music was only added much later, and it changed the dances once more. "First the dances are created without music. Then comes the music. It should be like a partner and the dancer like one more instrument in the music. This interplay between dance and music then creates an entirely new perspective and a completely new form of listening."[22]

Matthias Burkert and Andreas Eisenschneider, musical collaborators since 1979 and 1990 respectively (→ COMPANY), attended the rehearsals, discretely observed what the dancers were doing and began choosing music, a small selection of which they suggested to the choreographer, but only upon her request.

Pina Bausch selected material from what she had been shown and placed it in a choreographic context, which only gradually developed over the course of many attempts and alterations. About the montage-like method used, she said: "That is then ultimately the composition. What you do with the things. After all, at first it isn't anything. It's just answers – sentences, little scenes – that someone performs. Everything's separate to start with. At some point or other, I combine something I think is right with something else. This with that, that with something else, one thing with various others. Then, when I've again found something that works, I've already got a slightly bigger little something. Then I go off somewhere else completely. It starts really small and gradually gets bigger."[23]

Her pieces, as she emphasized, did not develop linearly, from beginning to end: "Pieces do not grow front to back but inside out."[24] Only by juxtaposing and connecting the scenes and through rhythmic dramaturgy did individual elements gain significance, thus allowing the piece to emerge.

In *1980 – A Piece by Pina Bausch*[25] (PREMIERE 1980), for example, an individual movement phrase became a group dance and a rehearsal break-time activity – namely the eating of soup – became a central scene. Pina Bausch did not engage in a dialogical process with the dancers in order to alter, amplify, estrange, duplicate, multiply, superimpose or displace what she had been shown, nor to develop the collage or montage-like composition of the choreographies, which characterized her earlier pieces in particular. She did it alone, in a process of constant experimentation, alteration and rearrangement, sometimes up to the day of the premiere or even after. It is thus misleading to assume that the dancers developed the choreographies together with Pina Bausch. The choreography was her work alone. The dancers usually did not know the piece from an audience's perspective, only from the perspective of the stage. At most, they observed it from backstage or onstage, and they mainly concentrated on their own parts and cues. This only changed when dancers became assistants and took on the responsibility of directing the rehearsals necessary for restagings.

Research trips – artistic research

Over the course of a total of 15 international coproductions, which began with *Viktor* in 1986 and finished with *"…como el musguito en la piedra, ay si, si, si…"* in 2009,[26] the company put something into practice for which there was no concept and no discourse at the time. This novel practice has since become both ideologically charged and politically contested. What I am referring to is: artistic research. Today, it is usually defined as a contemporary form of knowledge production. Artistic methods are considered to be more than mere processes that target perception. Like scholarship itself, artistic research is viewed as a discursive, knowledge-generating practice. The paradigm of artistic research thus calls into question the established, over 200-year-old opposition between art and academia in terms of, e.g., the knowledge being gained and produced.[27]

Pina Bausch's working method of 'asking questions' was not the only way in which she demonstrated that everyday experience can be productively regarded as knowledge, aesthetically translated into choreography and performed as aesthetically tangible knowledge. Her gaze as an ethnologist of the everyday grew with the international coproductions as she placed her 'questions' within the context of cultural experiences of difference. The company travelled – usually for around three weeks – to the coproducing cities and countries: to Rome, Palermo, Madrid, Vienna, Los Angeles, Hong Kong, Lisbon, Budapest, São Paulo, Istanbul, Seoul, Saitama, New Delhi, Mumbai and Santiago de Chile. The troupe had already been able to gain a wide range of experiences with local cultures during their extensive touring activities, some of which also provided the impetus for later coproductions. However, in the case of the coproductions, this travelling became a central component in the development of new pieces: the dancers collected impressions, sometimes by wandering about and making random discoveries, sometimes at events that had been organized for them in advance. Meanwhile, the musical collaborators Matthias Burkert and Andreas Eisenschneider browsed local archives and combed through record stores and secondhand shops – in search of, well… anything and everything that they could find locally in terms of music. Some travelers, including Pina Bausch herself, documented their impressions in photos and videos. Some of these photos later reappeared in the program booklets.

Would the dancers have created scenes and dances differently in response to a 'question' about longing in Korea, India or Brazil than they would in Lisbon or Los Angeles? Would the observations that they made in countries that publicly stage the gestural language of love in different ways have a different influence on them? How would the dancers translate publicly visible, gender-specific gestures during rehearsals if they experienced the atmospheres in the coproducing places differently due to their own cultural backgrounds and maybe also due to their own individual and situative moods? Would the cultural diversity of 'answers' to the subject of fear, for example, grow through local artistic research? Could something akin to an archive of feelings develop based on these different cultural perceptions and experiences – an archive that transcends situative perceptions and experiences and allows "suprahistorical kinship"[28] to reveal itself? In her acceptance speech for the 2007 Kyoto Prize, Pina Bausch pointed out: "And sometimes the questions

7 Research trip
for *Ten Chi*
Japan, 2003

8 Research trip
for *Wiesenland*
Hungary, 1999

9 Research trip
for *Wiesenland*
Hungary, 1999

10 Research trip for
Rough Cut
Korea, 2004

11 Research trip for
"*...como el musguito en la
piedra, ay si, si, si...*"
Chile, 2009

we have bring us back to experiences that are much older, which not only come from our culture and not only deal with the here and now. It is, as if a certain knowledge returns to us, which we indeed always had, but which is not conscious and present. It reminds us of something, which we all have in common."[29]

What the development of pieces looked like in connection with the research trips will be illustrated below using the example of two pieces: *Only You* (PREMIERE 1996) and *Wiesenland* (PREMIERE 2000).

ONLY YOU

The piece *Only You* was created in collaboration with four US universities: the University of California Los Angeles, Arizona State University, the University of California Berkeley and the University of Texas at Austin, as well as with Darlene Neel Presentations, Rena Shagan Associates, Inc., and The Music Centre Inc. It premiered on May 11, 1996, in Wuppertal.[30] The premiere of the piece was preceded by a joint rehearsal period from mid-January 1996 that covered a total of four work phases, the first phase beginning with rehearsals in Wuppertal. This phase was followed by a two-and-a-half-week research trip to the US in February 1996 and another rehearsal phase at the University of California Los Angeles (UCLA), ending with the fourth and final rehearsal phase in Wuppertal.

A total of 22 dancers contributed to the piece. As in almost all of Pina Bausch's pieces, men and women were equally represented, in this case, by eleven men and eleven women.[31] During the research trip, the company visited the Magic Castle, Universal Studios, Downtown Los Angeles at night and the tent cities of the homeless, and attended a Cassandra Wilson concert and the church service of an Afro-American congregation in LA. They went whale watching, talked to Paul Apodaca – a performer and Associate Professor of Sociology and American Studies at Chapman University, whose family comes from a Navajo reservation – went on a trip to Joshua Tree National Park, visited the redwood trees near LA, received a visit from Peter Sellars at the UCLA campus, rode public buses, went to jazz bars, striptease clubs, restaurants and gay bars, took open classes in rock and roll and swing, visited the Chinese Theater and the Believe It or Not Museum, and paid visits to the Walk of Fame on Hollywood Boulevard, Chinatown, West Hollywood, Santa Monica Boulevard and Venice Beach.

"When you see the questions, you know already what it's about, what I'm looking for,"[32] Pina Bausch explained. During the rehearsal phases for *Only You,* she asked a total of 99 'questions,' which she wrote down in shorthand. During the first rehearsal phase in Wuppertal, these were:

PRECAUTIONARY MEASURE · NO RESPECT · A FORM OF DEPENDENCY · HEAD CUDDLES · SURVIVAL ARTIST · DISTRUST · BOUNCING BACK · PROVISIONAL · PROVOKING · DEFENDING · BLUFFING · SOMETHING COMFORTABLE · ATTEMPT RECONCILIATION · BUT NOT COMPLAINING · CONSERVATIVE · POSITIVE · ASSERTING THE RIGHT TO · TEMPTING · BRAVE · STARTING FROM SCRATCH · DISARMING · ADDRESSING THE SENSES · WANTING TO MAKE ONE'S FORTUNE · DESPERATELY WANTING TO BE GOOD · BEING INVENTIVE · PROTECTIVE MEASURES · SIX TIMES IN NEED · SIGNALS · WITH RESPECT · SIX TIMES PUNISHMENT

During the second rehearsal phase in Los Angeles at the UCLA campus, they were:

GESTURES IN THE HOUSE · SOMETHING SMALL VERY IMPORTANT · FINDING A REASON FOR SOMETHING UNNECESSARY · SUPPRESSING · ANGEL · *Buffalo* · SIX LITTLE EXPLOSIONS ON THE BODY · IN FRONT – BEHIND · NOT YET PATENTED · SOMETHING WITH CENSORSHIP · SOMETHING THAT YOU'VE DREAMED · *Try to make the best out of it* · A MOVEMENT THAT YOU'D LIKE TO DO FOR AN HOUR · A MOVEMENT WITH BREATH · AFRAID OF NOT BEING BEAUTIFUL ENOUGH · REVEALING SOMETHING BEAUTIFUL · SOMETHING WITH THE ELBOW · SO BEAUTIFUL AND SO DESPERATELY LONELY · FEELING LOCKED OUT · PLEASANT · BEING ABLE TO ENDURE A LOT · MAKING SOMETHING POSSIBLE · PAUSE IN SPACE · SOMETHING THAT YOU'RE VERY GOOD AT · VERY PRACTICAL · IN ORDER TO BE LOVED · SUPER KITSCH · CONSTRUCTING A BOGEYMAN · YOU HAVE TO BE BRAVE 33 · PAUL APODACA · IT WAS WELL MEANT · *Working hard* · SOMETHING REAL · MOVEMENT WITH A STIFF NECK · SIX MOMENTS OF PLEASURE · WAKING UP FROM SOMETHING · DAMMED TO BEAUTIFUL LONELINESS · SLIDING MOVEMENT · MOVEMENT HEAD LEADS · SOMETHING SMALL THAT YOU'RE WORRIED ABOUT · JOIE DE VIVRE · SYMBOL OF HAPPINESS

And, during the third rehearsal phase in Wuppertal:

LITTLE FEAT OF JOY · WITHOUT PREJUDICE · HEAD MASSAGE · WORKING MOTION · BEING ABLE TO ENDURE A LOT · MOVEMENT PULLING IN PAIRS · LIKE FRESH WATER · MOVEMENT SWAYING · REALLY WANTING TO FEEL A BODY PART · CATCHING · UNCANNY MOVEMENT · LIFTING TOWARD A MOVEMENT · WELL-ORGANIZED · IDEALLY BEING AT HOME EVERYWHERE · *Western* · PUNISHING YOURSELF · REALITY AND ILLUSION · FIRST CLASS/SECOND CLASS · *Two jobs at the same time* · CALIFORNIAN LONGING · WRITING *Angel* IN MOVEMENT · WRITING *Pretty* IN MOVEMENT · WRITING MOON IN MOVEMENT · PORCH SWING · TABLEAUX · TROPHIES · PEACE PIPE · CIRCLES/CYCLE

These examples demonstrate, on the one hand, that the 'questions' were based on concrete observations, many of them directly relating to the location. Sometimes they were posed in English and included movement suggestions, such as writing 'pretty,' 'angel' or 'moon' in movement. On the other hand, some 'questions' could also have been posed the same way or similarly during rehearsals for other pieces – requiring a specific and thus different 'answer' in the US, in a different situative and cultural context. Moreover, the 'questions' were obviously not posed in a way that suggested that the piece was intended as kind of revue of the respective country. It was not about translating a representation of the host culture into the language of dance theater, which was what some critics and spectators expected, thus leading to disappointment (→ RECEPTION). The questions were too associative for that. Their openness alone

12 Research trip for *Bamboo Blues* India, 2006

provided a lot of leeway for finding answers, the range of which became unimaginably vast due to the dancers' subjectivities and situative sensitivities, through the use of props and materials and, finally, due to the option of choosing individual or group presentations.

Are the 'questions' still recognizable in the pieces? Can these starting points and thus points of reference to the coproducing country be detected in the respective scenes? Let us dive deeper into these questions by looking at another coproduction.

WIESENLAND

Wiesenland was created in collaboration with the Goethe-Institut Budapest and the Théâtre de la Ville in Paris. The piece premiered on May 5, 2000, in Wuppertal.[34] The rehearsal period encompassed five work phases from August 1999 until the premiere in May 2000. The first phase began in mid-August with a research trip to Budapest, followed by one- to two-week rehearsals in the Lichtburg in Wuppertal. Final rehearsals took place between March and May 2000. This rehearsal process was interrupted by performances of other pieces that the dancers were appearing in at the time: *Masurca Fogo* (PREMIERE 1998), *Arien* (PREMIERE 1979), *Kontakthof* (PREMIERE 1978), *O Dido* (PREMIERE 1999) and *Nelken*. In addition, they also rehearsed *Kontakthof with Seniors* (PREMIERE 2000) during this period. These performances and restagings not only repeatedly created distance to the rehearsal process but provided a basic frame for the generation of material for the new piece, as the dancers also had to reacquaint themselves with the material of the other pieces, to reembody them. This also guaranteed that dancers developed a connection to earlier pieces, especially dancers of the younger generation.

A total of 19 dancers contributed to *Wiesenland*, eight women and eleven men.[35] During the research trip to Budapest that took place from August 18 to September 6, 1999, the company visited Lehel Square and the 8th district in Budapest. They visited orphanages, discos, dance houses *(czárdás)*, numerous baths and horse races, and went to street parties with processions. Together, they went to a church concert by Félix Lajkó, to the open-air concert of a zither ensemble and to a dance performance by Ferenc Novák's Honvéd Ensemble at Trafó, a house for contemporary art in Budapest, which also served as the company's rehearsal space. They undertook a bus tour lasting several days to Nyírbátor, home of the Roma music ensemble Kék Láng, and received dance classes in Hungarian folk dancing at Trafó from Péter Ertl, who would later become the director of the National Dance Theater in Budapest.

During rehearsals, Pina Bausch asked a total of 96 'questions,' including the repeated prompt "Budapest" on different rehearsal days. Some were general 'questions' and others, especially during the rehearsals in Budapest, related to the experiences they had during their stay there and associations with Hungary, such as *Felix Lajkó, Czárdás, Sissi, Rear courtyards, Baths, En route, Rural, Hungarian nostalgia, Landscape* and *Péter*. Some terms were meant to be conveyed as movements, such as *Igen* (yes) and *Duna* (Danube). Another prompt was *Wiesenland* (meadow country), which later became the title of the piece.

Stephan Brinkmann was a dancer in the original cast. He carefully wrote down his 'answers' and can still trace them back to individual scenes: in reaction to the cue *Trance*, which Pina Bausch gave at rehearsals in Budapest, he developed an idea that was integrated into the first part of the piece and which he later implemented with Ruth Amarante and Michael Strecker. Ruth Amarente lies on her back in a plié with the soles of her feet touching the right-hand wall of the stage. As she smiles at the audience, Stephan Brinkmann and Michael Strecker come onto the stage and lift her up, until her legs are straight, but the soles of her feet still touch the wall. They then lay her back down again.

At the rehearsals in Wuppertal in January, Brinkmann responded to *Something with strength and energy* by throwing tulle dresses into the air while Aida Vaineri stood behind him, whooping as she watched. In answer to *How would you like others to treat you?* he created a scene in which he ran his fingers through his hair. Then there was the second part of the "pullover scene," which Stephan Brinkmann performed with Nayoung Kim: Nayoung Kim slowly comes onto the stage; Stephan Brinkmann walks toward her and pulls the back of his black sweater over his head, with his arms still stuck in the sleeves of the sweater. He sinks to his knees and places the back of the sweater on the floor so that she can step onto it. Standing on the sweater, she stretches out over his shoulders and Stephan Brinkmann lifts her up and leaves the stage. This scene was based on an idea that he developed in connection with one of the prompts that Pina Bausch gave during one of the last rehearsals. It was the poem *Szóváltás* (Exchange of Words) by Hungarian poet and translator Sándor Kányádi (1977), which she recited as follows:

> *I carried you on my back*
> *when you had no feet*
> *and ungrateful as you are*
> *you let yourself grow wings*
> *you carried me on your back*
> *when I had no feet*
> *so as not to have to thank you forever*
> *I let myself grow wings.*[36]

Pina Bausch probably rewrote this poem, which becomes evident when it is compared with the version translated into German by Franz Hodjak, which starts, "I carried you piggyback." ("Ich trug dich huckepack"). Maybe she felt that this was too explicit to be transformed into movement.

These examples show just how inquisitive, open and multifaceted Pina Bausch's process of developing pieces was – and that it is impossible to conclusively connect scenes to 'questions.' For even when the phrases are known, it is only possible to situate them properly by examining and reconstructing them with the help of the people who were involved at the time, who remember the 'questions' as well as the 'answers' or who wrote them down, with the notes helping them to remember even years later. But not all dancers did this, and while assistants may have written down all the 'questions', they did not necessarily write down all the 'answers'.

Does exploring the relationship between the 'questions' and scenes in the pieces make any sense at all? Yes, it does, for these steps in the process allow us to pursue an inquiry of general importance for the theory of art and dance: is knowing what Pina Bausch wanted to say with the piece, what it personally meant to her, important for the reception of that same piece? The choreographer always refused to answer this question. In *1980*, she explained to the journalist of a youth magazine: "People say it's all so easy, that we should simply perform for the audience. But that's precisely the difficulty: for which audience? The audience is so very diverse. Everyone sees differently, everyone has different thoughts. So, who are we performing for?"[37] Nevertheless, audiences and critics (→ RECEPTION) kept asking her, the dancers and themselves these questions over and over again. The audience wanted to know what Pina Bausch was trying to 'say' with the piece, and they also wanted and still want to identify something of the coproducing places in the coproductions themselves. Interestingly, as our audience surveys have shown, spectators occasionally do also see what led to a scene, such as the "fountain scene" in *Viktor*. A female dancer sits hanging over the back of a chair with outstretched arms. Male dancers fill up her mouth with water from a plastic bottle, as she continuously spits that same water back out again like a fountain. Some spectators interpreted this scene as being the famous Fontana di Trevi in Rome. And in fact, the inspiration for this scene really was the prompt *Trevi Fountain*. However, direct connections between individual 'questions' and scenes in the pieces cannot always be established. Although the sum of all of the 'questions' asked for an individual piece provides us with some indication of the mood and color of the piece, the multiple steps of translating from 'question' to 'answer' and then into a scene are so productive precisely because the aesthetic quest is so ambiguous. The identical translation of language into movement or into a scene fails – or rather: is doomed to fail – and the aesthetic productivity of the process emerges out of this very failure.

Artistic practices of (un)certainty

One of the central aspects of Pina Bausch's method of developing pieces was to find a balance during rehearsals between certainty and trust on the one hand and practices of inciting both uncertainty and a willingness to risk showing something on the other hand. This balancing act is what differentiates the artistic work process from modern society's goal of providing people with more certainty and security – an idea embedded in the legally defined protection and observance of human rights, in social security and unemployment benefits, in pension plans, in safety regulations on roads and in the air, in security measures at government institutions and in labor protection laws. Consequently, insecurity and uncertainty in social contexts are considered something threatening, confusing, something that rocks the foundations of a society or of an individual – a transition, confusion or state of emergency.

Two positions are commonly found: one that claims that we are facing growing uncertainty, observing and critically commenting on this fact with concern and suspicion, the argument being that we lose social certainty in times of detraditionalization. Increasing mobility and flexibilization, and the acceleration of communication due to the development of digital media are intensifying this process. The result is a loss of routine, making the social increasingly susceptible to crisis. Social security, state provisions, sedentariness, social involvement and reciprocal duties disappear in favor of a lack of commitment, a loss of attachment, nomadic lifestyles and social disintegration, leading to increasingly anxious and insecure individuals and uncertain social and government institutions. In this diagnosis, the discourse of uncertainty has one core thought: we are living in a time of crisis.

Diagnoses of crisis are omnipresent. The list of postulated crisis scenarios ranges from the financial and debt crisis and government and legitimacy crises to the crisis of the political, the public sphere and the education system, of art and of culture. In Europe, interpretations of a global crisis are intensifying once more. All kinds of uncertainty are being postulated under the label "Euro(pean)crisis": the globalized economy is eroding the securities that workers previously relied on and, in politics, we are seeing the disappearance of European solidarity. In the wake of a worldwide financial crisis, we are encountering renationalization, everyday social upheavals, irreversible social asymmetries and aggravated movements of inclusion and exclusion. All of this is creating a range of social, cultural, economic, generational and ethnic uncertainties.

Unlike this position of historical diagnosis, one sociological perspective argues that crisis and thus uncertainty are fundamental elements of every society.[38] This position does not conceive of uncertainty as an irritant or as a state of emergency in processes of social transformation. Instead of describing tendencies or one-sided developments, this idea looks at the fundamental structure of the social fabric. In this sense, it inquires into the potential of uncertainty, which can also be viewed as a prerequisite of possibility, breaking up routines and searching for ways into the open. This social theory thus argues that the topos of (un)certainty has been a constant presence throughout modernity. This has several consequences: on the one hand, the uncertainties generated by crisis potentially unsettle the assumption that existing systems are safe and questions the inevitability of associated, 'entrenched' social structures. Ongoing uncertainty therefore also opens up opportunities to criticize the system and discover alternatives. However, the possibility of an open future is always accompanied by the certitude of ongoing uncertainty as well.

Art history deals with the topos of uncertainty in a similar way to these sociological approaches. On the one hand, it considers the task of art in modernity to be the questioning of certainties and perceptual habits and expects art to undermine, confuse, criticize, scrutinize and reflect upon them. In other words: certainties, mainly understood as routines of perception in aesthetic discourse, need to be brought into crisis. Thus, in art, uncertainty has potential; it is a path into the open, into what is coming.

Dance in particular can be understood as a phenomenon of uncertainty par excellence. In this respect, dance studies have – in short – developed three main positions. The first considers dance to be ephemeral, something that evades language and writing and, in this sense, every form of rationalization and categorization as well.[39] It is thus the last form of magic in a disenchanted world. The second position defines dance as that which undermines the order of choreography, as productive resistance against choreography as prescription, as 'law.'[40] The third stance considers dance to be a special experience of movement, which, unlike sport, is not movement as purpose, but rather as "pure mediality."[41] It is thus capable of representing the unsettling of incorporated patterns of social experience. Accordingly, recent theater, dance and performance studies research has inquired into dance's potential to cause crises of perceptual habits. Where and how do these productive ruptures, demarcations and transgressions reveal themselves in artistic work? So far, this question has mainly been pursued in performance and stage analyses in the field of dance studies. However, what has received less attention is how uncertainty influences the actual artistic practice of production itself. How is uncertainty generated in such processes? What relevance and productivity does uncertainty in artistic processes hold for participants and for the development of pieces and their aesthetic positings?

These issues of (un)certainty are especially pertinent to the working methods used by Pina Bausch with the Tanztheater Wuppertal. The long period in which the company worked together generated specific routines that provided certainty: the consistency with which the dancers performed their roles over many years, thus developing specific characters and a distinct movement language in their solos. Members of the company worked and traveled together for many years, sometimes even decades. They relied on one another and had to find a good balance between intimacy and distance. In spite of occasional changes in the composition of the ensemble, this closeness produced a specific collective identity – the "Bausch troupe" – as well as a canon of values that provided the foundation for their work and their reliance on one another (→ COMPANY). The fact that Pina Bausch very rarely personally dismissed any of her dancers also provided security, and, ultimately, it was the trust placed in the principle of passing on material from generation to generation that promised certainty. So far (as of 2020), most dancers have been able to personally pass on the roles that they themselves developed to other dancers. Thus, they have it within their power to ensure that the roles are translated well.

All contributors to a production were allowed to watch rehearsals, but only very rarely was anyone present who did not belong to the company. This allowed a feeling of collective security to grow over the years. The familiar spatial environment during rehearsals at the Lichtburg, where everyone had a "corner," reinforced this sense of certainty. Open rehearsals, still on the Saturday program during the first season of 1973/74 in the old ballet studio of the Wuppertal opera house, were quickly scrapped. During rehearsals, the company utilized this safe space to play with practices of uncertainty. These included the choreographer's 'questions,' but also the 'answers' of the dancers. They were constantly challenged to transcend their own routines (the inscribed character roles or their personal repertoires of movement) and to explore the boundaries of safe performance. Since some 'questions' were repeatedly posed throughout the rehearsal period, dancers were also challenged to set them in relation to each new situation. What did, for example, *earning trust* mean for dancers in November 1996 in Hong Kong, when the 'question' was posed during a research trip for the piece *The Window Washer,* as opposed to in October 1997 in Wuppertal, when it was posed once more during rehearsals for *Masurca Fogo*, this time after the research trip to Lisbon?

For Pina Bausch, asking the same 'question' again and again was not an act of repetition, but rather constituted a shift, a translation into another context, because the 'question' and the dancer's perceptions of it were constantly changing, prompting them to 'answer' differently each time. Some dancers made reference to their earlier 'answers'; some showed something completely different. All this was unsettling and sometimes unnerving as well – as some dancers recalled in their interviews with me – but it also led to creativity: what can I show and what do I want to show? This 'question' again? What can I develop in response to it today? The others always think of something new – why can't I? Uncertainty was also generated due to the fact that it was unclear for many months which 'answers' Pina Bausch would choose, which scenes would find a place in the piece and who would be allowed to dance a solo. Even after the dancers had been asked to reconstruct and continue working on what they had previously shown, they still could not be sure that the scene would actually be chosen for the final version of the piece.

Moreover, there were key moments of uncertainty for those with a dance solo in the piece. The solos were developed without music or occasionally with music that they had chosen themselves. However, Pina Bausch would decide for herself much later what music to use, determining what she considered to be appropriate for the piece and for the solo. She was the author. The quality of the music changed the solo once more, and the dancers were asked to simply deal with it. Dominique Mercy remembers not at all liking the music that Pina Bausch first tried out and then selected for his solo in the piece *Ten Chi* (PREMIERE 2004). He thought it was too intense, which unsettled him and made him react angrily. Only over time did he grow to like it and consider it productive for his dance.[42]

The set (→ PIECES, COMPANY) was another thing that the dancers were only confronted with during final rehearsals. The reason for this was that Pina Bausch only made her decisions about the set at a very late point in time, meaning that the scene shops had to produce it at very short notice. This forced the dancers to situatively deal with their surroundings; they were not able to prepare. More often than not, the set was conceived of as an action space and, in many pieces, its materials presented new challenges. For example, in *The Rite of Spring*, the dancers have to dance on peat; in *Nelken*, they wade through a field of artificial flowers; in *1980*, they walk across a lawn; in *Palermo Palermo* (PREMIERE 1989), they balance on stones; in *Ten Chi*, they slide through water; and in "*...como el musguito en la piedra, ay si, si, si...*", they jump over the cracks that open up in the stage floor. As a result, their costumes become full of soil, wet and heavy with water; the materials help to shape the movements, resisting and challenging the dancers anew in every performance. The set thus plays a significant role in adding to the unique, unrepeatable character of every performance, drawing attention to its spatial and temporal situatedness. Long before the performative turn in scholarship and contemporary art, Pina Bausch believed that it was the performance that made the piece.

Questions such as, 'What is the quality of the peat like? Is it wet, dry, hard, muddy, sandy?' have been important throughout the 40 years that *The Rite of Spring* has been performed worldwide so far, and they have constantly helped to create uncertainty. The dancers only receive an answer to this question once they feel the peat under their feet onstage. The same applies to *Palermo Palermo*, because the stones of the fallen wall scatter across the stage differently in every performance, and the dancers have to walk and dance on them wherever they fall.

Thus, specific uncertainties in the rehearsal process came from long periods of not knowing what Pina Bausch would want to see again, what she might choose for the piece and when she would finally decide for sure. In other words, a dancer's position in the piece was not certain for a very long period of time. The aesthetic principle of uncertainty meant keeping the dancers from developing routines, making them stay 'fresh' and preventing them from lapsing into routinized patterns, from reproducing or representing.

Even after the premiere, the piece was not finished: "Sometimes I realize that it can't be done before the premiere. But I know that I won't stop changing it until it's right. Otherwise I wouldn't be able to go on such an adventure with myself. There are some things that I don't touch after the premiere, simply because they just evolved that way. But there are other areas where I know that I have to do something, which I then try out in the next performances, because you can only ever determine whether it's right in relation to the whole thing."[43]

In this respect, the work process was in fact a consistently unsettling work in progress. Confronted with new situations (stage designs, materials, rearranged choreographies), the participants were forced to act situatively and performatively. For the dancers, this meant that they could not simply rehearse and perform their 'parts,' but rather had to recreate them in each respective situation.

The work process of the Tanztheater Wuppertal under Pina Bausch shows how practices of uncertainty influence the artistic production process. Even though the working method of 'asking questions' and the temporal structure of how the pieces were developed became routine over time, it did not change the liberating, productive power of situative practices of (un)certainty. Pina Bausch's working methods reflect a performative understanding of dance and choreography: individual scenes were not intended to be acted out, depicted or presented, but were rather meant to be made, created and generated anew in every performance. Perhaps the methods of the Tanztheater Wuppertal are the realization of the idea that (un-)certainty is not an essential term and can be described not as a state, but as a constant practice of (un)settling, which challenges the subject to show itself in new and different ways. Ultimately, the production practices of the Tanztheater Wuppertal also give rise to a fundamental consideration: that certainty is inherent to every uncertainty and that the production of certainty must be conceived of from the margins, from the idea that becoming secure and being assured can only ever be achieved through performative practices of uncertainty.

Choreographic development as translation

Developing pieces with the Tanztheater Wuppertal under Pina Bausch was a constant and complex process of translating: from situative, everyday, cultural experience into dance and choreography, between language and movement, movement and writing, between various languages and cultures, and between different media and materials. Pina Bausch developed an artistic working method with the Tanztheater Wuppertal, whose practices – on-site research, 'asking questions,' trying out ideas – have been adopted by choreographers and directors worldwide and thus have in turn themselves also gained many new facets of translation. This working method was an initial act of aesthetic positing. It was followed by a second act of aesthetic positing, which was just as radical for its time: the introduction of the compositional method of montage – which had previously been used in film, especially in Russian constructivist films, and in the plays of Bertolt Brecht – to choreography, as it was also being attempted in dance at the time by artists such as Merce Cunningham, albeit in a different way. Not only did this new working method abandon the dramaturgy of linear narrative structure and introduce the fragmentary into dance dramaturgy, it also decentralized theatrical space, replacing the central perspective with multiple centers. It found ways to allow differences to stand side by side while also making them compatible with each other, and balanced out the subjectivity of individual dancers and the collectivity of the ensemble.

The working method used by the Tanztheater Wuppertal to develop pieces were process-oriented and not bound to a specific topic. They aligned with the needs of the company members and their subjective, everyday perceptions, experiences and specific skills. Pina Bausch once said: "I do always have to think of my dancers as well, and if one of them only has one big scene in a piece,

I can't throw that scene out as long as the dancer is still a member of the ensemble."[44] However, in the interviews that I conducted with dancers, a few of them admitted that they were ashamed if they could not come up with good responses to the 'questions' posed during rehearsals and that there were cases of silent jealousy when other dancers were given strong roles. They also confirmed that they were sometimes afraid that what they had shown would not be selected for the piece or would only be considered in passing. In a public talk organized for the exhibition *Pina Bausch and the Tanztheater* at the Bundeskunsthalle in Bonn,[45] which included a 'faithful' reconstruction of the Lichtburg and thus a musealization of their current workplace, the dancers Azusa Seyama, Fernando Suels Mendoza and Kenji Takagi vividly described this precarious situation of uncertainty, which could sometimes stretch for months and even up until the day of the premiere. In some cases, the disappointment of some dancers when their material was not considered led them to leave the company. While it was rare for Pina Bausch to directly dismiss a dancer herself, not including or only tolerating their material in the piece was a means of encouraging them to move on. Sometimes, a particular passage was then cut out in retrospect.

The artistic working method also required a radical collaborative approach, which, especially in the early years, was extremely unusual at the time. "Dare More Democracy" – this important slogan, which summed up chancellor Willy Brandt's 1969 governing policy at the peak of the student movement, also began making itself felt in dance: a young generation of artists began to loudly question the classical German theater system while shaking up its rigid, hierarchical structures. As chief choreographer of the Tanztheater Darmstadt, Gerhard Bohner (1936-1992) and his company developed the piece *Lilith* in 1972, featuring in the role of Lilith and as a kind of anti-ballerina the well-known ballerina Silvia Kesselheim, who had joined Gerhard Bohner after dancing with the Staatsoper Hamburg, the Stuttgarter Ballett and the Deutsche Oper in Berlin. The choreographer and his ensemble viewed the Darmstadt company's first production as an experiment. With participation as its theme, the performance attempted to involve the audience in the creation of the choreography by making the rehearsal process transparent and thus exposing ballet as a theatrical illusion of superficial beauty. The experiment in Darmstadt failed, and Silvia Kesselheim went on to join the Tanztheater Wuppertal in 1983, as did Marion Cito (→ COMPANY). Formerly first soloist at the Deutsche Oper in West Berlin, Marion Cito moved to Darmstadt in order to specifically work with Gerhard Bohner. In 1976, she accepted a position as a dancer with the Tanztheater Wuppertal and later assumed full responsibility for the costumes of the company after the death of Rolf Borzik. Overcoming power structures within theater institutions was immensely important to the artistic work of both Gerhard Bohner and Pina Bausch. At the same time, it provided a constant source of conflict, especially during the early years, with the orchestra and the choir, who found the new dance aesthetics to be extremely suspect, and the stage technicians, who did not want to go down this new and unfamiliar path with her. Thus, the artistic collaborators who really did accompany and support her were all the more important. Using her working method, Pina Bausch sought to achieve a balance between the individual and the collective, the latter becoming very diverse due to the multiculturalism of her dancers. Of course, other companies have had similar structures, but in the case of the Tanztheater Wuppertal under Pina Bausch, the collaborative method of working across cultures on the basis of individual experience meant that cultural translation itself became a fundamental aesthetic principle.

Moreover, certain routines established themselves over the long periods that artistic collaborators such as Hans Pop, Marion Cito, Peter Pabst and Matthias Burkert, and organizational staff members such as Claudia Irman, Sabine Hesseling and Ursula Popp worked with the company. Some dancers, such as Jan Minařík, Dominique Mercy, Lutz Förster and Nazareth Panadero, who were members of the company for far longer than an average dancer's career, namely for 20 to almost 40 years – in some cases, with interruptions – made a significant contribution to generating, establishing and passing on specific behaviors, practices and routines that proved to be crucial to and influential on the aesthetics of the Tanztheater Wuppertal and the collective identity of the company. These included dancers' spots and "corners" in the Lichtburg, the standard workday as it evolved over decades with training and "critique" of the previous night's performance,[46] the research trips, and the way that rehearsals and performances were run. The consistency with which dancers performed their roles and staged specific characters over the course of many years – such as Julie Shanahan's "hysterical woman" and Eddie Martinez's "happy boy" – and the way in which dancers like Rainer Behr and Kenji Takagi were able to develop their own incomparable language of movement in their solos, was and is also unusual, if not even unique for dance companies of this size.

In particular, the decades of collaboration within the company illustrate that forms of artistic collaboration are always 'models of reality' as well. They reveal which practices have been possible for artists in which periods of history: a company the size of the Tanztheater Wuppertal, with some of the same people working together for decades, is a historical relic at the beginning of the 21st century, in the age of neoliberal arts policies and project- and network-based working methods. The forms of collectivity that have been practiced in the ensemble and that have found their way into the artistic practices are therefore different to the collective practices generated within the context of project- and network-based artistic work. Against the backdrop of the difficulties that renowned choreographers such as William Forsythe and Sasha Waltz had continuing their companies in the 2010s,[47] it seems all the more remarkable that Pina Bausch was able to retain and finance her large dance theater ensemble of more than 30 dancers and employees for so many years. The generous support of the Goethe-Institut, which no longer grants such assistance to choreographers, not even to the Tanztheater Wuppertal, made a significant contribution to these developments. And so, the extent of the company's touring activities and the extremely broad international response to this singular German dance company remain unrivalled to this day.

Passing on choreographies

In November 2018, the company performed the piece *Nefés*, which had premiered in 2003, at the Teatro Alfa in São Paulo, Brazil. At that point in time, the piece had 20 performers (at the premiere there had been 19), ten female and ten male dancers. It was a special piece in the history of the Tanztheater Wuppertal, for in 2009 the company had been toured the same piece in Poland. On the day of the third and final performance of *Nefés* at the Opera House in Wroclaw, the members of the ensemble learned that Pina Bausch had died that morning in Wuppertal. It quickly became clear that they would not cancel the show that evening in spite of their deep shock. The dancers wanted to dance – for Pina Bausch. They performed the piece that evening and then finished the tour, which subsequently took them to Spoleto and Moscow. As Cornelia Albrecht, general manager of the Tanztheater Wuppertal at the time, remembers, it was an "unforgettable event and experience, the way this wonderful company danced after its great loss."[48] *Nefés* means 'breath' in Turkish – living, living on, even if Pina Bausch, the unquestioned heart of the Tanztheater Wuppertal cosmos, had stopped beating.

When *Nefés* was shown in São Paulo, the piece had already completed 15 tours[49] and had been shown repeatedly in Wuppertal. In São Paulo, the premiere began at 9:00 p.m., which was rather unusual for Pina Bausch's long pieces. Starting earlier would not have made sense in São Paulo in general and especially not at the beautiful, remote Teatro Alfa, located to the south of the urban metropolis. Given the constant traffic chaos on a weekday, the trip to the theater promised to be long and grueling for most of the audience members after their normal workday. However, the late start also meant that the presenters had to choose a piece that did not last for four hours, like many other Pina Bausch pieces. *Nefés* only runs for 2 hours and 50 minutes. As in the case of other pieces, the roles of the individual dancers in *Nefés* had also been passed on over the years, sometimes even two to three times. The situation in São Paulo was special, as only eight of the dancers from the original cast were still performing. Around half of the group now consisted of young dancers who had joined the company after Pina Bausch's death, most of whom had therefore never met the choreographer in person. Héléna Pikon and Robert Sturm, who had already assisted Pina Bausch in the original development of the piece, now conducted the rehearsals. For weeks and months, individual roles and dances were passed on and rehearsed in Wuppertal, with another two rehearsals and a general rehearsal in São Paulo.

How are pieces, roles, scenes and dances passed on and what happens during this process? These kinds of questions are of particular importance to the artists who feel responsible for this process of 'passing on.' But these questions have also become an important subject of discussion in dance studies within the contexts of other questions such as: what are the aesthetic limitations that reveal themselves in the process of passing on choreography? How is it possible to pass on material, and what means and methods are required? In this respect, passing on dance and choreography is not only an everyday practice of the Tanztheater Wuppertal but also a central object of discourse in contemporary dance. However, academic debate has so far mainly concentrated on archives, and forms and cultures of memory.[50]

Since the birth of modern concert dance at the beginning of the 20th century, from the postmodern dance of the 1960s to the contemporary dance that has emerged since the 1990s, the crucial question has been: how can works that are intimately bound to the subjectivity, life experience and individual style of specific choreographers be preserved and passed on? For unlike in the visual arts, a 'work' of dance is physically linked to individual authors, choreographers or dancers, and to the dancing bodies that make it visible and tangible in performance. Unlike dramatic theater – which is a spatial and temporal art form that, like dance, only exists in performance – modern and contemporary dance pieces like those of Pina Bausch are not based on a script or text that requires translation into a theatrical language or framework. The difficulty in passing on choreography and dance lies in the fact that, unlike in the case of ballet, they are only rarely based on a fixed movement technique. Moreover, in contrast to classical ballet, there is usually no notation of the works – even of the pieces of Pina Bausch – that might help to reconstruct them. Film recording technology developed almost parallel to the emergence of modern dance, which is why there are film recordings of early modern dance. At almost the same pace as postmodern dance, VHS and digital video recording technology developed from the early 1970s and mid-1990s respectively and were also used intensively by the Tanztheater Wuppertal from the 1970s. However, there has been little consistency in the quality of this film material; moreover, most of it was not systematically compiled nor produced or archived for the specific purpose of passing on dances. This shortcoming became painfully obvious at the beginning of the 21st century, due in part to the death of great and important choreographers of Western dance history such as Maurice Béjart, Merce Cunningham and Pina Bausch, who had worked with their companies for decades. It also brought up the question of how and whether these works, which were paradigmatic and groundbreaking in the history of dance as an art form, could be passed on and thus kept alive for future generations. Some choreographers have responded to this question in the negative, emphasizing the transitory nature of dance and the historical and cultural contextualization of choreographies, which resist the musealization of dance. Merce Cunningham, who like Pina Bausch died in 2009, decreed that the Merce Cunningham Dance Company, which he founded in 1953, would go on a final two-year farewell tour after his death and then disband.[51] The estate of the Cunningham Dance Foundation and the intellectual property rights to his pieces were then transferred to the Merce Cunningham Trust, which now grants leading dance companies the rights to perform Cunningham's works and thus facilitates the dissemination of Cunningham's choreographies.

The legacy of Pina Bausch presents a very different case. Passing on her material was not a major, challenging task that the Tanztheater Wuppertal was only confronted with after her death. The passing on of roles and choreographies had already played a major role in the work of the choreographer, her assistants and the company for many years prior to her death. Pina Bausch's credo was to preserve the pieces, to keep them in the repertoire and to perform them again and again. She wanted the 'old' to constantly be translated into something 'new.' In this way, she also introduced younger generations of dancers to each respective piece and its specific performance practices and socialized above all those who came from other dance traditions into the corporeal and dance aesthetics of the Tanztheater Wuppertal.

These restagings, which sought to perpetuate the temporal art of dance, distinguished Pina Bausch from other choreographers. The Tanztheater Wuppertal replaced the idea of the 'new' – which

13 Pina Bausch's worktable
Wuppertal, approx. 1983

had been so central to modern avant-garde art, but had always simultaneously insinuated an assault on tradition – with the idea that pieces would always become different and encounter specific audiences, that they would be received in other ways – due to changing casts and varying historical, political, cultural and situative contexts – but would still be the same pieces. Identity and difference have therefore always been one genuine component of the processes of restaging and passing on.

One central aspect of the artistic work of Pina Bausch and the Tanztheater Wuppertal was the passing on of roles, scenes, solos and group dances to new, often younger dancers, but also of entire pieces to other companies – such as *Orpheus und Eurydike* (PREMIERE 1975) and *The Rite of Spring* to the Opéra national de Paris – and to amateur dancers – such as the passing on of the piece *Kontakthof* to teenagers and senior citizens – as well as the transfer of her artistic work to other media – such as Pina Bausch's own feature film *The Plaint of the Empress* (1987) and Pedro Almodóvar's *Hable con ella* (2002) as well as countless documentary films like *What are Pina Bausch and Her Dancers Doing in Wuppertal* (1978), *One day Pina asked...* (1983), *Coffee with Pina* (2006) and *Dancing Dreams: Teenagers Perform "Kontakthof" by Pina Bausch* (2010).

In principle, acts of passing on expertise, life experience or acquired knowledge, artistic decisions or aesthetic styles all pursue the same intention: to pass on as much as possible as correctly as possible, while ensuring that the recipients understand, accept and adopt it as intended. The process of passing on – e.g., from one generation to the next – can take place orally (through narratives), in writing (through recorded statements, autobiographies, documentation, academic work) or visually (through photo, film and video material). Images and writings that document and record knowledge are especially relevant when it comes to practices of passing on across generations and cultures. This process transfers something from the communicative memory of an oral narrative culture into enduring, long-term cultural memory as described by Aleida Assmann[52] and Jan Assmann.[53]

In the process of being passed on, material but also immaterial things – such as choreographic and dance knowledge, dance and choreography – change their meaning and their value. This is above all due to the way that each individual attaches a different level of importance to and takes on a different level of responsibility for what they receive. Moreover, each time something immaterial is passed on, it is placed within a new personal, historical, social and cultural context, constantly generating new meanings and values through new framings. The relationship between translation and its framings is of great importance in this regard,[54] i.e., the questions of *how, what, when, where* and *through what* something is passed on and *how* meaning is generated in the process. Unlike material things, immaterial things are never the same once they are passed on; they lack thingness and objecthood. But like material things, which are sometimes refurbished, renovated or restored before being passed on, the aspects of immaterial things that have been lost are often reconstructed in the process of being passed on, e.g., through new sources, oral history and/or historiographic research.

Passing on dance therefore does not simply mean transferring the same object or content. Passing on is in fact a process of translation, subject to the paradoxical relationship between identity and difference: passing on is meant to transport something identical, but it can only do so by simultaneously producing difference. It is precisely this tension between identity and difference that makes the process of passing on so interesting to both artistic production and scholarship.

Passing on is based on a process of give and take. Giving and taking do not necessarily have to be a consciously designed process, as in the case of inheritance. Often the giver decides what they wish to pass on how, to whom and when. These decisions are rarely mere cognitive acts; unconscious, emotional, affective and irrational factors tend to play quite an important role. However, all these decisions made by the giver are ultimately meaningless without a taker, without someone willing to accept the legacy, to make it theirs, to bear responsibility for it. It requires people who are willing to accept something, to give it meaning, to attach value to it, to classify it as important, to nurture it and to take it into the future. Passing on thus also has something to do with transfer, transmission, distribution and dissemination, and these processes are connected to ethical and moral issues and sometimes even to aspects of sociopolitical and cultural responsibility.

These aspects of passing on have had an impact on the work of the Tanztheater Wuppertal. Passing on roles, scenes, solos and group dances to new, often younger dancers is an everyday practice in an ensemble whose members have worked together for what is now more than 40 years. The practice itself is ambivalent, as it has become a routinized workflow on the one hand while, on the other, always producing new, unstable and uncertain situations for the individual dancers passing on their dances or learning dances from others.[55] "Yes, but that has to do with the fact that some moods – say, after a cast change – simply aren't right any more. That you're then disappointed because you feel it. Time and again, pieces have slid away. But then, all of a sudden, they've been back again, and then everything has made sense again."[56]

After she became director of the Tanztheater Wuppertal, Pina Bausch did not develop any new choreographies with any other ensembles, and she only passed on two choreographies to one other company, namely *The Rite of Spring* and *Orpheus und Eurydike* to the Opéra national de Paris. Only after her death did the Pina Bausch Foundation, directed by her son Salomon Bausch, decide to pass on further pieces: *For the Children of yesterday, today and tomorrow* (PREMIERE 2002) to the Bayerisches Staatsballett for the 2016/17 season; *The Rite of Spring* to the English National Ballet in 2017; *Café Müller* (PREMIERE 1978) to Ballett Vlaanderen, the royal Flemish ballet company, for the 2016/17 season[57]; and *Iphigenie auf Tauris* to the Semperoper Dresden in 2019. In a joint project carried out in cooperation with the École des Sables of Senegalese choreographer and dancer Germaine Acogny, dancers trained in African dance studied and performed *The Rite of Spring* in spring 2020.

How is it possible to pass on art – something that is not explicit, something that cannot be categorized or objectified, but rather that claims to be open, ambiguous, polysemous, sensory, emotional, affective? How is passing on possible in the performing arts, which emphasize the momentary, the eventful, the situational? And how does the process of passing on take place in the case of dance, which is generally considered to be fleeting, ephemeral, unspeakable, the Other of language?

Practices of passing on

"Yes, of course it is very difficult to find someone to take over these different roles when dancers leave the company. Of course, you give a lot of thought to certain qualities, but you don't find the same person again. Thank God, I won't ever have to do that with some people, that would be unthinkable. [...]. Of course, if I know that someone is leaving, I try to get that person to teach the part to the other person. That's the ideal situation. The very best thing is if they study the role together before I intervene at all."[58]

The process of passing on Pina Bausch's choreographies is complex, long-term, multilayered, elaborate and expensive. It took a total of nine years to pass on the piece *For the Children of yesterday, today and tomorrow*. As she describes in an interview,[59] Bettina Wagner-Bergelt, deputy director of the Bayerisches Staatsballett at the time and artistic director of the Tanztheater Wuppertal since 2018, first considered acquiring the piece after its restaging in 2007 and even spoke with Pina Bausch about it at the time. After Pina Bausch's death, Bettina Wagner-Bergelt resumed the conversation with her son Salomon Bausch. Rehearsals began in 2014. The rehearsal phase then lasted, with interruptions, for one-and-a-half years, from fall 2014 until April 2016. It was a collective process of remembering that involved many people, including 14 dancers alone from the Tanztheater Wuppertal and – in the end, after all the dancers of the Bayerisches Staatsballett had learned their various initial roles – 28 dancers from the Bayerisches Staatsballett, i.e., two full casts. In total, the process probably involved more than 100 people, taking into account all of the other artistic and technical staff members.

There is usually notation available of choreographies from the classical ballet repertoire that companies can use. Even neoclassical ensembles, such as the Hamburg Ballett, and some modern companies work with notators or choreologists who set the pieces down in writing. The relationship between movement and writing inherent to choreo-graphy *(choros:* round dance; *graphein:* to write), which always locates choreography at the crossroads between performance and writing,[60] is not evident in Pina Bausch's choreographies. As with many modern and contemporary choreographers, there is no notation and thus also no 'script' of the movement event – and similarly, there is great skepticism on the part of choreographers toward 'postscripts,' i.e., dance reviews and academic writings, and toward their own spoken words. As translator Michel Bataillon says, Pina Bausch's words can be understood as an analogy to her pieces: "Pina Bausch's sentences are only reluctantly completed; they remain open, hovering. Strictly speaking, they even deliberately elude German syntax. They are both resolute and fragile and always clearly understandable. They are a reflection of her thoughts and thus in motion. It is this very freedom that suffers when transferred to written form, this unnatural procedure."[61] Nor did Pina Bausch herself exaggerate her own words: "In this sense, I would like to consider everything said during this conversation as a verbal attempt to understand, to encircle the unspeakable. And when this or that word is spoken then I don't want people to hold me to it; I want them to know that it was meant kind of like that, that it is only an example, but one that can mean a lot more,"[62] for, "it's something quite fragile. I'm afraid of not finding the right words for it; it's far too important to me for that. How it feels, how something is expressed or what I'm looking for – sometimes I can only find it when it finally emerges. I don't want to infringe upon that."[63] The auratic quality of dance here appears to lie in its eventfulness, singularity and unrepeatability, in the way that every single performance is sensed and felt out, which is set in opposition to texts meant for eternity.

However, passing on pieces (also) requires documentation using various media – and in the case of the Tanztheater Wuppertal, this is accomplished by means of a heterogenous range of sources and materials. It is a process of collective remembering. The way that the Tanztheater Wuppertal passes on pieces clearly demonstrates that it is a paradoxical process of translation. On the one hand, the act of passing on is intermedial, intersubjective and different every time. On the other hand, this very difference is what creates something identical: the piece that has now been passed on. The paradox between identity and difference in the translation process manifests itself in the relationship between piece and performance in particular, as well as between images and writing, video material and written records, especially considering the fact that this translation paradox is already inherent to the specific medialities of the media used to record images and words.

DANCE AND VIDEO

The Pina Bausch Archive, a suborganization of the Pina Bausch Foundation, houses approx. 7,500 videos. It is a rich and extensive collection of recordings of the rehearsals and performances of Pina Bausch's pieces. The material differs greatly in terms of its technical and aesthetic quality: for example, the condition of the images on the early videos, recorded using VHS cameras in the 1970s, is worse than more recent material. Moreover, in some cases, the camera only recorded part of what was happening onstage (especially in the case of performances, which were usually recorded using medium long shots). This is inevitably the case for pieces in which there was a lot going on at different places on the stage, in particular for Pina Bausch's early pieces, which, as is well known, were arranged using the compositional methods of montage and collage that were so innovative in the dance and theater of the 1970s. What is more, some recordings of performances were cropped at the beginning or at the end.

The longer the period of time between premiere and restaging, the more important the video recordings become, for the pieces themselves tend to vary as casts change. In other words: practices of passing on are based not only on the original production and choreography but on every single performance. Thus, the recordings of each performance – and the cast lists – become relevant when material needs to be passed on. For example, 14 dancers were involved in the premiere and development of the piece *For the Children of yesterday, today and tomorrow,* which then toured nine times between 2003 and 2015 to Paris, Tokyo (both 2003), Barcelona, New York (both 2004), Venice (2005), São Paulo (2006), Lisbon (2007), Geneva (2011) and Paris (2015). Thirteen years later, only eleven of the original cast members were still dancing in Paris. However, five new dancers had since joined the ensemble, because two roles had been split up, thereby increasing the number of dancers in the piece from 14 to 16.

Video as a medium for passing on material also harbors a fundamental translation problem: the piece is recorded from the audience perspective, which is a perspective with which most dancers are not familiar because they have always danced in the piece and, if they have seen the piece at all, have only occasionally watched from the wings. In addition, a video recorded from the perspective of the audience has to be inversely retranslated into its mirror image by the dancers in the studio. After all, video is a two-dimensional medium attempting to depict a three-dimensional performance that is a theatrical and spatial art form on the one hand and a choreography on the other, i.e., an art form of movement in time and space. Even the best video cannot properly convey the spatiality of dance, the spatial dimensions and distances that are of such elementary importance to dancers. Temporality is also a problem, because cinematic depiction has its own temporality: movement generally appears to be faster or slower, because the camera is moving along with it. This distinct temporality intensifies with shifts between close-ups and long shots. In addition, lighting conditions tend to appear differently through a camera lens and on film than when standing onstage (and different again in photos of the set, for example). Last but not least, film editing techniques can also change the timing and spatial positions of recorded movements.

As these examples show, video does not reproduce something. Instead, the specific mediality of video, i.e., its mode of representation, already inscribes a difference into what it seeks to depict. Video promises identical reproduction, a visual depiction of the real, but actually produces a simulacrum (→ THEORY AND METHODOLOGY). Due to these disruptions in media translation, video can only be a starting point that conveys a first impression of a piece or a scene when passing on pieces, providing an overview of the piece or helping to clarify a detail.

DANCE AND PHOTOS

Photos of pieces by the Tanztheater Wuppertal, of which tens of thousands exist, can be another productive source of material for passing on pieces, for example in relation to costumes or props. Most photos of the pieces have been taken by a few professional photographers who have worked with the company for many years, such as Ulli Weiss and Gert Weigelt. From the beginning, dancer Jan Minařík also took many photos, as did set designer Peter Pabst later on. In addition, there are countless photos that have been taken by dancers, but also by Pina Bausch, who took photos – and shot some videos – during research trips. However, these photos are only stills of movements, situations and scenes, or snapshots of research

Nazareth walk dance Daphnis kungfu scream

When everyone gets up the music starts again. Daphnis walks portal left, then he goes into the center and begins dancing. Nazareth begins her "walk" again. She walks around Daphnis.

Daphnis dance

*At the end of his dance
Daphnis sits down by the heap (1) and moves his left arm. (Clap-dance movement) He watches Nazareth while doing so. Then he walks in front of the heap (2) and repeats the arm movement
Nazareth goes to the back in the center,
Daphnis goes to Nazareth.
Daphnis carries Nazareth with his left arm on her back, his right hand under her legs
Daphnis walks with Nazareth to the front.*

14 Prompt book for *The Window Washer* compiled by assistant Irene Martinez-Rios

Nazareth Gang   Tanz Daphnis Kungfu Schrei

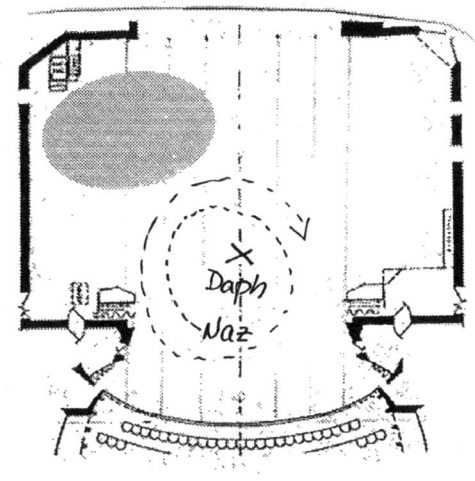

Wenn alle aufstehen setzt die Musik wieder ein. Daphnis läuft Portal links, dann geht er in die Mitte und fängt an zu tanzen.
Nazareth fängt mit ihrem "Gong" wieder an. Sie geht um Daphnis herum.

Tanz Daphnis

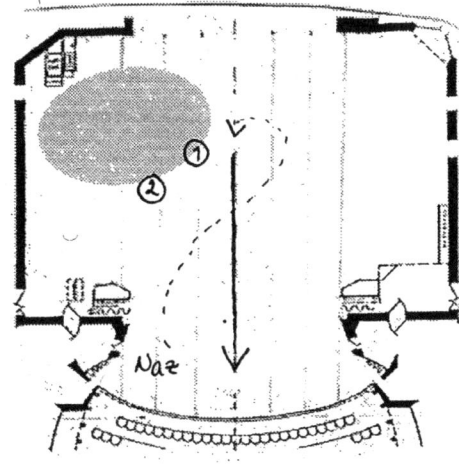

Am Ende seines Tanzes setzt sich Daphnis an den Berg ① und bewegt den linken Arm. (Klatschtanzbewegung) Dabei guckt er Nazareth an. Dann geht er vor dem Berg ② und wiederholt der Armbewegung. Nazareth geht nach hinten in der Mitte, Daphnis geht zu Nazareth.

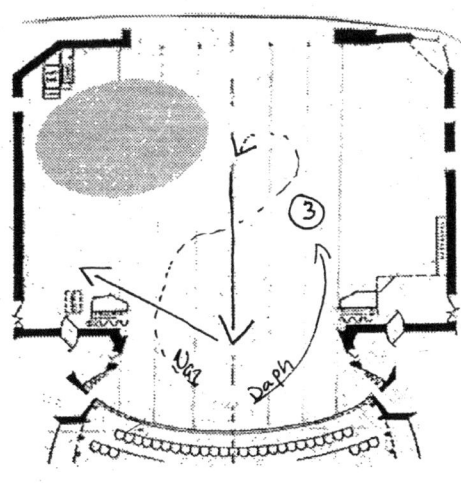

Daphnis trägt Nazareth mit seinem linken Arm an ihrem Rücken, die rechte Hand unter ihren Beinen. Daphnis läuft mit Nazareth nach vorne.

Palermo Nov. 2000 + São Paulo Dez. 2000

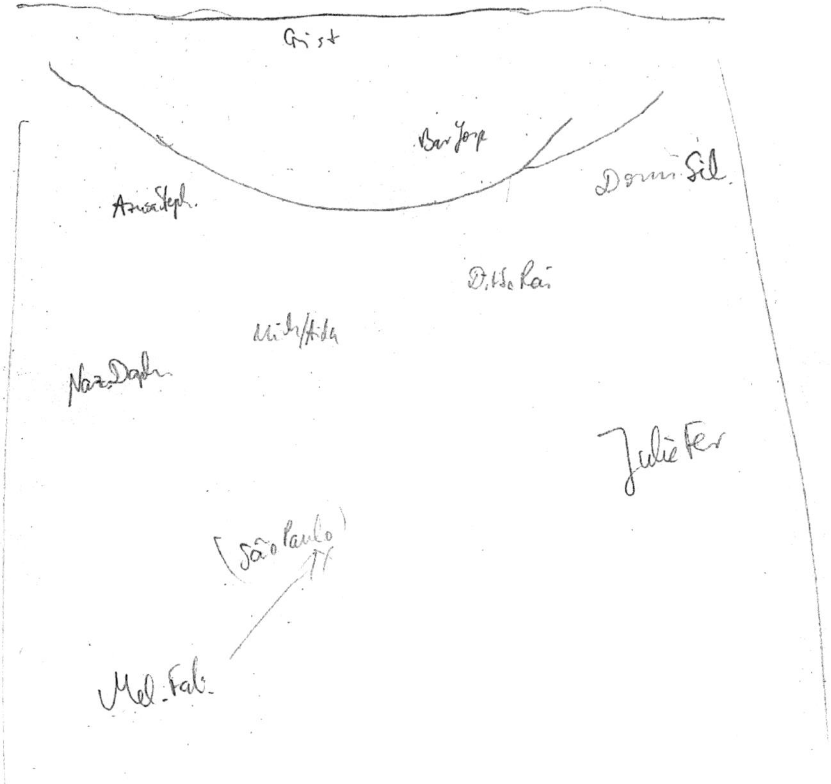

Gist

Bar/Jorge   Dorin-Sil.

Anna/Steph.

D. Ilse/Rai

Mich/Ada

Naz/Daph

Julie/Fer

(São Paulo)

Mel-Fab.

Hong Kong getaucht   Mel - Jorge
                      Anna - Fab.

Chile: Jorge - Sil
        Ken - Az
        Daph - Naz
        Pan - Ana
        Rai - Ditta
        Fer - J St.
        Dori - Ruth

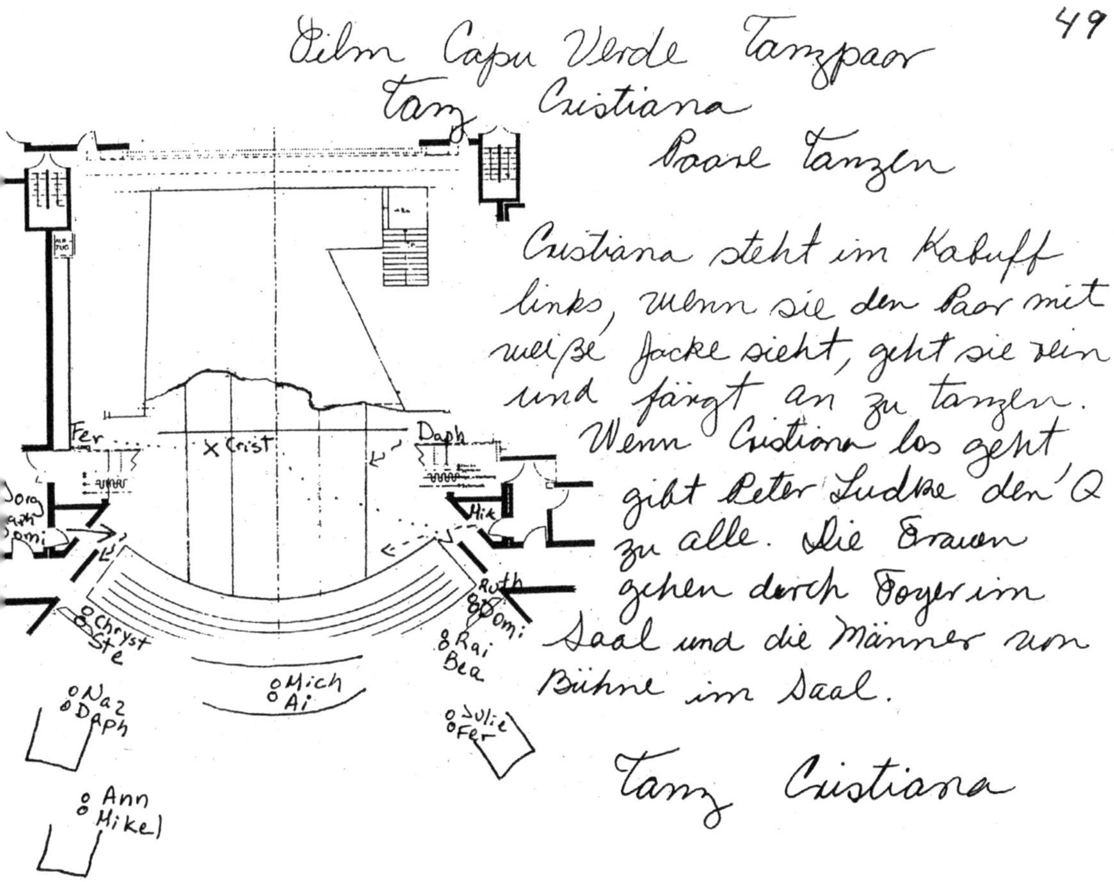

Film Capo Verde Tanzpaar
tanz Cristiana
Paare tanzen

Cristiana steht im Kabuff
links, wenn sie den Paar mit
weiße Jacke sieht, geht sie rein
und fängt an zu tanzen.
Wenn Cristiana los geht
gibt Peter Ludtke den Q
zu alle. Die Frauen
gehen durch Foyer in
Saal und die Männer von
Bühne in Saal.

Tanz Cristiana

15 Prompt book for *Masurca Fogo* compiled by assistant Irene Martinez-Rios Notes (LEFT PAGE) penciled in by Robert Sturm while passing on the piece

Film Capu Verde   Dancing couple
Dance Cristiana
Couples dancing

Cristiana stands to the left of the hut,
when she sees the couple with
the white jacket, she goes in
and begins to dance.
When Cristiana starts,
Peter Lütke gives everyone the Q.
The women
go through the foyer into
the auditorium and the men in front of
the stage into the auditorium.

Dance Cristiana

16 Translation of prompt book
   for *Masurca Fogo;*
   SEE PREVIOUS PAGE

trips, which merely provide an indication of what the company saw and what individual company members may have incorporated into a particular production. The paths of translation are once more twisted and tangled: the dancers never directly translated their experiences one-to-one, nor did they reflect on the relationships between what they came up with during rehearsals and what they had seen, experienced or learned. The 'why' question that occupies reception – the audience, critics (→ RECEPTION) and academia (→ THEORY AND METHODOLOGY) – is not only of little relevance to the artistic process but is in fact detrimental to it, because it is too restrictive, too authoritative, too definitive.

All things considered, these insights into the available written and visual material demonstrate one of the fundamental problems of passing on choreography using media: there is a vast amount of images, films and written material available that not only need to be collected, digitized and archived but also generated, e.g., by using oral history methods to interview dancers. The next necessary step would then be to evaluate them in order to judge their relevance for the long-term reconstruction of dance pieces. This requires academic expertise on the one hand and, on the other, intense collaboration from those who originally created the material – the dancers and the people responsible for costumes, set designs, stage technology and props – as well as the people who accompanied the production every night (stage managers, etc.). In this respect, the activity of processing and completing the materials used to pass on pieces is also subject to a severe time restriction, namely the presence of 'generation Pina,' if I may call it that: the people who personally accompanied the choreographer's work.

DANCE AND WRITING

There is no notation and there are no scores of Pina Bausch's pieces, but there are a large number of written and visual notes made by various people. The written materials that exist for individual pieces are therefore also extremely different. On the one hand, there are vast notes written by Pina Bausch herself and kept in her still inaccessible, private archive. I gained some idea of what these notes look like during the various interviews that I conducted and from a few photos that I was allowed to see, fragments of which are reproduced in the book *Tanz erben*.[64] Further insights were provided in the exhibition *Pina Bausch und das Tanztheater*.[65] Other written material that can be important for passing on pieces are dancers' and assistants' rehearsal notes and stage managers' logbooks and scripts, as well as the lists of the music featured in the performances, although the latter still need to be completed and compared. Moreover, Andreas

Eisenschneider tended to combine pieces of music into larger musical collages with fluid transitions – especially in later pieces – thus making it difficult to clearly distinguish individual pieces of music from one another (→ COMPANY).

DANCE AND LANGUAGE

The translation paradox between identity and difference is already evident in the written, visual and film material. However, in the process of passing on choreographies, these only have an introductory, commemorative and control function. In the case of the Tanztheater Wuppertal in particular, where many scenes and all solos were developed by the dancers themselves, the process of orally and physically passing on material from person to person is crucial. It is here in particular that the fragility and ambiguity of translation in processes of passing on, which are accompanied by the paradox between identity and difference, reveal themselves, together with their artistic productivity.

When pieces by Pina Bausch have been passed on, it has been a multistep process. Former dancers took on responsibility for passing on material while the choreographer was still alive. Bénédicte Billiet and Jo Ann Endicott did so for *Kontakthof with Teenagers*, as did Dominique Mercy for the process of passing on *The Rite of Spring* to the Opéra national de Paris. Of course, Pina Bausch as the choreographer of the piece and the final authority had the last word in the rehearsals that she attended. A wonderful scene in the film *Dancing Dreams* (2010) illustrates this: excited and nervous, Jo Ann Endicott, Bénédicte Billiet and the young dancers wait for Pina Bausch to comment on the results of the rehearsals. She says: "[...] like introducing yourself, with the hips or step with the hips. Such things, where the eyes are really looking straight ahead ... and, and that's, like ... so we put on a poker face ... You don't know what someone is thinking. Cold, isn't it ... and actually serious. But in some cases, ... your eyes are wandering around too much..."[66] but also: "I have a lot of confidence in them. What could go wrong? They will do their very best, and I love them, and even if something is wrong, it doesn't matter."[67]

Sometimes, Pina Bausch directed these rehearsals herself, for example in emergencies, like when the dancer who was meant to dance the victim/sacrifice in *The Rite of Spring* became unavailable and Kyomi Ichida quickly had to learn the role. The various physical and linguistic practices used here clearly demonstrate that passing on dance is a process that mixes dancing and speaking, therefore taking place as a hybrid process of speaking and dancing. However, both are only hinted at, only merging into a comprehensive whole that the recipient can understand during the act of passing on.

In addition, passing on takes place very differently with even the use of language varying widely. While Jo Ann Endicott uses imperatives to pass on her solo from *Kontakthof* to the teenage dancer Joy Wonnenberg – "Joy, you must [...]"[68] – attempting to teach her the movement quality in this way, Pina Bausch concentrates on the movements when passing on the "Sacrificial Dance" of *The Rite of Spring,* which she demonstrates perfectly – wearing gumboots, with a cigarette in one hand and an old aviator's cap on her head – without charging them thematically, emotionally or visually. Instead, she accentuates her movements with sentence fragments and snatches of speech:

"Pina Bausch: The second time... you take up your position,
　　　　make yourself rounder and stretch... too far... think about
　　　　not going too far. Yes... yes, that's it... and then... two...
Kyomi Ichida: Ok: fine.
Pina Bausch: Tata tata ta ta, there. But you don't have to...
　　　　Don't think about it. Don't do the arms extra. You didn't
　　　　do it right with the music just now. It's really two...
　　　　and well accented, okay? Yes. Tata ta ta. Yes. Spare yourself here
　　　　for a moment, perhaps just do it from somewhere here...
Kyomi Ichida: Yes.
Pina Bausch: And then we'll carry on with this one.
Kyomi Ichida: Too late.
Pina Bausch: Yes, overall you were a bit late this time,
　　　　compared to last time you took a different...
Kyomi Ichida: At this moment?
Pina Bausch: Yes, you were too late. But you also have to
　　　　mark a difference here, so... Play, play it again,
　　　　where there's a... that's the trumpet, isn't it?"[69]

While this was a face-to-face situation between two people, the differences that manifest themselves in different modes of passing on are all the more pronounced when several translators come into play, for example, when solos, essentially developed by individual dancers, are passed on and the new dancers experience different approaches to their part in the piece. Passing on takes place very individually from dancer to dancer and also differs in each partner constellation: one couple might communicate its role through form, the next through technique and the other using a richly metaphorical language, while some do it analytically. Some speak a lot about what the dance or the scene means to them, what they feel doing it; some do not speak about it at all. Nazareth Panadero remembers passing on her role in the piece *For the Children of yesterday, today and tomorrow* to the dancers of the Bayerisches Staatsballett: "It was difficult for us in the beginning, because Marta and Mia had never done anything like it. I wanted to encourage them. They should discover their talents [...]. What was important to me wasn't the external similarities, but rather whether we could discover a similarity in temperament and character."[70]

It is not just when working with other companies but also within the ensemble of the Tanztheater Wuppertal that dancers sometimes pass their roles on to other dancers who may have learned and habituated another technique, such as company members who have not trained at Folkwang Hochschule and are therefore not really familiar with the Jooss-Leeder method, or the dancers of the Bayerisches Staatsballett, who were trained in classical ballet techniques. Some dancers have attempted to explain the technique and quality of a movement using the vocabulary of the Jooss-Leeder method, like Stephan Brinkmann, who impressively demonstrated during his lecture at the international conference *Dance Future II*[71] in Hamburg how he passed on his solo from the piece *Masurca Fogo* to dancer Julian Stierle. Moreover, due to the dancers' different countries of origin and varying command of German and English, additional language barriers have led to things being understood in different ways. It is not possible to identify any supraindividual routines or schemata in terms of how things are passed on. What we do see are practices that are individual, personal and intimate, that are based on direct physical acts of passing on in face-to-face situations and that view this approach as the basis of a high-quality process of passing on that remains true to the original.

DANCE AND BODY/VOICE

Aside from cultural and technical difficulties, differences between generations ultimately play a decisive role as well: even within the Tanztheater Wuppertal, younger generations of dancers are more athletic than the first generation was at the same age in the 1970s. This athleticism – which found its way into concert dance in the 1980s and which younger dancers have since incorporated as a habitual disposition, much like the techniques in which they have trained – influences how they interpret roles. As Pina Bausch herself said, it is less about understanding than it is about corporeally grasping the role: "I am interested in grasping something, perhaps without understanding it."[72] The dancers now assuming the roles also have different body types: they are larger, smaller, thinner or fatter; they also have different bodies when it comes to, for example, their proportions, the length of their limbs or the strength of their bone structure. Figures of movement change as a result. One example of this is the way that Marta Navarrete and Mia Rudic, dancers from the Bayerisches Staatsballett, adopted Nazareth Panadero's role, dancing in the A and

B casts of the piece *For the Children of yesterday, today and tomorrow*. Even scenes in which the relationship between body and voice plays a decisive role change, as in many of the scenes by Mechthild Großmann, Lutz Förster and Nazareth Panadero, as it is the voice that creates and names the subject by making subjectivity audible.

Pina Bausch gave the following analogy of voice and dance: "I don't really know why singing, the human voice is so important to me. It affects me in a similar way to dance, it is so fragile, so vulnerable, so touching or soothing. I love bringing both of them together."[73]

How would Marta Navarrete and Mia Rudic be perceived if they were not speaking onstage? How does the character with the harsh, staccato-like High German voice change that Lutz Förster developed for pieces such as *1980* or *For the Children of yesterday, today and tomorrow* when someone speaks his text with a softer voice and a distinct accent?

Moreover, in many of Pina Bausch's pieces, the person passing on the solo is no longer the same person who originally developed it, but a member of the second cast or even of the third generation of dancers. In other words, the solo has already repeatedly undergone a multistep process of translation. This was different when the piece *For the Children of yesterday, today and tomorrow* was passed on to the Bayerisches Staatsballett: here it was the original cast of the world premiere that passed on the material to the dancers in Munich, aiming to make it 'authentic,' 'real' and 'original.' Some of the dancers contributing to this process of passing on the material were therefore dancers who had not danced for quite some time and now had to readjust to the situation of being a dancer and of finding their way back into their specific roles.

Even the dancers still dancing in the company had to reconstruct, or better: reenact their part and their dance at the beginning of rehearsals in 2014, twelve years after the premiere of *For the Children of yesterday, today and tomorrow* – in other words, they had to relearn their roles using their bodies. This was not an easy thing to do, for minor details (like where they should be looking when their eyes are closed) determine the quality of the individual movements. Perhaps they even reconstructed the 'questions' that Pina Bausch had asked during the original rehearsals for the piece, such as *Shaking someone awake*, *Something on your mind*, *Making yourself small*, *Joyfully destroying something* and *Children playing grown-up*.

In this respect, the authentic should not be regarded as something essential, but rather as a creative practice that is framed differently by each dancer. On the other hand, we also see here that passing on is always based on determinants that only allow the original and the authentic to be identified in retrospect. Walter Benjamin said the same in his paradigmatic text *The Task of the Trans-*

lator: "For in its continuing life, which could not be so called if it were not the transformation and renewal of a living thing, the original is changed."[74] In this sense, passing on presents itself as a permanent process of translation, a constant series of new positings.

These translation steps clearly reveal that the idea of an 'authentic copy,' of a 'primary original' becomes obsolete in the process of passing on, even though the company meticulously pursued norms of authenticity and of being true to the original, especially after the death of Pina Bausch. Instead, the practice of passing on takes into account the paradox between identity and difference: differences are accepted in the interpretation of a role, but dance parameters such as movement quality, expressiveness, intensity, accentuation and timing should be identical. Authenticity and identity are in turn generated by the fact that the dancers, for example, use their own names onstage while retaining the language of the original cast, even if it is not their 'mother tongue,' as in the piece *1980*, which begins with a scene in which Polish dancer Janusz Subicz spoons soup out of a large terrine, saying, "Pour Papa, pour Maman," while raising the spoon to his mouth. American dancer Eddie Martinez, who later assumed this role, still recites the text in French.

Between identity and difference

This play between identity and difference also refutes the criticism of those who claim that it is impossible to pass on roles tied to individual dancers. For the sheer number of roles passed on for restagings clearly demonstrates that the issue is neither the subjectivity nor the specific character of an individual dancer, in spite of the fact that both were of central importance in the original development of the piece, for the choreographer as well. However, what ultimately constitutes the piece is its colors, contrasts and oppositions, fleshed out by the various subjective 'answers' to the 'questions.' Journalists, critics and scholars have often argued that Pina Bausch's dancers developed their roles from their situative, personal worlds of feeling and experiences and in their own names. However, what is passed on in practice is the form and above all the specific movement quality that the form requires in order for it to become dance (→ SOLO DANCE). Personality and character are embedded in this form. Bringing it to life means having the ability to recreate the specific quality of expression and movement associated with the form.

If we were to consider the choreography or the individual solo as a purely subjective affair, it would be nothing more than the private matter of the person who made it. But such a point of view is too simplistic and beside the point, for the private here transcends the realm of subjective experience, not only by becoming the political (→ PIECES) but also because of the way in which the private translates itself into a form that takes on different "colors," as Pina Bausch called her dancer's movement qualities, while moreover revealing itself as a work of art to the public eye.

There is no doubt that passing on individual solos and scenes also changes them. Translating these individual parts in the piece in such a way that the choreography retains its quality and identity is something that Pina Bausch always took the liberty of doing – modifying, rearranging the piece and sometimes even leaving out sections. Since her death, this single, all-decisive voice has been missing. No one has come forward (yet) to claim authority over the one, correct interpretation of her choreographic oeuvre, since nobody, neither dancers nor close collaborators, had decision-making power in the development of the choreography itself. Up until her death, few dancers had seen the pieces from the outside or in their entire length. This has since changed, as many dancers have assumed responsibility for rehearsals, usually those who were already involved as assistants in the development of specific pieces and/or who have passed their roles on to other dancers. In the same way that artistic productions rarely manage to get by without explicit hierarchies or clear power structures, so does the process of passing on require a clear assignment of responsibilities and distribution of power, even when it is collectively organized.

In this respect, a first point of orientation was chosen after Pina Bausch's death: the last version of the piece, the last performance before her death is generally taken as a frame of reference. However, this fixes something in place that Pina Bausch herself would probably have opened up again, as she consistently did during her lifetime when roles had to be recast or other stage requirements needed to be met. Being faithful to an ostensible original in terms of fixing it in place therefore would not have corresponded at all to her own artistic process. As nobody has yet come forward who is able and willing to manage this alone, rehearsal management teams have been formed to organize the process of passing on the pieces, such as the team comprising dancers Ruth Amarante, Daphnis Kokkinos und Azusa Seyama for *For the Children of yesterday, today and tomorrow*. Daphnis Kokkinos had already assisted in the development of the piece in 2002, Azusa Seyama danced in the original cast, and Ruth Amarante joined them to pass on the piece to the Bayerisches Staatsballett.

Other protagonists involved in the development of the pieces have also helped to pass on these pieces to other companies and theaters: for example, the general manager of the company; set designer Peter Pabst; costume designer Marion Cito; Robert Sturm, artistic collaborator on all of Pina Bausch's new pieces since 1999; and Matthias Burkert, who was always responsible for stage management. The latter three were also the people who most frequently saw the pieces from the outside, but they too have clear areas of responsibility: the clothes have to be tailor-made for the new dancers, which can be difficult if the fabric is no longer available, the set has to be transmitted into a new stage design, and the choreography of the lights readapted to the set. Since Peter Pabst's sets often contain mobile elements or elaborate materials, someone has to verify whether the venue will be able to implement the original design at all. The tasks of the stage manager have to be passed on, even though stage management in Pina Bausch's pieces is a very dynamic, musical and rhythmic responsibility that encompasses the lighting, the set, the music and elaborate choreographic structures in which temporality plays a major role. What is being carried out here in the artistic practices of passing on a piece is a kind of oral history.

In this respect, the variance and openness, fragility and delicacy inherent to the process of passing on are affected by various temporal layers that combine with each other during this process: the first one is the 'here and now' in which, firstly, the piece is passed on and, secondly, a piece is performed that has to hold its own onstage with these dancers. The second temporality is that of the choreography, the memory and reenactment of Pina Bausch's art and her dancers' inventiveness at the time. The third and final temporal layer is that of the dancers of the Tanztheater Wuppertal themselves, who last danced these roles in 2016, i.e., 14 years after the premiere – at almost the same time as the dancers of the Bayerisches Staatsballett. Generally speaking, 14 years is almost half of a dance career, and the piece once specially developed with the younger dancers of the Tanztheater Wuppertal is now being danced in a completely different way by the same dancers 14 years later; changes in physical energy and physique, but also in experience, and shifting relationships to their own bodies make it different. And the young dancers of the Bayerisches Staatsballet dance it differently yet again to the way that it was danced by the young dancers of the Tanztheater Wuppertal back then, as they have received a different kind of technical training and have not experienced the entire collective work process.

The program booklet of the Bayerisches Staatsballett notes that the choreography of *For the Children of yesterday, today and tomorrow* was passed on on a one-on-one basis. However, 14 dancers from the Tanztheater Wuppertal passed on their roles to 28 dancers from the Bayerisches Staatsballett, so 'one-on-one' here in fact means one person passing on their role to two people. However, what the phrase actually means is that the material was passed on directly in interpersonal encounters. The goal was to adopt the finished role that is associated with a specific person exactly as is while simultaneously staying true to oneself. The paradox between identity and difference was thus experienced in practice. A decision was made in order to allow the dancers to appear as subjects onstage: they would dance the roles of others, but use their own names. And so, the paradox between identity and difference also reveals itself in the relationship between giver and taker, between the Other and the Self.

In all conversations and interviews, the dancers of the Bayerisches Staatsballett emphasized how important and unusual this personal process of passing on was while they were learning the choreography, especially in contrast to other prominent choreographies by artists such as Gerhard Bohner, Mary Wigman, Richard Siegal, John Cranko and Jerôme Robbins, whose works the Bayerisches Staatsballett had previously studied. In interviews and conversations, dancers from both companies describe the working process as being once in a lifetime, unique, open, intense, stimulating and surprising. The dancers of the Bayerisches Staatsballett believed that they had discovered new possibilities within themselves. They felt inspired and deeply touched by the rehearsal period – precisely because they were able to work so directly with individual dancers and in this way become familiar with the aesthetics of the Tanztheater Wuppertal. Passing on always entails a transfer of values, identities and perceptions as well. In the age of digitalization and anonymous communication, this corporeal practice of passing on is a privileged and almost anachronistic process, not only because the procedure is immensely expensive, but also because young dancers can directly learn from famous role models and have the chance to personally work with them one-on-one.

Practices of learning: *The Rite of Spring*

The choreography *The Rite of Spring* is far more than just a piece.[75] It is an ephemeral historical document that connects the transience of the individual performance with the choreography itself and with the longevity of its performance over a period of what has now been more than 40 years. *The Rite of Spring* is an artistic masterpiece and simultaneously, with the sacrificial victim and social sacrifice as its subject matter, a "surface phenomenon," as defined by Siegfried Kracauer,[76] something singular that provides insights into the general, into the substance of the society and culture in which the piece is shown and perceived by an audience. In this sense, although the piece stages the sacrificial victim as female, the question of what a sacrifice means and how sacrifice takes place in the community is perceived differently in different cultural, political, social and situative contexts, which is demonstrated by the piece's decades-long reception history.

The quantitative data on *The Rite of Spring* alone is overwhelming: the piece, which originally premiered on December 3, 1975, in Wuppertal, is Pina Bausch's most frequently performed choreography so far and has been shown in almost every country to which the company has ever traveled.[77] It was performed more than 300 times in total in 74 cities, 30 countries and on four continents between 1976 and 2013. Sixteen couples, a total of 32 dancers, dance in every performance. A total of almost 300 dancers have performed this piece onstage so far; many more have rehearsed it. Some of the dancers who have been dancing the piece for years have performed it together with more than 100 other people.

For some time now, *The Rite of Spring* has been performed by three groups of dancers: the dancers of the Tanztheater Wuppertal, members of the Folkwang Tanzstudio (FTS) and dance students at Folkwang Universität. All third- and fourth-year students at Folkwang Universität and all FTS dancers learn the piece, not in a workshop or as a part of the curriculum, but with view to actually performing it. Since Pina Bausch's death, those in charge of rehearsals have met with the artistic director of the Tanztheater Wuppertal and professors at Folkwang Universität to jointly select the group of students and FTS dancers who will be allowed to dance the piece.[78]

The quantitative data on this piece is relevant as it reveals an abundance of material and methodological approaches. In light of these 'facts' and the rich accompanying rehearsal and performance material alone, how can we access this 'masterpiece of the century' if it is not enough to examine just one performance or a single recording of the performance because the piece has been danced by so many dancers?

There is clearly an abundance of production material relating to *The Rite of Spring:* countless videos of rehearsals and performances; notes written and sketches drawn by the choreographer, rehearsal directors and dancers; correspondence between local organizers regarding, for example, the required supply of peat; stage managers' lists, technical directions, program booklets, reviews and interviews, mostly in foreign languages; countless photos by various photographers with different aesthetics; and films such as the German television documentary (ZDF) first broadcast on March 11, 1979,[79] and the excerpts shown on Franco-German free-to-air TV network Arte in 2013 to mark the 100th anniversary of Stravinsky's composition and Nijinsky's choreography.

Given the profusion of materials, which are largely stored in the Pina Bausch Archive in Wuppertal, it may at first seem like it would be more than enough to analyze this material alone – if it were accessible, that is. But even if the materials were to be 'released,'[80] it would not be possible to adequately answer certain questions using just the materials at hand. Additional empirical material would be important for a praxeological production analysis (→ THEORY AND METHODOLOGY) that also takes into account the artistic work practices: how were rehearsals run? How did new dancers learn the piece? How were dancers selected? How were pieces translated to other companies, for example, to the dancers of the Opéra national de Paris or the English National Ballet, to which the piece was passed on in 2019? How did the four generations of dancers who have now danced the piece in Wuppertal learn it?

Barbara Kaufmann, member of the Tanztheater Wuppertal since 1987, dancer in 28 pieces and one of Pina Bausch's artistic assistants, managed the restaging of *The Rite of Spring* as rehearsal director. She has talked about how rehearsals were run,[81] allowing us to gain insight into the specific practices of studying *The Rite of Spring*. These practices follow intersubjectively shared orders of knowledge and routines that have been practiced for years: first, the movement vocabulary is learned without music. The dancers learn the music by heart, listening to it on headphones over and over again and counting the beats. For unlike in the early years, when the piece had not yet been counted out and rehearsals were accompanied by music right from the start, the steps have now been meticulously noted. The piece is arranged in 30 sections, which are first learned separately. Sequences are rehearsed first, then formations, then sections.

In order to better communicate the individual parts (or "Stellen," as Pina Bausch called them) of the dance, they have been given names such as: "Little Solo," "Cloud," "Big Part," "First Men's Diagonal," "Ground Part" "Circle," "Chaos," "First Lifts" and "Pune Part."[82] The movements are learned in a synthetic process. After rehearsing the movement phrases and matching them up to the timing of the music, dancers clarify and rehearse the arrangements of the groups and their paths through the space. Men and women first rehearse separately with a male or female rehearsal director. Later, they rehearse together, especially the sequences that involve lifting.

Although the movement material is generally passed on by the rehearsal directors, media also play a central role in the rehearsal process. They have always been important, but now they have taken on a more decisive role, since Pina Bausch is no longer alive to make the final decision. The last version of the piece as recorded on video before Pina Bausch's death has become the gold standard for restagings. Other media include written materials such as the prompt book and video recordings, which are mainly used to decide who will adopt which dancer's position and who will take which paths through the space. Finally, dancers make their own notes about their paths in order to visualize the spatial dimensions, whose three-dimensionality cannot be recognized on video.

The Rite of Spring deals with the controversial discussions about the relationship between community and the individual that took place in the 1970s during a renewed surge in individualization. This is also a recurring theme in other pieces by Pina Bausch, for example, in the first part of *1980* (→ PIECES), where all of the dancers stand facing one other as they stage various individual, habitual and culturally specific farewells. This moment is repeated in the final scene of the second act, but without it ending in a farewell or any other resolution of the situation: the final, closing image is that of a tension-laden confrontation between the individual and the group.

In *The Rite of Spring*, this theme unfolds on the choreographic, dance, dramaturgical and narrative levels as a relationship between perpetrators and victim, between men and women, but also between women themselves. From a choreographic point of view, it takes place in line with the music, interweaving the polyphony of the music with various variations on the movement motifs. On the level of dance movements, the balance between stability, strength and tension on the one hand and instability, weight and relaxation on the other creates the tense sensation of being thrown back and forth. There are sequences in which the movement motif is prescribed, but not who dances the motif when or where, thus providing the individuals with a certain range of motion while also imposing constraints and duties on the community. There is a sense of connection, but also of exclusion. There is individual 'freedom,' but the group also makes certain demands.

The dramaturgical structure illustrates the relationship between individual and society by mixing group scenes, dances in unison and individual actions. Ultimately, it builds on a narrative widely understood in patriarchal societies: a man is chosen to select a woman to be sacrificed in the presence of all. The radical division between male and female dances and the sacrifice of the woman enact a specific relationship between the sexes: women and men are separated from the outset, not only in the piece itself but also during the rehearsal process.

"Standing as close together as possible and making the movements as big as possible"[83] – these words by Pina Bausch probably best sum up the relationship between individual and society. The figure of the sacrificial victim embodies the social repositioning of the individual: on the one hand, the individual longs to be chosen, to stand out from the community, to free herself from it and to occupy center stage – specifically: to be allowed to dance a great solo. On the other hand, being chosen also means giving oneself up for the community, the fear of being the chosen one, experiencing responsibility and its consequences, and dancing oneself to death for the good of the community.

The habitus and the incorporated knowledge of the dancers of the Tanztheater Wuppertal are specific and differ from those of other dancers and dance companies. This is also evident in the dance techniques used in *The Rite of Spring*, which are characterized by driving actions like pushing and whipping, by body curves and waves, by pulsating and sculptural movements, and by the interplay between central and peripheral movements. Therefore, when the classical dancers of the Opéra national de Paris learned "the Sacre," as the dancers call the piece, it was not surprising that they were not only unfamiliar with Pina Bausch's movement vocabulary but also realized that their bodies were not 'formed'[84] for these movements. Even just running barefoot on the flats of one's feet – over peat at top speed, as required by this piece – is something that classical dancers are not accustomed to.

The reasons behind Pina Bausch's dance aesthetics are the motifs and themes of the piece,[85] but the work of the dancers concentrates on the form and the quality of movement (→ SOLO DANCE), as emotion is generated by the form of the movement. Only when the form is danced precisely, only when the dancer finds a balance between controlling the form (their body, their breath, the distribution of weight) and experiencing the movement and its flow does emotion emerge – for the dancers, as well as for the audience. It is therefore of elementary importance for the rehearsal process that the dancers work in detail on form.[86] The dancers develop this form through the relationship between their body parts and the dynamics of the movement.

However, form is not just created in the movement of the bodies, but also in the way that they encounter materials, space and light. The stage floor is covered with peat. This peat turns the stage into an action space where every dancer has to struggle with resistance. The peat symbolizes communion with nature, roots, an intimate love of nature and down-to-earthness. But above all, it does something: it provokes struggle, it makes the movements more difficult, it resists, it is unpredictable, it confuses the trained form. This is why dancers often cry when they dance "the Sacre" for the first time on the peat[87] – because they have to find a new form. The peat forces the dancers to do more than simply repeat the movements they have learned, to dance them 'beautifully,' to re-present these movements. Instead, it makes demands on the performativity of the situation, its eventfulness, momentariness and uniqueness, which the dancers experience with the audience: being in the (performance) situation, generating the form over and over again in a corporeal confrontation with the peat.

Dancers consider *The Rite of Spring* to be an extreme piece, uncompromising, strenuous, an "inner earthquake." The physical exertion that it induces is the result of the fast tempo and immense energy that it requires. The emotional exertion comes when, as Barbara Kaufmann says, "you let it happen,"[88] when you let yourself be carried away by the movement sequence, when you experience it. Only then do the dancers encounter the full emotional range of the piece: struggle, passion, limitations, horror, compassion, grief, insecurity, loneliness, fear, death.

The side lights narrowing the stage, the costumes that become heavy with peat during the 35 minutes, sticking to the body and smelling of earth, peat on naked, sweaty skin, poignant music, the immense speed of the performance – all of this makes a significant contribution to the dancers actually being in the situation, not just performing the spring sacrifice, but truly experiencing it. It is no wonder that many dancers feel that the piece is a performative ritual: executed in that specific moment and not for the umpteenth time.

Passing on and inheriting

The performative aspect of passing on is particularly relevant in the case of immaterial cultural heritage such as dance, which, as an 'art of the moment,' evades definition. The meaning of dance heritage is also contingent. People, performances, rehearsals, company constellations and audience reactions are all subject to the laws of perception and interpretation, which are constitutively open and incomplete. The meaning of Pina Bausch's artistic legacy is not clear. It has to be renegotiated each time it is passed on, in different places at different times, between the dancers themselves and between the dancers, the audience and the critics, while also being reinterpreted in research. Here, different individual interests, cultural-political power constellations and research policies play a significant role. Given the possibilities, conditions and limits of passing on choreography and in light of the state of existing materials, these acts of communication constitute a difficult and fragile process of learning and understanding that is performative and can be successful, but can always fail, too. As a process of translation, its productivity lies in its very potential for failure, for missing the mark, in the (im)possibility of preserving a legacy in a way that is 'true to the original' and thereby musealizing it.

In his book *Specters of Marx,* French philosopher Jacques Derrida writes: "That we *are* heirs does not mean that we *have* or that we *receive* this or that, some inheritance that enriches us one day with this or that, but that the *being* of what we are is first of all inheritance, whether we like it or know it or not."[89] This inheritance refuses to put itself at our disposal: it cannot be chosen, you cannot 'be' an heir, and what has been passed on does not belong to you. However, Derrida does not relieve the heirs of their responsibilities. On the contrary: for him, responsibility is not conceivable outside of inheritance. *Respons(e)-ibility* always means: giving a response. Inheritance thus obliges us to constantly respond to the question of what it means to us here and now and how we can use it to shape the future. This responsibility is especially present in the passing on of dance as art, of a corporeal art form. It is not a compulsive act of 'keeping the pieces alive' nor a standstill, but a movement: a fragile transformation at the intersection between identity and difference. And this transformation takes place against the backdrop of what is culturally, socially and politically relevant, and (also economically) acceptable in order to promote contemporary art.

For What Tomorrow... is the promising title of a collection of conversations between Jacques Derrida, who died in 2004, and the psychoanalyst and historian Élisabeth Roudinesco.[90] In the section "Choosing One's Heritage,"[91] Derrida situates heritage at the crossroads between tradition and the critique of conservatism. For him, heritage is always an ambivalent process, one that oscillates between actively approaching something that has always come before and passively accepting it. On the one hand, it is the finitude of life that requires both giving and accepting inheritance. On the other hand, it is precisely the imbalance between the brevity of life and the longevity of art that calls for the well-considered selection and critical exclusion of certain kinds of inheritance. By linking the received gift with autonomous continuity, and external commission with self-determined responsibility, Derrida, making recourse to Emmanuel Levinas, opens up a conceptual realm of thought in which inheritance/heritage, tradition and responsibility are caught up in a tension between the dignity of the Other and the singularity of the individual, in other words: a tension where the attitude toward inheritance is an ambivalence between preserving tradition and desiring change.

How is it possible to feel responsible for a legacy when that legacy issues contradictory instructions? On the one hand, Pina Bausch was a pioneer, and she revolutionized dance history in many respects. Her legacy could therefore be precisely this bold innovation and courage to overcome boundaries. On the other hand, her pieces should be preserved and her work maintained. In legal terms, Salomon Bausch is the only heir to his mother's work. Although she had already told him that she wanted a foundation to care for and protect her work, her death came suddenly and unexpectedly. It radically changed his life. He accepted his inheritance, interrupted his studies and, together with his father Ronald Kay, founded the Pina Bausch Foundation, which he still manages today. Although he had previously had little involvement in his mother's artistic work with the Tanztheater Wuppertal, he honored her wishes and, just one year after her death, developed the archive concept "An Invitation from Pina"[92] with a small team that included Marc Wagenbach, research and development manager of the Pina Bausch Foundation; Dirk Hesse, general manager of the Tanztheater Wuppertal at the time; and Nataly Walter. This concept laid the programmatic groundwork for further activities. Bernhard Thull, Professor of Information Design at the Darmstadt University of Applied Sciences, supplied the software for the archive in Wuppertal, which houses all of the materials pertaining to Pina Bausch's work. The archive's first and most important goal is to keep the work alive, to make restagings possible and to make the pieces available to other companies.

Pina Bausch herself began setting up the archive. Bénedicte Billiet and Jo Ann Endicott had already started examining the video material that had been stored in a video archive looked after by Grigori Chakov for decades. Nevertheless, the digitization of the archive since Pina Bausch's death has been a Herculean task: 7,500 videos of performances and rehearsals, technical stage instructions, lighting plans, GEMA lists,[93] stage managers' notes, the documentation of stage sets, costumes, props, program booklets, and posters of performances in Wuppertal and of guest performances in 47 countries and in 28 languages, press kits, reviews, interviews, speeches, film and television documentaries, 30,000 photos, Pina Bausch's private archive and much more – all of this is still being digitized and organized using the linked data method. Years of work still lie ahead just to deal with the materials that already exist. There are also plans to generate more material, for Salomon Bausch knows that in addition to the written, audio and visual documents that can be digitized, it is above all the dancers and long-standing employees of the Tanztheater Wuppertal who carry a treasure trove of memories within them. They are the "living archives."[94] Collecting their memories with the help of oral history techniques, translating them from communicative into cultural memory and thus making them accessible to future generations are other tasks that the archive has always considered to be an essential part of its work.

Salomon Bausch is aware that the legacy of Pina Bausch only truly becomes visible when her choreographies are being performed. He considers it his responsibility to create conditions that make this possible. "I am neither a dancer nor a choreographer," says Salomon Bausch in an interview, "so others have to take responsibility for the rehearsals. I can just be grateful that there are people at the Tanztheater Wuppertal who can make the pieces come alive, who do so and want to do so, and who can inspire audiences all over the world. We want to collect and process their experiences for the archive. We can't predict what will happen in fifty years' time."[95]

What is the best way to store the materials? How and when should they be made public? How should which pieces be passed on to other companies? There are no already trodden paths for the foundation to walk down in any of these respects, there are no clues from the choreographer and no predecessors who have paved the way.

A legacy so great that it shaped the dance history of the 20th century has many heirs: the dancers and collaborators, the audience, the city of Wuppertal, the state of North Rhine-Westphalia, the German cultural landscape, the global dance community. Lutz Förster, born in Solingen like Pina Bausch, a dancer with the Tanztheater Wuppertal since 1975 and a permanent member since 1978 (with brief interruptions) as well as its artistic director from 2013 to 2016 does not like the word 'legacy.' "I don't like to talk about legacies; for me they have too much to do with death. Pina's pieces are living. I prefer to talk about assuming responsibility for the pieces in order to keep them alive. We have to be careful with this responsibility. We shouldn't lose sight of the bigger picture."[96] Lutz Förster is used to resistance: he told me of the Tanztheater Wuppertal's early pieces in the 1970s and early 1980s, about feeling certain that they were doing the right thing at the time, although the critics wrote scathing reviews and spectators slammed doors as they left the theater. From 1991 until 2013, before he succeeded Pina Bausch as artistic director of the Tanztheater Wuppertal, he was head of the dance department at Folkwang Universität, where he defied Bologna reforms in a fight for more artistic freedom. After months of intensely discussing the future of the Tanztheater Wuppertal, the dancers decided to make him their artistic director in 2013. This also meant finding a new director at the end of his own term of office, someone who could take on this great task. For the future, he envisioned an artistic director who would create something new and give the dancers creative responsibility while also maintaining the pieces of Pina Bausch. And this required the expertise of those who knew the pieces from the inside.

In January 2019 in Hamburg, Kampnagel, Europe's largest center for contemporary performing arts, presented the piece *1980*. Almost 40 years after its premiere, the piece had been passed on multiple times. In Hamburg, only one dancer from the original cast was still performing in the piece (→ PIECES), which plays such an important role in the history of Pina Bausch's work: Ed Kortlandt was hardly recognizable as he played the organ. Rehearsals were managed by Dominique Mercy and Ruth Amarante, neither of whom had been part of the original cast, and by Matthias Burkert, who joined the Tanztheater Wuppertal in 1979 as a pianist and quickly became an important musical collaborator in all further productions (→ COMPANY).

The piece was performed on a regular basis at home and abroad between 1980 and 1994, going on tour again in 2001. From then until the death of Pina Bausch, the piece stopped touring. The first artistic directors of the company, Dominique Mercy and Robert Sturm, decided to resume touring the piece after Pina Bausch's death. Lutz Förster was in charge of the rehearsals. Can Pina Bausch be replaced? "People often overestimate that," says Lutz Förster, "in principle, our work today is not that much different from when Pina was still alive. Unlike other choreographers, Pina herself had already tried to perform her pieces as much as possible and to keep her ever-growing repertoire alive. That was never an easy process, and it was wrought with discussion, but even today, someone ultimately has to lend the piece a face."[97]

Pina Bausch worked closely with the same people for many decades (→ COMPANY), and this too is a legacy in itself: a group of artists closely interweaving work and life, trusting and valuing each other, and travelling the world together. This model put into practice what contemporary art discourse now calls collaboration, collectivity and "complicity."[98] However, in the face of networked structures and project-based working methods, new forms of mobility and precariats, this has now become a historical model. Pina Bausch assigned responsibilities, but there is no doubt that she had the final say and last word in everything. How did she master all of this – a new choreography each year, in the 1970s and 1980s as many as two or three new pieces a year, guest performances, restagings, films, documentaries, speeches, interviews, etc.? She never spoke about it. It remains her secret.

For Derrida, the secret is where inheritance and responsibility overlap. "One always inherits from a secret – which says 'read me, will you ever be able to do so?'"[99] Inheritance always means two things: on the one hand, a responsibility that oscillates between tradition and reform and, on the other, misgivings about whether one will be able to adequately carry out the task set by the inheritance. Doubt is part of a legacy's interminable character: it is necessary to filter, classify, select and criticize. Sometimes the only way to honor this responsibility and remain faithful to the legacy is to use the inheritance to counteract the inheritance – in other words: addressing the legacy over and over again in different ways in order to keep it alive. Ultimately, nobody can say for certain what truly makes this great dance legacy what it is and what it has to say.

25 März 2000

Pina vermißt etwas "Ernstes".

Sie stellt eine neue Frage

(96) Verzweifelte Sehnsucht

Kuß mit Salzstreuer

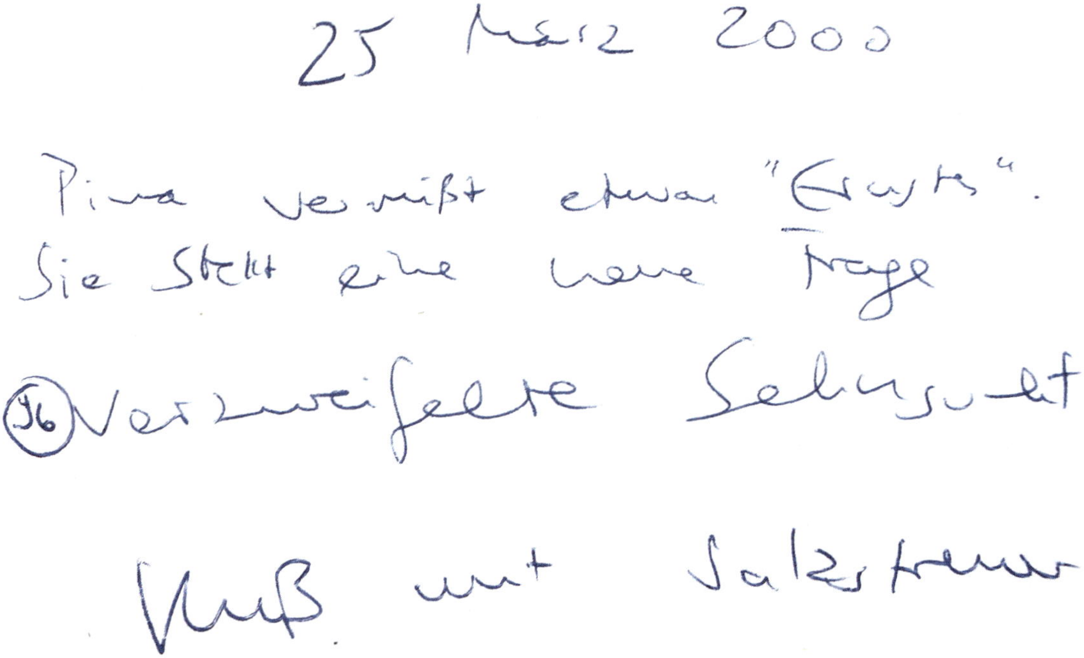

March 25, 2000

Pina thinks something "serious" is missing

She asks a new question

96. Desperate longing

Kiss with saltshaker

17 Excerpt from Stephan Brinkmann's notebook for *Wiesenland*

1 Rainer Behr
in *Nefés*
Madrid, 2006

Almost anything can be dance. It has to do with a certain awareness, a certain inner, physical attitude, a very high degree of precision: knowledge, breath, every little detail. It always has to do with the how.[1]

Solo

Dance

When Anne Martin was asked whether Pina Bausch had given her "psychological pointers" when passing on the very personal main role in *Café Müller* (PREMIERE 1978), she replied: "Not at all, it was actually very technical. And it was only once I had totally mastered the form that I understood everything that Pina had brought to this role."[2]

It is a constantly repeated mantra that the Tanztheater Wuppertal translates emotions into dance, that Pina Bausch was less concerned with how people move than with what moves them. So while she posed her 'questions' so as to incite inner emotion (→ WORK PROCESS), the composition and rehearsals of individual dances were actually all about how bodies moved; the development, study and passing on of dances at the Tanztheater Wuppertal has always meant, above all, working on form, on the quality of the movements. Only once the form has been mastered and the dance is perfectly performed can it grip the audience; only then can its 'meaning' be felt. What can be felt is often described by the audience using metaphorical and associative words charged with semantic and symbolic meaning – thus revealing the special ways in which the paradox between identity and difference comes into play in the translation of dance into language (→ RECEPTION). Dance reviews also reveal that the translation of dance into writing remains vague, since even most professional descriptions mainly focus on individual 'theatrical' scenes, but rarely on the dances themselves. This is particularly evident in reviews of pieces from the 1990s onward, as the pieces from this artistic phase are more likely to feature a succession of individual solos (→ PIECES, RECEPTION).

Translating dance into writing is by no means a new problem, but rather a practice that ballet masters have been dealing with for centuries. In order to be able to reconstruct dances, they developed forms of dance notation that allowed them to archive dance and document it in more detail. The history of dance notation, which goes back to 16th-century Europe, with its origins in Thoinot Arbeau's *Orchésographie* from 1589, illustrates the translation of dance into writing. Even today, some dance ensembles work with choreologists who meticulously notate dance movements and choreographic formations. But this was not the case for the Tanztheater Wuppertal under Pina Bausch. There was no specific notation system, only a corpus of images and texts that comprised video recordings, schematic diagrams and notes written by Pina Bausch, her assistants and dancers (→ WORK PROCESS). Sometimes, dancers also wrote down their positions and roles in the piece before they left the company. This written and illustrative material has formed the basis for the company's collaboration and has been used by dancers to pass on their dances to other dancers. How might we translate the solos of the Tanztheater Wuppertal, which are so individual in their language, into a form of notation? How can they be documented and archived in translations like these and thereby made accessible both for artistic reconstruction and academic analysis?

This chapter deals with the translation of body/dance into writing/text. I will begin by briefly presenting examples of different positions from the field of dance studies and setting them in relation to the approach taken in this book. After that, I will outline the method that we developed and refined to analyze videos of dance during this research project,[3] namely the translation of specific dances into the digital notation software Feldpartitur. Finally, I will illustrate how dance is translated into notation using three solos as examples. Because solo dance gained in importance and took up more and more space in Pina Bausch's last artistic work phases (→ PIECES), I have chosen solos from three different coproductions, which premiered over the course of three decades between 1986 and 2009. They were each produced eleven to twelve years apart. The first is a dance solo by Anne Martin from the first coproduction *Viktor* (PREMIERE 1986), the second was danced by Beatrice Libonati in *Masurca Fogo* (PREMIERE 1998) and the third by Dominique Mercy in Pina Bausch's last piece "*…como el musguito en la piedra, ay si, si, si…*" (PREMIERE 2009).[4] The analyses were carried out on the basis of video recordings of each respective premiere. We chose to use these recordings because they feature the original casts of dancers, i.e., those who were involved in developing the piece. These were the dancers who actually created and first danced the solos. This selection of videos itself constitutes an act of methodological positing (→ THEORY AND METHODOLOGY) and demonstrates how one singular performance, which has been recorded in a specific way, can be translated into notation. For the solos were often changed again after the premiere, but above all, they transformed when they were passed on to other dancers, sometimes being modified once more by Pina Bausch as a result. The final section of this chapter will reflect on the methodological process.

Body/dance – writing/text: Positions in dance studies

Various 'turns' in cultural studies and the social sciences such as the linguistic turn, the performative turn and the practice turn have had a strong influence on dance theory concepts that deal with the relationship between body/dance and writing/text. The linguistic turn, which began at the beginning of the 20th century and was then conceptualized in an anthology published by Richard Rorty in 1967,[5] replaced the idea of language as a 'transparent medium' for grasping and communicating reality with the notion that all human knowledge is structured by language and that reality cannot be understood outside of it. Language is thus defined as a discourse that obeys certain rules, and it is only within this discourse that it is possible to make statements in the first place. In this understanding, dance must also be seen as a language that can be explored semiotically. It was on the basis of this approach that Susan Foster suggested a perspective in the 1980s that regards the dancing body as something that is always discursive, 'legible' and that is a continuous producer of codes that can be read and interpreted as cultural signifiers.[6] In the 1990s, Gabriele Brandstetter in particular drew parallels between dance and writing in German-language dance research when, by taking a cultural-semiotic approach, she described the movements of the dancing body as writing in space, thus conceiving of body/dance and writing/text as "écriture corporelle" and "lecture corporelle," both representing different, but not contradictory, interrelated physical modes of production.[7]

In the 1990s, the performative turn and the practice turn brought about a change of perspective on the relationship between body/dance and writing/text. The performative turn, whose origins go back to the 1950s and various strands of cultural anthropology, sociology and language philosophy,[8] rejected the idea of representation and led to a renunciation of semiotic approaches, even in dance studies. The focus shifted to the performative production of reality in the interplay between performance and execution, as well as to the relationship between a specific performance, the context in which it takes place and the public (i.e., audience) that authenticates it. In the early 1990s, Judith Butler made a radical poststructuralist contribution to the debate by making reference to theories of subjectivity.[9] According to her, there is no performer behind the performance; subjectivity is in itself only created by and in the act of performance.

While the performative turn was transforming the social sciences, the practice turn – which favors practice theory over structural and system theories and takes its theoretical point of departure largely from Alfred Schütz, Harold Garfinkel, Erving Goffman, and Pierre Bourdieu[10] – heralded in a rejection of the structuralist thinking associated with the linguistic turn, according to which the social and the cultural are conceived of as (immaterial) ideas, worldviews, normative systems or linguistic forms of communication. The practice turn brought the corporeality and materiality of practices to the fore and, with them, the performative act of execution into a material environment.

In the 2000s, dance scholar Isa Wortelkamp took a performative approach by describing the process of writing in analogy to dancing. In her examination of Brandstetter's approach, she defines the ephemerality that characterizes both dancing and writing as "movement that is perpetually emerging and disappearing."[11] She does not understand the transfer of body/dance into writing/text as an immobilization, as the fixing of movement, but considers writing about dance to be a choreographic, corporeal dance process in itself.[12]

Another aspect of the performative, namely the context and, in this regard, above all the audience, features in the works of Janet Adshead-Landsdale, who questions previous writing practices and regards texts as unstable, mosaic-like conglomerates. Using the concept of intertextuality, she views the reading and interpretation of dance as a process of the spectator interacting with the dance.[13] Katja Schneider in turn suggests a hybrid concept that links approaches from media semiotics and practice theory with the performative, thus describing the relationship between body/dance and writing/text as semiotic and mutually dependent. Moreover, her approach takes into account aspects of performance and practice theory by viewing dance and text as equal media in a performance, seeking to emphasize material factors in addition to semantic ones.[14]

Whereas these approaches mainly take academic debates as their points of reference and have failed to develop a genuinely methodological procedure for translating body/dance into writing/text, Claudia Jeschke's scholarly approach derives from artistic practice. She focuses on dance as 'pure' movement, which she conceives of as motor action and attempts to translate into signs using analog notation methods. Her aim is to make it possible to reconstruct and analyze dances.[15]

The approach advocated in this book ties into different aspects of performance and practice theory and attempts to combine them with methodological approaches from qualitative social and cultural research (→ THEORY AND METHODOLOGY). In contrast with the classical linguistic notion that words function like labels – that is to say: that there is 'real' dance, followed by the image of dance (the signified) and then the word dance (the signifier) – the approach advocated here is based on the theory that there is no 'real' dance beyond its image and that this image is only produced in, with and through language: it is only in the process of translating dance into language, in the process of designating and describing it, that meaning is ascribed to the perceived dance movement, that it is charged with significance and that this process is authenticated by the public. In other words: it is only in the translation between body/dance and writing/text that 'dance' is created – understood as a medium, a generator of significance and meaning, a transmitter of emotions, which sometimes includes the idea of 'real,' 'authentic' dance, depending on the respective (dance) discourse. This translation always takes place through framings, i.e., references to socially or culturally shaped semantic complexes. The approach presented in this book does not understand translation in the tradition of a linguistic model of describing a linear transfer from A to B, from the original ('real' dance) to the translation (writing/text) that regards text as an illustrative or representative medium of dance. Instead, the translation of body/dance into writing/text is defined here as a reciprocal movement that has no clear beginning or end (→ THEORY AND METHODOLOGY). It does not presuppose the existence of 'real,' 'authentic' dance that precedes language as a kind of essential starting point. Instead, the approach taken in this book is based on the presupposition that 'dance' can only be identified as such through the reciprocal translation of body/dance into writing/text and vice versa. This performative and praxeological reading of translation focuses on the mode of translation. It does not ask *which parts* of dance can be decoded or read, but rather *how* 'dance' is produced in the interplay between dance and text.

Translation manual: Feldpartitur

The notation of the three selected solos was carried out using software developed in qualitative social research for the analysis of actions: Feldpartitur.[16] This digital notation software allows the user to work with characters (marked as CS in the score), symbols (NS) and text (TXT for shorter or TS for longer descriptions) to record movements. Since the description levels and sign and symbol systems that had already been developed for Feldpartitur did not provide enough differentiation to record a detailed dance piece, we refined and reworked them to meet the requirements of a dance studies analysis. This was itself an act of positing, for regardless of whether a dance is translated into text in order to artistically reconstruct or academically analyze it, this process always has something to do with inclusion and exclusion.

Before a dance is transformed into notation, the first preliminary translation step has already taken place: the dance has been recorded on video, meaning that the situation onstage has been converted into a two-dimensional image from a specific camera position and perspective using different aspects of film technology (zooming, etc.). In this case, employees of the Tanztheater Wuppertal had made the video recordings of each respective world premiere for documentation purposes with the explicit aim of using these recordings to reconstruct, restage and rehearse the pieces. The premieres were filmed from a medium long shot perspective in the auditorium, with the camera following the movements of the dancers along their spatial paths and constantly being readjusted by zooming in and out (FIG. 2). There is no use of film technology (editing, etc.) in the video to interfere with the dynamics of the actions onstage. During their solos, the dancers are always at the center of the image, even when other actions are taking place onstage. The quality of the video recording makes smaller head movements and facial expressions difficult to detect.

2 Camera movements, spatial paths and levels. Excerpt from the score; solo by Beatrice Libonati in *Masurca Fogo*

In order to transfer the video recording into the digital Feldpartitur software, the movement sequence is divided into shorter film stills or frames. The score is generated on the basis of these frames (FIG. 2). The basis of this method is an ambivalent translation process: on the one hand, this transfer fragments the dance movements into movement images, thereby immobilizing them. However, on the other hand, it is precisely this image technology that allows detailed movements to become visible and makes description possible, as the frames can be looped, slowed down or sped up.

The frames are arranged chronologically and sequentially on the horizontal x-axis, usually at intervals of 0.3 to 1 second. The smaller the time interval, the more differentiated the description of the individual dance movement. However, if the score is divided into shorter units of time it becomes increasingly complex and stretches out the linear sequence of frames, meaning that the individual frames can no longer be seen at a single glance as one unit of movement on the screen.

On the y-axis, the Feldpartitur software offers the possibility to establish various levels of analysis and, within them, to differentiate between different categories using symbol, code and text lines based on the subject of inquiry. For example, the symbols are divided into categories such as video dramaturgy (e.g. symbols for long shots, medium long shots, zoom), music (e.g. symbols for notes, pauses), body (e.g. hand gestures), expression (musical expressions for quiet/loud, faster/slower) and group (e.g. the arrangement of people relative to one another). The code lines, allow the user to enter more concise descriptions using short words.

		00:00:00.0	00:00:00.4	00:00:00.8	00:00:01.2	00:00:01.6	00:00:02.0	00:00:02.4	00:00:02.8	00:00:03.2	00:00:03.6	00:00:04
CS: Parts		Trans°	Trans°	Trans°	Trans°	Trans°	Trans°	Move_1	1	1	1	1
TXT: Situation		dancer in the background, wearing a black dress, giggles, throws stones in direction of the camera/			second dancer enters the cutout from the bottom right. She remains in the foreground	dancer in the background is still visible		dancer in the foreground arrives in the center of the cutout, only visible from the waist upwards	she begins to move, her body now visible in the cutout down to her thighs			her body nearly vis down to h knees, sh standing center of cutout
NS: CameraMov												
NS: MusicSound												
NS: Movement												
CS: Body_Actio			Forw.Mo.	Forw.Mo.	Forw.Mo.	Motion	Motion	Standing	Motion	Motion	Motion	Motio
TS: Mov_Design												rising
CS: Body_Use									lift		forward	
TXT: Body_Use			steps to the front edge of the stage					parallel feet, arms close to the body, only the upper body is visible	both forearms lifted, first left, then right, upper arms close to the body	palms and forearms moving, upper arms only slightly away from the body	right hand palm at face level facing front, towards audience	palms a forearms moving, upper ar only sligh away fro body
CS: HandMov										Slip Off	Stop	
TXT: HandMov										direct, quick 'slip off', sustained effort, two directions	associations of stop signs, also in combination with spoken 'No', light effort, flighty	
TXT: Touch									palms rubbing each other from the center of the body, repeatedly	palms rubbing each other from the center of the body, repeatedly		palms r each oth away fro center, sideway (left/righ upwards
TS: Head_Face											determined	
TXT: Head_Face			not yet visible				focussed	visible – without recognizable expression			mouth opens - 'o' shape	
CS: Torso											Twist	
TXT: Torso			upright posture								movement of the arm affects the position of the torso/ twist, left shoulder comes slightly forward	
CS: Axis_Scale												
TS: Symmetry									asymmetrical			
TXT: SpacialRef			spatial intention, direction, lateral axis, depth axis					place level middle, transverse kinesphere, transversal pathways			place le middle central here, pe l pathwa
CS: Accents											Terminal	
TXT: Dynamic									strong central quick guided movement			

In order to translate the dance into language in the text lines, the researcher requires clear vocabulary that has been adapted to the respective dance technique. In the case of the Tanztheater Wuppertal, it makes sense to utilize the vocabulary of the Jooss-Leeder method,[17] as this method, which Kurt Jooss and Sigurd Leeder developed out of Rudolf von Laban's movement analysis, was emphasized in the Folkwang training of many Tanztheater Wuppertal dancers, especially some of the earlier dancers and also the choreographer herself. The influence of classical ballet, which also played an important role in the company's training, is used for movements where this influence is especially striking, as in the solo by Dominique Mercy, who also studied ballet. The code lines, an example of which is shown here in the excerpt from the score of Anne Martin's dance in *Viktor* (FIG. 3), illustrate the use of the Jooss-Leeder vocabulary. It is supplemented by terms that describe the movement more concretely, for example, hand movements such as 'showing' and 'stripping.' The different symbol, code and text lines and their juxtaposition also allow for different "editing modes" and "multicode transcriptions."[18] On the vertical Y-axis, written annotations, condensed codes and symbols used to describe spatial paths, spatial levels, the music, camera movements and individual body parts, for example, can be noted down and combined in different ways, allowing for alternative interpretative approaches.

3 Excerpt from the score; solo by Anne Martin in *Viktor*

I will now use the following example of a solo by Dominique Mercy to outline the structure of a score: the first two lines of the score (FIG. 4) divide the dance into individual parts. This makes it possible to, for example, identify individual movement sequences that are repeated in different variations later on in the solo. Lines 3-7 (FIG. 4, VERTICAL LAYOUT) show how the dance solo has been structured and visualized for the analysis. In symbol line 3 ("Movement"), spatial paths are indicated by arrows. Code line 4 ("Position") records the alignment of the dancer's body: by dividing the movement sequence into 'front,' 'back' and 'side,' it is possible to record when and how often the dancer is facing the audience, turns laterally in profile or moves with his back to the audience. Symbol line 5 ("Axis_Scale") describes changes in the body's axis, for example when movements or floor paths break the vertical alignment of the body. The relationship between music and dance is noted in symbol line 6 ("Music"). Does the music support the movements, i.e., does the sound or rhythmic quality of the music amplify their effect? Is there a contrast between the music and the movements, e.g., does the music provide a counterpoint to the quality of movement? Or does the music accompany the dance, in other words: is it synchronous with the movement? To record

	00:00:33.0	00:00:34.0	00:00:35.0	00:00:36.0	00:00:37.0	00:00:38.0	00:00:39.0	00:00:40.0	00:00:41.0	00:00:42.0	00:
CS: Parts	17b	18	18/19	19	19	19	20 a	20 a	20 a	20 b	20
CS: Repetition										REP	RE
NS: Movement	↗	↗	●	●	●	●	⊙	→	↗	⊙	
CS: Position	SIDE	SIDE	SIDE	SIDE	SIDE	SIDE	TURN	SIDE	BACK	TURN	S
NS: Axis_Scale											
NS: Music					⋮̇>			⋮̇>	*sfz*		
TXT: Dynamic	LIGHT PERIPHERAL QUICK	STRONG CENTRAL QUICK	LIGHT CENTRAL QUICK	LIGHT CENTRAL QUICK	LIGHT CENTRAL QUICK	LIGHT CENTRAL QUICK	LIGHT PERIPHERAL QUICK	LIGHT PERIPHERAL QUICK	LIGHT CENTRAL QUICK	LIGHT PERIPHERAL QUICK	LIGHT PERIPHERAL QUICK	LI CE QI

4 Parts, repetition, variation, structure. Excerpt from the score; solo by Dominique Mercy in "*...como el musguito en la piedra ay si, si, si...*"

this, Feldpartitur offers symbols for musical analysis (e.g., the symbols for piano, forte, crescendo, decrescendo, adagio and allegro), but because they do not fully characterize the relationship between music and dance, we introduced further terms that describe specific qualities (as mentioned above: supportive, contrasting, accompanying). In addition, we listed the respective musical genre and the instruments used, since Pina Bausch's pieces typically feature a wide selection of music from different cultures. Text line 7 ("Dynamic") illustrates the movement dynamics of the solo using the vocabulary of the Jooss-Leeder method: the power with which the movements are performed is defined as either "strong" or "light," the direction of the movement as "peripheral" or "central," its tempo as "fast" or "slow." In spite of how difficult it is to fully grasp the individual movements using these conceptual antagonisms, they allow for a rough definition of the movement dynamics.

After the symbol and code lines, the text lines 8-18 (FIG. 5, VERTICAL LAYOUT) contain detailed movement descriptions that use the Jooss-Leeder vocabulary for choreographic structure. When do certain motifs repeat themselves in the music and/or in the movement sequence? Which movements and spatial paths does the dancer make and take? In addition to this spatial perspective, the movements of different body parts and areas of the body are noted. Accordingly, this section of the score is divided into two lines each for torso movements, leg movements, arm movements and head movements. Particularly striking hand movements are noted in the additional symbol line 16 ("Hands").

The Jooss-Leeder vocabulary is also used to provide differentiated descriptions of the movements of individual body positions (FIG. 5, lines 9 ["Torso"], 11 ["Legs"], 13 ["Arms"], 15 ["Hands"], 18 ["Head"]). A description like "The weight of the right leg lies on the flat foot, while the left leg lifts forward and upward" can thus be translated into the short phrase: "Single Medium Support (R), Forward High Gesture (L)."

Each of the lines above (FIG. 5, lines 8, 10, 12, 14, 17) translate these small descriptions into an abstract level of code. The movement sequences that were described in detail before are thereby condensed with the aim of determining a characteristic feature of this moment of movement. "Single Medium Support (R), Forward High Gesture (L)" becomes "High Gesture." By using these codes, the choreographic structure of the solo can be described in a highly condensed form: when, where and how often does a "High Gesture" occur in this solo? Where is the "starting point"[19] of a movement? Where does a movement 'end'? The score is varied and further aspects added when solos feature more dynamic spatial paths, as in the solos by Beatrice Libonati and Dominique Mercy (compared to Anne Martin's solo).

5 Body parts. Excerpt from the score; solo by Dominique Mercy in "*...como el musguito en la piedra ay si, si, si...*"

	00:00:12.0	00:00:13.0	00:00:14.0	00:00:15.0	00:00:16.0	00:00:17.0	00:00:18.0	00:00:19.0	00:00:20.0	00:00
S: Torso		Flex Tilt Forw	UP / FTF	UP / FTF	Upright Post.	FTF	Upright Post.	Upright Post.	Upright Post.	Uprigh
XT: Torso		Flexible Tilt Forwards	Swing in Upright Posture, Flexible Tilt Forwards	Swing in Upright Posture, Flexible Tilt Forwards	Swing in Upright Posture, Flexible Tilt Forwards	Flexible Tilt Forwards	Swing in Upright Posture, Flexible Tilt Forwards	Upright Posture	Upright Posture	Upright Postu
S: Legs	Upright Pos.	Down, Up	Down	Up	Down, Up	Down, Up	Upright Stance	Upright Stance	Upright Stance	Uprigh
XT: Legs	Parallel Double Medium Support	Parallel Double Medium Support	Single Support left, step sideways with hip guidance in slide tackle, Double Deep Support	Two little steps forward, slide tackle, Double Deep Support	Slide tackle, Double Deep Support	Single Support left, right, pulling towards center, soil contact	Parallel Double Medium Support	Parallel Double Medium Support	Parallel Double Medium Support	Parallel Double Mediu Suppo
S: Arms		Deep Swing	Deep Swing	Deep Swing	Deep Swing	Deep Swing	Narrow	Narrow	Narrow	Wide
XT: Arms	Arms close to the body, hands grab the pants	Both arms Deep Pendulum Swing	Both arms Deep Pendulum Swing	Both arms Deep Pendulum Swing	Both arms Deep Pendulum Swing	Both arms Deep Pendulum Swing	Both arms bent/kinked sideways in a square angle, hands guided at mouth level	Both arms bent/kinked sideways in a square angle, hands at the shirt collar	Both arms bent/kinked sideways in a square angle, hands at the shirt collar	Both a expan wide s
S: Hands	FLY	Scoop/Touch	Touch		Scoop/Touch	Touch	HAND MOUTH	FLY	FLY	Relax
XT: Hands	Hands grasp the pants on their sides, pulling the pants quickly form side to side, away from the body	Hands scoop from the floor, palms touch	Hands slip off the pants while coming upwards		Hands scoop from the floor, wandering/ sliding on the floor towards the front	Hands scoop from the floor, wandering/ sliding on the floor backwards	Both hands shaping a gesture, fingertips guided towards each other, towards the mouth	Hands grasp the shirt collar, pulling it quickly from side to side and away from the body	Hands grasp the shirt collar, pulling it quickly from side to side and away from the body	Hands and o palms upwa
S: Hands		👆					👆	👆	👆	
S: Head	Back	Flexible	Flexible	Flexible	Flexible	Flexible	Back	Back	Back	Back
XT: Head	Head tilted back	Head follows Pendulum Swing	Head follows Pendulum Swing	Head follows Pendulum Swing	Head follows Pendulum Swing	Head follows Pendulum Swing	Head tilted back	Head tilted back	Head tilted back	Head back

ANNE MARTIN IN *Viktor*

The dance solo by Anne Martin that has been translated here into a score comes from the piece *Viktor,* the Tanztheater Wuppertal's first coproduction, which was produced in 1986 in collaboration with the Teatro Argentino in Rome, Italy (→ PIECES). Anne Martin, born in 1953, studied music at the Lausanne Conservatory and trained as a dancer at the Centre international de danse Rosella-Hightower in Cannes. From 1978 to 1991, she danced with the Tanztheater Wuppertal and performed in numerous world premieres. In the 1980s, she began working as an independent dancer. After Anne Martin left the Tanztheater Wuppertal, she increasingly turned toward music and performed as a singer before returning to working as a dancer after a long break. She has also been working internationally as a dance teacher since 1998, in particular at the Conservatoire national supérieur musique et danse de Lyon in France.[20]

Our video analysis is based on a video recording of the world premiere at the Schauspielhaus Wuppertal on October 9, 1986. The piece lasts a total of 3 hours 15 minutes and includes one intermission. The solo is 2 minutes 23 seconds long. It is danced after the intermission during the second part of the piece. The score is divided into time intervals of 0.4 seconds and thus encompasses a total of 348 intervals.

Before the solo begins, another dancer (Melanie Karen Lien[21]) moves in the dark at the rear left-hand side of stage.[22] She has curly flowing hair and wears a black, close-fitting dress, with white lingerie visible at the neckline. She quietly giggles to herself while throwing cobblestones on the floor, but every time she leans back to throw a stone, she lets it drop from her open hand, which is tilted backward. Meanwhile, Anne Martin enters from stage right. The camera moves to focus on her. She is wearing everyday clothes: a tight black pencil skirt, a flowery, short-sleeved blouse and black heels, unlike Beatrice Libonati and Dominique Mercy, who wear 'dance dress' *(Tanzkleider;* → COMPANY, WORK PROCESS) in their solos. Pina Bausch describes her choice of costumes as follows: "It was always important to me that the dancers did not wear leotards or stylized costumes. On the one hand, the clothes are normal clothes and, on the other, splendid, beautiful dresses. There is a certain elegance, but the elegance is also disrupted."[23]

Anne Martin stands with her feet slightly turned out, heels together. When the music starts, she begins a dance of gestures, which she performs exclusively in one spot, standing at the front edge of the stage facing the audience. Her movements are mainly concentrated on her upper body, the communicative part of the body, with arm and hand movements dominating, sometimes allowing everyday gestures to appear. She addresses the audience directly and sometimes even speaks at the same tempo as her arm and hand movements.

As she dances the solo, a figure in a black cape (Dominique Mercy) comes onto the stage, bent over a cane. The figure later leads another dancer (Jakob Andersen) onto the stage as well. Four other performers come onstage during Anne Martin's solo, although not all at the same time. However, the camera focuses on Anne Martin throughout the solo, placing her at the center of the video image. The other performers provide the solo with a temporal frame and contrast. The actions taking place at the same time create tension: the hysterical, giggling woman in the background, the person wielding the cane loudly and threateningly, and the dancer who is later led onstage and jumps across the stage with his legs tied together once Anne Martin's solo has finished. The person with the cane approaches the two women and leads them off the stage, rushing them slightly, one after the other.

There is no contact between the two women; there is no spatial relationship between their actions. Both direct their attention exclusively toward the audience. They embody different types of women, which is evident not only in their appearance and clothing but also in the quality of their movements: the woman throwing the stones is strong, hysterical and impulsive. Her actions appear to be disorderly with no clear purpose, unplanned and spontaneous. She staggers restlessly back and forth to pick the fallen stones back up again. She seems desperate and undecided: on the one hand, she wants to throw a stone, i.e., carry out a deliberate plan, which evokes associations with violent clashes between police and demonstrators at the illegal squats, peace marches and anti-nuclear protests of the 1980s (→ PIECES). However, her feminine appearance and hysterical laughter contradict this intention, as does her failure to follow through with the throwing movement. Although she repeatedly prepares to throw a stone, it always lands on the ground next to her without having any effect. She only ends her Sisyphus-like actions when the person with the cane pushes her offstage. The dancer in the foreground, by contrast, is slim, small and austere with short hair. She performs fast, gentle movements. Her complex and extremely detailed dance gives the impression of well-rehearsed movement material that has been mastered and is meant to be presented. The polarity between the two women can also be heard in the sounds that they make: one hysterically giggles, her tittering sounds contrasting with her ostensible intent while underlining the actual action; the other dancer repeatedly says, "No, No, No," in the foreground in a clear French accent, uttered rhythmically in time with her movements and also in part with the music. Over the course of her solo, she repeats this multiple times at increasing speeds.

The person with the cane creates another layer of dramatic tension. This is mainly due to their audible gait and the impact of the cane striking the stage. Their posture is bent. Their body and face are completely hidden beneath a black cape. The person does not reveal their identity. Due to their stooped gait, this person is clearly smaller than the other dancers. First, they cross the stage in the background, interrupting the woman throwing stones, then they walk away and fetch another dancer onto the stage. Their purposeful actions, the quality and rhythm of their movements contrast with the movements of the two other dancers. Toward the end of Anne Martin's solo, they position themselves directly in front of her. She examines them, but does not interrupt her dance. Even when the music stops, she continues dancing and remains in eye contact with the audience. Then she pauses with a deep sigh, looks at the person with the cane and turns to the dancer in the background, who starts jumping with his legs tied together. The person with the cane now tries to push Anne Martin off the stage, touching her in the process, but she recoils from the undesired contact. Neither she nor the other dancer can completely finish their parts on their own; both are prevented from doing so by the person with the cane. The person with the cane takes on the function of directing and creating order, and retains this role over the course of the piece, for example, in the male and female dances, which they also direct, arrange and ultimately bring to an end. Hidden under the black cape, they are the only performer without an identity of their own. Their performance comes across as the anonymous, but concrete dominance of seniority, and their behavior toward the dancers resembles a generational conflict. Since buying and selling, offering oneself and something as goods are central themes of the piece, the figure could also be described as someone who regulates the presentation of the goods (in this case, the dancers and the dances).

Several kinds of relationships reveal themselves here, for example, between different characters, their performances and the types and qualities of their movements, between the visible and the invisible, between presence and absence, and between what is said and what is shown ("No, No, No" and giggling). Contrast and tension are not only central dramaturgical elements of Pina Bausch's pieces on the whole, but are above all essential characteristics of the piece *Viktor*, which begins with a corresponding opening scene that is often mentioned in reviews of the piece (→ RECEPTION). In this scene, a dancer, Anne Martin, comes onstage beaming in a red, tight-fitting dress. Smiling, she walks straight towards the audience, stopping at the center of the apron – and it is only at a rather late point in time that it becomes clear that she apparently has no arms.

The solo described above is danced by the same dancer, who opens the piece dressed in a red dress. In her solo, she does not allow herself to be disturbed by any other actions onstage. As in the opening scene, she stands directly in front of the audience at the edge of the stage. In this way, the apron is once again marked as both an in-between space, a place of transition and a border between the stage and the audience. The dancer communicates something directly to the audience. Her dance of gestures is marked by repetition, variation and loops as well as by the acceleration of fairly asymmetrical arm and hand movements. She executes the movements quickly, easily, fluently and rhythmically. There are no abrupt transitions. The movements start from the torso, moving in curves, sometimes in twists and tilts.[24] The acceleration causes the movements to become "lighter," "fluttering" more as the solo progresses. As she dances, she keeps touching her own body over and over again in stroking and wiping movements while also playfully touching her hair. Some of the movements from this dance will later reappear in the women's and men's group dances. Or to put it another way: the solo unites the group's movements. The individual dance is thus singular and simultaneously a microscopic image of the group dances.

Arms and hands are the dominant, mobilizing body parts in her dance (FIG. 6), which mainly features arm and hand movements such as lifting, lowering, widening and narrowing, pulling forward and back:

6 Moving her hands and touching her body. Screenshot of the score; solo by Anne Martin in *Viktor*

The dancer lifts and lowers her arms. The upper arms and forearms are at different distances from the upper body. She opens and closes them and brings them back toward the torso by tightly crossing her arms in different ways and touching herself. However, she does not pull them so far sideways or downward that the upper body has to give way and follow or that she is forced to take a step, squat or jump. Her flowing arm movements draw circles in the air. Different body parts and joints take over the task of guiding the arms. Movements start from the wrist, elbow or shoulder. The dominant qualities of movement are opening, scooping, modelling, swinging ("curving swings"/"figure-of-eight swings"), falling, rising ("fall and recovery"), finishing.

The dominant hand movements are: 'show'/'offer,' 'wipe'/'rub,' 'drop' and 'stop,' "fluttering," 'psst,' 'face circle,' 'measure' and 'wave' (FIG. 7-15). This is exemplified by a short movement phrase: For

7 'Show'/'offer'

'show/offer' (FIG. 7), the dancer opens her palms to the audience, which looks like she is offering something or revealing a secret. It is a movement performed by all of the dancers in a 'chorus line.'

8 'Wipe'/'rub'

'Wipe'/'rub' (FIG. 8) is an accentuated, precise and controlled rubbing of the hands. It is carried out by rubbing the palms of the hands away from or toward the body, or by using the hands to wipe down the arms in a powerful movement like rubbing – a similar movement also appears in the men's dance. It looks like something is being wiped off, wiped away, cleaned or put in order, much like a nervous tick.

9 'Drop'

For 'drop' (FIG. 9), which also appears in the men's dance, two fists fall onto the head or shoulders, where they begin "fluttering," or they move further down, where the hands then trace the shape of the chest, a movement that is then looped several times.

10 'Stop'

For 'stop' (FIG. 10), the dancer opens her palms toward the audience or places her hands next to her head in an accentuated way. Both movements are accompanied by the words "No, No, No," spoken in a French accent. Body movements and language thus reinforce each other and are overall clearly defensive.

11 'Fluttering'

When carrying out the "fluttering" movement (FIG. 11), the fingers are placed lightly on the shoulders, the elbows alternate, moving sideways away from the body and then returning to it. This movement is looped several times, performed rhythmically to the music and accompanied by a spoken "No, No, No."

12 'Psst'

'Psst' (FIG. 12) is a hand movement where the fingers wander to the mouth and open and close in front of or at the mouth, while the other fingers are clenched in a light fist. This is right after saying, "No, No, No."

13 'Face circle'

The 'face circle' (FIG. 13) follows directly after the 'psst' hand movement. The dancer draws a circle around her face using her index finger. Her head is turned to the side. Her chin points toward her shoulder. This hand movement appears shy but also playful or flirtatious.

14 'Measure'

During the 'measure' movement (FIG. 14), the dancer uses her arms to measure her upper body. Her head moves from right to left, as if she is shaking it. She says "No" in a French accent.

15 'Wave'

The 'wave' movement (FIG. 15) is a gentle movement using the fingers, hands and wrists. Both palms are pointing downward and wander to one side. The upper body twists slightly in the opposite direction of the movements of the hands. This movement is also looped several times. It reappears, albeit in a different mood, during the seated dance of another performer, Héléna Pikon.

The arm and hand movements are performed while the dancer speaks. In many of the hand movements, the dancer also pulls up both shoulders or just one or the other. Touching mainly takes the form of stroking the palms of the hands, wiping down shoulders or forearms, fists falling onto the head or fingers twirling hair or tracing the shape of the mouth. In spite of being executed at a relatively high speed, all of the movements are performed with great precision.

The facial expressions support the arm and hand movements. The dancer maintains eye contact with the audience, smiling timidly and shyly, but she also appears determined. Her expression charmingly oscillates between a confident showing and a sharp gaze on the one hand and a playful, shy withdrawal of movement while turning the gaze inward on the other. Her dancing demonstrates and performs something at the same time. It tells a story by showing it and shows it by telling. This multiplicity is generated by the fact that the dancer's arm and hand movements are dance-like/rhythmic and at the same time suggestive/expressive, which makes plural and also contradictory readings possible, for example, when something is rhythmically coherent and at the same time semantically confusing.

This solo changed when the role was passed on to Julie Shanahan in 1991 and later, in 2010, to Clémentine Deluy. Julie Shanahan danced it less shyly and more self-confidently than Anne Martin, while Clémentine Deluy's performance appeared more one-dimensional, at least in the video recording of the 2010 restaging, possibly because she placed greater emphasis on the dance aspect, allowing the rhythmic quality of the movement to emerge more strongly at the expense of the semantic content of the gestures. In this case, the dance was executed rather than performed.

Since individual elements of the solo also appear in other dances in the piece, it can be assumed that the movement material probably came from Pina Bausch herself. Unlike other solos such as the dances by Beatrice Libonati and Dominique Mercy that I will discuss in the following, there is therefore reason to believe that Anne Martin did not develop this solo herself. While the solos featured in later pieces tend to showcase the respective person dancing them (→ COMPANY, WORK PROCESS), the movement material here reappears again and again throughout the piece in new variations, combinations and figurations from different perspectives. In various solo and group formations, the dancers lend different colors and moods to the material, which is condensed into a specific color and mood in Anne Martin's solo.

BEATRICE LIBONATI IN *Masurca Fogo*

Beatrice Libonati's dance solo originated in the piece *Masurca Fogo*, which was coproduced with the Expo '98 Lisbon and the Goethe-Institut Lisbon, Portugal. Beatrice Libonati is Italian and was born in 1954 in Belgium. She studied dance at the Accademia Nazionale di Danza in Rome. In 1977, she worked with Susanne Linke, who at the time ran the Folkwang Tanzstudio in Essen together with Reinhild Hoffmann. From 1978 to 2006, she was a member of the Tanztheater Wuppertal ensemble both as a dancer and as a personal assistant, dancing in many pieces up until the 1998/99 season. *Masurca Fogo* was the last piece that she helped to develop and of which she was part of the original cast. She has also created her own solo dance pieces, paints and writes poems.[25] Beatrice Libonati is married to Jan Minařík, who first worked as a ballet dancer at the Wuppertaler Bühnen under Ivan Sertic, then joined Pina Bausch as a member of the Tanztheater Wuppertal from her first season there and stayed until 2000/01.

This analysis is based on a video recording of the world premiere at the Schauspielhaus Wuppertal on April 4, 1998. The piece lasts for 2 hours 30 minutes and includes an intermission. The solo is 2 minutes 39 seconds long. It is danced twice in the second part of the piece, the second time in front of a video projection. The solo is accompanied on both occasions by the Portuguese fado "Naufragio", sung by Amália Rodrigues (1920-1999), a world-famous fadista who helped popularize fado all over the world and whose work remains highly influential even today. Amália Rodrigues made her last public appearance during the Expo '98 in Lisbon, where the piece *Masurca Fogo* was also shown. Before that, she visited the company during rehearsals in Lisbon. The scene in which Nazareth Panadero bids farewell, saying, "Goodbye, where do you come from?" makes reference to this visit. Fado is often associated with the Portuguese word *saudade,* which describes a melancholy feeling of longing, desire, homesickness and wanderlust. In this piece, the singing is performed rubato with melismatic melodies. The music acoustically accentuates and rhythmically accompanies the dance solo, partly reinforcing it acoustically, partly in slight contrast to it.

The solo is embedded between two fast, dynamic dance scenes. It follows a movement scene based on the cue *sharp turn,* which Pina Bausch gave to the dancers at rehearsals in Lisbon in September 1997. It also appears under this name in the written scene order of the piece. In 'sharp turn,' the men run and catch each other and turn the person that they have caught around on his axis at a very high speed. The musical accompaniment is Baden Powell's "Batuque No 'B'" (1971), which mainly features fast, rhythmic percussion instruments. The scene changes abruptly when the dance solo begins: the stage becomes bright and empty. The dancer enters from stage left, and the music changes at the same time. On several levels, the previous scene is an antithesis to the subsequent female solo: there is a musical contrast, a shift from male group dance to female solo, opposite tempi, a contrastive use of space and lighting. There is another contrast after the solo: the music changes abruptly once more to a polyrhythmic string quartet (Alexander Balanescu Quartet, "The Model" [1992]), which quickly and loudly follows after the slow fado. At the same time, another dancer (Chrystel Guillebeaud) races down from the grey mound of rock that towers in the background of what is otherwise a white stage in order to begin her solo. Beatrice Libonati rolls herself off the stage and exits through the auditorium.

The second time that the solo appears is at the end of the piece, once again embedded between contrasting dynamic scenes. First, the 'sharp turn' is repeated once more, followed by the rapid construction and dismantling of a wooden barracks in which all the dancers gather to dance the salsa, accompanied by the sounds of Bantu Tupi Nago and a video projection showing a herd of running bulls. After the dance hut has been rapidly dismantled again, the sequence 'lift/turn' begins, in which several dancers lift and turn a female dancer (Ruth Amarante) by the legs from right to left. The scene ends on the left-hand side of the stage, where Beatrice Libonati's solo also begins, accompanied by projections of water and the sounds of the sea. During her dance, a deceptively real walrus crosses the stage in a casual, lonely manner. A dancer (Dominique Mercy) throws fish at it. The projection and sea sounds also dominate the next scene. After having once more repeated her solo, Beatrice Libonati again leaves the stage through the auditorium.

The solo's starting point is the 'questions' (→ WORK PROCESS) that Pina Bausch asked all dancers during rehearsals. These included: *Juicy movement, Floating movement, Brutal, Beautiful wistful violin sounds, Hurt movement, Slipping, Unfolding* and *Fado*. Beatrice Libonati used them to develop her solo, which begins in a squatting position in which she alternately leans on her left or right hand. As she pulls her legs forward, her pelvis almost touches the floor. She is wearing a light blue, floor-length dress and has dark hair, which hangs down just above her shoulders and often covers her face. As in Anne Martin's solo and in the entire movement vocabulary of the Tanztheater Wuppertal, the arm and hand movements in her dance are striking and determine the overall style of the dance (FIG. 16). Alfredo Corvino (1916-2005) – a Uruguayan ballet dancer and former member of the Folkwang Ballet under Kurt Jooss who, as a ballet master, trained numerous world-famous companies, including the Tanztheater Wuppertal – once said that the company had the best arms in the world.[26] This is also visible in Beatrice Libonati's solo: small recognizable gestures, such as scratching her arm, putting a finger in her mouth or wiping off a foot, are supported by sweeping arm movements and contractions of the torso. In addition, gestural and abstract movements incessantly alternate in this solo. All are executed slowly, gently and fluidly, which, together with the fado music, produces a quiet, rather melancholy atmosphere and a sense of calm that unfolds its own poetry.

16 Arm movements and torso. Excerpt from the score; solo by Beatrice Libonati in *Masurca Fogo*

	00:00:16.0	00:00:16.8	00:00:17.6	00:00:18.4	00:00:19.2	00:00:20.0	00:00:20.8
TS: Torso	Curve Back	Curve Back	Curve Back	Cambré	Tilt Side		Tilt Forward
TXT: Torso	Backwards Curve	Backwards Curve	Backwards Curve	Flexible Tilt Backwards/Cambré backwards(Chest Guidance)	Flexible Tilt Sideways		Flexible Tilt Forwards

The movements of the arms constantly alternate between closing and opening. When they are not stretched out to the side or upward, the dancer draws her arms toward her body at a tight angle, often leading to twists or contractions of the torso. The quality of the movement is soft and fluid throughout the solo. The accentuated arm and hand movements contrast with large flowing arm circles and swings, and the soft torso.

Throughout the solo, the torso provides central momentum for the movements (FIG. 16). Most of the time, it is at a slight tilt, in a backward or forward bend. Together with the arm movements, the tilt initiates turning movements. The tilt of the torso also plays an important role in transferring weight. The arm movements start from the torso, which supports their flowing quality – even in moments of contraction, which usually follow a backbend, the movements of the torso remain flowing and light.

	00:00:36.0	00:00:36.8	00:00:37.6	00:00:38.4	00:00:39.2	00:00:40.0	00:00:40.8	00:00:4
TS: Legs	Deep Transfer	Deep Transfer	Deep Transfer	Turn	Leap	Step Forward	Step Forward	Upright P
TXT: Legs	Transfer, Single Deep Support left, lift right	Double Medium Support, slightly turned back diagonally, left leg wide sideways	Single Deep Support left Transfer Single Deep Support right	Left leg lifted, turn over, Single Medium Support right	Transfer to Single Deep Support left - Jump	Double Support fist right, then left follows Single Support left, Gesture with right	Single Support Right Gesture with left	Double Medium Support - Stand

17 Transferring weight

Slow steps and constant transfers of weight characterize the solo (FIG. 17). Together with the tilted posture of the torso, this gives the impression that the dancer is constantly wobbling, falling out of balance. The transfer of weight from the right to the left leg via a deep plié is often supported by arm swings as well. Dynamic changes mainly occur between arm movements toward the center or to the periphery of the body, i.e., toward or away from it, which encompass or sometimes emanate from her torso.

	00:01:32.8	00:01:33.6	00:01:34.4	00:01:35.2	00:01:36.0	00:01:36.8	00:01:37.6
TS: Hands	Palm Deep	Palm Deep	Palms Side	Palms Side	Circle	Palm Side/Fist	Fist/Down
TXT: Hands	Right finger touches left elbow, shaking the wrist - accenting	Right finger touches left elbow, shaking the wrist - accenting	Palms of the hands facing each other, traveling down, slightly offset	Palms of the hands facing each other, slightly offset - then on the same level	Wrist joints circling ones	Right hand moves like a wave, hands meet above the head	Hands come together, light fists, from above the head the hands drop down to chest level

18 Hand movements

Her accentuated hand movements (FIG. 18) are integrated into the slow flow of her arms. They are primarily characterized by the varied positioning of her palms, which are directed upward, downward or forward, and by the way that her palms are positioned toward the body. Both hands are brought together to form a light fist, which she places in front of her sternum, lifts over her head or drops into her lap (FIG. 19). This is different to the position of the torso, which is either in an open backbend or in a rounded contraction, thus producing a humble and/or begging posture.

19 Hand movement and fist. Screenshot from the score of Beatrice Libonati's solo

The dancer also gently strokes her own arm with her fingers. This is performed relatively inconspicuously, like a slight intermediate movement (FIG. 20). At one point, she repeats and intensifies this touching until it can be interpreted as scratching.

20 Finger touch

At two points in the solo that occur in quick succession, she uses both palms to smooth her dress out down her leg. She also places her palms in front of her face or on top of or behind her head and uses them to stroke back her hair (FIG. 21).

21 Touching the palms of the hand – body

In a very conspicuous movement, the dancer touches the sole of her own foot with her hand. Here, functional and abstract movements meet: the dancer sits on the floor and strokes her foot then keeps holding on to her heel while standing up. She pats it with her hand before letting her leg fall to the ground, allowing it to immediately bounce back up again with the help of her hand in the very next moment (FIG. 22).

22 Touching hand – foot

Her head movements (FIG. 23) follow the movements of her torso. Her head is therefore often stretched backward during a backbend or tilted to the side. In some tilts, her head and torso make opposite movements: the head rotates from front to side, which also changes the relationship between chin and shoulders.

	00:00:18.4	00:00:19.2	00:00:20.0	00:00:20.8	00:00:21.6	00:00:22.4	00:00:23.2	00:00
TS: HeadMov.	Back/Central	Central/Side		Forw.	Side/Deep	Side/High	Central/Side	Centra
TXT: HeadMov.	Head Backwards High Flexible Tilt Sideways frontal face	Head aligned with the spine Flexible Tilt Sideways frontal face		Chin extended forwards	Head aligned with the spine Flexible Tilt Sideways face to the side (Head sideways)	Head aligned with the spine Flexible Tilt Sideways Head Sideways and High	Head aligned with the spine frontal face, Head moves sideways	Head a with the Head n sidewa

23 Head movements

The dance is characterized by a constant 'stagger' or 'swaying,' by a winding, turning and twisting, a falling out of balance. It is a self-referential dance, melancholy and lonely, calm and self-confident, struggling, but showing itself as such, forming a strong contrast to the dynamic dances of the younger dancers before and afterward. It was the last solo danced by Beatrice Libonati in a piece by the Tanztheater Wuppertal. This is also evident in the way that she exits: at the end, she literally leaves the stage and departs through the auditorium.

DOMINIQUE MERCY IN "*...como el musguito en la piedra, ay si, si, si...*"

On the multilingual website Bachtrack (bachtrack.com), Philippa Newis describes Dominique Mercy's solo as follows: "Dominique Mercy's solo is a lynchpin in the first half of the piece. His pale hands and bare feet are exposed against the black backdrop and his dark clothes. Mercy moves with a fine calligraphy. Skating across the space, his glass-cut shapes melt into the floor. A dancer with Tanztheater Wuppertal since 1973, Mercy wears Bausch's legacy like a second skin. He is mesmerising to watch, imbuing the space with a mature confidence and an easy, generous manner."[27]

Dominique Mercy has been a member and one of the main protagonists of the Tanztheater Wuppertal since its beginnings in 1973. Before that, he danced at the Grand Théâtre de Bordeaux and from 1968 at the Opéra national de Paris under the direction of Carolyn Carlson. He had his first important role with the Tanztheater Wuppertal in the piece *Fritz* (PREMIERE 1974), in which he danced while constantly coughing gently throughout (→ PIECES), but it was above all his solos in the two Gluck operas *Iphigenie auf Tauris*

(PREMIERE 1974) and *Orpheus und Eurydike* (PREMIERE 1975) that became milestones in his dance career. Nevertheless, he left the Tanztheater Wuppertal together with Malou Airaudo in 1975. He then returned once more in 1978 and, from then on, performed in all other pieces by the Tanztheater Wuppertal. In retrospect, he describes his relationship to Pina Bausch as always having been characterized by the fact that he stayed aloof from her throughout their many years of collaboration.[28] Nevertheless, he often developed dramaturgically important solos. Until the 2016/17 season, he danced in various pieces and also conducted rehearsals, which he has continued to do since he retired as a dancer. After the death of Pina Bausch, Dominique Mercy took over as artistic director of the Tanztheater Wuppertal in October 2009 together with Robert Sturm, a position that he held until 2013.

His solo, analyzed below, is from the piece *"…como el musguito en la piedra, ay si, si, si…"*, the company's last coproduction and also the last piece by Pina Bausch, who died shortly after the premiere. The analysis is based on a video recording of the world premiere at the Wuppertaler Opernhaus on June 12, 2009. The solo lasts a total of 5 minutes 10 seconds and thus, due to its duration alone, occupies a special position in the company's œuvre.[29] In the relatively short piece *"…como el musguito en la piedra, ay si, si, si…"* (2 hours 40 minutes), all 16 participating dancers dance a solo. Considering that there are also other group dances, it is therefore a very dance-intensive piece. Unlike the other solos, which tend to follow one another in the piece, this solo is framed by 'theatrical,' non-dance scenes. Right before the solo, a man (Fernando Suels Mendoza) calls to a woman (Anna Wehsarg) and kisses her. She slaps him. Then she kisses him back, whereupon he slaps himself. After Dominique Mercy's solo, two dancers (Clémentine Deluy and Azusa Seyama) simultaneously take off their bras; one of them measures her body. About ten minutes before his solo, Dominique Mercy dances a duet with Rainer Behr – who, born in 1964, is 14 years younger than Dominique Mercy and only became a dancer with the Tanztheater Wuppertal in 1995, 22 years after him. Rainer Behr energetically, powerfully and quickly moves back and forth from side to side along the front edge of the stage, but his movements also make him look like he is struggling and being hounded. Dominique Mercy runs after him and tries to grab him, but is unable to catch him for a long time. Eventually, he manages to grasp his jacket and tears it off his body. They stay in physical contact throughout their subsequent duet, leaning on each other. This duet shows the ambivalent relationship between the generations of dancers (powerful, determined but also disoriented on the one hand, physically weaker, needing assistance but also prudent on the other), but it also shows how being together compensates for weaknesses. Moreover, it introduces to the stage Dominique Mercy, who is 'older' compared to the other 16 dancers. Dominique Mercy, born in 1950, was 59 years old at the time of the world premiere and the only member of the first generation of Tanztheater Wuppertal dancers to perform in this piece.

His solo is accompanied by Andean music, which comes from the Andean countries of northwest South America, in particular from Bolivia, Peru and Ecuador. This specific piece of music was written by Mauricio Vicencio (1958), a composer and musician who was born in Chile and lives in Ecuador. He has dedicated himself to the dissemination of Andean music and also conducts research on the shamanism of his ancestors, on ancient cultures and pre-Columbian instruments, in particular wind instruments. The instrumental piece uses panpipes, string instruments such as the charango and guitar, bowed string instruments such as the violin and the cello, and percussion instruments like the bombo (similar to a bass drum). It also features samples of birdsong and jungle sounds. It has a homophonic texture; the rhythm of the music contrasts with the dance, while the sound is accompanying and supportive.

The solo is characterized by dynamic shifts between standing erect (stretching/reaching upward) and a strong connection to the ground (falling, long periods spent on the ground). The dominant movement quality is "fluttering" (at one point in the solo, which repeats itself, the dancer actually 'flaps' his trousers). As in the case of Beatrice Libonati, his solo also plays with free and fixed flow. The free-flowing quality conspicuously dominates. The energy of his movements is largely directed outward.[30] At one point, the dancer speaks during the dance. He calls, "Hey!" into the wings. There are gestural movements, especially of his hands and arms. One hand movement, which is performed in a "fluttering" manner, could be read as despair, with the back of his hand placed on the forehead as if he is about to faint.

Like Anne Martin's solo, this solo also constantly introduces new movement motifs while at the same time revisiting parts of what has already been shown in order to present them again in other variations and combinations. Movement variations are the result of changes in spatial position, changing the direction of movement (e.g., toward the audience or away from the audience), changes in tempo, shifting movements to other parts of the body, altering movement impulses (e.g., variations with his arms), (slight) variations of longer movement sequences, the reframing of movements (e.g., individual movement figurations emerging from different movements than before and merging into new ones) and variations in movement quality, direction and posture.

The soft, fluid quality of the movement does not lead to collapse or to the complete yielding of Dominique Mercy's body. After an impulsive 'aftershock' and 'compliant reaction' of the body, it falls, following the forces of gravity, which in turn provoke an upward countermovement. This creates the impression of great flexibility and free-flowing (movements that start from his shoulders, torso or elbows reverberate through the rest of the body), although the dancer is upright. A fall is always directly followed by coming back up to a standing position, in forward tilts that swing back up again, and by a floor part, where his whole body falls to the floor, only to immediately get back up again.

The solo fills the entire space and mainly features diagonal spatial paths. The first part is danced at the rear left-hand side of the stage, which is also where the solo begins. The recurring spatial paths, performed dynamically at high speeds, are striking. The spatial orientation of his body is also distinct: there are many turns and changes of direction. He dances a large part of the solo facing away from the audience. The calmer end of the solo forms a strong contrast to the dynamic sections: the dancer slowly walks to the back of the stage with his back to the audience. He makes wide arm movements, which he transforms with each step. With a last swing to the right and a few diagonal steps forward, he finally leaves the stage.

Dynamic shifts in movement quality are typical of this solo. If we use the conceptual pairings of the Jooss-Leeder vocabulary – energy/intensity ("strong"/"light"), form/design ("droit"/"ouvert"/ "tortillé"/"rond"[31]), spatial initiation ("peripheral"/"central"), and speed/time ("fast"/"slow") – the basic dynamics of the solo can be noted as dominantly "shivering" ("light"/"central"/"quick"), partially "thrusting" ("strong"/"central"/"quick") and "slashing" ("strong"/"peripheral"/"quick"). More rarely, a movement quality like "gliding" ("strong"/"central"/"slow") or "floating" ("light"/"peripheral"/"slow") appears. This use of movement qualities makes the solo appear rather fast and, in terms of its emotional disposition, "shivering" or trembling. However, it also repeatedly contrasts with moments of 'heaviness' (e.g. falling to the ground). The impression of trembling is also brought about by the fact that movement phrases are not broken off or interrupted. The dance also has many off-center, flexible turns, and transitions between peripheral and central movement motifs, which are rarely carried out in a jerky manner.

Torso movements typically feature flexible forward tilts, slight twists, and side- and backward curves. Sequences of bending forward and then quickly straightening back up again dominate the solo. Dominique Mercy's upper body is usually flexible, remains loose and 'fluid,' but there are also moments when his upper body leads. In some of these moments, the torso tilts to the side on his body's vertical axis. His body falls and then catches itself in the next step. Here, too, the torso loosely follows the falling movements of the entire body or itself determines the course of the falling movement. An important feature of the solo is the backward curve. In turns, steps and jumps, his chest opens upward and his head points backward and upward.

As a former ballet dancer, Dominique Mercy also includes some ballet movements in his solo. His legs are bent; he rarely completely extends them and does not hold them there. He shifts his weight in pliés; glissade jumps end in soft pliés. The jumps are never accentuated in the air. This creates a connection with the ground and with gravity, which, due to his upward turned chest and the many backward curves, gives the impression of an easy upward striving movement. In terms of leg positions, wide straddling movements (also jumped to the side or backward) alternate with croisé positions (legs crossed in a deep plié). Another motif is the turns performed on one leg, with ronde de jambes (one leg drawing circles on the ground or in the air). The quality of his leg movements is characterized by soft, 'floating' movements of the feet over the ground that use only little energy. Since strong leg movements with a lot of energy are rare, they are particularly striking when they do take place (e.g. stomping on or dropping to the ground).

The dance solo also features arm movements that alternate between movements toward the center and toward the periphery, merging fluidly and easily. Characteristic aspects include wide, high arms, crossed, narrow arm positions (hands crossed in front of the body/hugging oneself) and many arm swings, where the arms follow the momentum or are held in a curved position (FIG. 24).

24 Arm movements. Screenshot from the score solo by Dominique Mercy in "...*como el musguito en la piedra ay si, si, si*..."

The arm movements allow the sequence to be interpreted as leaning/resting/converging on or as being exhausted, as gestures of resting and pausing. Dominique Mercy slowly 'tilts' his head off its axis and brings it back, lowers or turns it slowly as his gaze is directed upward or sometimes in the opposite direction of the movement, both suggesting instability in the dancer's body.

The tilting back of the head, the frequent backbends and often the high, wide "scattering" arms, especially in turns that are performed bending backward with the head thrown back, evoke feelings of instability and insecurity. There is something searching/lost that pervades the solo. This impression is supported by the part in which Dominique Mercy sits on the floor, slowly looks around and then turns to the wings with a quiet "Hey!"

The soft, fluid movement quality of this solo is striking. This is reinforced by the fact that the dancer's hands are always held slightly apart, loosely 'hanging' in their joints; the movements of his hands can be read as culturally coded gestures of 'keeping watch.' The most striking hand movement is one in which the dancer brings both hands to his mouth in a "scooping" movement in different variations (FIG. 25).

25 Scooping movement

The dancer's hand position, movement quality, speed, direction of movement and the relationship between hand movements and other body movements vary. Dominique Mercy either "scoops" his hands up from below (with his upper body curving forward) and then brings them to his mouth, with his hands lying on top of each other as if scooping water, or the movement is one of "pulling," with his arms and hands pulling sideways toward his mouth (with his upper body in a side tilt). There is also a movement in which only his fingertips touch, scooping from below, and his upper body and head then slowly bend backward with his hands in front of his mouth, which are then gently released to the side. In these variations, it looks like he is bringing something to his mouth in his hands. This allows for interpretations ranging from astonishment to being frightened. However, the dynamics of the movement distort this interpretation. When he repeats the "scooping" movement directly in front of his mouth, it resembles a drinking movement. Seen within the context of the movement material as a whole, this central and also intimate act of coming into close contact with one's own mouth – with the instrument of speech, the opening that connects outside and inside – stands in contrast to his wide arm movements, which extend outward, making his body reverberate, and to the wide and "scattering" jumps and leg movements. These contrasts are also evident in the transitions from open to closed, crossed arms.

The constant transitions between fall and recovery, between above and below, the transitions between "scattering" and swinging arm movements, and the central "scooping" and guided arm and hand movements produce a sense of fluidity. Certain hand movements (from the hand to the mouth, "fluttering") and the specific alignment of the dancer's head create a sense of tension between openness and lightness on the one hand and a feeling of wandering and searching on the other. The reciprocal ambivalences in the qualities and dynamics of different movements do not allow for a one-sided or clear interpretation: the dance is a dance of despair, of being lost, of uncertainty and instability, but also of leaving behind, of relinquishing, of searching and of a (continued) will to fight.

Like all other dances, Dominique Mercy's solo also took Pina Bausch's 'questions' as its starting point, posed during the rehearsals for her last piece after a collaborative relationship that spanned 35 years (although it was interrupted at one point). Dominique Mercy himself describes the research trip to Chile (→ PIECES) as one of the most wonderful research trips that he ever had with the company and, apart from *Nefés* (PREMIERE 2003), *Rough Cut* (PREMIERE 2005) and *Bamboo Blues* (PREMIERE 2007), he had been a member of almost every original cast since the first coproduction and had always been involved in the development of the pieces. "I don't know if it had something to do with the country or with some kind of maturity on my part, or with Pina already being so weak that there was no room for any unnecessary arguments. I actually had a really nice time."[32]

To summarize, the three solos are prime examples of how dance can be presented and described in a differentiated way at a number of levels by translating it in detail into a score. The dances from the three different phases (→ PIECES) presented here differ individually and contextually – both in terms of when they were created and their position within the respective piece. Moreover, they each relate very differently to the audience: Anne Martin addresses the audience directly, while Beatrice Libonati's solo is more introverted, and Dominique Mercy partially dances with his back to the audience at the back of the stage.

It seems that Anne Martin's solo was developed not by her alone, but rather largely by Pina Bausch herself. The elements of its movements are dramaturgically linked to other (group) dances in the piece *Viktor*. In contrast, Beatrice Libonati and Dominique Mercy created their own solos. The individual movement language of each dancer alone means that they are already very different, but they tell us something about the respective person as well. "You are always yourself," is how Dominique Mercy characterized the dancing of a solo,[33] and that was also Pina Bausch's wish: "I think it's really nice to feel a little closer to everyone at the end of a performance because they have shown something of themselves."[34] Getting closer to the person in the dancer was one of the aims of her work (→ COMPANY). However, what the dancers developed in their solos had a clear starting point and a distinct framing: it was all related to the "movement questions" (→ WORK PROCESS) that Pina Bausch asked all her dancers during the rehearsals for each piece and that each individual answered differently in their own respective movement language. In the same way that Pina Bausch's 'questions' arose based on the situation, the respective time period or the research trips, and represent a circular searching process, the solos are based on her 'questions' translated into the situational moods of the dancers. What they show in their dances is sometimes related to the roles, positions and dances they performed in previous pieces as well. But most of all, it tells us something about them. Their dances appear as a gesture of touch[35] that opens up an indirect space of interaction with the audience, where dance emerges as action, showing and grasping.

In the same way that the solos are based on a reciprocal process of translation carried out by the individual and the group, by the choreographer and dancers, similarities also become apparent in these individual, situational, contextually bound dances, which are characteristic of the Tanztheater Wuppertal's specific dance language: hand and arm movements dominate in all three solos, to which small, clearly legible gestures and instances of touching the mouth have been added. Also conspicuous are recurring scenes in which the dancers touch themselves and say singular words. The tensions and dynamic shifts in movement qualities, as well as the relationship between the arm movements and the periphery and center are equally striking. The bodies appear 'fluid.' The movements are executed gently and start from the torso. All three solos are characterized by the repetition or variation of movement material that translates a movement motif into something different or makes it appear different through repetition alone. The dancing body is the medium that iteratively continues the danced loops of translation.

Translating dance into writing: Methodical reflections

The translation of dance into writing does not just help us to reconstruct dance; it is above all a decisive, indispensable process of analysis in dance studies. There are various methods that can be used to carry this out, some of which are described in the anthology *Methoden der Tanzwissenschaft* (Methods of Dance Studies) and shown using the example of Pina Bausch's *The Rite of Spring*.[36] As this chapter has demonstrated, one such method is the translation of dance into a score. This methodological approach, where parts of a piece like solos are presented and examined in detail in frame-by-frame analyses, is one aspect of praxeological production analysis (→ THEORY AND METHODOLOGY).

Applying methods always means developing methods as well, which is why the respective methodological steps should be comprehensible and intersubjectively verifiable. Since dance analysis involves several steps of translation, for each of which decisions have to be made, it makes sense to document and transparently present the analysis process. This ranges from the research question to the justification for selecting certain methods, from the adaptation of those methods for the respective analysis to the actual analysis itself. Here, it is particularly important to explain how the material was evaluated and interpreted, which I have carried out in this chapter using the example of the solos, although somewhat cursorily. Accounts like these are part of every analysis and are necessary in order to meet a second criterion, intersubjective verifiability, which is ensured by plausibly demonstrating how the video material was evaluated and the interpretative conclusions drawn. This procedure is not only relevant for the presentation of the results, but is also useful during the analysis itself as well, as it allows one's own first reading and interpretations to be discussed and their plausibility to be checked in a scholarly context and for the researcher to reflect upon his or her own position as such in terms of "reflected subjectivity" (→ THEORY AND METHODOLOGY). The Feldpartitur software is a methodological tool that makes the steps of translating from body/dance to writing/text reproducible and comprehensible. In the context of hermeneutic video analysis[37] and grounded theory,[38] translation takes place on three levels of abstraction: firstly, the distinct encoding/description, secondly, the categorization of what has been encoded and, thirdly, its interpretation. From each level to the next, the content of the analysis becomes increasingly condensed, leading to differentiated descriptions. As in ethnographic research, the constant writing of memos, i.e., records that present the current state of analysis in relation to certain phenomena, categories or events, is likewise an indispensable component of the analysis process. These memos help the researcher to develop ideas, establish structures, review positions and develop concepts. They accompany the researcher throughout the analysis process and are always produced at the same time as the score, while continually being expanded and elaborated upon.

In the act of writing a score, dance is translated into notation and recorded in a differentiated way. What we also see here is *how* this methodical step of translation generates something new and different. At the same time, the respective score and its particular media-specific, aesthetic and technical qualities produce a distinct kind of knowledge about dance that materializes in the form of writing and images, and is represented through the specific mediality of the score. Due to its specific form of visualization, a score like the one produced using Feldpartitur turns dance into something different to the scores produced by, for example, Benesh Movement Notation, which records dance movements in a system of musical stave lines; digital notation software such as Synchronous Objects,[39] an artistic project that translates the organizational structures of William Forsythe's dance *One Flat Thing* into digital notation and thereby transforms them; or the Motion Bank project,[40] which visualizes dances by various choreographers such as Deborah Hay and Jonathan Burrows.

In this respect, this methodological process of translating body/dance into writing/text should not (only) be understood as a loss in the sense of the fixing or fragmenting of movement, as is sometimes feared. Rather, it also has the potential to grasp the form and shape of a dance in detail, to reconstruct it and, in doing so, to generate meaning and alternative knowledge about dance that is not only associative, metaphorical or symbolic, but which instead sets form in relation to what it 'says,' thereby establishing a relationship between movement and being moved, between doing and saying. In the case of notation-based dance analysis, this is carried out by translating dance into language with the help of a distinct vocabulary that is suitable for the specific case that is to be analyzed and then differentiating between the movements of the respective body parts and examining them in detail. Here, we chose the Jooss-Leeder vocabulary, which was expanded to include ballet terms and concepts capable of grasping the relationship between dance and music. The score functions as a medium with a logic of its own, whose qualities and readings differ not only from the live performance onstage but also from the video recording. The specific mediality of the notation software evokes a dance that is a simulacrum of dance onstage, both real and imagined, that is related or similar to the dance onstage. However, this should not to be seen in a negative light as an illusion, but rather regarded as something positive against the backdrop of the translation theory presented in this book. Like Roland Barthes, I interpret it as a process that recreates dance through selection and recombination. The result is "a world which resembles the primary one, not in order to copy it but to render it intelligible" and that "[...] makes something appear which remained [...] unintelligible in the natural object."[41] Accordingly, the software representation of the score brings to light what is not tangible in the perception of the ephemeral dance movement.

This step of translating dance into notation is already preceded by another step of media translation: recording the video of the live performance onstage. In order to assess the relationship between the video recording and the piece onstage – whether the video 'leaves something out' or emphasizes it, whether something is not visible due to the quality of the video material or appears in a different light – it is necessary to attend the performance in person as well. However, this is often impossible as the piece is no longer being performed or, as in the examples selected here, it is now being danced by other dancers. But even if the piece is still being performed, it is difficult to imagine any detailed dance analysis without the translation of dance into text and images. In this respect, notation-based dance analysis, like the one presented here, is essentially video analysis. As is the case here, each video-based dance analysis is already the result of an initial media translation and should therefore reflect upon the specific mediality of the recording medium.

Translating the video image into the score creates frames, a step that also requires decisions to be made. The categories that are used to define a frame depend on the movement sequence and its dramaturgy, but also on the research question. Another act of positing consists in the fact that, in order to be able to describe how a movement is carried out, it must first be understood and identified. Where does it begin? Where does it end? Which part of the body guides the movement? In order to pursue these questions, it is helpful to mimetically reproduce the dance using one's own body and/or to trace or draw figurations or spatial paths. In this respect, one way of verifying movements is to 'comprehend' the movement with and through one's own body. In the case of dances whose original creators we can still talk to, their specific knowledge and 'insider's point of view' can also be used to determine and correct the score. For example, a dancer might perceive the beginning or the end of a movement very differently to the way that it is interpreted by a scholar watching the video footage: while dancers usually begin with the (invisible) movement impulse, the movement in the recording only begins with the visible physical action.

Scores force researchers to reflect on how they design the translation process by fixing and immobilizing movements. On the one hand, these positings challenge researchers to embark on a search for repetitions in the movement material that has already been captured. On the other hand, they also serve as the precondition for further translations, as each translation begins with an act of positing that marks out a boundary, a standstill (→ THEORY AND METHODOLOGY). These positings in media translations ultimately touch upon an epistemic question, as movement in dance – as something that has little to do with instrumentally rational movement – cannot simply be described or examined as a spatial or temporal movement from A to B. Rather, it is precisely the aesthetic form of movement in time and space that characterizes dance.

The analysis of the dances presented here was thus preceded by several steps of media translation: first, by the translation of the dance from the stage – through the 'eye' of the camera – to video, then of what had been seen in the video to one's own body and sketched figures, which in turn were translated into the Feldpartitur score. Each step of translation from one medium to another makes something disappear while simultaneously making something visible that was previously unknown. The decision to use a specific vocabulary, here the Jooss-Leeder method, was another act of positing, as it was bound to a distinct framing, i.e., interpretations, that shape the design of the score. It is also useful to (self-)reflect and intersubjectively examine this decision in order to avoid only seeing in the dance what the conceptual toolkit suggests or using terms that do not reflect the movement. However, at the same time, the conceptual classifications also allow for new interpretations, for only through a term such as "scooping" in relation to Dominique Mercy's solo can specific qualities of movement be analyzed. The paradox between identity and difference, between the alleged 'original' and 'copy' that is inherent to every translation, is also evident in this methodological approach: dance only becomes recognizable and 'readable' in its gestalt or basic form through difference, through its translation into writing.

It is not just the vocabulary used by the 'translators' that frames the step of translating dance into a score, but also the technical specifications of the software, which play a decisive role in the identification of a movement. These include, for example, the linearity of the score's structure and the technical specifications required for transcription, as well as the division of a dance sequence into movement stills and time intervals, which are reflected in the image segments (frame by frame). The linear temporal structure of the score illustrates the possibilities but also the limitations of using video analysis software for dance and movement analysis: on the one hand, the linear structure allows us to visualize the temporal flow of a movement sequence. On the other hand, the software can only depict dance in the temporal succession of movement motifs. The analysis of the dance therefore remains the task of the researching 'translators.'

These translation steps reveal that movement is identified above all through its fixing in the process of translation, which changes the way we perceive dance. We see this in the logic of the Feldpartitur software and in all the individual steps required to translate a dance into a score. The productivity generated through this process allows something different to emerge and for dance to appear as an object of research. This approach develops its 'object' in order to make what is ephemeral and dynamic, that which is always already in the past, negotiable at all. In this way, it becomes possible to identify the dance, the 'original,' in retrospect. The various readings produced in the course of the different steps of media translation and the associated production of written material generate an interpretative construct. It is this construct, this process of 'producing' dance, that allows it to become identifiable at all, allowing the dance, the 'original' to become recognizable and comprehensible through the detailed analysis of the form and quality of movement. How are the 'poignant' or 'moving' effects of the dance, how are the audience's emotional reactions to it (→ RECEPTION | AUDIENCE) generated in the interplay between doing and saying, showing and telling? Score-based dance analysis is methodologically significant, as it is a detailed methodological translation process that allows us to apprehend dance for the purposes of documentation, artistic reconstruction and academic analysis. I have introduced score-based dance analysis in this book as part of the methodological canon of praxeological production analysis, which also includes other methods that accompany this translation step, such as descriptions by dancers and the analysis of their personal notes (→ COMPANY), the investigation of work processes and 'questions,' the observation of rehearsals (→ WORK PROCESS) and, finally, inquiries into audience perceptions (→ RECEPTION). In this pool of methods, score-based dance analysis turns its attention to the practices of creating dance, to the 'craft.' However, it cannot grasp the poetry of dance itself, for this remains the aesthetic 'surplus' that ultimately constitutes the art of dance.

1 Public broadcast of Pina Bausch's memorial service Wuppertal, 2009

The audience is always part of the performance, just as I myself am part of the performance, even when I am not onstage [...]. We have to have our own experiences, just like in life. No one can do it for us.[1]

Rece

ption

The Tanztheater Wuppertal can look back on several generations of spectators around the world. These spectators have seen, felt, experienced, interpreted and processed the ensemble's pieces, some of which are now over 40 years old, embedded them within the context of their own lives and connected them with what they already know and have experienced themselves. Some of them have written about their experiences, composed reviews and communicated what they have seen to a wider public. All of these activities have been acts of translation between the piece, the respective performance, its situational framing and the audience's perceptions and (prior) knowledge. This interplay has given rise to a variety of interpretations, which are part of the dance production insofar as they also generate knowledge about a piece. These audience interpretations continue to be updated over time, become entrenched and change.

The following chapter takes the perspective of the recipient and inquires into the relationship between piece, performance, perception and knowledge. On the one hand, it examines how dance critics have positioned themselves over decades, the interpretations they have developed and how they have translated the pieces and their respective performances into text. On the other hand, it also focuses on the audience and investigates what spectators expect of a piece after 40 years of the Tanztheater Wuppertal, and how they perceive performances and convey their experiences in words.

Dance criticism

"Critics simply have to come to terms with the fact that they are nothing but critics, not unlike mustard on warm sausages, not unlike aestheticizing weather frogs, loudly croaking out their judgments."[2]
Klaus Geitel, music and dance critic

"Critique has to be an open system [...]. Nowadays a critique is not an art judge in the old sense, but he/she holds some responsibility as a participant in the shaping of a complex discursive dynamic. To define this, to assert oneself with respect to the artists and the audience, is an ever-challenging exercise of life. Writing about dance performance means continuous investigation of representations of alterities in an ephemeral structure of reception."[3]
Helmut Ploebst, dance critic

Klaus Geitel and Helmut Ploebst belong to two different generations of critics – and they differ in their views about the role, status and purpose of journalistic criticism. They exemplify the transformation of dance criticism's own concept of itself, which is what this chapter will discuss and examine using reviews written about the work of Pina Bausch and the Tanztheater Wuppertal.

Klaus Geitel, an influential Berlin-based music and dance critic, came to know and love ballet in Paris. In 1959, he wrote his first dance review – about Maurice Béjart. In the 1970s, he also reviewed pieces by the young Tanztheater Wuppertal, such as *Bluebeard: While Listening to a Taped Recording of Béla Bartók's "Duke Bluebeard's Castle"* (PREMIERE 1977; → PIECES). After the premiere, he noted: "Pina Bausch's works are anxieties set in motion: nightmarish visions, scornful gymnastics classes, bitter lessons. What Pina Bausch does has little to do with dance, ballet or choreography. Hers is a silent theater. A staged bludgeon to the head. [...] Bausch makes no concessions: neither to herself, nor to the dancers or the audience. She knows how to use her art to bewitch. There has been nothing like it on German stages for quite some time. Pina Bausch storms all traditional theater divisions."[4]

The ambivalence expressed in this review repeats itself in many others – and their overall numbers are overwhelming. The Pina Bausch Archive boasts 2,372 reviews about the 15 international coproductions alone – and this collection is most certainly not complete. By the early 1980s, every new piece by the Tanztheater Wuppertal had already become an event. Dozens of critics from all over the world would travel to Wuppertal to attend the world premieres. And everywhere the company performed, renowned critics expressed their opinions in respected national newspapers, even if the performance was merely a restaging of a piece that had originally premiered years ago. However, despite the vast and immense number of reviews published worldwide, it is just a small group of critics above all in the German-speaking world who have actually followed Pina Bausch's work through the decades and who have written reviews about every single one of her new pieces.[5] Unlike US dance criticism of the 1970s, which was primarily shaped by women like Marcia B. Siegel, Arlene Croce and Deborah Jowitt, in 1970s (West) Germany, most of the dance reviews printed in the most important periodicals were penned by male authors. For this reason, the majority of the people writing about Pina Bausch were men like Klaus Geitel, Rolf Michaelis *(Die Zeit)*, Jochen Schmidt *(Frankfurter Allgemeine Zeitung/*FAZ) and Norbert Servos (e.g., *Ballett International, Die Zeit,* FAZ, *Der Tagesspiegel, Theater heute, Die deutsche Bühne, tanzdrama, tanz affiche,* as well as various radio reviews). One exception to this rule was Eva-Elisabeth Fischer *(Süddeutsche Zeitung/*SZ), who reviewed the company for years.

Dance critics are the stewards of discourse: it was the reviews of the 1970s in particular that played a major role in shaping how the world would come to speak about the art of Pina Bausch. Even today, these narratives, interpretations, explanations and judgments are still constantly referred to and repeated by audiences

3 Raimund Hoghe
Cantatas
Brussels, 2013

2 Pina Bausch
press conference
Düsseldorf, 2008

(→ RECEPTION | AUDIENCE), other critics, scholars and speakers, in Internet forums, magazines and blogs. As I will show in this chapter, the knowledge that critics have produced about the Tanztheater Wuppertal over the course of decades still influences the prior knowledge of audiences and shapes their expectations. The audience surveys that my team and I conducted for this book with specific questions related to audience expectations have confirmed as much (→ RECEPTION | AUDIENCE).

Dance reviews translate a stage event into the public sphere through media. They are paratexts,[6] i.e., texts that accompany or complement a piece and steer its reception. And against the backdrop of this book's definition of 'production,' they are also constitutive parts of a choreographic production (→ THEORY AND METHODOLOGY). In particular, the reviews published in the arts sections of newspapers hold special sway over the complex of power and knowledge surrounding the discursive knowledge of dance. Even though digital media have been breaking arts sections' exclusive position of power since the turn of the 21st century, thus diminishing the influence of individual journalists and dance critics, the arts sections in serious national print media around the world continue to mold public opinion. They still shape discourse, the reputations of artists and companies, the interest of potential host venues in a special production or in upcoming works by an artist, as well as the relevance generally afforded to dance as an art form. Dance critics and the media in which they publish occupy (differently recognized) positions of power. Dance reviews are significant written and publicly accessible sources of material for understanding the connections between performance and reception. So, while there are also other types of texts such as academic inquiries available as well as other journalistic resources – e.g., paratexts such as reports, interviews, documentaries and even texts written by the artists themselves – dance reviews, especially in the form of performance critiques, make it possible to gain special insights into the ways in which a respective piece has been perceived, contextualized and judged by a professional audience, that is, dance critics. In addition, they also reveal how the respective publications wanted to present the specific piece, the dance genre, the artist or venue. As reflective written statements, they form a counterpart to but also provide guidance for the oral statements made by the audience immediately after a performance (→ RECEPTION | AUDIENCE).

The dance reviews written about Pina Bausch and the Tanztheater Wuppertal also reveal themselves to be central components of the dance productions insofar as they fundamentally shape public opinion about their artistic work. Reviews have been divided since the outset: some have viewed Pina Bausch as a revolutionizer of dance, as journalist Ursula Heyn wrote on the occasion of the premiere of *Viktor* (UA 1986) in 1986: "The dance-theater revolutionizer [...] has struck again."[7] Others believed they were seeing no more than endless repetitions, such as Helmut Scheier from the newspaper *Nürnberger Nachrichten,* who stated in 1986: "Almost all of it has been seen before in some way or another."[8] A third faction in turn has considered Pina Bausch's art to be sublime, for instance, Martin Töne in the *Westdeutsche Zeitung:* "Nobody presents the world as an eternal spiral of hopes and desires quite as magnificently as Pina Bausch."[9]

These three positions – that Pina Bausch showed nothing new and repeated herself, that Pina Bausch always had new ideas and is still groundbreaking, that Pina Bausch is a timeless pioneer of dance – have shaped the range of different judgments made in the arts sections since the company began over 40 years ago. They are components of the power-knowledge complex that defines the social value of dance according to the bourgeois understanding of art and decides whether the aesthetics of Tanztheater Wuppertal are innovative or not. This is especially striking when we look at its historical dimensions: the established critics of the 1970s, who were above all music critics, used the Tanztheater Wuppertal as an example to write about how a new aesthetic was infiltrating the reigning art establishment, which still adhered to the aesthetics of ballet at that time, a dance form that was considered to be subordinate to music within the hierarchy of the performing arts in Germany.[10]

This chapter deals with journalistic dance criticism and examines how critics have translated Pina Bausch's art into writing, how these acts have established and perpetuated dance theater discourse and the repercussions they have had on public opinion and perception. How is a piece translated into dance criticism? What kinds of writing practices can be found in such reviews? And in light of the opening quotations: what concept does dance criticism have of itself in relation to dance as an art form? How does dance criticism formulate critique? The following chapter pursues these questions by first outlining the different historical positions of dance criticism. This overview forms the framework for the subsequent presentation of central positions adopted by critics about Pina Bausch's artistic work with the Tanztheater Wuppertal. I will present these positions using reviews of the piece *Viktor* written between 1986 and 2017 and writings by critic Jochen Schmidt about all international coproductions (1986–2009).

Dance criticism has been an integral part of the European history of arts and culture since the public sphere moved into the media in the 19th century and journals took on the role of shaping opinion, to begin with in bourgeois circles.[11] Although newspaper scholar Wilmont Haacke emphasizes that the character of the arts sections of newspapers has repeatedly changed throughout history, he still essentially defines it as engaging in personal, subjective forms of writing, as "inner involvement."[12] In fact, the early days of arts-section dance criticism – which began above all in France with Théophile Gautier around 1830 – were characterized by translations into subjective, illustrative and poetic writing. Men wrote about the 'fleeting,' enchanting dances of the famous ballerinas of romantic ballet, and they did so with great passion and empathy. Dance criticism meant translating the imaginings and fantasies one experienced while watching dance into writing; it was less about formulating objective descriptions of what had actually been seen.[13]

After the Second World War, dance reviews in Germany primarily dealt with ballet and as such played a marginal role in arts sections. As the third and least valued art form in the hierarchy of the performing arts in Germany, it was assigned a subordinate status. And like all art criticism at the time, dance criticism was dominated by men.[14] Even in the early 1970s, when dance theater was revolutionizing the German theater landscape and calling the reigning hierarchical system of ranking the arts into question, only men – with the exception of Eva-Elisabeth Fischer – were writing about Pina Bausch and the Tanztheater Wuppertal, and most of them were actually music critics, among them 'pontiffs of criticism' *(Kritikerpäpste)* like Klaus Geitel and Horst Koegler. While other artistic genres have taken for granted that music, opera and theater critics possess practical experience and specialized knowledge in their respective art forms, even today, there is little to no discussion about what dance critics should know. Perhaps this is because so few have made the switch from the profession of dancer or choreographer to the profession of dance critic. On the contrary: if at all, they have generally gone in the opposite direction, like dance critic Norbert Servos, or Raimund Hoghe, who was once a critic, then became a dramaturge for Pina Bausch and is now an internationally respected choreographer.

The turning point in dance criticism came not in the 1990s, as claimed by Esther Boldt,[15] but as early as in the 1960s – and it was radical. Unlike in Germany, where newspaper arts sections mainly focused on the bourgeois institutions of a state-subsidized art scene, it was young American dance critics who first recognized the analogies with the new forms of dance being produced by Merce Cunningham and Judson Dance Theater, and who attempted to translate them accordingly into dance reviews.[16] For some, dance was an expression of emotion, for others a physical act. However, representatives from both sides agreed that "[t]he one inescapable thing about dance criticism is that you have to be in contact with the real live thing as it is performed."[17] Here, the idea that dance cannot be accessed discursively is connected to a kind of anti-intellectualism in dance criticism, which would soon be followed by a countermovement in the late 1970s that would attempt to grasp dance theoretically.[18]

In 1970s West Germany, dance theater's radical aesthetics triggered a crisis in dance criticism. The older, established critics rallied against dance theater. Although they recognized it as a radically new performing art form, they were unwilling to accept it as an artistic form of dance. In the meantime, a younger generation seized the chance to reinvent dance criticism and its institutional structures. In 1982, Rolf Garske founded the magazine *Ballett International,* which focused on new dance aesthetics. Young critics such as Norbert Servos and Hedwig Müller became important allies of Pina Bausch and the authors of a new way of writing about and interpreting her work. As young theater studies students, they developed an entirely different, more open approach to dance theater than the one practiced by their older, musicologically schooled colleagues. Their writings referenced current theater discourse, thus questioning the previous hostility of ballet criticism toward theory. They built a bridge between criticism and academia, reading this new art form through the eyes of theater scholars, thus developing a narrative about the work of Pina Bausch that has been replicated and translated for decades,[19] meaning that dance reviews about Pina Bausch are primarily characterized to this day by semiotic and semantic descriptions of individual scenes. This new generation of dance critics searched for new forms of writing and for analogies between dance and text – thus making a significant contribution to improving the reputation of the new art form of dance theater and, above all, to viewing the work of the Tanztheater Wuppertal as not just a purely aesthetic dance phenomenon but also a sociopolitically relevant art form.

In the 1980s, the founding of two new dance journals, *Tanzdrama* and *Tanz Aktuell,* gave German-language dance criticism another boost in the transformation of its self-image and the establishment of a critical writing practice. *Tanz Aktuell* in particular styled itself as a companion to contemporary dance and made a significant contribution to examining the problem of translation between dance and writing, between the aesthetic and the discursive, and to understanding dance itself as a special, corporeal expression of social and cultural knowledge while also discussing its political potential. This intellectual opening up of dance criticism, also and above all in relation to the emerging field of dance studies, initially led to broad and diverse coverage of dance in German arts sections. National newspapers employed 'permanent-freelance' dance critics, some of whom wrote detailed dance reviews, also about the work of Pina Bausch. Since the 1990s, this situation has changed, due in part to the crisis in publishing brought about by digitalization. Today, only a few arts sections publish dance reviews, most of which are short, often standardized descriptions that barely allow for any adequate translation of the experimental, any critical reflection on one's own writing practice or 'open writing.' At the same time, digital formats and platforms such as tanzkritik.net, tanznetz.de and corpus-web.net have established themselves in the German-speaking world with the aim of developing new forms of presentation, appealing to alternative groups of readers and producing new forms of knowledge through their distinct mediality.

Since the 1960s in particular, dance criticism has undergone a number of decisive changes within the scope of the paradigm shift that has occurred in dance, developments that have taken place in the media landscape and in light of digitalization: in the 1960s, the artwork itself and its performance formats were regarded as objects of criticism (→ PIECES), but since the 2000s,[20] 'conceptual dance' and dance research have shifted the focus toward artistic practice, which is now in itself considered to be the "site of criticism."[21] From the point of view of conceptual dance, criticism is not so much judgment as a mode of working that makes 'other' experiences and approaches to the world possible. However, some theoretical positions in turn define certain artistic working methods as 'critical' based on the fact that they allow new forms of community,[22] friendship,[23] "complicity"[24] and new collective working methods to be tried out and tested. These experimental and experiential spaces enable the exploration of 'different,' alternative or subversive social practices, in that they address a 'different' mode of individual and collective socialization.

Not just artistic practices but also journalistic practices of dance criticism have redefined themselves since the 1990s as critical practices, as the opening quote by Helmut Ploebst illustrates. Their critical potential lies in how they carry out the various steps of translating the perceptions of a piece into written text and what effects perception, knowledge and power, as well as the critics' own position, the performance situation and the (institutional) context (recipients, conditions of publishing outlets, etc.) have on each other. There are a number of translation steps between choreography, writing, description and judgment, each of which generates undeniable difference. By demonstrating its awareness of said difference, criticism becomes both a special practice of judging and a critique of judgment itself. Instead of relying on knowledge-based judgment, writers question what they think they know in a continuous attempt to approach artworks with fresh eyes. This attitude is not one of certainty; rather, it is based on an awareness of disruption. The act of judging a work of art can thus be read as the inextricable tension between translating dance into writing, balancing the interplay between the singular and the general, between experience and idea, moment and concept. The process of judgment itself thus appears to be a practice that is subject to open steps of translating between choreography, performance, perception and writing that must constantly be reconstituted.

These more recent concepts of a critical writing practice differ from the practices of established and traditional journalistic critique. But it would be wrong to assume that they were only developed and formulated in the 2000s – following the paradigmatic upheaval brought about by conceptual dance in the 1990s. Instead, we should regard them as the practices of a young generation of critics, who used the crisis of artistic dance provoked by dance theater in the 1970s and 1980s to productively reorient dance criticism.

These positions have redefined the concept of practice, which is usually considered to be antecedent or in opposition to theory. Practice theory's concept of criticism, on which this chapter is based in keeping with the framework of a praxeology of translation introduced in this book (→ THEORY AND METHODOLOGY), questions this duality between (dance) theory and artistic practice. Practice theory's concept of criticism thus also breaks away from the privileging of (dance) practice over theory, which is based on the dualistic notion that artistic practice is the real site of criticism. On the one hand, this thinking contradicts contemporary dance practice, which generates theory precisely in and out of that practice. On the other hand, however, it does not do justice to a way of thinking that understands the reception of a piece as a component of dance production and in itself a practice of generating knowledge. In this sense and as this book argues, practice is a complex and interdependent act of translation within the framework of an artistic production, which is defined as the interplay between developing, performing and perceiving a piece.

From this point of view, the concept of practice serves as a collective term for the techniques and "arts of existence,"[25] as Michel Foucault calls them, that play a role in dance production and that are generated in working methods (→ WORK PROCESS), forms of collaboration (→ COMPANY) and discursive fields of knowledge, such as those produced in journalistic and scholarly texts. Practices – artistic, journalistic and scholarly – form subjects. They also create difference between different types of subject, for example between dancers, choreographers, dance critics and scholars.

THE TANZTHEATER WUPPERTAL AND DANCE CRITICISM

Although the Tanztheater Wuppertal is a world-renowned company and Pina Bausch is undoubtedly considered a choreographer who has influenced various cultural, national and regional dance histories around the world, dance critics have always been divided in their opinions of her achievements. During her first artistic phase and right up until the first coproduction *Viktor* (→ PIECES), the guardians of the holy grail of traditional ballet were facing off with her fans. As the initial excitement, bewilderment and outrage over her revolutionization of dance began to die down, voices began emerging in the late 1970s that called Pina Bausch outdated, conventional and canonized. For example, in his 1978 review of *Renate Emigrates* (PREMIERE 1977), Jens Wendland claimed that he was unable to find anything other than "[...] sparse monomaniac dance sequences with rigid creeping, tearing and gyrating movements, which provide no further variation to Pina Bausch's well known barefoot dance litanies."[26] Arlene Croce stated with disappointment in 1984: "Bausch's publicity has exaggerated the scandal and salaciousness in her work. Some mild ribaldry, some rather unappetizing nudity are all she has. As a theatre terrorist, she achieves her main effects through repetition."[27] And, back in 1979, Horst Koegler wrote that, "What we need is a new Bausch,"[28] reiterating this opinion 30 years later in 2009, when he stated on the occasion of the premiere of *"...como el musquito en la piedra, ay si, si, si..."*: "It cannot be denied that the Wuppertaler Tanztheater Miracle has lost some of its original electrifying magic."[29] While our recent audience surveys confirmed the assessment of a growing conventionalization of Pina Bausch's works, they also revealed that the audience now takes particular delight in recognizing the familiar and expected (→ RECEPTION | AUDIENCE).

Until the very end, critics were divided about Pina Bausch. There were just as many exuberant voices emphasizing the unique, revolutionary or scandalous qualities of her art – more so internationally than in Germany. While Croce lamented the repetition, *Ballett News* issued the following praise in 1984: "Her work inhabits a self-created category that pushes into uncharted territories. Theater, dance, spectacle, elements of psychoanalysis, comedy and sheer terror are welded into grandiose, oversized, overlong epics of considerable impact."[30] And while Koegler longed for a "new Bausch," Johannes Birringer emphasized the radicality of her art in the *Drama Review* in 1986: "But when Pina

Bausch's Wuppertaler Tanztheater, still unknown in this country outside of New York, opened the Olympic Festival with such emotionally devastating pieces as *Café Müller* (1978) and *Bluebeard* (1977), the Festival had its first unpredicted scandal."³¹

THE WRITING ROUTINES OF ARTS-SECTION DANCE CRITICISM In their writing practices, critics are subject to selective practices of perception framed by experiences, tastes, preferences and discursive traditions. Dance critic and scholar Christina Thurner has emphasized that critics are required to take a step that translates perception into writing: "Perception, as well as the manner of its communication are, however, fundamentally shaped by discursive traditions, i.e., by the specific description of movement that is, by writing the effect of artistic movement in dance into being *[Er-Schreibung]*. In my opinion, it is a myth that movement onstage can be directly, immediately received, written down and communicated. In actual fact, we perceive that for which we have the perceptual tools. Discourse is what provides us with this toolkit – not exclusively, but to a decisive degree. Describing dance (in the arts sections or in academia as well) is thus not, as is often assumed, a purely parasitic matter, but an act whose retrospective and anticipatory effects cannot be detached (any longer) from the entire process of perception."³² Accordingly, writing routines, i.e., conventionalized, recurring practices of writing, and established discursive tropes can be identified in articles about pieces by the Tanztheater Wuppertal, as we will now show using the example of reviews of the piece *Viktor*,³³ Pina Bausch's first coproduction.

The reviews of *Viktor* all begin by situating the piece within Pina Bausch's overall oeuvre, with critics who have followed her work for years referencing their own personal or 'professional' history of visual experience. They then contextualize the piece by placing it in relation to a 'before' or 'previously.' A 1999 review of a guest performance of *Viktor* in London reads: "The Sadler's Wells season sold out weeks ago, because she is 'a legend.' Yet some of Bausch's targets are beginning to look rather obvious, not to say old hat – the destructive sexualizing of women with their cleavages and high heels: the inability of the sexes to communicate on things that matter, the blotting out of uncomfortable truths."³⁴ Often reviews distinguish between 'old' and 'new' parts. Comparisons are made with earlier pieces, and what has just been seen is accordingly characterized as being 'new' or 'typically Pina Bausch.' In 1997, Gerald Siegmund wrote in the FAZ on the occasion of a performance in Frankfurt: "Nothing human is strange to Pina Bausch. That's why her pieces are just as fresh and enchanting as when they first came out, even after more than a decade. They live and breathe with the people who never tire of looking for the strand under the pavement."³⁵

These classifications are not only formulated in reviews of restagings of the piece years after its world premiere, but can also be found in reviews of that premiere. In 1986 for example, critics judge what is new in *Viktor* to be innovative and praise it by saying, for example, that "the old phobias (reappear) in new form" and "new ideas."[36] In contrast, the elements identified as 'typically Pina Bausch' are either indifferently accepted – for example, the "carrying around of men and women," which is part of the "indispensable grammar of the Bausch stage"[37] – or are classified as outdated and a thing of the past – for example, when the piece *Viktor* is described overall as "the swan song of the last ten years of dance and theater" and its stage as "a powerful museum."[38] But even when critics claim that *Viktor* is nothing new, they still simultaneously emphasize the innovative power of Pina Bausch's art and its status within the context of contemporary art, as in 1986, when reviewers write that "her pieces have a long-term effect"[39] and that "Pina Bausch's Tanztheater Wuppertal's radical abstinence from conventional form means that it now has a reputation to defend."[40]

These classifications describe aesthetic routines in Pina Bausch's choreographies that are critically called into question against the backdrop of expectations relating to the 'new,' especially when reviews are written about restaged pieces, sometimes years and decades after the original premiere. The outcome can be positive, like when a critic for *The Jerusalem Post* writes about a performance of *Viktor* in Tel Aviv in 1995: "Pina Bausch is at her best, perhaps even her greatest, in *Viktor*."[41] Twenty-two years later, in 2017, after a performance in Hamburg, a newspaper reviewer stated: "Anyone who doesn't know that Pina Bausch's legendary piece *Viktor* was created in Rome in 1986, would consider it contemporary. […]. *Viktor* is a splendid example of this. It is also an example of how timelessly modern Pina Bausch's pieces are. Still avant-garde, even after 30 years."[42] These examples show that each respective piece is measured less against the standards of contemporary dance aesthetics than against a backdrop of questioning the overall contemporary relevance of the work of the Tanztheater Wuppertal (and these voices have multiplied even further since the choreographer's death). It is an ongoing struggle with the icon Pina Bausch and her almost mythological status in recent dance history. Hence, in 2001, Hungarian writer Péter Esterházy wrote about the performance of *Viktor* in Paris: "Pina Bausch fait partie de ces grands artistes. À travers elle, l'art acquires a raison d'être; nous regardons la scène, sa scène, au plus profond de notre cœur (ou d'un autre organe interne), et nous voyons alors à quoi sert l'art."[43]

The categorizing judgments of 'contemporary' and 'new,' 'outdated' and 'historical,' or 'timeless' and 'unique,' which are also made by the audience (→ RECEPTION | AUDIENCE), can be read as evidence of the close juxtaposition of performance, perception and knowledge. This is a juxtaposition that makes reference to the paradox between identity and difference inherent to every translation – and in particular to its temporal aspect. While restagings show the same piece and are thus identical with the past, they also create something 'new' and 'different' at the same time by shifting the piece during the performance into another present with other dancers and another audience in another place. In these new contexts, in temporary retrospectivity, dance critics measure what they see against its antecedent. In other words, the supposed original is only created during its translation into a restaging and in the reviews. And there are different positions on this matter: for example, in 1999, a reviewer for *The Daily Telegraph* complained:

"[...] I was bored stiff. The poetic scenes were few and far between, listlessness and dull parody everywhere else: the sad nondescript men in drag; and the bitchtarts in stilettos, seemed like overfamiliar Bauschian archetypes."[44] On the other hand, a critic in the *Süddeutsche Zeitung* wrote: "Pina Bausch's *Viktor* has not only survived the years well, but it has even increased in importance, dealing as it does with an internally torn society."[45] The *Frankfurter Rundschau* issued the following praise: "[...] but respect also grows for this dance and theater maker, whose pieces have aged like good wine."[46] Finally, in 1995, the writer for *The Jerusalem Post* stated: "*Viktor*, though created nine years ago, couldn't be more up to-the-moment."[47]

However, there was not only praise for the passing on of roles to other dancers (→ WORK PROCESS) and the translation of elements from the piece to other productions. For example, Jochen Schmidt wrote about *O Dido* (PREMIERE 1999) in the FAZ: "The magnificent gargoyle being force-fed bottled water, portrayed by Kyomi Ichida in *Viktor*, has now turned into the banal moistening of a chair by Ruth Amarante."[48] And in 2001, once again in the FAZ, he regretted that "there is as yet no one who could compete with the old fighters in terms of personality."[49]

Moreover, the dance reviews reveal various writing routines that evolved and solidified over time – over a period of 30 years in the case of *Viktor*: 1986-2017. During this period, writing conventions changed. For instance, the general eruption of dance criticism in the 1980s also becomes visible in the reviews of Pina Bausch's work as dance is placed in a political context – for example, Rolf Michaelis compares *Viktor* to German chancellor Helmut Kohl's environmental policies: "The gentle but determined, often comically, more often sorrowfully expressed – and clearly politically motivated – protest against the established world order is unmistakable on the evening of this premiere. During the rehearsals, no one could have foreseen the nuclear disaster in Chernobyl. Now, the perplexing image of a smiling girl with no arms not only awakens memories of thalidomide victims, but above all fears for the future. But what is the chancellor, who is 'sojourning' at the 'economic summit' in Tokyo, transmitting to his men in Bonn, who are musing over the citizens' critical questions about the purpose and benefits of having so many nuclear power plants in the densely populated Federal Republic of Germany? 'Don't wobble!' is the slogan of Viktor Kohl, who craves victory in the impending elections. Just how masculinely stupid are policies that only fend off the consideration of new facts, the critical examination of previous guiding principles in the categories of military, front-line thinking and soldier jargon? The other point of view, which does not consider it a weakness ('wobbling') to abandon potentially false positions, but rather sees it as a strength necessary for survival – this is what you can learn in the way that Pina Bausch plays with eternally 'broken' victors, who have been victorious to the death."[50]

Writing routines also changed in that, compared with later critiques, reviews of the 1980s allotted more space to a critical writing practice in the sense of critics reflecting on their own subjective positions and to descriptions of the audience's perceptions. At the same time, the text dramaturgy of dance reviews has been conventionalized over the years and has become routine. It now consists of routine text modules and follows a succession of descriptions of the stage, costumes and music, as well as individual, above all 'theatrical' scenes related to established aesthetic narratives such as 'dancing everyday movements' or 'male/female relationships.' Finally, most reviews end by assigning the piece a position within Pina Bausch's overall œuvre.

Another writing routine is the attempt to create analogies between choreography and writing by translating the dramaturgy of the pieces with all their tensions, contradictions and surprises into the dramaturgy of the text. For example, the opening scene of *Viktor*, into which all of the tensions of the entire piece are condensed, is reproduced by critics in reviews of the piece as a temporal succession of observations. A beautiful woman enters from the back right-hand side of the stage (from the audience's point of view). She walks toward the middle of the stage. She is wearing a tight red dress, which is described in detail using adjectives such as "brilliant,"[51] "vibrant,"[52] "elegant"[53] and "fiery red."[54] She smiles confidently at the audience, an act that is described as "showy"[55] and "triumphant."[56] As if attending the actual performance, the reader is only informed later that the woman's arms are missing, after having first been given an interpretation of the scene and a description of the tension, confusion and surprise felt while watching it. Moreover, these writing routines are often self-referential: reviews refer back to past reviews and to established and habituated styles of writing.

Dance criticism makes a significant contribution to the production of discursive knowledge about dance theater and to the framing of future perceptions. Expectations about a Pina Bausch piece feed on the discursive knowledge generated by the media in addition to personal experiences. This knowledge is translated and framed according to the situation and is thus continuously updated, consolidated or transformed in situational perception. Thus, there are situatively different readings of *Viktor's* opening scene, which I have described above: reviews of the premiere in May 1986 – like the review by Michaelis quoted above – link the "woman without arms" to the thalidomide scandal and to the catastrophe of Chernobyl in April 1986, thus placing her within the sociopolitical context of current affairs. In addition, cultural framings interact with expectations. The dance reviews of the coproductions thus ask what statement the piece wishes to make about the respective coproducing countries and whether something culturally 'typical' can be recognized in it. One example of this is the "restaurant scene" in *Viktor,* which critics have interpreted as being "typically Italian" for years – at its premiere, on tour and even in restagings – as well as the "fountain scene," which is read as a reference to the Fontana di Trevi and thus to the coproducing city of Rome (→ PIECES). Interpretations differ depending on the social, cultural and aesthetic sources, as well as the local frameworks of the respective dance critics. In reviews of *Viktor's* 1999 London performance, for example, the "restaurant scene" is interpreted as an homage to dancer and choreographer Antony Tudor. Even *Viktor's* stage design has been interpreted differently: for some, it is a Roman archeological site or a grave; for others, it is a symbol of the post-industrial Ruhr region or a coal mine.

Pina Bausch herself reacted to the different situational readings by referring to the wall that collapses at the beginning of *Palermo Palermo.* German audiences associated this with the fall of the Berlin Wall, Italian audiences with the fall of the Mafia or Sicily's distance to Europe. Pina Bausch said: "The wall means something different to everyone, every day."[57]

Such different interpretations of individual scenes depend on the various situational, political, social and cultural framings. They prove that discursive translation is a historically, culturally and regionally distinct and fragile process, which is also subject to both historical transformation and changes in perception and reception. Together, these framings and reframings contribute to the fact that the discourse and narratives surrounding the aesthetics of the Tanztheater Wuppertal have become entrenched while remaining metaphorically open. This in turn has helped each piece to be perceived as both historical and yet contemporary.

Writing routines do not just reveal themselves in reviews of individual pieces. They can also be found in the collected works of individual critics who have written about the Tanztheater Wuppertal for decades while developing and conventionalizing their own writing practices. One prominent example in Germany is Jochen Schmidt, who has been a critic for the *Frankfurter Allgemeine Zeitung* (FAZ) since 1968. As such, he has played a decisive role in shaping opinions about the art of Pina Bausch in one of Germany's most important newspaper arts sections. He recognized the rebellious potential and controversial artistic nature of her art early on and began regularly writing dance reviews of Pina Bausch's pieces in the 1970s. He also published reviews of all of the 15 coproductions produced between 1986 and 2009. These articles primarily appeared in the FAZ, but some of his reviews were also published in other newspapers such as *Die Welt*, on the online platform tanznetz.de and in *tanz aktuell / ballett international,* which merged in 2010 to become *tanz*. Schmidt also conducted regular interviews with Pina Bausch[58] and has published a book on the choreographer entitled *Tanzen gegen die Angst* (Dancing Against Fear).[59]

Jochen Schmidt has occupied a position of power in the media discourse surrounding Pina Bausch since the 1970s. His opinions have been influential – more so in the past, when the media landscape was not yet as decentralized and the newspapers and magazines of the educated middle class held a near-monopoly, especially the arts sections. Although this example is almost historical in light of recent radical changes in the media landscape, I would like to use his critiques here to illustrate the sustained influence of an established journalistic writing practice on Pina Bausch's work: what are the characteristic attributes of his practice of writing dance reviews about the Tanztheater Wuppertal over decades? Which writing routines can be found here?[60]

The writing routines in Jochen Schmidt's reviews can be identified above all by their dramaturgical structure. They follow a routine text dramaturgy. His dance reviews often use the titles as a hook: Schmidt points out that the piece does not yet have a title and that this is typical of the works of Pina Bausch. 'Typically Pina Bausch' therefore means premiering an unfinished piece, showing a 'work in progress.' While he and other critics read and praised this at the beginning of Pina Bausch's career as a critique of notions of artistic authorship, allowing the focus to be directed toward the processual rather than the finished work, this positive attitude changed over the years, morphing into a tired dismissal of the familiar.

Set design, music and costumes are the central categories mentioned in his reviews, always in connection with the names of Pina Bausch's long-standing collaborators, such as stage designer Peter Pabst, former ballet dancer and costume designer Marion Cito, and Matthias Burkert and Andreas Eisenschneider, who were responsible for the music (→ COMPANY). His descriptions of individual scenes usually characterize dancers, describe props or categorize the piece in terms of its main theme. Rarely does he mention actual dances – Jochen Schmidt does not have a dance background – but such references have become more frequent over the years. The ratio of solo to ensemble dances is always mentioned, but mainly in terms of quantitative distribution, i.e., the total number of solo and group dances in the piece, the length of the solos or the ratio of solos to group dances. In Jochen Schmidt's texts, dance is rarely discussed in terms of rhythm, dynamics, form, quality or the synchronization of movements. Instead, his writing tends to ascribe meaning to the dance. One example of this is the description of a scene in the piece *Only You* (PREMIERE 1996): "The dances, which begin almost entirely in the area of the arms, are of a disturbing, hectic immediacy. Their movements change directions in a matter of seconds, twitching here and there, and then withdrawing even before they have been performed completely. They seem to want to confirm the existence of the world, while simultaneously rejecting it using circling and beating movements, like trying to drive away a swarm of flies or mosquitoes. But these dances are neither embellishments nor divertissement. Their self-preoccupation and isolation are the actual theme of the piece."[61] On the one hand, this literal 'rewriting' of the dance scenes reveals a metaphorical openness. On the other hand, Schmidt attributes meanings to the dance which – in his opinion – fulfills dramaturgical functions in the piece.

Thematic, theatrical, symbolic, semiotic or material references to the coproducing country are also central criteria in his dance reviews of the coproductions. It is the common theme that runs through them. Like other dance critics, Jochen Schmidt searches for references to the culture of the coproducing countries in the music, stage, costumes and scenes that he describes. However, one exception is his descriptions of the dance sequences. He classifies them in terms of Pina Bausch's entire œuvre, comparing them to earlier dances from other pieces by Pina Bausch or to dance theater as a genre. In his review of *Masurca Fogo* (PREMIERE 1998), for example, Schmidt states for the first time that "the return to dance that has been pursued for years is now pushing ahead"[62] and then repeats this in almost every review that follows. Likewise, he regularly refers to "earlier spiral dances" or "line dances" that, he regrets, no longer appear in more recent pieces. In his reviews, dance is emphasized as something absent; the "search for the vestiges of dance" is more present in his reviews than descriptions of dances performed in the pieces. He combines this with an ambivalent attitude, criticizing on the one hand those pieces that only feature "beautiful dance" in "beautiful clothes" to the detriment of controversy and sociopolitical relevance while, on the other, yearning for a return to more dance.

Over the years, his reviews play with this ambivalence, as exemplified in his change of opinion: in the years between *Masurca Fogo* and *Nefés* (PREMIERE 2003), Schmidt describes pieces as being "dead" and as a rehashing of "waste."[63] He comments on the piece *Ein Trauerspiel* (1994) as follows: "This is the logical end of the piece, after which only dead material is accumulated in the transport of civilization's garbage and many a repetition."[64] Then from *Ten Chi* (PREMIERE 2004) up until Pina Bausch's last piece *"...como el musguito en la piedra, ay si, si, si..."* (PREMIERE 2009), he continuously praises what he sees as the positive trend toward the Tanztheater Wuppertal gaining a new identity thanks to a new generation of dancers, a trend characterized above all by the "rediscovery" of dance. The new generation of dancers in the Tanztheater Wuppertal ensemble, which he initially described as being "too athletic" and "too professional" while also complaining about a lack of "strong personalities," now appears as a ray of hope thanks to the new motif of rediscovering dance. We see here that, while his opinions change, his practice of forming those opinions remains constant: his point of reference is not the piece itself or other contemporary pieces, but earlier phases of Pina Bausch's oeuvre, which he as the 'expert' establishes as the normative standard.   In his reviews, Jochen Schmidt thus forms his opinions based on his own classifications of Pina Bausch's oeuvre. Finally, he contextualizes the piece in relation to earlier pieces. He usually refers to specific examples or the central narratives of Pina Bausch's aesthetics, such as the 'incompleteness' of the piece, the social and political relevance of the piece's theme or the number of dances in the piece. Schmidt describes the piece's effect on the audience by generalizing his own experience and by describing its entertainment value and the expectations of the audience from the point of view of an "experienced Bausch spectator."[65] His judgments are mainly based on classifications and, in these classifications, the dominant discursive tropes are those of the 'old' and the 'new,' as, for example, in his review of the premiere of *Viktor:*

"Occasionally the old phobias reappear in new form. Again and again – and increasingly exhausted – Monika Sagon steps out onto the stage and tries to briefly greet the audience after having made her rounds of the auditorium: an element of insisting on one's own obsessions seems to be deliberately implanted into the new piece in the form of this dancer. At some point, Anne Martin, who had previously verbally attacked a colleague, asks the audience to leave, saying she doesn't need them. But alongside the variations on the familiar, there is an abundance of not only new but also very carefully and masterfully worked-through ideas. A woman receives new high-heeled shoes as if being shod like a horse; but the blacksmith does not simply shoe her using a few symbolic gestures, turning it instead into an act of extremely meticulous craftsmanship. When Kyomi Ichida, hanging over the back of a chair with her arms outstretched, turns into a living gargoyle, it creates the full image of a fountain alongside the ghostly symbolism; two men use the stream of water emitting from Ichida – as she is constantly filled back up again by force – for a thorough wash."[66]

That the process of rating something as 'new' is relative and subjective reveals itself in the fact that the "fountain scene" from *Viktor* in 1986 (→ RECEPTION | AUDIENCE) can also be read as something 'very familiar.' The appearance of water is a common element in many of Pina Bausch's pieces, as for example in the "Macbeth Piece" (PREMIERE 1978) and in *Arien* (PREMIERE 1979), in the water pistols in *Legend of Chastity* (PREMIERE 1979), a water sprinkler in *1980 – A Piece by Pina Bausch* (PREMIERE 1980) and also in later pieces, such as *Masurca Fogo, Nefés, Ten Chi* and *Vollmond* (PREMIERE 2006).

Jochen Schmidt's reviews of Pina Bausch's dance pieces are a prime example of an established practice of dance criticism. They adhere to a routinized writing practice, which reveals itself in the reviews' text dramaturgy and how their criteria are based on history and œuvre, Pina Bausch's development as an artist and the overall genre of dance theater. Last but not least, they show themselves in the use of recurring discursive tropes that aim to convey the performance to an audience through a text, with the critic as translator.

Schmidt's critiques are precise, concrete, differentiated and based on profound journalistic knowledge of, above all, the Tanztheater Wuppertal. Schmidt does not write scathing reviews, nor does he indulge in polemic extravagancies or hymns of praise. His language is prosaic. Unlike early French and American dance critics, he does not attempt to find a metaphorically rich, associative language that is itself in motion and that still characterizes some academic approaches to dance.[67] His style of language is educational: he wants to document, recount and classify all at the same time, to deliver an interpretation and perform his knowledge of and his relationship with the Tanztheater Wuppertal. Not only does he allocate a place for each respective piece in Pina Bausch's œuvre, but he also references the judgments that he himself has already made about her work in earlier texts – and comments on whether he was proven right. While the work of the choreographer changes over time (→ PIECES), as he himself asserts, he changes neither the text dramaturgy of his dance reviews nor his standards or frames of reference. Jochen Schmidt is not one of those critics who reveal the criteria on which their judgments are based. His descriptions of how the audience receives a piece are shaped by his own subjective perspective; his attitude is that of a 'pontiff of dance criticism' who does not question himself or his 'expert' authority.

TRANSLATING BETWEEN PERFORMANCE, PERCEPTION AND TEXT

Dance criticism is characterized by the paradox between identity and difference inherent to translation, which reveals itself here in specific ways when perceptions of a dance and theater event are transferred into the medium of text. Dance reviews are characterized by translation steps that are different to those taken in translations of dance into dance studies texts, which take more time, rely on other types of data and source material, and usually address smaller, more specialized audiences. These structural differences in the fields of journalism and academia still exist even when individuals simultaneously work both as dance critics and dance scholars, as Christina Thurner explains, describing the relationship between dance criticism and dance studies on the basis of these personal identities.[68]

The act of translating perceptions into spoken language, in turn, is fundamentally different to the act of translating them into writing, as becomes clear in a comparative analysis of dance criticism and audience surveys (→ RECEPTION | AUDIENCE). The latter take place immediately after a performance. Audience statements are spontaneous, fast, impulsive and often 'amateurish' in terms of their technical terminology. Dance reviews, on the other hand, are written by professional viewers (in most cases) with the vast visual experience, specialist terminology, linguistic skill and specific technical knowledge of dance that are expected by their readers. Dance reviews are also created at a spatial distance to the performance situation, but unlike academic texts, still within temporal proximity of it. Although they are often penned under the pressures of a deadline, they strive for professionalism and are written with a broad media public in mind, the respective readers of their publications. They are typically based on specific writing routines, which reveal themselves in the dramaturgical structure of the reviews and in recurring linguistic choices, for example in the description or emphasis of certain scenes, which are usually only referenced in terms of their meaning and – as in the case of the international coproductions – are more often than not interpreted as being 'typically' Italian, Turkish, Portuguese, etc. At the same time, dance critics substantiate their judgments by assigning the individual piece a place within the overall œuvre of Pina Bausch and by characterizing them as being 'typically' or 'untypically Pina.' In this way, aesthetic discourse about the Tanztheater Wuppertal is conventionalized, and these conventions are thus constantly updated as well.

Dance criticism demonstrates that translating dance into writing can be seen as not only a loss but also as a productive way of dealing with the limitations of translation (→ THEORY AND METHODOLOGY). We see this in the ways in which clear attributions are avoided and descriptions are 'suspended in limbo' in order to keep them ambiguous. For example, dance reviews of *Viktor* feature passages such as: "Something Roman shines through,"[69] "One seems to be able to recognize the 'Roman' here, much in the same way that Fellini portrayed it in his films,"[70] or "So you can choose to see Rome in *Viktor*, or to share (or endure) Bausch's eternal preoccupation with the way that men and women treat each other, wherever they happen to be."[71]

At the same time, these reviews are dominated by classifications and conventionalizations of the 'Pina Bausch aesthetic,' the descriptions of the dances in particular reference stylistic elements considered to be characteristic of Pina Bausch's choreographies, such as 'everyday movements,' 'everyday gestures' or dance as a means to an end, as the medium of a statement that she supposedly wishes to make: "She explains herself through dance – delicately, tenderly and enchantingly choreographed to the end."[72]

The reviews are characterized by interpretive writing. In them, the performative aspects of the pieces only play a minor role: criticism is not interested in *how* a scene is created, choreographically constructed or performatively generated, but in *what* the scene represents. The "fountain scene" is, for example, described as a dancer portraying a "water dispenser" or as a representation of the famous Fontana di Trevi. What is not being described is how this happens in and through movement, i.e., that this is a performative process created by a dancer using her body to portray a source of water – and not a case of representation. This is precisely where the difference to Pina Bausch's artistic practice becomes evident (→ PIECES), as said practice is primarily characterized by a performative approach to choreography and less by a choreographic style that uses movements, materials or scenes to represent something else, something underneath.

This focus on the representative level is also reflected in the descriptions of what the respective pieces are 'about.' Dance reviews tend to not discuss the choreographic aspects of the tensions that characterize Pina Bausch's choreographies – for example, the relationships between dance and music, movement and stage, speech and action, theatrical scenes and movement scenes. They primarily translate them thematically, for example as tensions between death/

life, human/world, man/woman, body/object/sexuality, mourning/ love, the struggle for survival/a lust for life, while most dance critics believe – as do large parts of the audience (→ RECEPTION | AUDIENCE) – that the main focus is on issues of gender, used to illustrate all other themes.

Perceptions are framed by experience and knowledge. Describing dance or, as Thurner puts it, "writing [it] into being *[erschreiben]*,"[73] has always been bound to context and situation. Dance reviews demonstrate that the genealogy of the Tanztheater Wuppertal has been generated within a complex of power and knowledge that – together with other forms of writing (scholarly texts, interviews, artist portraits, commentaries, overview articles), but also with visual material such as film documentaries, photo volumes and their reviews – helps to produce the perceptions and interpretations of a performance, thereby also (re)updating and consolidating the discourse surrounding Pina Bausch's dance theater. It is above all these reviews that translate the knowledge of her art from communicative to cultural memory.[74]

The audience

"Everybody is part of the performance."[75] Pina Bausch

In 2008, about ten years after the publication of his paradigmatic book *Postdramatic Theater*, Hans-Thies Lehmann drew the following conclusion: "The spectator has practically, but even more so aesthetically, become the central topic of theatre, of its practices and its theory."[76] However, at the time, as others like Jacques Rancière were also declaring the audience to be the coauthors of every performance,[77] the "rediscovery of the audience"[78] was really not that new. Debate surrounding this topic had actually pervaded much of 20th-century art. For example, it had already played a major role in the works of Bertolt Brecht and Antonin Artaud. Since the 1960s, the artistic and theatrical avant-garde and, above all, young performance art had been claiming the discovery of the audience for themselves, as they sought to no longer understand art as a 'product,' but rather as a situation, an action, as performance, as an event.

In interviews, Pina Bausch also repeatedly stressed that it was not important for spectators to know or understand what she as a choreographer thought about her piece or what she saw in it. In her opinion, the audience should be open to their own perceptions, interpretations and points of view about the piece: "When I make a piece, I am the audience […]. But I cannot speak for everyone. The pieces are actually made in such a way that everyone in the audience can search for and perhaps find something of their own. Each individual in the audience becomes creative in this state or that movement, or in the mood that he or she is in at that very moment."[79] To avoid restricting this openness, the Tanztheater Wuppertal has always rejected discursive formats such as introductions to pieces before performances or subsequent discussions with the audience, and has designed almost all of its programs to consist mainly of pictures and photos instead of explanatory or associative thoughts based on the theme of the piece. "The audience is always part of the performance, just as I myself am part of the performance, even when I am not onstage. [...]. Our programs never hint at how the plays are to be understood. We have to have our own experiences, just like in life. No one can do it for us."[80]

Regardless of this interest in the audience, theater studies has claimed that the renewed interest in the audience was only sparked by the advent of "postdramatic theater"[81] in the 1990s, thereby discovering the issue of the interplay between the stage and the audience. In current debates on the theory of theater, dance and performance, this interplay thus refers to forms of theater that attempt to open up the classical proscenium stage toward the darkness of the auditorium and to allow spectators to actively participate in the action onstage. It also refers to theater projects that occupy public spaces and define them as theatrical or performative. The issue of the interaction between the stage and the audience is also raised in connection with artistic awakenings that seek to overcome the established concept of the 'artwork' and situate the creation of the piece in its reception through spectators. This entails a change of perspective, from how a piece is staged to how it is performed,[82] and with it an understanding of the audience as not just a prerequisite to and genuine component of a theatrical performance but also as something that helps to constitute the performativity of the performance situation.

It is no coincidence that this change of perspective is taking place at a time when digital space is expanding, enabling new forms of interactivity and collectivity, and assigning a more active role to individual 'users.' Theater and dance discourse have also begun debating such digital forms of interactivity by discussing the relationship between mediality and theatricality, media and dance,[83] and by seeking to prove that theater is a special case by ascribing theater performances their own specific logic.[84] The focus has thus shifted from the staging of a piece, which was central to the discourse of the 1980s and thus deciphered by means of semiotic methods,[85] to the performance, to its eventfulness, uniqueness, singularity, unrepeatability[86] and thus also to the way that it is perceived situationally, which has become the center of theoretical debate about theater and dance and the focus of cultural and philosophical discussions about art in general since the 1990s.

4 *Viktor*
Lyon, 1994

While concepts such as those of the "emancipated spectator"[87] and "relational aesthetics"[88] developed within the scope of the performative turn, "corporeal copresence"[89] has played a major role in discussions in the field of theater studies. Theater performances are thus considered unique in comparison to other media formats in terms of the simultaneity of the physical presence of performers onstage and members of the audience.[90] This also extends to a broader definition of stage presence that is applied to the auditorium. For Erika Fischer-Lichte, 'copresence' means sharing time and space through physical presence and corporeal experience. I should add that corporeal copresence is framed and takes place in the theater in specific ways: through the performance situation, which can, on the one hand, differ due to the various types of architecture and atmosphere in theaters and, on the other, through the specificity of spectators' perceptions, which are based on their distinct forms of habitus, their perceptual habits, visual experiences and knowledge, and situational moods during one and the same performance. These differences in audience perception increase when a piece like *The Rite of Spring* (PREMIERE 1975) is performed over the course of more than 40 years, thus generating multiple audiences in different places and at various points in history.

This increased interest in the audience has also prompted reflection on the previous methods of theater and dance studies, and performance theory. The focus of research has shifted from the 'piece' to its perception, bringing up the question of how to best empirically capture audience perceptions. An empirical approach to audience research has already been firmly established in art sociology[91] and performance studies, which evolved out of cultural anthropology, where ethnographic methods such as participatory and non-participatory observation and interview methods have been applied since its inception in the 1980s. While audience surveys are quite common in these fields and at events such as sports matches, theater and dance studies have so far struggled to take an empirical approach to audience research. Only recently have they begun to make use of ethnographic methods and practice theory.[92] These methodological approaches constitute the process of praxeological production analysis that this book is based on (→ THEORY AND METHODOLOGY). Inspired by concepts used in media theory such as the uses-gratification approach,[93] the encoding/decoding model[94] and the concept of bricolage,[95] praxeological production analysis focuses on the relationship between performance and reception. Audience perception plays a central role in this, i.e., how the spectators are affected and how they adopt and translate their perceptions into their own lifeworlds.

Praxeological production analysis assumes that work process, performance and audience perception are closely connected. A 'dance production' thus emerges out of the interplay between different sets of practices: practices of developing a piece, restaging and rehearsing it, training and performance practices, and practices of spectator perception. The practices of spectator perception depend on the work process and the performance, but also on the cultural habits of each theater audience. Since choreography and dance are rarely clearly encoded, it is similarly impossible for the audience to uniformly decode them. In addition to this diversity of interpretation, which is embedded within the piece itself, the audience's perceptions are not purely individual and subjective, because they are bound, firstly, to complexes of knowledge, which include discursive knowledge, i.e., knowledge that is generated by and acquired through language, texts and images. However, the situational perceptions of the audience members are also framed by cultural and social patterns of perception, which are habituated and thus differentiated, physically manifesting themselves in relation to social and cultural categories such as gender, ethnicity, class and age. Finally, several temporalities are inscribed into the situational perceptions of a performance. As theater scholar Erika Fischer-Lichte explains, while a performance is "always executed in the present,"[96] it is simultaneously connected to the past and the future: "For it is past experiences and expectations of the future that the perceiving subject has made or cherishes that make it perceive the present in a given constellation."[97]

The situative aspect of performance, that which theater studies defines as instantaneous, momentary or unrepeatable,[98] thus encounters patterns of perception, knowledge and visual experience as well as the expectations and the situational mood of the audience. It is this interplay that allows the specific atmosphere that makes a performance unique to emerge in the theater. Philosopher Gernot Böhme defines 'atmosphere' as a spatial carrier of moods[99] that help to shape the realities of the perceiver and what is being perceived. Böhme defines perception as a modality of corporeal presence and, like phenomenologist Hermann Schmitz,[100] as a feeling of presence or an atmosphere that is neither objective nor purely subjective. "In my perception of the atmosphere, I feel what kind of environment I am in. Thus, this perception has two sides: on the one hand, the environment that radiates the quality of the mood and, on the other hand, me, by allowing my state of mind to share in this mood, thereby assuring that I am here now. [...]. Conversely, atmospheres are the way in which things and environments present themselves."[101] Elsewhere, he writes that atmospheres are "not thought of as free-floating, but rather inversely as something that emanates from and is created by things, people or constellations between them. Conceptualized in this way, atmospheres are neither something objective, namely the properties that things have, although there is a thingness to them, they are something that belong to a thing, inasmuch as things articulate the spheres of their presence through their properties – conceived of as ecstasies. Nor are atmospheres something subjective, determined by a state of mind. And yet they are subjective, they belong to subjects, insofar as they are felt by human beings in corporeal presence, and this feeling is simultaneously a corporeal feeling that subjects have of being in space."[102]

If we take this approach, it is almost impossible to maintain the separation between a theatrical performance and its reception. Instead of defining two separate entities, more recent approaches to the philosophy of art and the theory of theater performance have viewed performance as something in-between, that which Jacques Rancière calls a "third thing." It is something that only constitutes itself in interaction with the audience: "Performance […] is not the transmission of the artist's knowledge or inspiration to the spectator. It is a third thing that is owned by no one, whose meaning is owned by no one, but which subsists between them."[103] It follows from these basic propositions that the polarization between staging and performance on the one hand and the audience on the other – still evident in the theater studies of the 1990s, above all in semiotic approaches to theater[104] – cannot be maintained if we wish to adequately grasp the complex interactions between performance and audience perception both theoretically and methodologically.

How can we methodologically understand the performance situation from the point of view of the audience? Theater scholar Stefanie Husel has given some thought to the issue of how to analyze performances. As yet, she has only discovered two distinct possibilities: "'from the outside,' by describing text-like, possibly predetermined structures of meaning, and 'from the inside,' by making recourse to the experiences made by those participating in the situation."[105] Dance and theater studies have so far tended toward an external view of the performance with the aim of examining artistic intent or concepts of staging by analyzing production processes, employing hermeneutic methods of performance analysis or examining the connections between an underlying (dramatic) text and its theatrical execution.

Theater scholar Jens Roselt attempts to methodologically reverse this external perspective by proposing an approach 'from within' the performance that conceives of the performance in terms of its eventfulness in order to understand the simultaneous presence of audience and performers as more than just a "media condition of reception," instead making it visible as something independent in the "execution of the event"[106]: "The examination of performances should not stop at amazement, but should take this state as its point of departure. My proposition is that performances can be analytically accessed in a meaningful way through these moments of experience."[107] In order to implement this methodologically, he proposes writing performance logbooks: "Spectators are given the task of recording what they can still remember after a performance. It is expressly not about retelling a story, distilling stage directions or repeating the dramaturgy, but about taking a direct look at immediate memory. [...]. Writing a logbook is a kind of experiment, not a test, but a self-experiment whose outcome is uncertain and through which the writers of logbooks can find out how a performance has affected them, free from preconceived interpretations."[108]

In contrast to Roselt's approach, which attempts to capture the situativity of the performance from the perspective of the audience, Husel proposes an ethnographic approach that focuses on the interactions between performance and audience and proceeds in a theoretical and empirical manner: "The performance situations [...] should be reformulated and reflected on in a dense 'back and forth' of description and theoretical reflection."[109] For this, she examines materials such as audio recordings, which record audience actions such as clapping, laughing, the clearing of throats, giggling and complaining during a performance, and then relates them back to the dramaturgy of the piece.

Both research approaches, from the 'inside' and from the 'outside,' are attempts to overcome the separation between staged piece and audience perception. Nevertheless, as Husel notes, the vocabulary of theater studies still reflects "the distinction established by academic practice between staged piece and performance, production and reception, even if overcoming this epistemic divide has long been aspired to and approached in specific ways (post-structuralist or phenomenological)."[110]

This is also evident in the fact that audience research – with the exception of Bettina Brandl-Risi, who explores applause from a historiographical perspective and postulates that the emotional dimension of a performance can also be observed from 'the outside'[111] – has so far been literally non-existent in theater and dance studies. This book seeks to respond to this research desideratum by presenting the approach of praxeological audience research. How does the 'piece' translate into audience perceptions? What is the best way to describe the copresent relationship between perceivers and what is being perceived? Our methodological starting point is ethnographic and practice-theory-based research; both are more than familiar with the constant changes of perspective between the 'inside' and 'outside,'[112] something that only Husel's work has so far reflected upon methodologically in theater studies.

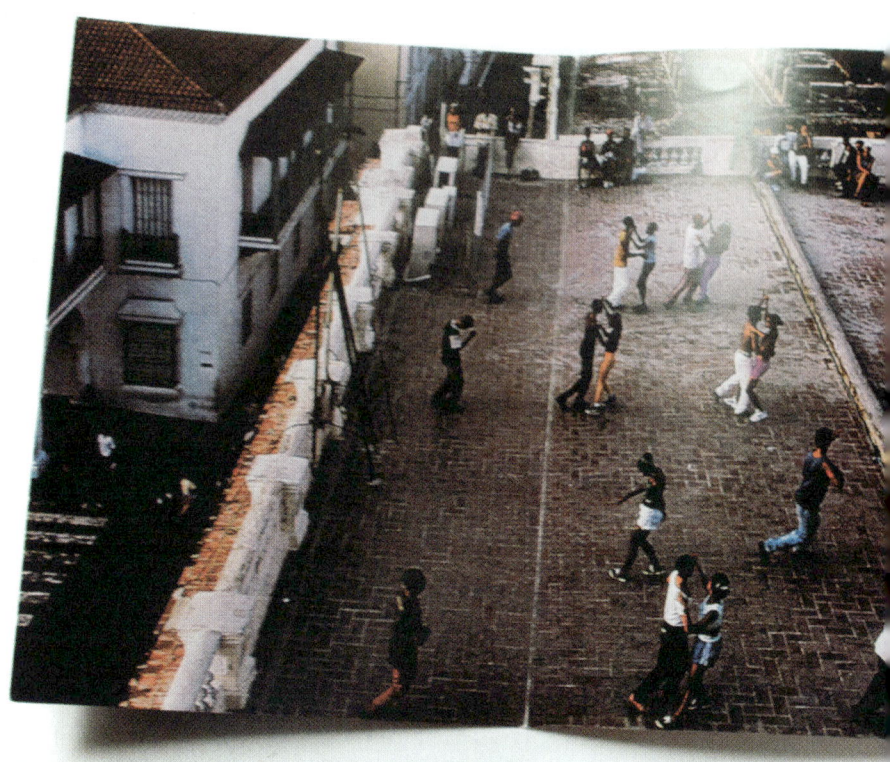

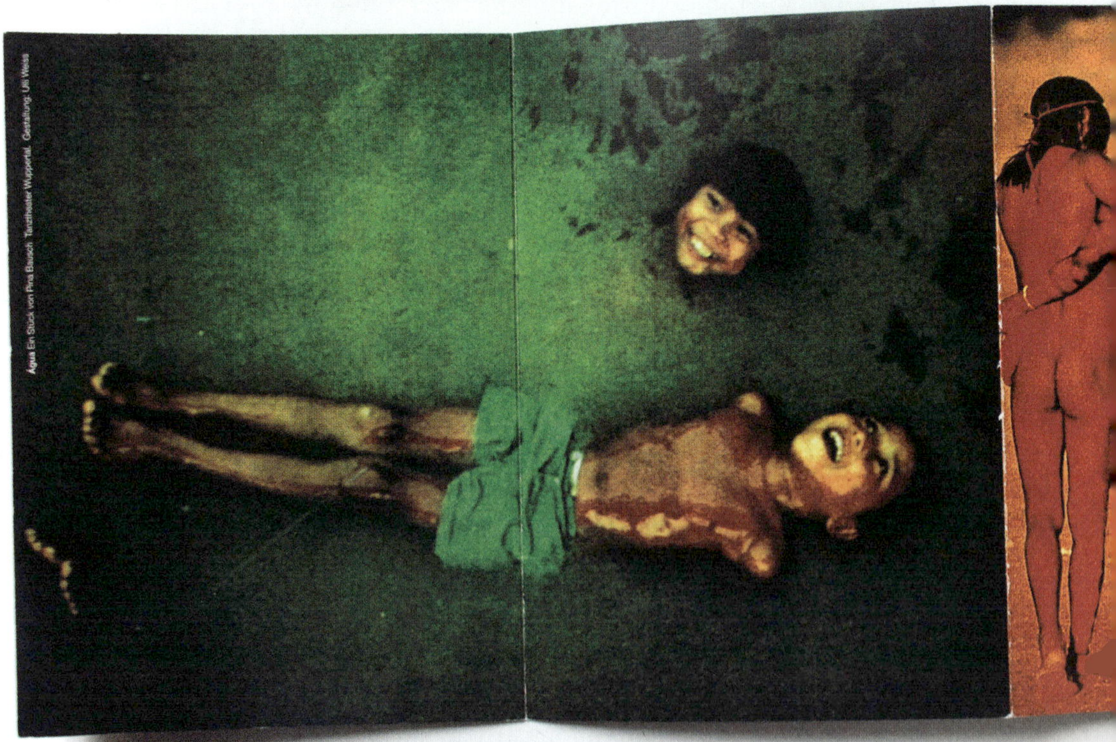
Água Ein Stück von Pina Bausch Tanztheater Wuppertal Gestaltung: Ulli Weiss

5 Program booklet, restaging of *Água* 2005

By abiding to sociology's tradition of qualitative research methods (→ THEORY AND METHODOLOGY), praxeological production analysis attempts to take an empirical approach to audience perception using ethnographic methods of participatory and non-participatory observation and audience surveys. My team and I therefore conducted a total of four audience surveys in connection with four coproductions, each of which first premiered during one of Pina Bausch's four different artistic phases (→ PIECES): *Viktor* (PREMIERE 1986), *Masurca Fogo* (PREMIERE 1998), *Rough Cut* (PREMIERE 2005), *"…como el musguito en la piedra, ay si, si, si…"* (PREMIERE 2009).[113] The four audience surveys were conducted at the Opernhaus Wuppertal at restagings of the pieces between 2013 and 2015. In short interviews (max. five minutes), spectators were asked three questions before and after the performance.[114] A total of 1,553 spectators were interviewed at various locations in the opera house (in the foyer, in the cloakrooms and in front of the bar).[115] In each case, four to five interviewers conducted the interviews simultaneously and recorded them using audio equipment. At the same time, observation logbooks were drawn up for the events in Wuppertal before, during and after the performances.

AUDIENCE ROUTINES

"Yes, oh goodness me, they've been around for so long. It just feels like I'm a part of it,"[116] is how one spectator described her relationship with the company in an interview before the performance of *Masurca Fogo* at the Opernhaus Wuppertal in 2015.

A performance is a situational and situated practice, and both aspects are constitutive of the translation of a perceived piece. Dance studies and social research have each developed a different understanding of 'situativity' and 'situatedness,' which are combined in the approach presented here. In dance and performance studies, situativity is generally used to describe the momentary, the unrepeatable, the fleeting, that which is always already absent as it emerges. It is not its embeddedness in the situation, but rather its non-availability, its non-graspability, the non-categoriality of situativity that is focused upon here. The specific criterion of copresence is therefore ascribed to the situativity of theatrical performance. However, at the same time, it is important to point out that situativity presents a number of epistemological problems, such as permanent absence[117] and constant non-presence, which can only be grasped via "presence effects,"[118] i.e., can never be observed themselves. This approach also disregards the framings of situativity, be they social or cultural or framings based on knowledge systems and expertise or on the visual experiences of the spectator. On the other hand, sociological practice theory (→ THEORY AND METHODOLOGY) defines situativity as itself socially structured, i.e., interspersed with patterns of social order. It emphasizes its situatedness, which is here meant as that which embeds, constitutes and frames the situation. Accordingly, the basic assumption of practice theory is that practices reveal themselves in their situatedness. Hence, the counterpart to situativity can be found in the routines and habits that characterize practices – including perception.

A copresent audience at a theater, dance or opera performance, but also at a sporting event, has different routines than an audience attending, for example, a movie at the cinema or watching it on television. These habits are not only brought about by the mediality of the performance format and by the performance venue (theater, cinema, private residence), but have also been established by tradition. As a place of bourgeois representation, the theater has been producing a specific audience for generations. One spectator described it this way: "Oh, I've been going to Pina Bausch ever since I was nay high. So, I don't know, since I was four, five, six years old. That's why it's a tradition."[119]

The Tanztheater Wuppertal has a global audience. In addition to being performed in Wuppertal, the piece *The Rite of Spring*, for example, was performed almost 400 times in approx. 80 cities and more than 40 countries on four continents between 1977, when it went on tour for the first time, and 2019.[120] This clearly shows that the audience of the Tanztheater Wuppertal not only spans several generations but also includes people with very different cultural and social patterns of perception and experience, and with a broad range of specific (dance) knowledge and personal expectations. In this respect, that which practice theorists Alkemeyer, Schürmann and Volber ascribe to human perceptions and actions also specifically applies to theatergoers: "They are affected differently, bring their own distinct experiences and expectations to the table, develop disparate views, interests and desires based on their respective physical, mental, linguistic and personal situatedness, can be addressed in different ways and, as participants, invoke 'cognitive artifacts' (Norman 1993) such as rules, criteria, systems of knowledge and justification that reference disparate contexts in order to lend emphasis, plausibility and legitimacy to their points of view."[121]

Although the perceptions of different audiences are heterogeneous, it is the specific, respective atmosphere of the performance situation that has an ongoing community-building effect, not only on the dancers but also on the audience. At the same time, historically specific routines have emerged that pertain to theater as an institution on the one hand and to the specific art of Pina Bausch on the other. This juxtaposition of institution, theatrical atmosphere and specific aesthetics is particularly apparent in the Wuppertal audience, which has grown and aged together with the members of the ensemble. "We know most of them – not personally, but for us, it's as if we're part of the family; they've grown old with us."[122] Spectators from Wuppertal tend to emphasize the aspects of family and local tradition in particular: "As a resident of Wuppertal, I have a natural predisposition for it. My parents took me with them to performances when I was just a child."[123] In this respect, many people have developed routines and habits of attending performances. These are framed by the architecture of the venue (forecourt, foyer, buffet, bar, etc.). In Wuppertal, the central meeting point before the event is the entrance foyer, where there is a bar, a booth that sells posters of Tanztheater Wuppertal pieces and a bookstand that exclusively sells in-house publications by the Tanztheater and its members.

The audience obeys the (unwritten) rules and regulations of the theater as a traditional place of bourgeois representative culture: unlike at the movies, coats are left in the cloakroom, drinks and snacks are not taken into the auditorium, and three chimes of the bell remind the audience that the performance is about to begin and that they need to take their seats. You take your allocated seat – and apologize if you arrive late and the other spectators have to get up from their seats, forcing you to embarrassingly push your way past them down the narrow aisle. The latter in particular is an audience routine that the dancers repeat and perform in the piece *Arien* (PREMIERE 1979), thus demonstrating that the audience and its habits are part of the piece itself. The audience also shares this point of view: "The Tanztheater Wuppertal doesn't just perform pieces onstage. The Tanztheater Wuppertal plays and performs with the audience."[124]

In Wuppertal, routines and habits have been established over decades. This is a rare phenomenon, because there are hardly any companies anywhere in the world that have resided at a specific theater and worked exclusively with one choreographer for as many decades as the Tanztheater Wuppertal or the Hamburg Ballett under John Neumeier. The majority of the audience has seen multiple pieces by the Tanztheater Wuppertal – and this unites them: "I think it's great that they've actually grown old with me."[125] The knowledge gained over long periods of time by reexperiencing pieces together or observing the changes effected by new cast members in restagings are therefore not just one of the experiences of copresence in the theater, but are always an updating of memories as well. Behaviorisms such as quietly laughing, silently mouthing the texts, murmuring a dancer's name and whispering about what comes next are not merely due to the situation onstage, but are always an indication of what is already known to the audience, demonstrations of knowledge about the piece.

In Wuppertal, conversations with others in the audience before the performance thus already follow special routines: many people know each other; they usually talk about the piece they saw last, whether they have already seen the piece being performed that evening, how long ago it was, whether they liked it or not, and what their relationship is to the Tanztheater Wuppertal. This is already a kind of initiation into the community of the audience and into the shared theater experience, the beginning of which is signaled by a strict announcement: unlike in many other theaters, at the Opernhaus Wuppertal, a tape-recorded voice draws attention immediately before the beginning of the performance to the fact that the cell phones must be switched off and that video and audio recordings are prohibited during the show. Aside from making the audience aware of copyright issues and of what would be disruptive behavior, it also indicates to the audience that, when the auditorium lights go out, they will be witnessing an event that, unlike mediatized 'events,' should only take place in the here and now as a shared experience between those physically present. The fact that the audience's attention should be focused solely on the performance situation is also demonstrated by the fact that, unlike in movie theaters, disturbances during the theater performance such as conversations with neighbors, the use of cell phones, the rustling of candy wrappers or constantly sliding one's backside back and forth are usually negatively commented upon by neighboring viewers, as one spectator in particular emphasized in his interview: "The stupid cell phones that people opened next to me during the performance; two women looking at their cell phones in their pockets and scrolling through them, writing text messages – it's annoying. It upsets and angers me, because I can't concentrate on the show. But that's probably just how it is these days."[126]

It is above all these disturbances that penetrate the almost meditative silence of the auditorium and clearly reveal the habits and routines of the theater audience. And unlike audiences of contemporary dance, spectators in Wuppertal largely adhere to the traditional bourgeois ideal of passive and silent observation. The Opernhaus – where the company has performed since the more modern Schauspielhaus closed down – its architecture and atmosphere make a significant contribution to this.

Performances by the Tanztheater Wuppertal can last for up to four hours. As a rule, there is an intermission of approx. 20 minutes, during which the audience is not required to exit the hall, although the majority does. Immediately after the performance, there is always frenetic applause in Wuppertal – no matter which piece is being performed and no matter how well the respective performance went. The applause is a tribute to the dancers, to Pina Bausch, to the Tanztheater Wuppertal's decades of artistic work:

"Yes great, I can tell you, but we are also die-hard Pina Bausch fans."[127] Many spectators jump out of their seats and immediately offer the ensemble respectful standing ovations for minutes on end, which the members of the ensemble, standing closely together in a row, arm-in-arm, accept gratefully, but also benevolently and as a matter of course. The audience surveys that we conducted in Wuppertal also give the impression that the audience is celebrating 'their' dance theater company. Thus, the audience tends to emphasize not the individual piece, but the 'overall event of going to see the Tanztheater Wuppertal,' as one spectator said after *Masurca Fogo:* "It was another magical evening. I have seen three pieces so far and I always find it wonderful how you can immerse yourself, how you have to first find your way into it. When you leave, you're terribly sad that it's over, and you really don't want it to be over. It's magical to me to see how different the dancers are. It feels much more unique than in other companies, and it's as if you know the people. That's kind of absurd, but very beautiful."[128] People are proud of 'Pina' and 'Pina Bausch,' names that have now been trademarked and whose fame has long since outshone the reputation of the suspension railway, Wuppertal's most famous listed landmark in this impoverished city so rich in tradition. This final gesture of standing ovations also ritually concludes the event. In this liminal phase, which can be described in the tradition of anthropologist Victor Turner as a ritual transition between the end of the performance and the state of still being present in the theater, the collective excitement demonstrated by the applause evokes a community comprising the dancers and the 'Pina fans.'

EXPECTATIONS AND KNOWLEDGE

From a cultural-sociological perspective, habits of perception and audience expectations are not merely individual. Instead, subjective perceptions depend on cultural and social patterns. As habituated knowledge, they are persistent and powerful. From this perspective, a dance piece does not exist by itself, but is confronted with the audience's respective habits of perception and expectations during the performance situation. This interaction creates a specific performance atmosphere that is not always supportive, but rather can sometimes be confrontational and full of conflict. The Wuppertal ensemble was forced to experience this in the 1970s, when a number of spectators in Wuppertal angrily and loudly left the auditorium, slamming doors on their way out. At the world premiere of the "Macbeth Piece" *He Takes Her By The Hand And Leads Her Into The Castle, The Others Follow* (PREMIERE 1978) at the Schauspielhaus Bochum (→ PIECES, WORK PROCESS), the performance was nearly stopped due to the tumult taking place in the audience only half an hour after the piece had begun. Thirty years later, Jo Ann Endicott, who was in charge of restaging the piece in 2019, remembers the uproar: "All hell broke loose in the auditorium! It was impossible to perform during the first half hour. It was terribly loud. The audience kept booing. In the first scene, I stood right at the front of the stage, and after 30 minutes I thought to myself: I can't stand it anymore. I got up and yelled at the audience: 'If you don't want it, then go home, but we can't continue our performance up here on this stage.' Then I left the stage and thought: 'Oh, no, what have I done?' I quickly returned and, from then on, the audience really was quieter. Maybe I saved the premiere."[129]

During the India tour of 1979, the performance of *The Rite of Spring* in Kolkata had to be stopped because the audience was so horrified about the barely dressed dancers that they stormed the stage.

Unlike in the 1970s, audiences today have high expectations of the Tanztheater Wuppertal. "A sensational spectacle,"[130] "To have a great experience,"[131] and "Another form of dance, the magic of Pina Bausch"[132] are just some examples of what spectators are looking for. For them, there is a dazzling range of reasons to see pieces by the Tanztheater Wuppertal: to pay homage to a great artist and to a world-famous ensemble, to express gratitude for decades of outstanding dance, to see their own process of aging reflected in the aging dancers still standing onstage, fearing that it might be 'the last time' before the ensemble is dissolved, going to see something that their parents' generation admires so much. Finally, there is also the aspect of seeking to educate oneself, since Pina Bausch has now become part of the canon of knowledge about modern (dance) art. Performances thus attract not only individuals but also cultural associations, school groups, educators, scholars and young international artists who are interested in the work of Pina Bausch and want to add the live experience of seeing an actual performance onstage to the theoretical knowledge they have already acquired about the company. Some spectators have simply been inspired to see a show after seeing Wim Wenders' film *PINA* (2011), which has undoubtedly introduced the Tanztheater Wuppertal to new audiences. Many people now want to experience the ensemble 'live,' like the spectator who came to see the piece *Viktor* after watching the movie: "Yes, to experience the dancing live for the first time in addition to having seen the film. It's very geared toward emotion, and I'm really looking forward to actually seeing it live."[133]

The expectations of most of the spectators in Wuppertal are closely linked to knowledge and experience. Most of them have specific dance knowledge that they conventionalize: they know what is "typically Pina Bausch" or "typically Pina." More than 75 percent of the 1,553 spectators interviewed said that they had already seen at least one piece by Pina Bausch before. Their knowledge is not only nourished by their own visual experiences but also by personal connections to their hometown of Wuppertal or to acquaintances who know the dancers. It was striking to hear just how many of the viewers mention that they think they know the dancers, as one woman did: "I know the dancers and have been following them for years, and I am interested in everything that has to do with Pina."[134] However, their knowledge is actually shaped above all by paratexts such as photos, films, DVDs, television shows, documentaries, reviews, books, scholarly articles, lectures, programs, merchandise such as calendars or posters, and video clips on the Internet. Linking perception with this discursive knowledge influences the supposedly 'open' perception of the pieces; it becomes tempting to search for what is 'familiar.' In this respect, the situation of perception is always permeated by experience and memory, and framed by knowledge. This is illustrated by the ambivalence formulated by viewers. On the one hand, they want to "be surprised," "completely open" and "unbiased," to "enter entirely without expectations." On the other hand, they expect to experience something "sensational," "spectacular," "fascinating" and "beautiful."

Whether the specific atmosphere affects the audience also depends on the habituated knowledge that shapes perceptions and expectations. This knowledge of Pina Bausch's signature style produces patterns of perception and routines of expectation that preform situational perception and bind it to past experiences and habituated knowledge. At the same time, perception itself helps to update patterns of perception and knowledge complexes when that which has just been seen coincides with what is remembered – in the words of one spectator: "I know a lot of it, I've already seen a lot of it several times before."[135] Even when audience knowledge of the Tanztheater Wuppertal's aesthetics is guided by experience, translations of this knowledge into language still take their cues from media discourse, which is above all defined by the critics who have continually refined and updated it for decades (→ RECEPTION | DANCE CRITICISM). The audience surveys show that audiences believe Pina Bausch's pieces are about "love," "interpersonal relationships," "humanity" or fundamentally about "humankind." It is above all guests who have not yet seen a piece by Pina Bausch before who are most likely to reproduce this discourse: "I only know that the piece is about the relationship between men and women or rather about the interactions between men and women,"[136] or about the "outstanding dancing of all human emotions,"[137] or "the difference between happiness and sadness."[138] If the guest has not yet seen the piece that is being shown that evening, they say that they will approach the evening with an open mind, without any specific expectations, while even rejecting any such expectations: they want to imagine "nothing," go into the performance "open minded," be "bowled over" and "let themselves be surprised." They say that they want to be astonished, which can also be viewed as an expectation routine of theater audiences.

REMEMBERING WHAT HAS BEEN PERCEIVED

How and what do viewers remember and *how* do they translate it into language? This question becomes particularly important when we assume that what is perceived becomes experience when it has meaning for the present of the perceiver, that is, when it can be related back to his or her lifeworld and identified there as relevant. But what parts of that which has been perceived are truly remembered? The interviews that we conducted show clear connections between dramaturgy, knowledge and perception: interviewed spectators primarily recall scenes that played a central dramaturgical role – such as the opening scene in *Viktor*, in which a woman in a tight red dress and high heels enters stage right with a charming, winning smile. From the audience's perspective, she then purposefully strides to the middle of the stage. Only then does the audience see that she has no arms (→ PIECES, SOLO DANCE). This is a scene that is also highlighted in many reviews. Alternatively, spectators recall parts of scenes that repeatedly reappear throughout the piece as well as scenes that they read as being "typically Pina." In this way, they seek to comprehend the complex choreographic process by ascribing meaning to what is already known and familiar, i.e., to habitual knowledge. Examples of such practices of description and ascription are the "line dances" – ensemble dances that are also referred to as "polonaises" in the audience surveys conducted after *Viktor* – and the women's dance in *Palermo Palermo* (PREMIERE 1989). Other examples include the very 'gestural' dance scenes, i.e., scenes that are charged with meaning and that are supposedly easy to decode, or scenes that tell a 'story,' such as the famous dance solo that uses sign language to illustrate George and Ira Gershwin's ballad "The Man I Love," featured in the piece *Nelken* (PREMIERE 1982).

Spectators tend to gives names to the scenes that they are able to recall according to their main narratives or images. Sometimes there are clear parallels to earlier reviews of the same piece. For instance, many mentioned "the fountain scene" in *Viktor,* which they associated with the Fontana de Trevi in the coproducing city of Rome: a dancer sits on a chair. She is bending forward over the backrest, her arms stretched out on both sides. Men continually 'fill her up' with water from a plastic bottle, which she then spits out in a high arc like a fountain. The men then wash themselves in this fountain. Others recall the "restaurant scene," which is often interpreted as "typically Italian." Three waitresses serve a male guest, probably a tourist, who is somewhat confused by the clumsy service as he attempts to order spaghetti and coffee. He is then served by the waitresses in a bored, slow and disinterested sort of manner, which is above all expressed in the posture and gait of the dancers, who do their job by performing slow, delayed movements with their feet turned out, their hips pushed forward, round backs and cigarettes hanging out of the corners of their mouths. In *Rough Cut,* the scene that most people remember is the "washing scene," in which the women wash and scrub the men. In *Masurca Fogo,* it is the "water scene"/"water slide," in which a clear sheet of plastic is stretched out across the stage, filled with water and held up on both sides, creating a water chute through which dancers dressed in swimsuits slide from one end to the other with childish joy. It is also striking that cultural associations with the coproducing countries are primarily triggered by the music, although it has usually been compiled from a broad cultural mix. Finally, spectators also react strongly to specific visual cues and images, such as the video images in *Rough Cut,* also referred to as the "escalator scene," which features video projections of escalators in a shopping mall in Seoul.

In contrast, dance solos are much less frequently mentioned by the audience and just as rarely talked about by dance critics. When they are, their translations are more unspecific and simultaneously more metaphorical and charged with emotion. Solos are not described in detail; the audience prefers to speak of "lots of dance" or of "particularly intense," "expressive," "emotional," "fascinating" and "inspiring" movements (→ SOLO DANCE).

BEING AFFECTED AND SPEAKING ABOUT BEING MOVED

When spectators are asked what they think of a piece, they tend to classify it in positive ways, placing what they have seen within the context of other pieces. They describe Pina Bausch's pieces as "beautiful," "inspiring," "fascinating," "impressive," "great," "wonderful," "indescribable," "unbelievable," "overwhelming," "outstanding," "lovely," "evocative," "splendid," "gripping," "emotional," "stirring," "exciting," "amazing," "superb," "moving," "profound," "touching," "phenomenal," "awesome," "fantastic," "delightful," "uplifting," "intoxicating," "extraordinary" and "unique." They use these adjectives to describe what they have perceived, while at the same time leaving it undetermined. They describe corporeal affective states brought about by the piece such as "palpitations of the heart," "goose bumps" and "taking a deep breath." They search for words for their emotions and use small gestures to show that and how the movements onstage moved them inside. They use expletives and words that allow them to grasp something intangible and indescribable, and that help them to convey their corporeal affective state. "I'm just still somewhere else, I really can't do this now. Can you?"[139] Yet even by hesitating, evading, paraphrasing vaguely and refusing to find words, they reveal the cracks in translation between 'being affected' and speaking about 'being moved.'

In our audience surveys, the audience spoke about what they had just seen directly after the end of the performance while they were on their way to the cloakroom, still in the theater. This is a kind of threshold situation, a liminal phase, a state of passing through, a floating transition between collectively being-with in the fleeting community that the audience constitutes during the performance and the individual processing of experience afterward. It is a phase in which what has just been seen is still reverberating. At the same time, the act of leaving the theater as a site of the extraordinary has already announced itself. In this liminal phase, the audience is in the atmospheric echo chamber of affect, in a state of 'being affected,' in which what it has witnessed has neither been processed nor become experience yet: "At most, we have emotionally absorbed it, but already calling it experience would be saying too much, I think."[140]

This quote makes it particularly clear that the distancing process required in order to translate an aesthetic perception into language has not yet taken place. In this respect, it is not surprising that emotionally charged descriptions, evasive remarks and attempts to withdraw from the situation typically characterize the interview situation. The many "ums," pauses, stumbles, groans, answers broken off mid-sentence, refusals to answer and the use of adjectives that attempt to capture the "overwhelming" effect of what has just been seen all indicate this. In this sense, words such as "incredible," "fantastic," "unbelievable," "monumental," "brilliant" or "terrific" should not be read as helpless, exaggerated descriptions, instead revealing the ambivalence of the untranslatable in aesthetic perception as a productive failure on the one hand and, on the other, as the potential, openness and incompleteness evident in the process of translating aesthetic experience into language.

This liminal phase between the end of the performance and not yet having left the extraordinary site of the theater can also be characterized as the relationship between 'being affected' and speaking about 'being moved.' Speaking about 'being moved' means wrestling for words that can be used to convey 'being affected' into language, thus allowing it to turn into 'being moved' by voicing it. For 'being affected' can only be communicated by translating it into language. Spectators are affected 'by something' and translate this feeling of 'being affected,' which they perceive as authentic, into

6 *Palermo Palermo*
Tokyo, 2008

the discursive figure of 'being moved.' Spectators speak of 'being moved' when they are affected by something, when something "concerns," "addresses," "touches," "grasps" or "grabs" them. The state of 'being moved' expressed in their statements is a discursive figure that has always dominated the reception and discourse history of the Tanztheater Wuppertal since its very beginnings. According to this narrative, Pina Bausch's pieces are moving because their everyday topics are so close to human beings and human feelings. The audience's feeling of 'being moved' is intensified by the re-cognition of the dancers and their personalities. From the audience's perspective, the affective state has little to do with dances that are performed perfectly or being moved by the perfection of the performance. Instead, one spectator spoke of "special kinds of behavior that are almost psychiatric, but very interesting. Physical and emotional exertion that manages to achieve wonderful harmony," concluding with: "and I'm still quite moved."[141] Another woman remembers "[...] the vitality, vibrations of the soul, everything that is communicated by the dancing."[142]

Speaking about 'being moved' can be understood as a linguistic transposition that allows spectators to negotiate their affective state. The step of translating from 'being affected' to speaking about 'being moved' can thus be understood as 'interpretation,' i.e., as a linguistic translation from a (prelinguistic) affective state.[143]

Phenomenologist Bernhard Waldenfels puts it this way: "What befalls us or chances upon us has always already happened by the time we respond to it. This is precisely why every reference to experiences has an indirect character. It takes place from a position of temporal distance. [...]. Being affected, which should be considered as something similar to being overcome, is preceded by an encounter with something. Only in *response to* what we have been affected by does that which affects us reveal itself as such."[144]

The reassurance of the affective state, of the supposedly authentic experience and of 'being moved' as something sublime beyond compare therefore only occurs in retrospect, that is, when it is translated into language. On the one hand, this transformation of aesthetic experience into language makes use of a knowledge of 'feelings' and a discursive knowledge of Pina Bausch's work, according to which her pieces generate a state of 'being moved.' On the other hand, this translation creates something constitutively new by generating knowledge, transforming patterns of perception and prompting ambiguous interpretations. Spectators describe the pieces as opening up spaces of thought and perception: "Oho, in the end I thought that it's actually unbelievable, because you suddenly drift off into your own fantasies and thoughts, and that's actually what I find so beguiling, which leaves so much space for association. Or it triggers you, let's put it that way. That's an even better way to say it."[145]

The productivity of this step of media translation lies in the way that something is transferred into language and thereby emerges as something new in perception and knowledge. For although something that cannot be grasped linguistically is lost in the distancing process of speaking, there is also something else to be gained in the new connection between perception, knowledge and experience. The translation of dance into language is thus always a two-sided process that creates new knowledge while simultaneously being doomed to fail from the outset. Moreover, translation is an important and decisive step in transforming what has been perceived into communicative memory and finally into cultural memory.

That which is generated in language continues the discourse surrounding the Tanztheater Wuppertal and creates mental spaces to question, change, adapt or re-posit previous discursive tropes. This is precisely what constitutes the potential and productivity of linguistic translation, which become most visible in linguistic disruptions. In addition to avoiding and refusing speech, these disruptions reveal themselves above all in the way that audience members speak about 'being moved' using words and concepts that document the failure of translation. After a performance of *Viktor,* for example, a spectator summed up the state in which she found herself using the words "tears, goose bumps and awe."[146] Another variation is emotional speech, which translates the tensions between joy and suffering, love and hatred, etc. in the piece into dramatic language – "an interplay between tenderness and brutality,"[147] "ebb and flow,"[148] "exuberant joy and deep despair,"[149] "chaos, vitality, trance, fatigue, exhaustion"[150] – or describes an experience of transformation – for example, of being "pushed" or "dragged along" or of "going along for the ride." With the help of kinesthetic terms and metaphors, spectators try to grasp the indescribable. Two people interviewed after *Masurca Fogo* emphasized: "Wonderful emotions were conveyed; I was deeply impressed by the music in combination with the dance, and it actually carried me off with it like a tidal wave."[151] The refusal, the inability or unwillingness to speak, and the way recourse is made to the vocabulary provided by existing discourse, points to potential disruptions in the translation process. When the "overpowering" effect reveals itself in people being overwhelmed, pushing those who have been 'moved' to the limits of their own linguistic abilities, it allows the aesthetic 'remainder' to show itself: the aesthetic surplus of translation, what is untranslatable in the aesthetic experience, that which is not immediately accessible through communication.

The practice of translation is a permanent process of negotiation and decision-making, which in the case of audience research is a multistep process. In audience surveys, the audience translates what they have just perceived into language, in this case in a face-to-face situation immediately after the end of the performance (in other approaches, this is accomplished using questionnaires or transcripts or even at a different place and time). Next, some form of media is used to document their spoken words (in this case, audio equipment) and the recordings are transcribed (using one of the various methods of transcription). Finally, the text that has been generated is treated as a piece of 'data'/a document that is analyzed (using one of many different methods, such as content analysis or discourse analysis), and the results of this analysis are in turn translated into a continuous text. Depending on the original question, there are different methods and ways to approach each and every one of these steps. Moreover, due to these multiple stages of translation that characterize the relationship between perception and writing, the process of negotiation fails in a special way due to the im/possibility of translation (→ THEORY AND METHODOLOGY). The reason for this is that it is only possible to record what spectators feel – what affects them, and when and how they are affected – communicatively, that is by essentially taking a linguistic approach, and to examine it in writing. The questions of who is observing when, where and how and who is conducting interviews where, when and with which spectators also shapes this translation step, as do the subsequent processes of transcribing and analyzing the audio material.

Researchers are translators, and empirical audience research must therefore transparently disclose and reveal the methodological *how* of their translation. It is only through this kind of reflection that the insights into and the handling of audience surveys can be substantially and soundly conducted as praxeological contributions to discourse about the audience, its perception and activities, and about the "emancipated spectator."[152] It is not the "work of the spectator"[153] and what he or she does singularly during a performance that is the focus of praxeological audience research, but rather the ensemble of practices that situatively allows an audience to become a specific audience, a kind of 'fleeting community,' as well as the way, in which we investigate audience perceptions and actions and their corporeal and sensory practices while they perceive a piece and thus translate them into another public sphere.

7 Advertisement for *Nefés* Istanbul, 2003

1 Premiere of the film *PINA*
Berlin, 2011

The closest thing to us is
our body, and every human being
is constantly expressing
themselves, simply by existing.
It's all very visible. When you
read it, you can see everything.[1]

Theor
Metho

y and
dology

In this age of economic globalization, multiculturalism and media interconnectivity, translation has become an essential everyday practice. Whether negotiating the customs of different cultures, dealing with different media aesthetics and approaches to them, or navigating the various possibilities of purchasing goods – people are constantly required to perform acts of cultural, social and media translation in their everyday lives. Mastering everyday activities is almost inconceivable without having good command of such translation skills. In this respect, it comes as no surprise that, since the 1990s, the concept of translation established by linguists has increasingly come up for discussion in cultural and media studies and the social sciences in the wake of the translational turn sparked by globalization and digitalization.[2] The theoretical approach taken in this book ties into those debates. Here, the concept of translation is introduced as a concept for use in dance and art theory, because – unlike the terms 'transmission' in information technology and 'transference' in psychoanalysis – it is able to capture the complexity of cultural, aesthetic and media transformations.

This book is based on the proposition that, even in increasingly nontransparent and abstract globalized societies connected by digital media, cultural translation fundamentally takes place through processes of physical and sensory, situative, (inter)corporeal and (inter)subjective adoption.[3] Pina Bausch's dance theater, which was dedicated both to exploring everyday life and finding inspiration in many different cultures – in their daily practices, their music, dances and languages – is especially well suited to illustrate this.

Today, hip hop is a globalized phenomenon, but it originally came from Black youth culture, while the understanding of gender inherent to tango is different to that of, e.g., the waltz or salsa – in other words: dances, their movement patterns, basic steps, figures and forms, rhythms and dynamics, are physical expressions of social conditions. In their aesthetic patterns of movement, dances embody the social status of gender, age, ethnicity and class. However, dances not only depict cultural patterns and social hierarchies, they are also performative. People acquire cultural knowledge through dance. They experience the culturally 'familiar' and 'foreign' through and in physical movements. They literally dance their way into cultures, thereby corporeally and performatively authenticating,[4] incorporating, habituating, conventionalizing and transforming cultural forms and practices.

While social relations, cultural patterns and gender norms are 'inscribed'[5] into the forms and figurations of popular dances and 'incorporated' (in the Bourdieusian sense) in acts of dance, dance artists reflect these inscriptions and incorporations of cultural, political and social experience using the aesthetic means of dance – but not without repercussions for both everyday life and popular dance culture. Since the 1970s, initiated in particular through Pina Bausch's dance theater, artistic dance has thus been turning its attention toward everyday patterns of movement and, in doing so, has transcended the strict boundaries between artistic and popular dance, aesthetic and social practices (→ PIECES).

Translation as a new approach to dance and art theory: Toward a praxeology of translation

In order to grasp the theory behind these transfers between everyday life and art, dance and media, and art and academia, this book uses the term 'translation' as it is discussed in cultural and media studies and the social sciences in order to compare for the first time these hitherto relatively unconnected discourses on translation. At the same time, I will be supplementing these discourses with the so far largely neglected corporeal dimensions of translation – with a focus on dance. This will culminate in the idea of the 'praxeology of translation' as a central concept for research in dance and art studies.

The praxeology of translation is less concerned with the *what* or *why* than it is with the *how* of translation. Thus, translation does not mean conveying or imparting – feelings, emotions, perceptions, thoughts, ideas or stories – through, with or as dance. Contrary to such a representative understanding of dance, the concept of translation used here seeks to understand how acts of 'passing on,' transfer and adoption take place. In fact, such processes of translation can be found all through dance as well as in the work of the Tanztheater Wuppertal: as acts of acquiring dance knowledge and skill, of corporeally passing on material between dancers (→ WORK PROCESS) and of bringing various dance cultures together (→ PIECES, WORK PROCESS), as well as of translating dance both into language and into various media and vice versa (→ RECEPTION), translating between artistic and academic practice and, in this chapter, between theory and methodology. This chapter will examine and reflect upon the process of translating dance into theory and methodology. First, I will introduce the basic characteristics of a praxeology of translation, after which I will describe the methodology of 'praxeological production analysis' upon which this book is based, which I developed during the course of my research into the work of Pina Bausch and the Tanztheater Wuppertal.

The concept of translation has its origins in several strands of social, cultural and media theory. Their central characteristics can be described as follows:

ORIGINAL AND TRANSLATION   Translation is a term that is in itself a translation, namely from ancient Greek *(hermeneuein, metaphrasis)* and Latin *(transferre, translatio)*.[6] Its imagery of 'carrying across,' 'crossing over to another shore' calls attention to the fact that translation can never be 'word-for-word,' is never identical with its point of departure and thus can never truly convey a supposedly authentic meaning. Argentine tango, for example, cannot be authentically transported into other cultures or transferred onto the stage. Raimund Hoghe remembers Pina Bausch saying, "If that is what one wants, then one would have understood nothing of the tango,"[7] during rehearsals for the piece *Bandoneon* (PREMIERE 1980). Hence, translating is always an act of negotiating and mediating between distinct elements and should thus per se be considered a cultural, media and social practice.

However, not only cultural and media translations but linguistic translations, too, are already "in the broadest sense reworkings and in the strictest sense transpositions."[8] Walter Benjamin said something similar in his ground-breaking essay on the philosophy of language, "The Task of the Translator," which was first published in 1923 and has since become required reading for researchers in the fields of cultural and media studies.[9] In this essay, Benjamin interprets the relationship between original and translation not as primary and secondary, but as one of constant interaction, of reciprocity, as a result of which even that which has been designated 'the original' only reveals itself in hindsight, in the act of translation.[10] Benjamin differentiates between languages according to their "mode of meaning."[11] Translation is thus "transparent"[12]: it does not obscure the original, but instead aims to "rediscove[r] the meaning of what was intended in one's own translating language."[13] Theories of cultural and media translation also pick up on this idea of semantic transparency and interpret it in terms of a theory of difference. In this reading, translation refers to neither a starting nor endpoint, nor even to an original. It does not focus on (supposed) source or target cultures, but rather aims to open up 'in-between spaces' that go beyond binary orders.

TRANSCRIPTIVITY AND REMEDIATION "Transcriptivity"[14] is the term used by German linguist Ludwig Jäger to describe his media concept, which is based on the idea that different media both refer to one another and are defined by constant "resemantizations" as well as "circumscriptions and transcriptions."[15] Jäger defines the process of translating between media as a multidimensional process of setting media in relation to one another. Meaning thus emerges in acts of making reference to something else, which, "firstly, take place between different (media) semiotic systems – i.e., intermedially – and, secondly, within the same semiotic system as well – i.e., intramedially."[16] Therefore, translations do not merely transfer 'content' from one medium into another; rather, they are performative in the sense that they, "to a certain extent, produce what is transcribed in the first place."[17] For Jäger, translation means transitioning "[…] from disturbance to transparency, from decontextualization to a recontextualization of the signs/media under focus."[18] Disturbance is not meant here as a communicative defect, but rather as "that aggregate state of communication in which the sign/medium is visible as such and can thus be semanticized,"[19] a state in which the medium itself comes to the fore and becomes perceivable. Jäger describes transparency as a "state of undisturbed media performance […], in which the respective sign/medium disappears, becomes transparent in relation to the content that it is mediatizing."[20] The medium remains invisible and the content or meaning steps into the foreground. In this book, the interplay between disturbance and transparency as described by Jäger is applied to cultural translation (in dance), allowing us to focus on the mediality of dance itself, on its specific qualities, techniques and forms of presentation during processes of translation. The interplay between disturbance and transparence is constitutive of practices of translation in dance either when the focus is on dance itself, which then becomes perceivable as such, or when it becomes invisible, and meaning, content and significance take center stage, as I have demonstrated in my analyses of dance critiques and the audience (→ RECEPTION).

In contrast to Jäger, the media scholars Jay David Bolter and Richard Grusin consider media translation from the perspective of "remediation"[21] and understand it as the representation of one medium in another. They emphasize the cyclical dependencies between different media, in which media imitate, outbid or otherwise make repeated reference to one another, thus both establishing and subverting the boundaries between individual media. "In appreciative as well as rival references, the represented medium is thereby both preserved and transformed. In this sense, remediation means transforming media in technical, narrative and aesthetic processes of incorporation."[22]

This remediation approach is important for a dance studies concept of translation, as it allows the specific corporeality and presence of dances to become visible in different ways in their respective translations into other media, whether into language, writing or images. However, remediation also becomes crucial when it comes to the failure of translation, namely when the impossibility of translating dance into other media becomes visible and comprehensible. This ambivalence of translating media reveals itself in artistic work processes, but also in their reception (→ WORK PROCESS, RECEPTION).

Like Jäger, Bolter and Grusin emphasize the way that media are viewed as transparent, as simulacra of non-media presentation.[23] They contrast 'immediacy' with the concept of 'hypermediacy,' which becomes relevant when the medium itself becomes the focus and is therefore perceived. "In every manifestation, hypermediacy makes us aware of the medium or media and (in sometimes subtle and sometimes obvious ways) reminds us of our desire for immediacy."[24] Theater as a "medium of presence"[25] and dance as a corporeal medium both deal with this field of tension: on the one hand, theater is understood as a place where, unlike in other media, immediacy dominates the stage and the audience. Dance is likewise considered to be a medium that is immediately corporeal. At the same time, the desire to understand what dance is seeking to express points to the hypermediality of dance itself. Together with Jäger and following Benjamin, Bolter und Grusin agree that the dynamics of the translation process create something new, which is either transparent or opaque in relation to the supposed original.

TRANSLATION AS TRANSFORMATION In the 1990s, concepts of cultural translation were being debated parallel to the discussion of the concept in media studies.[26] They predominantly came from three areas of theory: from a cultural turn in translation studies, from postcolonial studies[27] and from a translational turn[28] in the fields of cultural studies and the social sciences. In essence, they can be systematically traced back to four basic models[29]: (1) hermeneutic translation theories, which, based on the concept of understanding, consider translating something foreign into something familiar as an act of adoption; (2) the concept of translation in translation research, which emphasizes the way that translated texts remain foreign when the texts intended for translation are adapted to one's own language, thereby identifying the foreign in them or what cannot be translated in the translated texts; (3) the school of thought that considers all translations to be metaphors in the literal sense of *meta-phora*,[30] compiling similar terms of translation such as transfer, transmission, transposition, transduction and transcription, which all focus on the *trans-ferre* or the *trans-mettre*[31]; and (4) the concept that relates translation to alterity[32] and defines it as indeterminacy, as a reciprocal transformation, as the metamorphosis of the foreign into the familiar and of the familiar through the foreign, which views translation as something that remains foreign and 'monolinguality' as a signature of alterity or as a crack in the untranslatable/the intransitive.

Unlike translation research in media studies, approaches in cultural studies emphasize the "epistemological leap," whereby "the well-known cultural technique and practice of linguistic translation is expanded to include processes of cultural transmission and mediation."[33] Following Benjamin, none of these concepts consider translation to be the mere movement of cultural signs from a source culture to a target culture. Instead, processes of translation themselves become the actual engines of everyday cultural practice.[34] Their dynamics of processually negotiating meaning between cultures or cultural entities are based on practices, i.e., on translational acts of production, dissemination, interpretation and adoption. Translation scholar Susan Basnett writes: "Today the movement of people around the globe can be seen to mirror the very process of translation itself, for translation is not just the transfer of texts from one language to another, it is now rightly seen as a process of negotiations between texts and between cultures, a process during which all kinds of transactions take place [...]."[35]

The concept of cultural translation understands cultural processes as continuous processes of translation and views translation as the transformation of the cultural: (dance) culture can be read with literary scholar Homi K. Bhabha as something that has always been already translated.[36] His postcolonial understanding of culture is also fundamental to a concept of translation in dance theory: "Culture [...] is both transnational and translational. It is transnational because contemporary postcolonial discourses are rooted in specific histories of cultural displacement, whether they are in the 'middle passage' of slavery and indenture, the 'voyage out' of the civilizing mission, the fraught accommodation of Third World migrations to the West after the Second World War, or the traffic of economic and political refugees within and outside the Third World. Culture is translational because such special histories of displacement – now accompanied by the territorial ambitions of 'global' media technologies – make the question on how culture signifies, or what is signified by culture, a rather complex issue."[37]

According to Bhabha, it is not least this transnational dimension of cultural and media transformation that makes cultural translation a practice that is both complex and necessary. On the one hand, Bhabha emphasizes the 'in-between' state that characterizes migration societies constantly negotiating between the necessities of cultural translation and its inherent dimensions of untranslatability.³⁸ On the other hand, Bhabha fundamentally describes translation as "the performative nature of cultural communication" and describes its dynamics as a "movement of meaning."³⁹ From the perspective of performativity theory, translation is a twofold procedure – "translation as performance and in performance,"⁴⁰ both a practice of execution and of performance, which, in this binarity, constitutes a "practice of everyday life."⁴¹ This idea is important for dance research, since dancing is a corporeal practice that always takes place in the interplay between the act of carrying something out and the act of performing it.

IDENTITY AND DIFFERENCE   Translation is subject to the paradoxical relationship between identity and difference. The paradox lies in the way that difference is suspended in translation, that is, in the idea that the translated should be identical with the 'original.' At the same time, identity can only be established through difference. In other words, identity always requires a counterpart, an Other, in order to find itself. This paradox between identity and difference is one genuine component of translation, but there have been many efforts – in dance, too – to resolve it in one direction or the other. There are innumerable examples of attempts to resolve this difference, such as ostensibly faithful dance reconstructions, for example of historical material such as Nijinsky's *Sacre du Printemps* (PREMIERE 1913) or Kurt Jooss' *Grüner Tisch* (PREMIERE 1932). And there have also been a range of attempts to produce difference, to generate the non-identical: some dance reenactments are framed by other formats, such as *Urheben/Aufheben* (PREMIERE 2008), a lecture performance by the German choreographer Martin Nachbar that references Dore Hoyer's *Affectos Humanos* (PREMIERE 1962). Other choreographies, in turn, deal associatively or from the perspective of subjective experience with 'dance heritage,' for example the pieces developed as part of Tanzfonds Erbe, a project carried out by the German Federal Cultural Foundation (2011-2018).⁴²

Walter Benjamin solved the paradoxical problem of identity and difference by ascribing translation with two tasks, namely to generate difference and, at the same time, to bear witness to the "suprahistorical kinship of languages."⁴³ According to Benjamin, the goal of translation is therefore not to decipher the meaning of what was intended, but rather to touch "the original fleetingly and only at the infinitely small point of sense, in order to follow its own path in accord with the laws of fidelity in the freedom of linguistic development."⁴⁴

It would appear that Pina Bausch also addressed this paradox between identity and difference and consciously played with it, since she virtually made it the central issue of the Tanztheater

Wuppertal's artistic work – for example, with regard to the topic of age, by letting some dancers dance the same roles for decades (→ PIECES); or in the case of dancers from earlier generations passing on their dances to current members of the ensemble for re-stagings, which was common practice even during Pina Bausch's lifetime and which has continued since her death, with pieces being restaged without the choreographer's decision-making strength or power, but with the collective knowledge of the dancers – and with the help of media translations (videos, notation; → WORK PROCESS). Pina Bausch also had the piece *Kontakthof* (PREMIERE 1978) danced not only by the company but also by senior citizens (PREMIERE 2000) and teenagers (PREMIERE 2008), thereby allowing the same choreography to become different through the diversity of the performers (→ PIECES).

UN/TRANSLATABILITES AND THEIR PRODUCTIVITY Following Walter Benjamin, we can summarize that cultural translation (in dance) has two sides to it: it would be senseless and arbitrary without the assumption of kinship – even if fictive – between (dance) cultures, (dance) languages and (dance) pieces and their performances. Pina Bausch described this kind of translation as follows: "Getting to know completely foreign customs, types of music, habits has led to things that are unknown to us, but which still belong to us, all being translated into dance."[45] At the same time, cultural translation (in dance) establishes difference between, for example, different (dance) cultures and (dance) languages, and between the 'original' and the material that is passed on for the revival or restaging of a piece. The difference is the effect of uncertainty, which testifies to the failure to translate movement and dance as in a reproduction that is 'true' to the original in the sense of a direct copy. It becomes visible during the process of carrying out the translation, when the translated material pursues, in Walter Benjamin's words, its "very own path" – or, in the words of Pina Bausch: "Our pieces are definitely not about copying something. That would be completely wrong. It's about processing, about abstraction."[46]

As asserted by philosopher Alexander Garcia Düttmann,[47] cultural translation (in dance) can therefore be described as an act of translating the un/translatable. However, the concept of translation presented in this book does not negatively interpret translation as a diminishment, simplification or loss – and not just because even failed translations always reveal something translatable beside the untranslatable. In fact, it is the central proposition of this book that the productivity of translation lies in its very im/possibility. This applies above all to art and in particular to dance as an aesthetic medium of the body. Translation cannot be grasped as linear, unambiguous or in terms of semiotic theory, but must be understood instead as a movement – circling, cyclical, ambiguous, suspended – both in a corporeal dance sense and in a symbolic and metaphorical sense.

The productivity of the un/translatable reveals itself in particular in the Tanztheater Wuppertal's international coproductions (→ PIECES). For Pina Bausch, it was never about bringing the 'other culture' onto the stage. She thus frustrated the expectations of many critics and spectators who were searching for the 'authentic,' who criticized her when they found what they believed to be nothing, not enough or only clichés of the coproducing countries in her pieces (→ RECEPTION). In one of her rare interviews, Pina Bausch responded to this critique by stating, "[…] I have placed great value on the fact that we don't just see what is external or touristic."[48] In her attempts to 'grasp' the Other, whom she understood in a literal, aesthetic and corporeal sense, she insisted, on the one hand, on a difference between cultures, a difference that she considered to be rooted in the limits of understanding. On the other hand, Pina Bausch repeatedly pointed out the common ground, that which encompasses various cultures, but also the situatedness of the performance, as in her speech at the Kyoto Prize Arts and Philosophy Workshop in 2007: "Of course there are many cultural differences, but there is always something that we have in common […]. It's about finding a language […] that allows us to sense something of what has always been there […]. When something coincides, it's wonderful, with all these different people, on this one evening, then we experience something unique, something unrepeatable together."[49]

In the same way that translation is one of the foundations of (dance) culture, the untranslatability of cultures, media and languages is a prerequisite of human culturality. Thus, translation is itself culture, as culture is permanent translation.[50] In this interpretation, translation is not a special process – not in dance either. It neither refers to a starting nor endpoint, nor does it perform the relationship between original and copy. Instead, from this standpoint, the notion of (dance) culture as an authentic, originary or essential unit only emerges in the act of translating – that is, retrospectively, as Barbara Johnson explains in her book *Mother Tongues*,[51] in which she investigates Benjamin's text and reflects on his theories. It is precisely this retrospectivity that reveals the productivity of the un/translatable.

HYBRIDITY AND BOUNDARIES Thus, cultural translation (in dance) does not mean cultural understanding, building bridges between cultures or blending them. The 'space of translation' is, especially in the tradition of postcolonial studies, a hybrid one, a "third space"[52] of "transculture,"[53] in which translations are the rule rather than a disturbance.

Homi K. Bhabha introduced the notion of hybridity into the discussion he initiated about cultural translation, as he did the now inflationary concept of "third space." The term 'hybridity' has since become overused and ideologically charged. In his Vienna Lectures of 2007,[54] Bhabha draws attention to the fact that the hybrid subject should not merely be euphorically welcomed as a cultural globetrotter, as an intellectual nomad – that is, as a subject that generates hybridity by (constantly) transgressing boundaries. Instead, Bhabha locates the perspective of the unconditional 'trans,' of transgressing boundaries, in the experience of colonialism, which, citing Peter Sloterdijk[55] or Zygmunt Bauman,[56] can also be seen as rooted within the kinetic concept of modernity, which has declared movement, transgression and progress to be its leading metaphors. When taken to its logical conclusion, the dream of no borders or boundaries that follows on from these concepts of colonialism and modernity is actually totalitarian.[57]

In this sense, Bhabha points out that cultural translation is always a movement on the periphery, in both a direct and a metaphorical sense. A boundary always has two sides to it: it simultaneously separates and connects. It is the frontier, the wall, but also the contact zone, the in-between space, the rendezvous point. A boundary thus not only establishes difference but also makes contact and touch possible. A globally touring dance ensemble like the Tanztheater Wuppertal is composed of nomads. It is a 'travelling people,' a group of cultural translators (→ COMPANY). Their life and work are deeply influenced by migration, the global art market and the distribution machinery of the media. The professional mobility of artists is rarely chosen voluntarily or light-heartedly, but is usually the result of economic necessity. It is not just in artistic practices themselves, as the example of the international coproductions shows, but also in the relationship between artistic and scholarly practice, the aesthetic and the discursive, that the question of how to deal with the experience of the boundary becomes decisive.[58] This is just one of the reasons that German philosopher Bernhard Waldenfels, in the tradition of Jacques Derrida and Emmanuel Levinas, argues for an "ethics of respecting and violating borders [...]. In other words, transgressing the threshold to the Other, without suspending the boundary or leaving it behind."[59] Or, as Jacques Derrida writes: "One is never installed within transgression, one never lives elsewhere. Transgression implies that the limit is always at work."[60]

TRANSFERRING, POSITING, ENFORCING[61] The violation and transgression of boundaries is closely related to hegemonic factors. The German word for translation, *Übersetzung,* also means 'carrying something over,' 'ferrying something over.' It is important to pay attention here not only to the preposition *über* – 'over' or 'trans' – but also to the second part of the composite noun: *Setzung* means to posit or to plant. Thus, translation – *Übersetzung* – always begins with the positing of something. In media philosopher Dieter Mersch's words, it is "always a 'different beginning,' an act that must always be begun anew."[62] Pina Bausch likewise emphasized that, for every new piece, she had to start again from scratch, she had to forget what she knew: "With each piece this search begins anew."[63] The piece, as she said elsewhere, is always situatively embedded in time: "There is no piece, we actually start, and there is nothing but ourselves and the situation that exists – just our situation: how we are all here, here in this world, so to speak."[64]

The 'beginning' needed to be posited anew, again and again. What would be the starting point of a piece? How would the dancers understand Pina Bausch's 'questions' during rehearsals? What would they translate into scenes, movements and dances? What would they note down during their research trips to other countries? What would be integrated into the choreography? What would the company use as orientation for their restagings? (→ WORK PROCESS) These questions show the extent to which the development of pieces, but also the passing on and restaging of material were characterized by the interplay between translating, positing and enforcing. The same applies to reception: what is perceived by audiences and mentioned by critics? What is chosen as the starting point for a description or review of a dance piece? Whether it be the dance, the symbolism of the dance, the mnemonic image, a personal association, one's own experience of affect – everything that is conveyed in language, writing and images has already been translated (→ SOLO DANCE, RECEPTION). Contrary to the prevalent view that translating dance into language, writing and images merely diminishes something supposedly diverse, turning it into something clear-cut, forcing the ambiguous into the binary structure of language, this book focuses on the cracks and gaps in translation and their productivity while also asking: could it be that these translation steps are actually necessary in order to carry dance over into communicative and cultural memory?[65]

From this perspective, even the normative term for the genre, German dance theater *(Deutsches Tanztheater)* – used to categorize artists as different as Pina Bausch, Reinhild Hoffmann, Susanne Linke, Gerhard Bohner and Johann Kresnik[66] – is an attempt to posit a national imaginary in relation to dance. This position has been declared retrospectively and was only possible by positing a difference either historically – from expressionist dance as its historical predecessor to contemporary dance as its historical successor – and by differentiating it normatively from other dance aesthetics such as modern dance, postmodern dance, modern ballet and conceptual dance. Therefore, it is translation itself that exposes the attribution of a (national) identity to a (dance) culture as the act of asserting a political imaginary.

Thus, translation in dance can mainly be described using three prepositions: translating through, translating in and translating as movement. All three contain a metaphorical openness, as they describe the corporeal and sensory dimensions of practices that always involve, as in the philosophy of French philosopher Jacques Rancière,[67] something genuinely political. The political of translation reveals itself in the fact that every translation presupposes and entails an act of positing and that it takes place in a process of negotiation, during which something asserts itself. Yet even this assertion is ambivalent: on the one hand, it has an emancipatory potential, as translations are paths for negotiating difference and have the potential to overcome hegemonic conditions. On the other hand, there is the counter-aspect of establishing authority, making something one's own, stabilizing and reactualizing hegemony. This is the hegemonic side of translation, which is sometimes neglected in debates on translation in the arts. Art historians Hans Belting and Andrea Buddensieg have pointed out that it is only in the context of the battle for attention and recognition in the global art market that the concept of translation has gained such relevance.[68]

Whether it is a painting by Jan Vermeer, music by Johann Sebastian Bach or a play by William Shakespeare, Pyotr Ilyich Tchaikovsky's *Nutcracker* or Pina Bausch's *The Rite of Spring* – in all of the works of art that belong to the global art canon dominated by the West, it is always also about establishing cultural authority and asserting claims to hegemony. The same applies, for example, when popular dances from other cultures, such as salsa, rock and roll or Argentine tango, are standardized and squeezed into the corset of European dance culture by dance teachers' associations. Another example is hip hop, which has been welcomed into the context of contemporary dance and shown at renowned dance and theater festivals, but is still declared to be 'street art' or 'urban style.' Here, we once again encounter the paradoxical relationship between identity and difference and the two political sides of the boundary, namely separation and transgression, inclusion and exclusion. This is where the hegemonic aspect of translation manifests itself – but this is also an area of its productivity.[69] For even within these political practices of inclusion and exclusion, new choreographic forms and dance styles manage to emerge through translation.

3 Special issue stamp
commemorating Pina Bausch's
75th birthday, 2015

2 Advertisement for
   Masurca Fogo
  Hong Kong, 2001

4 Advertisement for *Bamboo Blues* Italy, 2009

The politics of translation reveal themselves in practices, in acts of negotiation. Practices of translation in turn reference the political dimensions of artistic practice and the political site of art. Translation thus also means, as Bhabha writes, "not simply mixing, but strategically and selectively adopting meanings, creating space for people to take action."[70] Precisely herein lies the relevance of understanding translation as an empirical project through, in and as dance, for a praxeology of translation prompts us to understand translation as negotiation, as a practice of the political on the boundaries between aesthetic and scholarly practice. Translating between art and academia is also a practice of negotiating and mediating between differences. The discourses into which the artistic dance practices have to be translated are thus always subject to the caveat that they are potentially untranslatable: they miss the mark, they posit something else, they cannot be identical to aesthetic processes. Accepting this irresolvable alterity between aesthetic and discursive practices involves upholding a boundary. This means, on the one hand, defending the logic inherent to the aesthetic while, on the other hand, continuing to question the scholarly, theoretical and empirical practices of discursive positing.

How are complex translation processes carried out in dance? A praxeology of translation does not define translations as stable, fixed formats or entities, but rather considers them to be transitory practices. The focus lies not on the question of *what* translation is, but rather on the issue of *how* translations are carried out and *how* we can examine practices of translation and their performative effects. These questions shift scholarly attention to the action, the "in-between"[71] and, with it, to the "mediality of translation's in-betweenness."[72] Translation is thus not an "artifact at rest within itself," but rather an "agile relationship"[73] between transmitting and conveying, between translation, transduction and transcription – in other words, something that is generally described using terms that all take processes of 'transfer' into account.

Whether reacting to 'questions' during rehearsals, recording dance using other media such as video or notation, 'passing on' dances, writing reviews about dance, etc. – practices of translation are an everyday part of dance, as this book shows. Their manifestations and applications diverge widely. Translations generate plural effects and misunderstandings. They exhibit patterns of inclusion and exclusion, of interruption, resistance, loss and reinterpretation and, moreover, generate their own respective boundaries and in/translatabilities. In practices of translating dance, corporeality and materiality[74] come to the fore as specific medialities of dance itself.

A praxeology of translation thus means accentuating new aspects of existing concepts of translation by circling back to the general problem of alterity in all translation theories in order to examine a specific 'act of translation,' its practices and performative effects. This also makes it possible to expand the concept of translation beyond its latent linguistic boundaries to include the corporeal and sensory dimensions so fundamental to dance and dance research.[75] At the same time, the question of the mode of translation requires us to take a praxeological research approach, which is here condensed into a praxeology of translation.

Praxeological research is the result of the practice turn in sociology and cultural studies, particularly in the sociology of the 1970s[76] In the history of the social theory of modernity, the term dates back to Karl Marx, who considered practice to be a "sensuous human activity."[77] Various philosophical positions, such as those of Hannah Arendt and John Dewey, are equally considered to be predecessors to sociological practice theories. Arendt elevated Marx's concept of practice by defining it as a creative rather than a reproductive activity.[78] Dewey's pragmatic position emphasizes sensory and material experience as one fundamental aspect of practically gained knowledge.[79]

351 ACTION AND PRACTICE The sociological notion of practice is fundamental to dance research, because it draws attention to physical activities, intercorporealities and to the interaction between human and non-human actors.[80] What has been essential to the career of the concept of practice in sociology is that it has abandoned mentalist concepts of action following on from Max Weber, who defined action as follows: "We shall speak of 'action' insofar as the acting individual attaches a subjective meaning to his behavior – be it overt or covert, omission or acquiescence. Action is 'social' insofar as its subjective meaning takes account of the behavior of others and is thereby oriented in its course."[81] Weber clearly differentiated 'action' from 'behavior,' which he described as being mere activity and – unlike action – not endowed with any subjective meaning. According to him, 'action' is the conceptual opposite of 'structure,' which provides order and – in keeping with the tradition of the philosophy of mind – is bound to intentionally operating actors. Practice theory deviates from this definition of action. Here, action is neither, as in Weber's case, instrumentally rational nor is it value-rational or moral, that is, affectively motivated. Rather, it is understood in an anti-rationalistic, non-intentional and non-motivated sense as corporeal and material coactivity and as a creative practice. Interaction is therefore not the exception to action, but rather its prototype.[82]

'Action' is defined in practice theory as a practice that is carried out or perceived by the body.[83] Practices always occur in coactivity with other subjects, things and artifacts, spatial, material and situational framings. This conceptualization is especially useful for dance research: dance cannot be described using an intentional, mentalist or in part instrumentally rational concept of action. Moreover, the concept of practice looks at (stage) interactions between actors and non-human artifacts, which are also characteristic of the works of Pina Bausch. For practice theory defines artifacts such as things, objects, props, set designs and costumes themselves as actors. Thus, practice theory can help us to grasp the interplay between the different levels of action relevant to rehearsals, performances and audience situations, which have hitherto not or only peripherally been looked at in theater and dance research, in performance theory and in the dominant concept of action used there.

Practice theories programmatically integrate the materiality and physicality of interactions as well as their performative aspects into a research system that innovatively shifts the conceptual clusters of action/situation/movement on the one hand and of structure/order/choreography on the other, thus also redefining the difference between micro and macro. Accordingly, the executive mode of practice can be derived neither inductively from mere subjective meaning or from a single relationship of cause and effect, nor purely deductively from a superordinate structure, a narrative, discourse or an order of representation. Instead, practice itself forms social order. Practice theories understand 'practice,' or "bundles" "complexes,"[84] "ensembles"[85] or "plenums"[86] of interconnected practices, as their basic theoretical units. Practices thus structure the social world and negotiate what is described in other sociological approaches as a structure or order, in the corporeal and material execution and in the actualization of incorporated, collectively shared orders (of knowledge).[87]

Moreover, practices are a central concept in experientially oriented, empirical dance studies, like the research presented in this book, which focuses on the production of and thus on the interplay between the development, performance and reception of a piece. Practice theory lets us identify ways in which a company's specific conventions establish themselves, e.g., during rehearsals and training or while developing, restaging or touring pieces, and how these routines are perpetuated over decades, even when the individual actors have been replaced.

ROUTINE AND TRANSFORMATION The work of a dance artist is made up of a sequence of practices such as rehearsal, training, performance, etc. These reoccurring processes are perceived as routines, because they allow for the development and consolidation of a stable, specific dancer habitus that combines, among other things, formative and expressive aspects of the body and self. Different branches of practice theory prioritize different aspects of these processes[88] – with various consequences for dance research. (Post-)structural practice theories, mainly represented by Andreas Reckwitz in Germany,[89] are primarily rooted in the French tradition of Pierre Bourdieu's *Outline of a Theory of Practice*[90] as well as Michel Foucault's writings on orders of knowledge and governmental strategies of the *Technologies of the Self*.[91] Here, practice is conceived of analogously to a linguistic model, inasmuch as cultural habits are regulated by their own 'grammar,' by orders of knowledge, by practices.[92] (Post-)structuralist practice theories emphasize the aspect of repetition in practices at the expense of performative shifts. The execution and performance of practices depends on "routines."[93] Thus, these theories focus more on consistency than on transformations: the orders inherent to the practices form a framework for evoking an embodied, practical sense *(sens pratique)*, which in turn creates, according to Bourdieu, consistency due to its habitual stability.[94] Here, practices are conceived of as a "continuous stream" of "repetitive formations," as a "culturally available and circulating repertoire that subjects can attach themselves to and cite from,"[95] as an "open spatially-temporally dispersed sets of doings and sayings organized by common understandings, teleo-affectivities (ends, tasks, emotions), and rules,"[96] as in the case of rehearsal, training and performance routines. However, unlike poststructuralism itself, (post-)structural practice theory locates the logic of practice not only on the discursive level but also in physical skills, the material properties of things and collectively shared schemata – and this is where it becomes interesting for dance studies. Aspects of subjectivation also come into play in that routines – such as daily classical ballet training or certain artistic working methods – always generate the types of subject[97] with which (dancer) subjects align themselves and which they continually become through continuous repetition. Routines thus not only help to consolidate and normatively strengthen the bonds of practice but also to shape habitus – in this case, a specific dancer habitus.

Unlike (post-)structural practice theories, microsociological positions, pioneered in the German-speaking world above all in Stefan Hirschauer's writings,[98] follow a radical concept of practice that is not guided by consistent orders (of knowledge) but rather by a knowledge that is performatively generated in practices, in doings. These positions thus aim to question, redefine or even dissolve the dualism of situation and structure, of micro and macro perspective. Microsociological approaches develop less a culture-theoretical interpretation than they do an interpretation based on the sociology of bodies and/or things – and are thus, with their focus on the corporeality of practices, important for dance studies. Microsociological approaches view practices as the corporeal realization of social phenomena,[99] as in the context of artistic work,[100] and define practices as observable forms of execution and realization that can be separated into various types of activities, modes of action and behavioral patterns,[101] as revealed in rehearsals (→ WORK PROCESS), pieces (→ PIECES), solos (→ SOLO DANCE), audience reactions and the habits of critics (→ RECEPTION).

Microsociological practice theories do not emphasize the self-formative, but rather the self-expressive side of practice due to their connections with the US tradition of Harold Garfinkel and ethnomethodology.[102] Garfinkel and conversation analyst Harvey Sacks dedicated themselves in the 1970s to examining the formal structures of practical actions,[103] which they defined as methods that everyday actors develop and use when performing actions. They were not interested in uncovering the reasons behind the actions, but rather in making visible the "accountable phenomena"[104] (of conversation) that constitute action. This approach is similar to the aesthetic practice of the Tanztheater Wuppertal (→ PIECES). Garfinkel and Sacks define 'accountable phenomena' as those that display in 'saying' what they are in 'doing' through indexical expressions. In order to examine this, Garfinkel developed "crisis experiments," in which he exposed the normative order of actions by means of practical interruptions, by disappointing expectations and by not obeying everyday rules. These experiments are reminiscent of how the Tanztheater Wuppertal designed its stages as situative action spaces meant to subvert conventions and continually challenge the dancers to overcome routines (→ PIECES, COMPANY).

Microsociological practice theories take these insights as a starting point by detaching social phenomena from the linguistic, textual and figurative levels of conversation. They are similar to the concepts of performativity developed in the philosophy of language and culture in that they view the difference between saying and doing – expressed, for instance, in Theodore Schatzki's phrase "nexus of doings and sayings"[105] – as outdated. In this sense, signs can be found in gestures and bodily and dance movements. Saying is thus embedded within doing, inasmuch as doing – dancing, performing, presenting – always reveals what it is as well. This is why (dance) practice can also be observed, because the meaning of doing is not assumed to be found or sought out in motives or intent, but is displayed in the visibility of forms of physical self-(re)presentation. Here, doing or acting is meant in both senses: something is being done, created, but what is being created is also being presented and performed. This links to the concept of performativity, which likewise emphasizes that performance is always also part of execution – and vice versa.

PERFORMATIVITY IN PERFORMANCE PRACTICES Erving Goffman's theory of theatricality and interaction and Judith Butler's theory of performativity have paved the way for most approaches in practice theory. Goffman's position can be seen as a turning point in the sociological concept of action,[106] which had previously been heavily influenced by Max Weber. Goffman's concept of theatricality also provides an approach to understanding the relationship between everyday gestures and their artistic translations, as is typical of the Tanztheater Wuppertal. Thus, it seems more than conceptually apt to look at everyday actions as performance and thus as theatrical and as movement. Goffman's work on the theatricality of everyday life therefore defines it as performance, with actors no longer the authors of an action, but rather performing as participants in interactive situations.[107] Goffman abandons the use of theatricality as a metaphor for the social, instead introducing it into sociology as a category for observing everyday life. In doing so, he prioritizes the category of the aesthetic, which Georg Simmel had also already advocated in sociological thought.[108]

In practice theories, theatricality is mainly examined in terms of its performativity. Unlike in theater, dance and performance studies, it therefore has less to do with the concept of performance and more with that of execution. Performativity, in turn, is considered the generative mode of practice. On the one hand, (post-)structural practice theories do not explicitly elaborate on the performative; however, it can be embedded within the matrix of practices and orders inasmuch as practices of the performative authenticate orders,[109] allowing us to read the performative praxeologically.[110] On the other hand, microsociological practice theories relate performativity to an action's representativity and expressivity. Performativity here becomes the engine of social transformation. For dance practices, the relationship between representativity, expressivity and performativity is central. Dance movements can but do not inevitably have to be expressive. Dance is always abstraction. Dance movements can represent, stand for something. But what really matters is how they are executed and authenticated. The performative is thus the driving force that allows dance to become 'real.'

(Post-)structural practice theories emphasize that the power of practices to generate reality lies in the way that they refer to supraindividual orders (of knowledge). If we take this stance, then (dance) practices can be understood as embodied cultural techniques, while (dance) discourses, which reveal themselves in paratexts – e.g., program booklets, posters and reviews – are the material forms of practices that frame artistic production. In microsociological positions, however, 'reality' is solely generated in performative execution. Discourses are not considered practices, but rather independent sources of meaning. On the one hand, they provide the semantic infrastructure for practices while also legitimizing what can be said and thought; however, on the other hand, they are also dependent on practices.[111] The focus here thus lies not on semiotic systems, but rather on the material repositories of communication, on bodies and things.

CARRYING OUT PRACTICES The routineness and regularity of practices are the focus of (post-)structural practice theories, which consider practices to be largely ahistorical, static and constant. The emphasis thus lies on the sustainability and stability of practices and of their associated normative orders of knowledge. The modes of their execution reveal themselves in the way they reference the orders stored in the routines. Thus, the performative is embedded between practices and these orders, opening up a perspective that microsociological positions in practice theory neglect or even reject. For microsociological theories locate the mode of execution in practice alone; they inquire into performatively generated knowledge and the relationship between the success and failure of the act of execution. This shifts attention to the relationship between stability and instability, thus taking a perspective that conceptualizes the social as something dynamic and concentrates on the relationship between conventionalizing and transforming practices. This approach shares much with artistic work processes – in rehearsals, restagings and acts of 'passing on' – which, at the Tanztheater Wuppertal, are characterized by the interplay between certainty and routine on the one hand and uncertainty and risk on the other (→ WORK PROCESS).

Just as these microsociological approaches assert that practice is generated through not just embodied knowledge but also through the knowledge revealed in the act of execution – through performed knowledge – performance theory describes the modes of execution through the performance of embodied knowledge.[112] Without actually reflecting on the theoretical concept of the practice itself, performance theory defines this knowledge as practice – in opposition to theory – inasmuch as a performative act must be publicly carried out, i.e., in orders of interaction, and authenticated. Within the scope of the performative turn, theater studies has differentiated between performativity (of the performance) on the one hand and representativity (of a staging) and expressivity (of the presentation) on the other. It is not overarching, retrieved knowledge or the knowledge that is stored and expressed in bodies that takes effect during a performance; rather, performativity is what produces the theatricality of a performance in the first place. Approaches in literary and cultural studies in turn make explicit reference to the representative when they position the performative as a series of executed acts.¹¹³ The dance studies concept of practice is based on these positions in that, unlike (post-)structural practice theories, it conceives of the performative as (radical) instability and relates it to phenomena such as unrepeatability, eventfulness, ephemerality and presence.

ACTORS IN PRACTICES The main point of tension and contradiction between practice and performance theories lies in the question of which participants – including human as well as non-human actors – contribute to the creation of a practice or performance and how it takes place. Performance theories and dance theory are more humanist and anthropocentric. They attribute great authority to the active subject, to processes of subjectivation and collectivization,¹¹⁴ and to situations controlled by agents, even when, as in the works of Pina Bausch, material, non-human actors (lights, stage, props, animals, things, objects) become important.

Practice theories, in contrast, are based on a less humanist understanding of doing: human action and individual agency are not elevated, but rather contextualized within an interactive structure comprising a chain of actions or an ensemble of practices. Following on from Pierre Bourdieu, in (post-)structural practice theories, practices are initiated by embodied forms of habitus, which are controlled by the *sens pratique*, without this process necessarily being a conscious one. The perspective taken here is heavily anthropocentric, to the extent that the process of incorporation always relates to the subject and the process of subjectivation.

Microsociological practice theories even more radically turn away from concepts of action that are bound to actors, toward the distribution of actions and the "participants"¹¹⁵ of practice. From the perspective of the sociology of the body, they simultaneously strengthen the communicative aspect of corporeal action by emphasizing what is socially visible. They do so in accordance with the Actor-Network Theory (ANT)¹¹⁶ developed predominantly by (technology) sociologists Bruno Latour, Michel Callon and John Law in the 1990s, which asserts that technology, nature and the social reciprocally attribute properties and the potential for action to each other within a network. ANT thus also takes into consideration non-human participants, creating a hybrid between the social actor and the material thing. This simultaneously calls into question concepts that limit their understanding of the subject to humans. If, for example, we examine in Pina Bausch's pieces the participation of animals in relation to human actors or the performance and inherent logic of stage elements and objects such as water, collapsing walls, turf, lawn and artificial carnations (→ PIECES, COMPANY), it is striking how these pieces formulate the question of agency from a new and different perspective, namely from that of objects. However, the art of Pina Bausch is not suitable for an application of ANT's broad concept of agency, of one that encompasses both human and non-human actors. Her pieces adhere to a humanist, anthropological concept that differentiates between human and non-human actors, even when the specific performative quality of the latter, such as that of the hippopotamus in *Arien* (PREMIERE 1979; → PIECES), tells its own stories. The concepts of incorporation and embodiment, of copresence and corporeality are therefore central to a praxeological approach toward dance studies. As in practice theories, these forms of embodiment are again best introduced via Bordieu's concept of habitus.

Moreover, for a praxeological approach, the relationship between situationality and contextuality is central when analyzing performances. 'Contextuality' here refers to the concrete material and spatial design of performance situations (theater architecture, etc.), but also to the broader, cultural, political and social frameworks (the political situation at a performance venue, the cultural significance of theater and art). Praxeological research assumes that these contexts become perceivable and visible in the performance situation. 'Situationality' means the 'presentness' and eventfulness of a performance. The focus is on the mode of execution, i.e., on the performativity of the performance.

The performance situation is characterized by a dialectics of observing and being observed. This is a constitutive structural feature of a performance's execution – in terms of actualizing and reconventionalizing norms, referencing cultural orders of representation and knowledge, and formulating and designing the execution itself. The public, or the audience, during a performance, is thus central to dance research that is rooted in practice theory, for the public performatively authenticates the execution of an action. The members of the audience are coactors in the realization of events, and a performance is consequently understood as an actor-observer relationship, as a network of actors standing in relation to one another.

Although there are some differences between the practice theories that have developed in the social sciences,[117] we can outline the basic premises of praxeological research as translated to dance studies as follows: taking a dance studies perspective based on practice theory does not mean primarily examining the ideas, values, norms or semiotic and symbolic systems of dance or choreographies; rather, it is about attempting to locate them in practices, in their situatedness. This means concentrating on the ways in which ideas, values, norms, and semiotic and symbolic systems are embedded within bodies, but also within things and artifacts such as spaces, materials, props, stage designs and costumes. This material embeddedness sets them in relation to the practical skill and implicit knowledge of bodies and to the framings provided by orders (of knowledge). How can we describe a praxeological approach toward translation in dance studies against this backdrop?

DANCING AS TRANSLATING: THOUGHTS ON PRACTICE THEORY

Approaching translation from the perspective of practice theory as it is discussed in this book means concentrating on the corporeal practices that are fundamental to translation. This is what makes this approach so important and attractive to dance research. The term 'practice' should not be confused with the term 'praxis.' Kant, Hegel, Feuerbach and Marx used 'praxis' in philosophical debate to describe the sensory or concrete activities of humans.[118] However, according to Andreas Reckwitz, practices are "meaningfully regulated bodily movements that depend on corresponding implicit, incorporated knowledge" and on regular "behavioral routines in dealing with artifacts."[119] They are based on complex collective knowledge, which is less *know-what* knowledge than it is *know-how* knowledge, "less a mental knowing/consciousness than something [...] incorporated through physical practice/study *[Übung]*."[120] In the same way that carrying out practices does not presuppose purposeful actors, practice theory does not consider the body to be a medium for executing a practice, it does not carry out or perform practices. In truth, "the body is embedded within the practices."[121]

A praxeological approach does not understand dance practices as the movements of individual actors, but rather sees them as interdependent activities, organized by collectively shared, practical forms of knowledge. Dance practices such as warming-up, training and rehearsals should therefore be understood as a bundle of physical and mental activities that cannot be reduced to individual motives or intentions. Even certain orders, such as the predetermined and routine course of a dance class, are not considered to exist independently beyond or outside of practices (of conducting a class). This means that practices are not framed by orders; instead, the praxeological perspective dissolves the relationships between orders and situations, between macro and micro levels: these orders are viewed as emergent phenomena that are embedded within and generated by practices. Praxeological dance research thus concentrates on the performative dimension, on the ways in which something is executed and how it is authenticated.

Dance practices reveal themselves in their situatedness, that is, in their materiality and corporeality. They can be observed. Practical skill and the implicit knowledge of (dancing) bodies show themselves, for example, in practices of training and rehearsing (→ WORK PROCESS). Daily ballet training and the specific research methods of the Tanztheater Wuppertal have thus provided the bodies of the company's dancers with practical skills that they can retrieve in research phases. Moreover, they have habituated a distinct movement aesthetic – a certain plasticity of movement figures, a specific relationship to center and periphery, a particular way of working with their arms and hands. This knowledge is implicit knowledge, inasmuch as it is not always accessible through contemplation.

A praxeological perspective thus focuses on *doing:* on artistic practices of warming-up, training, improvising, taking notes and recording material, of composing and choreographing, but also on practices similar to those in the academic field, such as observing, researching, evaluating, reflecting, documenting, archiving, etc. Practices are based on collectively shared, practical knowledge that, as physical and implicit knowledge, always creates difference as well. Not only do the working methods of the Tanztheater Wuppertal and therefore their practical know-how differ from those of other dance groups, the execution of the practices itself also generates other bodies and subjectivities. Practices of translating in dance should therefore be understood as a bundle of physical and mental activities where the mental is registered, ratified and validated in corporeal practices and can then be perceived.

From a praxeological point of view, dancing is not an intentional, subject-oriented action, nor is it a symbolically charged, communicative phenomenon or a process in which meaning is transferred through movement; rather, one *does dance,* i.e., it is a practice before it is translated into a symbolic act – in other words: it is an observable physical process. German sociologist Stefan Hirschauer explains the difference between acting and doing: "an action [in dance, G.K.] has to be initiated, it requires an impulse and a center that conveys meaning. That is why we inquire into it using questions like 'why' and 'for what.' However, a [dance, G.K.] practice is always already ongoing; the only question is what keeps it running and how 'people' practice it: how should it be done?"[122] This *how* does not just focus on the bodies of dancers; rather, the *how* already addresses the interplay between dance practices and material artifacts as well, such as stage spaces, materials, props, set designs and costumes. A praxeological perspective thus circumvents the dichotomy between the worlds of subject and object by taking into account the contribution made by artifacts to physical practices of translation.[123]

Practices of translation always take place in the paradox between identity and difference. They occur at the 'boundaries,' the junctions, the margins, the liminal phases and places; they are never definitive or identical, but are hybrid with a specific logic of their own. Aesthetic, media and cultural translations are circularly interrelated, whereby discursive knowledge is generated in diverse, also temporally overlapping translation processes and in different artistic, media and cultural practices that create patterns of interpretation. It is only through these media translations that discursive knowledge establishes and conventionalizes itself – creating, for example, a genealogy of the Tanztheater Wuppertal.

Translating as methodology: Praxeological production analysis

Taking a praxeological approach to dance research involves methodological considerations: how can we think, read, examine, analyze or write about dance? These questions seem difficult to answer when dance is described as a fleeting or ephemeral phenomenon. Dance is both present and absent, always already in the past, and we can only remember it as a trace. It cannot be fixed, is neither objectifiable nor concrete. The methodological considerations of dance analysis are therefore always linked to the epistemological problem of analyzing a dynamic form,[124] i.e., capturing what is ostensibly transitory, fleeting and absent, rendering it motionless and conceptually 'pinning it down.' An act of translation is carried out when dance, which evades the fixing and categorical grasp, is turned into an 'object,' a 'configuration,' a 'narrative' or a 'discourse' in retroactive contemplation or during the research process. In dance analysis, this is usually done from different perspectives, focusing on aspects such as the spatio-temporal relationships between the dancers, on the performances of the dancing bodies, the interactions between dancers or the theatrical, cultural and social framings of dance. Sometimes, the spatial and architectural contexts of a dance – whether it is performed onstage, in everyday life or during a celebration or ritual – are also examined. Translation is thus not only a theoretical concept but also one of the fundamental methodological principles of praxeological dance research. This chapter presents the methodological aspects of this concept.

It would be short-sighted and misguided to view the individual steps required to translate dance into research as a one-to-one mapping (→ SOLO DANCE). For what usually serves as the material for choreographic analysis is not the event, the performance situation, its momentariness or singularity, but rather the dance stored on various media, in recording systems such as videos or DVDs. Dance therefore cannot be translated 'one-to-one' into an object of research. Instead, it is something 'other,' namely dance as discursive knowledge, generated by the very acts of having been translated into other media – into film, images, sound, language, writing, notation, text or signs. In opposition to the arguments of some[125] and from the perspective of translation theory, these media transfers

5 Rainer Behr
in *Nefés*
Madrid, 2006

of dance should not be viewed as the loss of an inalienable 'remainder.' Instead, the question at hand is how dance as a cultural construction of interpretation and understanding is created in this kind of multifacted process of media translation. Media translations are thus the externalized cultural memory of dance.[126] Only in and through media translation and its discursive localization is it possible to create a cultural memory (of dance).

TRANSLATION AS A BASIC METHODOLOGICAL PRINCIPLE

A methodology and theory of dance rooted in translation theory assumes that describing and interpreting dance inevitably has to do with the generation of some kind of Other. For no matter whether we look at translations into images and film, into signs and symbols, or into language and writing, new media are constantly coming into play, attempting to understand dance through their own specific mediality, i.e., their (re)presentability. At the same time, they produce difference, which, in turn, always depends on the medium in question and its specific mediality. This paradox between identity and difference is an intrinsic aspect of every translation as described above in the sections defining the term 'translation.'[127] Identity can only be generated in translation via the Other, through difference.

The paradox between identity and difference and thus the im/possibility of 'faithful' translation in the sense of pure replication is also characteristic of the methodology of dance analysis. For, while the concept of translation is based on media difference, translation is not unilaterally understood as loss, as an inability to grasp the 'real.' Unlike positions that consider a transcription or notation to be something 'other' than the original and therefore as something diminished,[128] the methodological approach introduced here is based on the following two propositions: first of all, that the specific mediality of each medium creates added value by making polyphonic cultural patterns of interpretation and constructs of understanding possible; and, secondly, that this methodology does not assume that the individual methodological steps of translation depict dance itself – instead, they produce simulacra through each respective translation into a new medium.[129] Simulacra are considered here with Roland Barthes to be beneficial for the epistemological process inasmuch as they are ascribed a certain productivity. It is precisely these translation steps that make new patterns of interpretation and new constructs of understanding possible in the first place, which in turn have the potential to generate new dances and dance aesthetics.[130] We see such developments in popular dance forms, as in the global dissemination of hip hop, where 'moves' circulate worldwide through films, DVDs and websites, generating new local aesthetics.[131] The global dissemination of Pina Bausch's art was the result of both touring and the company's research trips (→ PIECES, WORK PROCESS), which repeatedly took the company to almost every continent, except Africa, where the reception and adoption of her work differed both regionally and situatively depending on the location (→ RECEPTION). Her work also achieved global acclaim through a wide variety of media framings such as reviews, films, DVDs, interviews, and journalistic and academic texts.

These two propositions – that media translations do not depict an original 'dance' and instead generate constructs of understanding that can initiate productive processes – form the basis of the 'praxeological production analysis' methodology that I have developed within the context of and during my research with the Tanztheater Wuppertal and that has become the basis of this book.[132] This methodology is guided by the parameters of praxeological dance research and combines choreographic analysis methods from theater and dance studies with methods from qualitative social research.[133] The focus of praxeological production analysis lies neither solely on the performance or staging – as hitherto conventional in theater and dance studies – nor on the examination of audience perceptions alone – as is established practice in the empirical approach taken in the sociology of art. Instead, praxeological production analysis bundles the development of a piece, its performance and its reception together under one term: 'production.' This is in line with recent insights in theater studies, i.e., that the 'performance' concept has made a shift toward the performative and that the relationship between process and piece has changed, attributing greater significance to the work process. This reorientation in theater studies has occurred in reaction to the rise of pieces that stage the processual in order to critique conventional understandings of the 'work' – and Pina Bausch was one of the pioneers of this development (→ PIECES, WORK PROCESS). A 'piece' *(Stück)*, as Pina Bausch also called her choreographies, is thus an open, mutable, complex, interwoven set of translation processes that only become visible in the performance.

PIECE, PERFORMANCE, AUDIENCE When dance research shifts its focus from artistic work (in the sense of a repeatable choreography) to performance (as an unrepeatable act), it is confronted with a central problem: what is the best way to approach performance methodologically? In order to answer this question, we first have to clarify what is actually meant by 'performance': is it the piece, the performance situation, the venue, audience perceptions? In theater and dance studies, performances are observable, temporally and spatially defined units with a clear beginning and end. However, works like Pina Bausch's pieces play with this clarity, for example, by dissolving the boundaries between ordinary life outside of the theater and the extraordinary life inside it: they stage things in quotidian places, create new spaces for the stage, make no reference to either script or literary template, and make it possible for the performers to be themselves rather than playing characters. In this sense, the pieces of the Tanztheater Wuppertal are models of reality. They demonstrate what is and what could be.

In recent theater studies scholarship,[134] a 'performance' is not a piece in the sense of a finished product, but rather designates the eventfulness, the situational and the singularity of the performance situation. By reforming the concept of the performance, theater studies has taken a performative understanding of what it means to present artistic work, one championed by artistic practices in dance as early as the 1960s as well as by the much younger genre of performance art – as in John Cage and Merce Cunningham's chance-based performances or in the performatively structured, improvised productions of Judson Dance Theater.

In the German-speaking world, Pina Bausch was one of the first to show that every piece is a work in progress and never finished when she premiered her first piece *Fritz* in Wuppertal (PREMIERE 1973). Pina Bausch's decision to call it a *Stück* – a 'piece' – was an apt choice of term to describe its processual and constantly developing qualities (→ PIECES). But it is not just the piece that continually develops, 'piece by piece' as it were. The context in which it is performed also constantly changes, which in turn alters the performance. For example, whether *The Rite of Spring* is performed at the world premiere in Wuppertal in 1975 or in 2013 in Taipei, the historical, cultural and social context, the spectators and their viewing habits, their understanding of the subject matter and their levels of knowledge differ (→ RECEPTION | AUDIENCE). This relationship between piece (choreography), the situationality and contextuality of the performance, and the specific audience watching a performance is especially relevant if we choose to interpret the piece in line with social and cultural theory, and subscribe to the proposition made in perception theory and reception aesthetics that a piece only ever truly comes to be in the eye of the beholder.

A methodological approach that does not consider a dance piece as a finished product but rather as a process that depends on the context makes the issue of empirical material especially topical. Which material is relevant? What material exists of which pieces? In which quality? Is there video material? If so, of what performances, of which pieces? From which perspective was the piece recorded – long shot, medium long shot, excerpts? Who dances in it? What material can and may we work with? Do we have access to it? Are there copyright issues? Praxeological production analysis, which focuses on the 'production,' is always contextual performance analysis. It therefore prompts further questions: are paratexts available, such as program booklets, photos or interviews with the choreographer or dancers? Have reviews, academic texts or lengthy journalistic articles already been published? If so, about which pieces? Do we have access to impressions or statements from the audience? Is edited film material of the piece available, such as documentaries? These questions reveal the problem of methodologically analyzing a piece and its paratexts – in other words: of combining the analysis of a piece with an analysis of its framing. This methodological problem has so far largely been neglected in theater, dance and performance research and has methodologically been given little thought. I have chosen to deal with it using the term 'production' in the various chapters of this book (→ SOLO DANCE, RECEPTION).

ARTISTIC PRODUCTION However, recent dance research has not only put up for discussion a broader concept of performance, but has also questioned the idea of the performance so fundamental to theater studies. This is why German performance studies has introduced the term 'production.'[135] The production concept on which the theory and methodology of this book are based also makes reference to the term 'artistic production' used in the arts in that it, as in an expanded concept of 'performance,' encompasses choreography and paratexts, the piece and its framings. In addition, the term 'production' addresses the relationship between process and product, working methods and the piece, as well as its reception. On the one hand, it takes into account the work process, valuing it as more than the mere process of developing a piece with the aim of attaining a finished product. From a production analysis perspective, the research interest is therefore, aside from choreographic analysis, artistic work practices and thus the sociality of the work process. From this point of view, the question of *how* collaboration takes place is central for the generation of the aesthetic. On the other hand, the term 'production' also includes the reception of a piece, its history and discourses, and social, cultural and media contexts. From the point of view of reception analysis, *how* a piece is perceived is central to the production of that which constitutes the discourse surrounding a piece.

If we define production in a way that encompasses creation, performance and reception, then empirical research has to deal with new and different questions to those which we would be dealing with if we were 'purely' looking at piece and performance analyses: how do we describe the production process as a synthesis of developing, performing and receiving a piece? What material is needed to examine a Pina Bausch production – the notes of the choreographer, the dancers, the dramaturges, the musical collaborators, costume designers, set designers, technicians and stage managers? What additional material do we need to collect, e.g., audience surveys (→ RECEPTION | AUDIENCE), interviews (→ COMPANY) or (non-)participatory observations (→ WORK PROCESS)? Which survey, interview and analysis methods should be applied? It is in particular the additional generation of empirical material in connection with a specific research question that requires knowledge of the appropriate methodological instruments of qualitative social research, be it proficiency in a wide range of interview methods and techniques, transcription and analysis methods, or practical knowledge of different observation methods, and the condensing of these observations into "thick descriptions."[136] It moreover requires us to reflect on these methodological instruments regarding their suitability for dance research. When does it make sense to conduct interviews? How can we methodologically assess translations of experience into language? When are observations appropriate, and how do we carry them out? How do we then translate them into notes, into text?

METHODOLOGICAL APPROACHES TO DANCE PRACTICE

Dance studies is a young academic discipline that can draw on the wealth of other established disciplines for its theoretical concepts and methods. But it also needs to modify the existing methodological instruments to meet the requirements of its 'object' and to develop its own specific, adequate tools.

PERFORMANCE AND MOVEMENT ANALYSIS IN DANCE STUDIES Since dance studies first began establishing itself internationally in the 1980s, various methods from different academic disciplines have been made productive for research – depending on the background disciplines of the pioneering academics. Photo, film and video analysis is an approach to dance analysis that predominantly emerged out of art history and media studies and that assumes that dance can only be examined as a media phenomenon. It examines, for example, the way dance appears in film, on video[137] and in digital media.[138] The methods used come from political iconography,[139] image composition[140] and fundamental epistemological and methodological considerations about media dance research.[141] In addition, it discusses methods such as camera ethnography,[142] which considers film to be more than mere documentation and instead defines the camera as an 'agent' in itself by reflecting upon the meaning of the technical aspects of media such as camera work and editing techniques for ethnographic research.

Literary studies have most notably contributed the method of (para)text analysis. Mark Franco[143] and Gabriele Brandstetter[144] have pioneered this method of interpreting dance as text and writing, an approach that has been applied in recent research (→ SOLO DANCE).[145] Other research in this direction has focused on analogies between dancing and writing as performative operations while also concentrating on reflexive processes of writing.[146]

The theater studies methods of performance and staging analysis have been adapted for use in dance research,[147] examining, on the one hand, the singular, non-repeatable performance, primarily concentrating on the performativity of the performance event,[148] while also focusing, on the other hand, on the (reproducable) choreographic and dramaturgical structure of the piece, such as the stage design or the relationship between music and dance.

Methods from the social sciences such as discourse analysis have also made their way into dance research since the 1980s.[149] Qualitative social research methods such as ethnographies and interview techniques[150] and methods used to study historical sources[151] – for example, in the analysis of historical sources of dance but also in dance reconstructions – have been applied to dance research in multiple ways.[152] Anthropological, phenomenological, semiotic and post-structuralist concepts, and approaches from social, cultural and art theory have also found their way into the study of dance phenomena. Although they are not actually methodological approaches or techniques for analyzing dance, they do provide theoretical concepts and terminology to better understand the basic concepts of dance – such as the body, movement, time and space – and theater – such as performance, presence, presentation, performance – which frame methodological approaches to analyzing dance.

While the methodological approaches mentioned above have been translated from established disciplines into dance research, dance practices have also generated their own methods of movement and body analysis,[153] drawing on traditions of dance notation that go back as far as the 16th century. However, dance does not have any established, conventionalized form of notation in a set code of signs that could be compared to those of language or music.[154] Instead, we have a multitude of notation systems, developed depending on the respective media used to document dance at a given time, reflecting specific dance aesthetics and styles. The oldest means of recording dance is graphic notation, which translates the order of the paths on the ground and the movements of the body or individual body parts into signs. In Western dance history, Canon Thoinot Arbeau's (1519-1595) writings on dance, which appeared in France in 1588, and Raoul-Auger Feuillet (1653-1710) and Pierre Beauchamps' (1631-1705) subsequent dance notation, published in

1700, paved the way for contemporary dance notation.[155] Modern dance at the beginning of the 20th century developed new methods of notation, able to record the non-canonical, i.e., the 'free' movements of dancers, but also the various emerging modern techniques (such as the Graham Technique and the Cunningham Technique). These include Laban/Bartenieff movement analysis,[156] the Kestenberg Movement Profile (KMP)[157] and the Movement Evaluation Graphics (MEG) method, as well as the more recent concept of *Inventarisierung von Bewegung* (the Inventorization of Movement; IVB).[158] Recently, computer science has been playing an increasingly important role in the exploration of methods to record motion. Since the 1980s, computer scientists and programmers have been developing computer-based systems, some in collaboration with dancers and choreographers, such as the Life Forms program used by US dancer and choreographer Merce Cunningham from the late 1980s on to develop his choreographies, or the various digital methods utilized by US dancer and choreographer William Forsythe, such as the *Improvisation Technologies* DVD (2003) for the study of his specific movement technique, the Synchronous Objects project (2009) for the development of a movement score and the Motion Bank project (2012-2016) for archiving dance and choreography. Since the advent of digitalized motion capture software, the notation of movement has developed into an experimental scientific research method, particularly in anglophone dance studies. It explores the movements of dancers by focusing on physicality and neuronal stimuli – thus also contributing in part to research on artificial intelligence.[159] In the German-speaking social sciences, primarily within the context of video analysis, the field of qualitative social research has developed digital software programs such as Feldpartitur,[160] which have been made productive for dance analysis (→ SOLO DANCE).[161]

While these lines of research treat dance as a textbook example of the eventfulness and ephemeral nature of movement, as well as corporeal intelligence and the affectivity of corporeal perception, it would be oversimplifying the matter to assume that 'the ephemeral' is only a specific, fundamental problem for dance and movement and thus for methods of dance and movement analysis. Ultimately, ephemerality is a phenomenon that is relevant in all historical, cultural, political, economic and social events, and therefore in all empirical social and cultural studies disciplines, such as sociology, ethnology, history and folklore studies, inasmuch as they deal with human figurations, i.e., with dynamic orders. It also affects the study of art and culture – such as theater studies, music and performance studies – in that they deal with spatio-temporal processes and situative, emergent orders, such as performances.

Translating the ephemeral, i.e., non-discursive phenomena such as presence, liveness, aura, vibe or coherence into an image or writing is thus by no means merely a specific difficulty faced by dance studies. Instead, dance illustrates a fundamental situation that all social and cultural studies share, for the 'event' – as a social or cultural practice onstage, in film and in everyday life – is always ephemeral, in the past and missing from the research process. Thanks to its genuine object of study – the exploration of spatio-temporal conditions, of dynamics and rhythm, of synchronization and the ephermal – dance analysis can thus provide important concepts and methods for the analysis of social interactions as orders of bodies and of movements.

ACADEMIC AND ARTISTIC APPROACHES TO PRACTICE RESEARCH Observing and documenting, researching, interviewing, taking notes; recording in words, in writing, on camera and video; transcribing, modeling, interpreting, analyzing, discarding and evaluating; grouping and arranging; reflecting upon, presenting, discussing, publishing and translating dance into different media and implementing it in fields of knowledge are just a few of the practices of knowledge production that are characteristic not only of praxeological (dance) research,[162] but also of the practices of artistic work and research.[163] Observing and analyzing practice on the one hand and performing and (co) developing it on the other are two heuristically distinct modes of research that art and scholarship carry out and interpret differently. However, acts of observing and analyzing as well as acts of performing and developing merge in the everyday operations and routines of both academic research and artistic practice.

Academic and artistic practice are two different fields of knowledge production. Both fields of knowledge – art and academia – are connected to the public spheres[164] in which they observe, perform, develop, present and "assemble"[165] practice. The public/the audience – as an action, performance, observation and authentication situation – is thus not only constitutive of theories of practice and performance, as demonstrated above, but also methodologically crucial to research based on practice and performance theory.

The method of praxeological production analysis picks up exactly where these thoughts leave off. It finds methodological reference points in performance studies (ethnographic approaches) and in theater and dance research (choreographic analysis), then merges them together. In performance research guided by sociology and cultural studies,[166] 'practice' is an unquestioned category for capturing what has already passed – be it artistic performances or cultural performances in everyday life. As ethnological research, performance studies borrows its methods from qualitative social

6 Research trip
for *Only You*
USA, 1996

7 Filming *The Plaint
of the Empress*
Wuppertal, 1988

research, in particular from ethnography. However, in the theater studies tradition, practice is situated in the field of art or theater and is thus set in opposition to the fields of academia and theory. Here, 'practice' is mainly used in a hermeneutical sense. 'Practice,' then, becomes an explicitly empirical term when attention shifts to production and rehearsal processes in artistic creation, as in recent theater, performance, and dance research,[167] or, for example, to the habits of the audience during performances and the rituals of actors before a show. While methods from the fields of sociology and practice theory are increasingly finding application due to the rising interest in artistic production processes, theater and dance performances are still primarily being examined with the help of performance and stage analysis.[168]

Finally, artistic research has also made 'practice' productive in hermeneutic ways, claiming since the beginning of the 21st century that art can also be considered research in that it generates originary knowledge. Here, the development of practice is tied to artistic and aesthetic, corporeal and material practices, which usually take place in places explicitly dedicated to them (for example, the dance studio, atelier, rehearsal space or stage, etc.). Moreover, practice is always dealt with in relation to historical or contemporary art, politics, society and everyday life, as well as to the cultural, political, social or aesthetic concepts and products necessary for the production of artistic artifacts (such as a theater piece, a choreography, a performative installation, an exhibition, a festival, etc.). Artistic research claims to combine theory and practice in the actual practices of research and artistic creation. Artistic research is thus based on an extended definition of 'research,' that is, on a definition that does not differentiate between the two different 'logics of practice,'[169] between artistic and academic 'doing.' However, the problem is that this approach does not take into account their differing temporalities: academic 'doing' always occurs retrospectively, at a different pace and in another, often longer time frame than artistic practice. Unlike practice theory, artistic research defines practice less as an empirical category that needs to be identified and analytically isolated than as a field of practices in which practical artistic practices and theoretical academic practices are so close that they can hardly be separated from one another. Accordingly, artists, academics, dramaturges and "experts of everyday life"[170] strive for performative collaborations, understanding their shared work to be a social and political field of experimentation.[171]

The political positioning of individual action in artistic research contrasts with academic practice theories that are methodologically more cautious about the political dimensions of their work and therefore find themselves subject to (sometimes self-critical) accusations of neutralizing their objects of study.[172] Conversely, artistic research establishes the interplay between knowledge production and truth publicly and simultaneously performs it. In this way, it also encourages us to see the performance as an explorative practice in itself, thus making research the responsibility of 'everyone,'[173] which raises new issues for civil society and generates its own form of activism. Artistic research practice thus legitimizes itself not only by examining aesthetic patterns of perception but also by dealing with normative orders of the social, which form the basis of the political in their interplay.

In both academic and artistic research, observations penetrate the compositional character of practices and their interactions. Accordingly, observation is a fundamental method both in artistic processes and in sociological practice theories.[174] However, their methodological premises differ: observations like those conducted during the research trips of the Tanztheater Wuppertal tend to be methodologically unsystematic, while methodologically sound forms of observation based on the techniques used in qualitative social research, such as expert interviews and group discussions, are constitutive of the approaches taken in practice theory, especially of those that make use of ethnological methods of observation. Observation is conceived of here from a multitude of perspectives: on the one hand, by situating observers in relation to their field of investigation[175] and, on the other, by fundamentally assuming that the object of study is constituted through the choice of method and the position of the inquiring researcher.[176]

Practices of (non-)participatory observation are implemented in different ways, especially in practice theory: for example, (post-)structural approaches, influenced by a combination of positions from cultural sociology and the sociology of the body, regard the performance in the sense of 'cultural performance' as a given category of observation[177]; the focus here lies on factors such as supraindividual schemata, orders of knowledge, rituals and performance conventions.[178] In contrast, microsociological positions do not consider the performance as a theatrical event or performing as a theatrical act to be categories of observation – not only because cultural theory plays a smaller role here, but above all because the emphasis is on analyzing the habits of everyday observations and conventionalized knowledge in a methodologically systematic manner.[179] Researchers examine what is ostensibly obvious and unquestionably given in order to translate the 'silent,' i.e., the corporeal dimensions of culturality and sociality, into language.[180] Instead of observing a theatrical act, they focus on a 'doing' that is visible to the observer, which thus first has to be performatively authenticated as doing by the researcher.

Since praxeological approaches acknowledge the researcher's embeddedness within his or her field of research as necessary for observation, they do not consider methods to be neutral or universally applicable. Instead, they presume that it is the scholar's methodical research and observations fixed in writing that give rise to the (academic) existence of the object of research in the first place, i.e., that it is itself performatively generated in the practices of research.[181] In some cases – depending on the object of study – observations have also helped to develop practice and thus led to a performative interplay between observing practices and shaping practices. In artistic research involving collaborations between artists and scholars, this interplay is considered to be one of the foundations of researching and "sharing expertise,"[182] such as when computer scientists help to develop digital technologies for set designs, dance scholars assist in the reconstruction of historical dances, or phoneticians turn their scholarly analyses of voices into soundscapes together with artists.

Other similarities between the methods used in academic and artistic practice research include the use of tools such as interview and dialogue techniques and the ethnographic use of video and photo cameras, the use and analysis of audio and video excerpts and other media interventions, and the systematizing practices of analysis such as memorizing and codifying. All these methods come from ethnographic research practices, which productively make use of media formats and social forms of knowledge in their respective fields of study and translate them into their research practice.

Academic practice theorists predominantly pursue a form of 'interpretative sociology' *(verstehende Soziologie),* inasmuch as they strive to systematically get to the bottom of both the phenomena they study and their own point of view. Like artistic researchers, they do not really aim to formulate universal explanations in terms of fact-based evidence seen from a (scholarly) bird's-eye perspective, nor should their work be confused with purely descriptive scholarship, for they employ their own strategy of making social phenomena visible. In this respect, they also share much with artistic research. Here, too, the process of understanding pertains not only to the act of observing but also and in equal part to the researcher's involvement in the associated, recursive research process: transcribing the data gained from observation in the form of minutes, memos and other notes, and analytical writing, reading and theorizing,[183] which leads to the development of works of art and, in the academic process, to the production of texts in multiple translation loops. Finally, it also pertains to the performance of artistic work or research results, to acts of speaking about them, for example in audience talks or with critics on the one hand or at congresses, conferences or in lectures on the other.

THE LOGICS OF ARTISTIC AND ACADEMIC PRACTICE

Praxeological dance research reflects on the relationships between academic and artistic practices, i.e., between the various logics of an academic research practice and of choreographing and dancing. In this respect, it differs from artistic research. Dance research should in itself be considered a practice, but one that follows a different logic to that of artistic practice, simply because the logic of artistic practice is subject to, for example, a different sense of urgency and different time constraints to those of academic practice.

Moreover, praxeological dance research reveals, in the Bourdieusian sense,[184] academic practices such as observing, describing, researching, documenting, analyzing and interpreting while also shedding light on its relationship to the artistic practices that it is observing, i.e., to the practices of training, improvising, rehearsing, composing, choreographing and performing, and to practices of spectating, visiting the theater, reading and writing reviews, reading program booklets and attending talks with the audience. Recognizing these different logics inherent to the practice of artistic production itself and between artistic and academic practice, relating them to one another, methodologically implementing and theoretically reflecting upon them, form the basis of practical theory as well as of theory-based practice, in other words: it forms the basis of praxeological dance research. Practices of choreographing – which include some of the same practices found in academic practice, such as researching, describing and observing, but which perform and embed them differently within the production process – demonstrate how fundamentally important it is to contextualize the logics of artistic and academic practices in order to identify the similarities between them.

In what ways does a choreographer's research practice differ from that of a scholar? What differences are there between practices of observing in the artistic and academic fields if, as in the Tanztheater Wuppertal's research trips (→ WORK PROCESS), the approach taken is ethnographical? It is precisely the ongoing, controversial debate on artistic research that shows that looking at the logics of practices in artistic and academic fields can encourage differentiated debate about the potentiality of artistic research. Practice theory is therefore a critical and analytical project that sets the logics of academic and choreographic practice in relation to one another. From a praxeological perspective, dance studies should be an experiential discipline. Praxeology thus provokes a redefinition of what dance

8 Pina Bausch
   Italy, 1994

studies could be. Conducted as empirical research, it demands a permanent relativization of theory. From this point of view, the development of theory cannot remain self-referential, but rather has to face its empirical obligations.

Practice theory destabilizes the separation between academic theory on the one hand and artistic practice on the other by revealing the relationality of the logics behind academic and artistic practices. Its point of departure is empiricism's attachment to theory as well as theory's attachment to empiricism. A praxeological perspective thus sacrifices the idea of what theory generally stands for, namely 'pure thought' or a model, a depiction of reality. But what it gains is an eye for diversity, for the wealth and the "silent language"[185] with which dance practices themselves create the object of study that dance scholars explore. Praxeology thus conceptually embodies a visionary idea: to undermine the dualism of theory and praxis, scholarship and art that is so characteristic of modernity, thus circumventing politics of inclusion and exclusion and the power relations between the artistic and the academic fields with and through praxeological research, which reveals itself – differently – in dance and dance research.

THE SCHOLAR AS TRANSLATOR: REFLECTING UPON ONE'S OWN ACTIONS

In a praxeological approach to research, researchers are called on to expose the historicity and culturality of their own points of view and to reveal their own interpretative positions. Not only has critical theory in the tradition of the Frankfurt School considered such self-reflection to be a fundamental task since the 1930s,[186] but it is also a fundamental principle of qualitative social research. Pierre Bourdieu and Loïc Wacquant further pursued the idea of self-reflection and coined the term "reflexive methodology,"[187] which they define as the complete objectification, not only of the object of study itself but also of the relationship between researcher and object, including personal patterns of perception and classification. For the interplay between being affected by the performance, habitual disposition, knowledge and situative emotional state not only determine a researcher's sense of perception but also simultaneously establish the conditions of possible objectification. Postcolonial studies similarly reflect on a speaker's position within society.[188] Accordingly, the (self-)reflexive investigation of artistic practice requires that which generally characterizes the concept of translation, which can be described with Bernhard Waldenfels as an ethics of respecting and violating boundaries.[189]

One methodological consequence of these theoretical considerations is a continual reflection on the *how* of translating during the dance research process. This takes place on two levels, as also attempted in this book: namely, in media, cultural and aesthetic translations of the pieces themselves (→ PIECES, COMPANY, WORK PROCESS, RECEPTION) and in their translations into academic methodology and theory (→ SOLO DANCE). Researchers thus become translators, engaging in a constant practice of negotiation. Herein lie both the challenges and the opportunities of experiential dance research, which aims to continually undermine and question its own points of view.

The production of knowledge depends on this kind of self-reflection, which cannot in turn be separated from constellations of power. Thus, attention must also be paid to the researchers themselves, to their proximity and distance to the field of research, to the way they are affected, their empathy and corporeality – in short: to their bodies as "subjects of cognition."[190] Researchers are themselves part of these practices. Not only are they compelled to engage in objectified self-reflection in the Bourdieusian sense, but due to their corporeal and sensory embeddedness within the research process, they are also called on to directly address and reflect upon the relationship between their own practices and the practices that they are examining (→ INTRODUCTION). As this chapter has shown, they are thereby confronted with various sets of practices in artistic and academic research that reveal similarities, but which differ in the ways that they are carried out: on the one hand, with the ethnographic methods used in academic and artistic work to generate knowledge and utilize its results in various ways and, on the other, with distinct modes of reflecting upon and processing their own methods, which find their own specific forms of translation in academia and art.

1 Pina Bausch during rehearsals for *Ahnen* Wuppertal, 1987

Conclusion

Translating (into) the Present: Doing Contemporaneity

"How and for how long can [dance theater's, GK] corporeal, speechless potential for protest assert itself against the market, against being marketed as an innovative form of theater? [...] When will dance theater pieces finally become monumental tableaus?"[1] Susanne Schlicher poses these questions in her groundbreaking book *TanzTheater* from 1987. As early as in the mid-1980s, academics were already asking how long it would take before an innovative art form created in the 1970s would be conventionalized, would become routine, part of the canon of established art forms, how long it would take until everybody got used to its artistic style, its working methods, its repertoire. In much the same vein, by the 1980s, some journalists and critics were already complaining that the Tanztheater Wuppertal's new pieces were not showing anything original, that they had become thematically and aesthetically repetitive (→ RECEPTION). Today, more than three decades after the publication of Susanne Schlicher's book, dance theater – including the dance theater of the 1970s – is no longer considered protest art. Now, the term 'protest art' itself seems outdated, although even in its early days, the term did not really reflect the way that dance theater saw itself. However, the questions posed by Susanne Schlicher are still – or once again – relevant. Since the death of Pina Bausch in 2009, there has been incessant and almost worldwide debate over whether her dance pieces can and should be preserved, whether they are still contemporary, whether performing older pieces will lead to their musealization and, finally, whether the pieces lose some of what once distinguished them when they are restaged: aesthetic innovation, the transcendence of the boundaries of individual art forms, the unpredictable, the performative, the non-representational and the non-theatrical.

The pieces are in fact characterized by three different temporal layers, all of which are interwoven into each performance: first, there is that which I deliberately differentiate from 'the present' and refer to as the 'here and now' *(Jetzt-Zeit)*, in which rehearsals take place and the piece is passed on to younger dancers (→ WORKING PROCESS). This practice of passing on pieces has now spanned several decades and some generations of dancers. This constant process of restaging the pieces has ascribed the temporal art form of dance with a timelessness; it can therefore potentially be performed over and over again, regardless of the respective historical context. The here and now is also when a piece is performed (again). The second temporality is historical time: the creation of the choreography and its premiere. The performance taking place in the here and now is a memory and reenactment of this choreography, a document of Pina Bausch's choreographic art and her dancers' ingenuity at the time, as well as a historical document of the translation of that period's political, social and cultural perceptions and experiences into dance. At the same time, the restaging repositions the piece in a different historical context with different performers, where it is received by an audience with different perceptual habits and visual experiences. The third temporality relates to the Tanztheater Wuppertal dancers themselves, who reperform the piece decades after its premiere. And it is also here, in the interplay between generations of dancers, that the temporal layers intertwine (→ COMPANY): some pieces are still being danced by members of the original cast, even 40 years after the premiere, a period of time that is generally longer than a professional dancer's career. The 2017 performances of *Viktor* (PREMIERE 1986), for example, featured 23 dancers, including three dancers from the original cast: Dominique Mercy and Julie Anne Stanzak, as well as a former member of the company, Jean-Laurent Sasportes, who performed as a guest. However, not one dancer from the original cast was still involved in the 2019 restaging of *1980* (PREMIERE 1980), although almost all of the performers had been working with Pina Bausch for years, unlike in the case of *Nefés* (PREMIERE 2003), where more than half of the dancers onstage in 2019 had joined the company after the choreographer's death and, in some cases, had never met Pina Bausch in person. Thus, there has now been a complete change of generations in all of the pieces (→ COMPANY), in some pieces even several. This process of transformation, which has sometimes spanned several generations of dancers, has not been abrupt, but has taken place step by step. These steps are constant acts of translation, for, in the last few decades, the pieces have been restaged and sent on tour over and over again, meaning that they have been repeatedly rehearsed, sometimes with new or different dancers, which – while Pina Bausch was still alive (→ WORK PROCESS) – also led to the pieces themselves being changed, shortened or individual parts rearranged.

Pina Bausch herself tried to keep her work alive by continually restaging it. On the one hand, she thus ascribed a timelessness to her pieces. On the other hand, she also showed that modernity in dance means more than (primarily) striving for innovation or dismissing what has already been accomplished as obsolete. Instead, it is about making the modernity that has become historical contemporary once more in and through dancing bodies. At the same time, she was able to show that her pieces can generate a different kind of relevance in other temporal contexts, even if they are based on the specific working processes of the company and the situative temporal experiences made by its members (→ WORK PROCESS). What is special about dance is perhaps that it is a temporal art form in this multiple sense, as dance is not just contemporary due to the fact that it only exists in the moment that it is being danced, but also because multiple layers of time overlap in that very moment.

From this point of view, Pina Bausch's pieces are historical, topical and timeless, all at the same time: they are closely tied to the everyday cultural and situational experiences of the company and the audience at the time they are created; they are performed in multiple presents, where they are perceived by each audience as being either topical, historical or timeless. It would therefore be short-sighted to simply regard them as monuments of dance history, like some classical works of ballet that are performed again and again out of respect for the history of 'high' European culture. Conversely, however, it would also be false to either assume that dance pieces are timeless or to view the restaging of a piece in another historical and situational context in front of a different audience per se as proof of its topicality. Instead, it is precisely the pieces of the Tanztheater Wuppertal and the way that they interweave various temporal layers in connection with their distinct translation processes that raises the question of what can be regarded as contemporary at all. This final chapter poses this very question by taking a look at the temporality of translation and considering it together with the concept of contemporaneity.

What is contemporaneity?

In Western cultures, the concept of contemporaneity first arose in the early modern period (1500-1800), in an era when the concept of time itself was being renegotiated in the wake of the invention of the clock and the ensuing objectification and linearization of time. In other words: 'time' has since been regulated by and through technical inventions, and globally controlled by the early capitalist, colonial European countries that initiated these technical developments. In the 18th century, with the advent of Western modernity, early industrialization, the Enlightenment and the French Revolution, the term 'contemporary' took on great importance. As early as in 1764,

Voltaire declared that all should "conformez-vous aux temps,"[2] i.e., establish a relationship to their own time and adapt to it, with the primary aim of being able to take a critical look at it. In his *Hyperion* from 1794, Friedrich Hölderlin addressed, "O you who share with me this age!"[3] while Johann Wolfgang von Goethe on September 20, 1792, proclaimed an often-repeated sentence to commemorate the Battle of Valmy that would have a lasting influence on our understanding of contemporaneity: "From this place and from this day forth commences a new era in the world's history, and you can all say that you were present at its birth."[4] According to historian Lucian Hölscher, since the Enlightenment, 'contemporaneity' has meant, "a temporal connection to the simultaneity of events and people."[5] However, this means not only being together in time but also self-reflective participation. A contemporary is somebody who sets him- or herself in relation to time – and this is not a purely individual affair.

Contemporaries are thus people who share something with each other, and that something is 'time.' This definition contains a dual promise: firstly, that it is possible to connect with someone in relation to time and, secondly, that it is possible to connect with time itself. But: does 'time' exist? Is 'time' not something that depends on people's perceptions and experiences, i.e., that differs historically, socially and culturally? And is it not precisely Pina Bausch's pieces – which were developed at different times and, in the case of the coproductions, in different cultural locations with an international company – that have proven the latter to be the case?

Contemporary art / contemporary dance

Works of art, in particular ephemeral works of dance, are paradoxical phenomena in terms of their relationship to time: on the one hand, they were created at a specific time and relate to that time, but, on the other, they are timeless and sometimes outlast epochs, like works of classical or romantic ballet. Unlike in the visual arts, works in the performing arts are bound to their performances and their forms of embodiment. Both artworks and dance pieces may lose historical relevance, but aesthetically they remain identical with themselves. Their value on the art market can fluctuate, which is also due to the way that different periods evaluate them in different ways and attribute different levels of relevance to them.

The established definition of 'contemporary art' that will serve as our starting point here is something that is produced by contemporaries and perceived by other contemporaries to be significant. This definition assumes that contemporaneity can only be produced in the present, in the here and now. It does not address what kind of relationship there has to be between artistic production and the here and now in order for art to be considered contemporary. But it does draw attention to one important aspect that is above all constitutive of the praxeology of translation presented in this book: contemporaneity is a performative concept that cannot just be asserted – it must also be authenticated. Contemporaneity is thus ascribed to a production in a performative process, thereby referring to the interplay between piece, performance, perception, knowledge and context. Three layers of temporality coincide in this interplay and what we usually label 'the present': what has developed into this very moment, what is happening here and now, and what is to come. Although the performance takes place in the present and presupposes copresence, it is also characterized by the translation of the piece into the present through the simultaneity of the here and now and historical time. The performance in the present also has an impact on what is still to come, for example, on future discourse about the piece.

This simultaneity of temporalities intersecting in the here and now also characterizes the audience's perception: just as the piece itself connects different temporal layers with each other in its performance, so are they, too, shaped by the simultaneity and entanglement of different temporalities in the audience's perception (→ RECEPTION) – in other words: they are clearly and unquestioningly regarded neither as topical nor as outdated or old-fashioned. In this respect, the entanglement between performance, perception and knowledge should not be understood as a mere conventionalization or historicization of a dance piece. For the aesthetic, media and cultural translations that take place back and forth between performance, perception and knowledge always have a transformational effect on situative perception and the future discursive positioning of the piece. Thus, they not only shape the perception situation, its eventfulness and aura but also preform the future – as expectations and as the production of new knowledge.

That which is ascribed the attribute 'contemporary' in the particular work of art therefore makes reference to more than just the respective contemporary art form. "All significant art, all art in the emphatic sense, is contemporary. It has significance for the present," writes philosopher Juliane Rebentisch, arguing against the attribute 'contemporary' as an "additional quality *(Zusatzqualität)*"[6] for works of art. Her position also contains another consideration: whether or not an artwork is perceived as contemporary depends on its frame of reference in the present, on the way that it is contextualized in the specific situation. But who determines whether a work of art has meaning for the present and when? The answer to this question lies in the cultural-political strategies of the global art market and in a number of positions in art philosophy. Today's concept of contemporaneity lies between these two poles, and this is also where we find its limits and potential.

As a strategic marketing term, the adjective 'contemporary' has become a criterion of distribution since the globalization of the art market began in the 1990s. As such, it has replaced the term 'modern art,' which is now bound to a specific aesthetic with its origins in historical modernity. "Today," as journalist and translator Henning Ritter writes, the contemporary is "not an artistic statement, but a property of the art system."[7] He criticizes the current art system's fixation on the contemporary. Accordingly, he says, 'contemporary art' indiscriminately refers to any artistic product or production that has been recognized and absorbed by the art system in any way. Following this train of thought, the contemporary is not an exclusively aesthetic concept, but is also a strategically relevant concept in art marketing.

So far, only a few authors have drawn attention to the relevance of the attribute 'contemporary' as an exchange value for art in the global art market. Contemporary art should therefore be distinguished from the concept of 'modern art' that is anchored in historical modernism, which claimed that it could create new worlds by means of aesthetics. Contemporaneity in art – or 'contemporary art' – is, however, a topos used to shape cultural policy, to include and exclude, to carry out various demarcations (for example, from modernity, from tradition, from other cultures and their arts) and to regulate the global art market. Current practices in the global art business remain Western. Historian Ljudmila Belkin therefore describes 'contemporary art' as "a value concept with a selective function: it determines what art is and what it is not."[8] The term 'contemporary art' is thus, in Pierre Bourdieu's words, a "mark of distinction"[9] in the globalized field of art that is used to conduct politics by classifying the respective work of art as new or as outdated, i.e., as (ir-)relevant to the present. In the performing arts as well, the administrators of this system are the legitimized spokespeople, curators, organizers, journalists and representatives of cultural institutions who operate according to the standards of the art market guided by Western principles. Even if modern art can no longer make claims to hegemony in the age of globalized artistic practice, where the relationship between modernity and tradition is no longer considered exclusionary (as it was in Western modernity), new hegemonic practices of inclusion and exclusion have (re)established themselves through the term 'contemporary.'

In the 1990s, Pina Bausch's pieces became a global commodity. The opening of the global art market on the one hand and the increasing number of coproductions on the other both played a part in this development. The aesthetics of the pieces changed from the

2 Program booklet for
"...*como el musguito en la piedra,
ay si, si, si*...", 2009

3 Reproduction of the Lichtburg, the Tanztheater Wuppertal's rehearsal space; from the exhibit *Pina Bausch and the Tanztheater* Bonn, 2016

mid-1990s – toward more dance, especially solos, increasingly beautiful and elegant evening gowns, more lightness – helping to facilitate and promote the global circulation of the pieces, which was in turn driven by the support of powerful cultural institutions such as the Goethe-Institut and other collaborating partners. This kind of politics asserted that the pieces had relevance for the present, which was legitimized above all by the working methods used in the coproductions. These were thus not only an economically necessary (→ PIECES) and aesthetically enriching (→ WORK PROCESS) tool for the company. The coproductions were also a political tool for national cultural policies aimed at drawing the attention of a global art market.

A contemporaneity open to the future

In addition to its significance in terms of art market strategy, the term 'contemporary' also has utopian potential, which has mainly been attributed to it by thinkers in the philosophy of art. As Giorgio Agamben says: "Those who are truly contemporary, who truly belong to their time, are those who neither perfectly coincide with it nor adjust themselves to its demands. They are thus in this sense irrelevant *(inatturale)*. But precisely because of this condition, precisely through this disconnection and this anachronism, they are more capable than others of perceiving and grasping their own time. [...]. The contemporary is he who firmly holds his gaze on his own time so as to perceive not its light but rather its darkness. [...]. The ones who can call themselves contemporary are only those who do not allow themselves to be blinded by the lights of the century, and so manage to get a glimpse of the shadows in those lights, of their intimate obscurity."[10] This understanding of contemporaneity, formulated in reference to Friedrich Nietzsche's *Untimely Meditations*,[11] is based on the latter's much-cited "pathos of distance." Contemporary art thus emerges where something is of 'concern,' where the goal is to have a true experience of the present. The production, but also the authentication of the significance of a dance piece for the present is therefore based on a relationship to the present that is shaped by critical distance. A certain distance to the here and now, an act of setting oneself in relation to one's own present is required in order to ask: what can a dance piece, even if it was developed decades ago, tell us about our present?

From a philosophical perspective, 'contemporary' means not only being able to distance oneself but also having a passion for the present.[12] As literary scholar Sandro Zanetti puts it, "only in a passion for the present that crosses one's own horizon but is registered as a transgression is it possible to foster a contemporaneity that is open to the present, but also open to the future (because it cannot be kept in the present)."[13] It should be added that this is a passion that is aware of the existence of multiple presents and thus of different understandings of temporality. If we follow this line of thought, contemporaneity in art is based on a practice of translation that sets itself in relation to the respective present. A practice of translation that is critical toward the present thus consists in creating temporal dis/continuities, in balancing distance and proximity, and in criticizing and empathizing with the respective present. With this practice of translation, contemporary art defines itself neither through its distance to a past that has been pronounced closed (modernity) nor through a culture that has been declared different (popular dance culture, coproducing country). Instead, contemporary art is defined by multiple relations to, extensions and refractions of history and cultures, which it acknowledges and processes, i.e., aesthetically and discursively translates and artistically and politically frames.

In this sense, Pina Bausch's pieces are contemporary in that they typically feature a balance between a distance to and a passion for the time when they were created. The coproductions in particular were created at a distance to and with respect for the foreign culture. The working process, with its methods of 'asking questions' and research trips, was based on the everyday empathies of all members of the company. Their cultural perceptions and experiences were then translated into an aesthetic form, the dance piece, meaning that it was not simply a matter of creating distance between the piece on the one hand and the situative perception and experience on which it was based on the other during the step of aesthetically translating everyday experience into dance. Rather, the constant restagings have also allowed the pieces to be translated (back) into each respective present by transferring the performances into other temporal contexts, where they provide different audiences with the opportunity to question the relevance of the pieces for the present. In this way, each performance creates space for the audience to examine the topicality of the piece by linking it to their own time. The audience decides whether or not the piece is relevant to the present in which they are experiencing it. Thus, from a practice theory perspective, the contemporary is not inherent to the piece itself, but is generated in the interplay between the performance and the audience. A contemporaneity that is open to the future thus requires not just the artist but also the audience to be able to distance themselves from and foster a passion for their own time. It is these qualities that above all enable audiences to translate pieces into their own here and now and to decide whether they are relevant for a critical relationship to the present or whether they contribute to the musealization of dance and choreography.

Audience perception is determined by the audience's own process of becoming or having become, for example, by its habits of perception, visual experiences, routines of expectation and (dance-specific) knowledge. However, these habits can also be undermined, as a piece is always perceived differently in different situative and cultural contexts at different times. Thus, a piece is not only updated and carried forward into the future in restagings and new performances. These practices can also contribute to the musealization of pieces, as is the case for works of classical ballet. In fact, it is the performative dimension that is decisive: the dance piece is an unstable, flexible and constantly changing, contingent production created in the interplay between piece, restaging, performance, perception and knowledge – and not a supposedly timeless work that is meant to be preserved as such.

Pina Bausch brought her pieces into the future by restaging them again and again and thereby constantly translating them. It is yet to be seen whether "keeping them alive" like this, as Pina Bausch called it, will merely serve to preserve or musealize her cultural legacy or whether hers is a contemporaneity that is open to the future. This ambivalence is a genuine component of passing on and restaging pieces, and is a question that must be posed again and again. The answer to the question of which of her pieces are still relevant for the present cannot be decided alone by those who continue to put her pieces on the market or who define the discourse surrounding them, but will also be decided by the audience, who performatively authenticate the relevance of the pieces for the present. Once again, it is of considerable importance how exactly the practice of translating the piece into the new present is carried out. The 'faithful' reconstruction of a piece neither necessarily leads to its musealization, nor does its complete deconstruction inevitably promise to produce contemporary relevance in terms of a critical distance to the historical material. Instead, the 'how' is also dependent on the complex, performative interplay between piece, performance, perception and context to decide what kind of relevance the piece will have. Inherent to this hybrid and multifaceted practice of translation is the potential for both the musealization of a once revolutionary art form and a reception with contemporary relevance.

Indexes

Notes

INTRODUCTION

1 Klein 1994 *(WomenBodiesDance: A History of the Civilization of Dance)*.
2 Brandstetter/Klein 2015a.
3 This book is based on a corpus of material that I examined using different methodological approaches. For the analysis of the work processes, I recorded, transcribed and analyzed the content of a total of 20 approx. two-hour-long interviews with dancers, focusing on the subjects of rehearsals and working methods, with a particular emphasis on their research trips to the coproducing countries. I also spoke with the artistic and technical staff of the Tanztheater Wuppertal (set designer, costume designer, music manager, stage manager, stage technician, managing director). I interviewed three long-standing staff members several times. During my research trips to Japan (Tokyo), India (Delhi, Kolkata, Chennai, Kochi), Brazil (São Paulo) and Hungary (Budapest), I interviewed the organizers of the Tanztheater Wuppertal's research trips as well as those of the premieres and guest performances. I also reconstructed the itinerary and research destinations of the Tanztheater Wuppertal ensemble using ethnographical methods.

PIECES and Performances: After reviewing the material provided by the Pina Bausch Foundation and the Tanztheater Wuppertal (videos, reviews, interviews, documentation), we (my research assistants Elisabeth Leopold, Anna Wieczorek and I) organized the international coproductions into three phases and analyzed each in relation to its aesthetic narrative. One piece was selected from each phase – *Viktor* (PREMIERE 1986), *Masurca Fogo* (PREMIERE 1998), "*...como el musguito en la piedra, ay si, si, si...*" (PREMIERE 2009) – and then extensively analyzed regarding its work process, performances and reception. In addition, we selected one solo from each of these pieces. The video recordings of performances provided by the Pina Bausch Foundation were examined in terms of how cultural experiences are translated aesthetically – and in terms of the stage representation of the dancers, the solos and group dances, and the choreography, its temporal and rhythmic, spatial and architectural, interactive and figurational, and dramaturgical aspects. This process was very detailed and time intensive, drawing on analytical methods that went beyond the performance, dance and choreographic analysis methods common in theater and dance studies. Instead, we took into account the fact that we were dealing with video, mostly recordings of the pieces taken from a medium long-shot camera perspective, shot in the Opernhaus Wuppertal from about the 13th row on the right. Accordingly, we employed the method of hermeneutic video analysis developed in qualitative social research, which we adapted in order to analyze the bodies, the movements and the dance. To do so, we used and altered the *Feldpartitur* software, originally developed for qualitative social research, for the first time in an analysis of choreography and dance.

RECEPTION: We conducted a total of four audience surveys in connection with the pieces *Rough Cut, Viktor*, "*...como el musguito en la piedra, ay si, si, si...*" and *Masurca Fogo*. Then we transcribed and evaluated them in a qualitative content analysis using the MAXQDA software. Audience opinions were sorted into emotional, analytical and metaphorical statements as well as into 'semantic fields,' understood as groups of similar words, i.e., words related in meaning. This way, we were able to extract narratives that show how perceptions are translated into language and also how and by which means translation 'resists.' This also revealed that parts of the pieces less accessible to symbolic interpretation evade language and thus remain invisible in verbal translation. By 'translating into language,' it was possible to more clearly define the characteristics of individual pieces and to relate them to other coproductions. At the same time, we wrote down our observations of the same shows before, during and after the performances. The results of the audience surveys were in turn cross-referenced with narratives extracted from reviews. Reviews compiled by the Pina Bausch Archive about all of the international coproductions (2,372 reviews in total) were systematically extracted and evaluated using the – as yet uncataloged – archive material of the Pina Bausch Foundation – and used to create a press report. We extensively analyzed the content of reviews about *Viktor, Masurca Fogo* and "*...como el musguito en la piedra, ay si, si, si...*" again using the MAXQDA software. We also analyzed reviews by critic Jochen Schmidt – who reviewed all of the coproductions (1986-2009) and published his reviews in a range of newspapers and journals – in order to examine the narrative consistency of a prolific, widely acclaimed critic, i.e., a voice with a hegemonic position in discourse for over 23 years.

PIECES

1. Bausch 2016: 328. Unless otherwise noted, all translations are by E. Polzer.
2. Cf. Linsel 1985, 1994, 2006; Linsel/Hoffmann 2010.
3. Fischer/Käseman 1984.
4. Akerman 1983.
5. Cf. Bentivoglio/Carbone 2007; Climenhaga 2008, 2012; Linsel 2013; Meyer 2018; Müller/Servos 1979; Schmidt 1998; Schulze-Reuber 2008; Servos 1996a, 2008; Weir 2018.
6. Wildenhahn 1982.
7. Cf Müller/Servos 1979.
8. Cf. Müller/Servos 1979: 1.
9. Cf. Schmidt 1998; Servos 1996a, 2008.
10. Servos 2008: 7.
11. Servos 2008: 8.
12. Servos 2008: 9.
13. Servos 2008: 14.
14. Servos 2008: 24.
15. Servos 2008: 29; translator's note: the German term "bewegt" used in the original denotes both the body in motion and a body moved, e.g., by emotion.
16. Klein 1994.
17. Klein 1994.
18. Cf. Bentivoglio/Carbone 2007, Linsel 2013; Meyer 2018; Schmidt 1998; Servos 1996a, 2008
19. Cf. the well-informed sections in: Meyer 2018; Schmidt 1998; Servos 2008.
20. Translator's note: "anähneln" – approaching similarity, toward semblance.
21. Marion Meyer's book also divides Pina Bausch's oeuvre into artistic phases. However, it concentrates on short descriptions of individual pieces and does not go into further detail about what characterizes these artistic phases (Meyer 2018).
22. Cf. Meyer 2018; Schmidt 1998; Servos 2008.
23. Bausch 2007.
24. Schitthelm, cited in Krug 2008, translation by E. Polzer and L. J. White.
25. Kresnik, cited in Meyer, F., 2008.
26. That theater was not just one of many social institutions being seized by the desire for democratization, but itself often triggered the initial spark for such developments, became evident in Warsaw, Poland. Here, student protests were sparked by the piece *Dziady* (Forefathers' Eve) by Adam Mickiewicz (1798-1855) being banned due to its anti-Russian content (cf. Spiegel Online: *http://www.spiegel.de/spiegel/print/d-46135831.html*, accessed February 4, 2019). Twenty thousand students were subsequently expelled from universities. Although this may at first have stifled the student protests in Poland, it did set the ball rolling and laid the foundations for the subsequent democratization movement, Solidarność.
27. Probst 2015, translation by E. Polzer and L. J. White.
28. Bausch 2007, translation modified by L. J. White.
29. Schmidt 1979: 5, also in: Steckelings 2014: 29.
30. Koegler 1973: 40.
31. Millet 2016: 24.
32. Cf. Betterton 1996.
33. Cf. Frei Gerlach, e.g., 2003.
34. Cf. Buikema/Van der Tuin 2009; West/Zimmerman 1987.
35. Cf. Klein 2004.
36. Gopnik 2007.
37. Hoghe 2016: 28.
38. Bausch 2016: 323-324.
39. Hereafter shortened to 1980.
40. From the program booklet to the piece *Fritz*, which premiered on January 5, 1974, at the Opernhaus Wuppertal.
41. Kuckart 2018.
42. Bausch 2007.
43. Bausch 2016: 324-325.
44. Bausch 2007, translation modified by L. J. White.
45. Howard 2014: 38, translation modified by L. J. White.
46. For a more detailed discussion, cf. Brandstetter/Klein 2015a.
47. Diers 2015.
48. In the following shortened to *Bluebeard*.
49. In the following shortened to "Brecht/Weill Evening."
50. At the conference *Dance Future II: Claiming Contemporaneity* in Hamburg in January 2017, Gerald Siegmund addressed the relationship between contemporary dance and dance theater, presenting Pina Bausch as a conceptual artist and, in doing so, significantly expanding the notion of conceptual, cf.: Siegmund 2018.
51. Bausch 2007.
52. Servos 2008.
53. Cf. Hoghe 1987.
54. Linsel/Hoffmann 2012.
55. Schmidt 1998: 69.
56. Bausch 2016: 331.
57. Bausch 2007.
58. Bausch 2016: 328.
59. *Fritz* (PREMIERE 1974); *Iphigenie auf Tauris* (PREMIERE 1974), *Zwei Krawatten* (PREMIERE 1974); *I'll Do You In* and *Adagio – Five Songs by Gustav Mahler* (PREMIERE 1974); *Orpheus und Eurydike* (PREMIERE 1975); *The Rite of Spring* (PREMIERE 1975); *The Seven Deadly Sins* (PREMIERE 1976); *Bluebeard: While Listening to a Taped Recording of Béla Bartók's "Duke Bluebeard's Castle"* (PREMIERE 1977); *Come dance with me* (PREMIERE 1977); *Renate Emigrates* (PREMIERE 1977); *He Takes Her By The Hand And Leads Her Into His Castle, The Others Follow* (PREMIERE 1978); *Café Müller* (PREMIERE 1978); *Kontakthof* (PREMIERE 1978); *Arien* (PREMIERE 1979); *Legend of Chastity* (PREMIERE 1979);
60. Cf. Schulze 2000.
61. Cf. Illies 2001.
62. *1980 – A Piece by Pina Bausch* (PREMIERE 1980); *Bandoneon* (PREMIERE 1980); *Walzer* (PREMIERE 1982); *Nelken* (PREMIERE 1982); *On the Mountain a Cry was Heard* (PREMIERE 1984); *Two Cigarettes in the Dark* (PREMIERE 1985); *Viktor* (PREMIERE 1986); *Ahnen* (PREMIERE 1987); *Palermo Palermo* (PREMIERE 1989).
63. Servos 2008: 81-86.
64. Hoghe/Weiss 2016: 104.
65. Bausch 2016: 332.
66. Cf. Schmidt 1998: 113.
67. Pina Bausch Foundation n.d.b, translation by E. Polzer and L. J. White.
68. Bausch 2007.
69. Wenders 2009.
70. Bausch 2007.
71. *Viktor* (PREMIERE 1986); *Ahnen* (PREMIERE 1987); *Palermo Palermo* (PREMIERE 1989); *Tanzabend II* (PREMIERE 1991); *The Piece with the Ship* (PREMIERE 1993); *Ein Trauerspiel* (PREMIERE 1994); *Danzón* (PREMIERE 1995); *Only You* (PREMIERE 1996); *The Window Washer* (PREMIERE 1997); *Masurca Fogo* (PREMIERE 1998); *O Dido* (PREMIERE 1999); *Wiesenland* (PREMIERE 2000); *Kontakthof with Seniors* (PREMIERE 2000);
72. *Ahnen* (PREMIERE 1987); *The Piece with the Ship* (PREMIERE 1993); *Danzón* (PREMIERE 1995); were not coproductions.
73. Bausch 1990.
74. Regina Advento, Ruth Amarante, Daphnis Kokkinos, Cristiana Morganti and Aida Vainieri joined the company for the premiere of *Ein Trauerspiel* (PREMIERE 1994) Rainer Behr, Andrey Berezin, Stephan Brinkmann, Eddie Martinez and

Fernando Suels Mendoza for *Only You* (PREMIERE 1996). For *The Window Washer* (PREMIERE 1997), it was Raphaëlle Delaunay, Na Young Kim, Michael Strecker and Jorge Puerta Armenta, for *Wiesenland* (PREMIERE 2000) Pascal Merighi and Fabien Prioville and for *Água* (PREMIERE 2001) Ditta Miranda Jasjfi, Azusa Seyama, Kenji Takagi and Anna Wehsarg.
75 Fukuyama 1992.
76 Casati 2015.
77 Casati 2015.
78 Meyer 2012: 94-112; cf. also its table of contents.
79 Waldenfels 1990: 39.
80 Kramer 1986.
81 Stiftet 1998, translation by E. Polzer and L. J. White.
82 Kuckart 1986.
83 Bausch 2007.
84 Servos 2008: 194.
85 Cf. Benjamin 2012.
86 Benjamin 2012: 78.
87 Servos 1995: 37.
88 Servos 2008: 153.
89 Bausch 2016: 331.
90 Gibiec 2016: 217.
91 Servos 2008: 168.
92 Gibiec 2016: 217.
93 Adolphe 2007: 38.
94 Siefer 2009.
95 Serwer 2009.
96 Mackrell 1999.
97 *Água* (PREMIERE 2001); *For the Children of yesterday, today and tomorrow* (PREMIERE 2002); *Nefés* (PREMIERE 2003); *Ten Chi* (PREMIERE 2004); *Rough Cut* (PREMIERE 2005); *Vollmond* (PREMIERE 2006); *Bamboo Blues* (PREMIERE 2007); *'Sweet Mambo'* (PREMIERE 2008); *Kontakthof with Teenagers* (PREMIERE 2008); "... *como el musguito en la piedra, ay si, si, si...*" (PREMIERE 2009);
98 Servos 1995: 37.
99 Cf. Meyer 2018; Servos 2008.
100 Servos 2008: 179.
101 Servos 2008: 189.
102 Servos 2008: 191.
103 Servos 2008: 202.
104 Due to the high threshold of 10 percent, only two parties, the AKP and the CHP, made it into parliament, although they only represented approx. 60 percent of voters. The KAP under Abdullah Gül formed the government alone. Initially, Recep Tayyip Erdogan could not participate in the elections due to a prison sentence, but he reentered parliament thanks to a constitutional amendment and the annulment of the election results through new elections in the province of Siirt, supplanting Abdullah Gül as Prime Minister in 2003.
105 Cf. Pritzlaff 2007; Schmöe 2007.
106 From the program booklet to the piece 'Sweet Mambo,' which premiered May 30, 2008, at the Schauspielhaus Wuppertal.
107 Parra 2015.
108 Ibacache 2010.
109 Pfeiffer 2009.
110 Keil 2009.
111 Bausch 2016: 317-318.
112 Cf. Althusser 2001.
113 Cf. Benjamin 2012.
114 Burkart 2018.

COMPANY

1 Gibiec 2016: 216. Unless otherwise noted, all translations are by E. Polzer.
2 Cf. Chabrier 2010; Linsel 2013; Schulze-Reuber 2008; Vogel 2000.
3 Cf. Bode 2004; Bonwetsch 2009; Internationale Liga für Menschenrechte 1995; Janus 2012; Winterberg S./Winterberg Y. 2009.
4 Rosenbaum 2014.
5 Arendt 2006.
6 Almost three-quarters of all the bombs released were dropped in this period between early November and the end of the war. In total, 3,753 heavy bombs including mines fell on Solingen, as well as 10,300 firebombs with a total weight of 2,116 metric tons. There are various figures, but the number of casualties incurred during the two major attacks is estimated to be at least 1,700 fatalities and over 2,000 injured, most of them women. Over 20,000 Solingen residents became homeless.
7 Rogge/Schulte 2003: 25
8 Bausch 2007, translation modified by E. Polzer.
9 Some publications use the Kyoto speech to depict the life of Pina Bausch, while neither pointing out the difference between reconstructing history and personal narrative, nor taking into account Pina Bausch's own style of narration and presentation of events. Cf. Linsel 2013.
10 Bausch 2007, translation modified by L. J. White.
11 Bausch 2007.
12 Bausch 2007.
13 Schwarzer 1998, translation by E. Polzer and L. J. White.

14 Schwarzer 1998, translation by L. J. White.
15 Schwarzer 1998, translation by L. J. White.
16 Kluge 2010, translation by E. Polzer and L. J. White.
17 Gleede 2016: 25.
18 Gleede 2016: 25.
19 Schwarzer 2010.
20 Schwarzer 1998.
21 Bausch 2007.
22 Schwarzer 1998.
23 Bausch 2007.
24 Jooss 1957.
25 Bausch 2007.
26 Schwarzer 2010.
27 Schwarzer 1998.
28 Schwarzer 1998.
29 Pina Bausch: Brief an das Kulturamt der Stadt Solingen [Letter to the Cultural Department of the City of Solingen], January 16, 1959, in: Stadtarchiv Solingen (StA) sg 3327, translation by L. J. White.
30 Kurt Jooss: Gutachten über Fräulein Pina Bausch zur Vorlage beim Kulturamt und Magistrat der Stadt Solingen [Report on Fräulein Pina Bausch for the Cultural Department and Municipal Authorities of the City of Solingen], in: Stadtarchiv Solingen, sg 3327.
31 Schwarzer 1998, translation by E. Polzer and L. J. White.
32 Robert Sturm, interview by Gabriele Klein, May 2, 2013.
33 Bausch 2016: 322.
34 Bausch 2016: 321-322.
35 Panadero 2016: 31.
36 Marion Cito, interview by Gabriele Klein, August 14, 2015, translation by L. J. White.
37 Vogel 2000: 84.
38 Bausch 2016: 322.
39 Jooss 1993: 76-77.
40 Borzik 2000: 99.
41 Bausch 2016: 329.
42 Hereafter shortened to *Bluebeard*.
43 Bausch 2016: 322.
44 Bausch 2016: 322.
45 Bausch 2016a: 309-310.
46 Marion Cito, interview by Gabriele Klein, August 14, 2015.
47 Großmann 2000: 93.
48 Großmann 2000: 93.
49 Rettich 2000: 89.
50 Tankard 2000: 87.
51 Bausch 2016: 327.
52 Tankard 2000: 88.
53 Marion Cito, interview by Gabriele Klein, August 14, 2015.
54 Marion Cito, interview by Gabriele Klein, August 14, 2015.
55 Marion Cito, interview by Gabriele Klein, August 14, 2015.
56 Bahr 2015.
57 Gsovsky 1985.
58 Wendland 1975, translation by L. J. White.
59 Marion Cito, interview by Gabriele Klein, August 14, 2015.
60 Marion Cito, interview by Gabriele Klein, August 14, 2015, translation by L. J. White.
61 Marion Cito, interview by Gabriele Klein, August 14, 2015.
62 Marion Cito, interview by Gabriele Klein, August 14, 2015, translation by L. J. White.
63 Cito, cited in Wilink 2014.
64 Cito 2014, translation by L. J. White.
65 Wilink 2014.
66 Marion Cito, interview by Norbert Servos, book presentation on November 16, 2013 within the scope of the jubilee season *pina40 – 40 years of the Tanztheater Wuppertal Pina Bausch*, Deutsche Oper am Rhein/Opernhaus Düsseldorf, translation by L. J. White.
67 Peter Pabst, interview by Gabriele Klein, October 9, 2015.
68 Pabst 2019: 22; cf. also Strecker 2010.
69 Manfred Marczewski, interview by Gabriele Klein, September 24, 2015.
70 Manfred Marczewski, interview by Gabriele Klein, September 24, 2015, translation by E. Polzer and L. J. White.
71 Pabst 2008, translation by L. J. White.
72 Tanztheater Wuppertal Pina Bausch GmbH 2010.
73 Bausch 2007, translation modified by L. J. White.
74 Matthias Burkert, interview by Gabriele Klein, May 3, 2013.
75 Fränzel/Widmann 2008.
76 Matthias Burkert, interview by Gabriele Klein, May 3, 2013.
77 Matthias Burkert, interview by Gabriele Klein, May 3, 2013.
78 Matthias Burkert, interview by Gabriele Klein, May 3, 2013.
79 Matthias Burkert, interview by Gabriele Klein, May 3, 2013..
80 Matthias Burkert, interview by Gabriele Klein, May 3, 2013.
81 Bausch 2016: 330.
82 Burkert 2019: 62.
83 Matthias Burkert, interview by Gabriele Klein, May 3, 2013.
84 Matthias Burkert, interview by Gabriele Klein, May 3, 2013.
85 Matthias Burkert, interview by Gabriele Klein, May 3, 2013.
86 Andreas Eisenschneider, interview by Gabriele Klein, September 27, 2014.
87 Andreas Eisenschneider, interview by Gabriele Klein, September 27, 2014.
88 Burkert 2019: 63.
89 Andreas Eisenschneider, interview by Gabriele Klein, September 27, 2014.
90 Andreas Eisenschneider, interview by Gabriele Klein, September 27, 2014.
91 Matthias Burkert, interview by Gabriele Klein, May 3, 2013.
92 Matthias Burkert, interview by Gabriele Klein, May 3, 2013.
93 Andreas Eisenschneider, interview by Gabriele Klein, September 27, 2014.
94 Schmidt-Mühlisch 2000.
95 Gibiec 2016: 216.
96 Gibiec 2016: 216.
97 Bausch 2016: 323.
98 Gibiec 2016: 216.
99 Cf. Gibiec 2016: 216; Bausch 2016: 325-327.
100 Gibiec 2016: 216.
101 Adolphe 2007: 36.
102 Fischer 2004, translation by L. J. White.
103 Stephan Brinkmann, interview by Gabriele Klein, May 2, 2013.
104 Schwarzer 2010.
105 Barbara Kaufmann, interview by Gabriele Klein, November 14, 2013.
106 Schwarzer 2010.
107 Berghaus 2016: 103.
108 Bausch 2007.
109 Bausch 2016: 326, translation by E. Polzer and L. J. White.
110 Seyfarth 2016: 126, translation by E. Polzer and L. J. White.
111 Stephan Brinkmann, interview by Gabriele Klein, May 2, 2013.
112 Kenji Takagi, interview by Gabriele Klein, August 26, 2013.
113 Cf. Bausch 2007.
114 Fischer/Käsmann 1994.
115 Gliewe 1992.
116 Schmidt 1996b: 302.
117 Michaelsen 2015, translation by E. Polzer and L. J. White.
118 Endicott 2009.
119 Endicott 2007: 43.
120 Bausch 2007.
121 Laurent Sasportes, interview by Marc Wagenbach as part of a series of talks entitled *Zeitlinien – Tänzer recorded*, Wuppertal, January 26, 2014 (unpublished transcript).
122 Anne Martin, interview by Marc Wagenbach as part of a series of talks entitled *Zeitlinien – Tänzer recorded*, Wuppertal, November 3, 2013 (unpublished transcript).

123 Anne Martin, interview by Marc Wagenbach as part of a series of talks entitled *Zeitlinien – Tänzer recorded*, Wuppertal, November 3, 2013 (unpublished transcript).
124 Michaelsen 2015.
125 Anne Martin, interview by Marc Wagenbach as part of a series of talks entitled *Zeitlinien – Tänzer recorded*, Wuppertal, November 3, 2013 (unpublished transcript).
126 Schwarzer 2010.
127 Schwarzer 2010.
128 Bausch 2016: 326.
129 Burkert 2019: 62.
130 Cf. Bausch 2007.
131 Seyfarth 2016: 126, translation by E. Polzer and L. J. White.
132 Bausch 2016: 321.
133 Fischer 2004. In the original: *Respektperson* – 'respected person.'

WORK PROCESS

1 Bausch 2016: 328. Unless otherwise noted, all translations are by E. Polzer.
2 Members of the Tanztheater Wuppertal actually used the English term "research" when talking about the ensemble's trips to coproducing countries.
3 Pina Bausch did not use the German term *Methode* (method) and preferred speaking of *Arbeitsweisen* (literally: 'ways of working'). However, since 'ways of working' is not terminologically clear in English, we have chosen to use the term 'working method' to describe the way that Pina Bausch worked in the English edition of this book for more clarity.
4 Hereafter shortened to the "Macbeth Piece."
5 Bausch 2016a: 309.
6 Hereafter shorted to *Bluebeard*.
7 Schmidt 1998: 87-89.
8 Bertolt Brecht later expanded the title into *The Seven Deadly Sins of the Petty Bourgeoisie*.
9 Bausch 2016: 325.
10 Bausch 2016: 325, translation by L. J. White.
11 Handke 2002: 28.
12 Schmidt 1983: 14.
13 Schmidt 1983: 13ff.
14 The 'questions' that Pina Bausch originally posed in English appear here in italics.
15 Cf. Brandstetter 2006; Müller/Servos 1979; Schmitt/Klanke 2014.
16 Pina Bausch either consciously or unwittingly translated the Chinese character ai as 'life,' although it actually means 'love.'
17 Bausch 2016: 328-329.
18 Schmidt 1983: 14, translation by L. J. White.
19 Schmidt 1998: 92.
20 Bausch 2016: 329.
21 Stephan Brinkmann, interviewed by Gabriele Klein, May 2, 2013.
22 Bausch 2016: 329.
23 Schmidt 1983: 14.
24 Schmidt 1983: 14.
25 Hereafter shortened to *1980*.
26 The coproductions were: *Viktor* (PREMIERE 1986), in collaboration with the Teatro Argentina and the City of Rome; *Palermo Palermo* (PREMIERE 1989), in collaboration with the Teatro Biondo, Palermo and Andres Neumann International; *Tanzabend II* (PREMIERE 1991), in collaboration with the Festival de Otono, Madrid; *Ein Trauerspiel* (PREMIERE 1994), in collaboration with the Wiener Festwochen; *Only You* (PREMIERE 1996), in collaboration with the University of California in Los Angeles, Arizona State University, the University of California in Berkley, the University of Texas in Austin, Darlene Neel Presentations, Rena Shagan Associates, Inc. and The Music Center Inc.; *The Window Washer* (PREMIERE 1997), in collaboration with the Hong Kong Arts Festival Society and the Goethe-Institut Hong Kong; *Masurca Fogo* (PREMIERE 1998), in collaboration with Expo '98 Lisbon and the Goethe-Institut Lisbon; *O Dido* (PREMIERE 1999), in collaboration with the Teatro Argentina in Rome und Andres Neumann International; *Wiesenland* (PREMIERE 2000), in collaboration with the Goethe-Institut Budapest and the Théâtre de la Ville Paris; *Água* (PREMIERE 2001), in collaboration with the Goethe-Institut São Paolo and Emilio Kalil; *Nefés* (PREMIERE 2003), in collaboration with the International Istanbul Theatre Festival and the Istanbul Foundation for Culture and Arts; *Ten Chi* (PREMIERE 2004), in collaboration with Saitama Prefecture, the Saitama Arts Foundation and the Nippon Cultural Center; *Rough Cut* (PREMIERE 2005), in collaboration with the LG Arts Center and the Goethe-Institut Seoul; *Bamboo Blues* (PREMIERE

2007), in collaboration with the various branches of the Goethe-Institut in India; *"...como el musguito en la piedra, ay si, si, si..."* (PREMIERE 2009), in collaboration with the Festival Internacional de Teatro Santiago a Mil in Chile and supported by the Goethe-Institut Chile.

27 Cf. Badura u.a. 2015; Peters 2013.

28 Benjamin 2012: 78.

29 Bausch 2007.

30 Performances in the USA in 1996: San Francisco, October 3-5; Los Angeles, October 10-13; Tempe, Arizona, October 17; Austin, Texas, October 22.

31 The original cast comprised Elena Adaeva, Regina Advento, Ruth Amarante, Rainer Behr, Andrey Berezin, Stephan Brinkmann, Chrystel Guillebeaud, Barbara Hampel, Kyomi Ichida, Daphnis Kokkinos, Bernd Marszan, Eddie Martinez, Dominique Mercy, Jan Minařík, Nazareth Panadero, Héléna Pikon, Julie Shanahan, Julie Anne Stanzak, Fernando Suels Mendoza, Aida Vainieri, Jean Guillaume Weis and Michael G. Whaites.

32 Schmidt 1983: 10.

33 In German, Pina Bausch's 'question' was, "Ein Indianer kennt keinen Schmerz," which translates as, "An Indian [i.e., Native American] knows no pain." This is equivalent to the English saying "Big boys don't cry." Since Pina Bausch was not targeting a specific gender with this question, we have chosen to translate it gender-neutrally.

34 Performances at Vígszínház, Budapest: May 26-28, 2000; performances at Théâtre de la Ville-Paris: June 7-9 and June 11-14, 2001.

35 The original cast comprised Ruth Amarante, Fernando Suels Mendoza, Michael Strecker, Julie Anne Stanzak, Julie Shanahan, Jorge Puerta Armenta, Fabien Prioville, Héléna Pikon, Jan Minařík, Pascal Merighi, Dominique Mercy, Eddie Martinez, Daphnis Kokkinos, Nayoung Kim, Barbara Kaufmann, Raphaëlle Delaunay, Stephan Brinkmann, Rainer Behr and Aida Vainieri.

36 Translated by E. Polzer on the basis of the version translated into German by Franz Hodjak (Kányádi, Sándor [1999]) and then edited by Pina Bausch.

37 Heynkes 2016: 61, 64.

38 Cf. Bauman 2004.

39 Cf., e.g., Brandstetter 2013; Wortelkamp 2006, 2012.

40 Cf., e.g., Lepecki 2006; Siegmund 2017; see also Klein's criticism in: Klein 2015a.

41 Cf. Agamben 2000: 58.

42 Dominique Mercy, interviewed by Gabriele Klein, November 14, 2013.

43 Bausch 2016: 328.

44 Schmidt 1998: 97.

45 Film *Ten Chi: A Piece by Pina Bausch* (PREMIERE 2004) and talk, moderated by Gabriele Klein, in conversation with Azusa Seyama, Fernando Suels Mendoza und Kenji Takagi, Bundeskunsthalle Bonn, April 26, 2016.

46 Cf. Brinkmann 2015, Klein 2015d.

47 In 2004, the Ballett Frankfurt, which had been directed by William Forsythe for 20 years, was dissolved. He then founded the Forsythe Company (2005-2015) as an independent dance company with the help of private sponsors and the cities of Dresden and Frankfurt, and with the support of the German states of Saxony and Hesse. The company was reduced to half its size. His more recent pieces have been exclusively performed by the Forsythe Company, but earlier works have been danced by other companies around the world, e.g., by the Mariinsky Ballet, New York City Ballet, the San Francisco Ballet, the National Ballet of Canada, the Semperoper Ballett Dresden, the British Royal Ballet and the Opéra national de Paris. William Forsythe's successor, the Italian dancer and choreographer Jacopo Godani, was a member of the Ballett Frankfurt ensemble under William Forsythe from 1991 until 2000. Since the 2015/16 season, the ensemble has been performing under the name Dresden Frankfurt Dance Company. The dancers of the former Forsythe Company have financial security at their Dresden location until late 2021. The planned joint dance company for Dresden and Frankfurt has failed due to the city of Frankfurt financially withdrawing from the collaboration.Sasha Waltz and Jochen Sandig founded Sasha Waltz & Guests in 1993 and worked with a wide variety of interdisciplinary guests. For her "Travelogue" trilogy, Waltz toured over 30 different countries with her dancers. She then replaced most of her company in order to continue working with a new generation of dancers. After establishing the independent theater house Sophiensæle Berlin and codirecting the municipal Schaubühne am Lehniner Platz theater in Berlin, Sasha Waltz resumed working with her own fully independent company in 2004. Since 2005, the company has mainly been rehearsing and working at the Radialsystem in Berlin. From 2010 to 2014, Sasha Waltz & Guests permanently employed 14 dancers. The group has been generating 50 percent of its funding by itself since 2014. In spite of Berlin's Department of Culture recognizing the company's need for funds to the amount of EUR 970,000, the city of Berlin decided on a ministerial and parliamentary level to abandon the pursuit of the company's institutionalization. In order to financially stabilize her ensemble, Sasha Waltz had to let her permanent ensemble go as well as approx. one third of her other employees. Since then, the company has continued to employ dancers on a freelance basis in order to internationally tour what are now about 70 performances per year of 20 repertoire pieces.

48 Albrecht, cited in Linsel 2009.

49 2012 London, 2011 Geneva, 2010 Istanbul, 2010 Athens, 2009 Essen, 2009 Breslau, 2008 Seoul, 2008 Lisbon, 2007 Ottawa, 2006 Madrid, 2006 New York, 2005 Tokyo, 2005 Helsinki, 2004 Berlin, 2004 Paris, 2003 Istanbul.

50 Cf. Brinkmann 2013; Cramer 2009, 2013, 2014; Thurner 2010, 2013; Thurner/Wehren 2010; Wehren 2016.

51 The world tour of the Merce Cunningham Dance Company ended on December 31, 2011, in New York.

52 Cf. Assmann, A. 1999, 2013.

53 Cf. Assmann, J. 2013.

54 Cf. Benthien/Klein 2017.

55 Klein 2015e.

56 Schmidt 1983: 15.

57 There is a trailer documenting how the dancers of the original ensemble like Dominique Mercy, Jan Minařík and Malou Airaudo passed on the material: *https://vimeo.com/216304728* (ACCESSED APRIL 15, 2019).

58 Adolphe 2007: 38, translation by E. Polzer and L. J. White.
59 Bayerisches Staatsballett 2016: 7.
60 Brandstetter 2002, 2013; Klein 2015g.
61 Michael Bataillon, cited in Koldehoff/Pina Bausch Foundation 2016: 272.
62 Gleede 2016: 31, translation by E. Polzer and L. J. White.
63 Servos 1995: 39.
64 Wagenbach/Pina Bausch Foundation 2014.
65 This exhibition ran from March 4 until July 24, 2016, at the Bundeskunsthalle in Bonn and subsequently from September 16, 2016, until January 9, 2017, at the Martin-Gropius-Bau in Berlin.
66 Linsel/Hoffmann 2010: 34:26-34:54.
67 Linsel/Hoffmann 2010: 01:16:49-01:16:58.
68 Linsel/Hoffmann 2010: 02:54-05:19.
60 Bausch 2013: 50.
70 Panadero 2016: 31.
71 International conference: *Dance Future II: Claiming Contemporaneity*. Focus Pina Bausch, Kampnagel Hamburg, January 26-28, 2017. Concept: Gabriele Klein/Hamburg University; organization: Gabriele Klein/Katharina Kelter; space design: Jochen Roller/Christin Vahl; speakers e.g.: Leonetta Bentivoglio, Stephan Brinkmann, Royd Climenhaga, Susan Leigh Foster, Claudia Jeschke, Barbara Kaufmann, Gabriele Klein, Susan Manning, Annemarie Matzke, Shigeto Nuki, Katja Schneider, Gerald Siegmund, Hirohiko Soejima, Christina Thurner, Marc Wagenbach, Bettina Wagner-Bergelt.
72 Bausch 2016: 331.
73 Bausch 2016: 329-330.
74 Benjamin 2012: 77.
75 Cf. Klein 2015c.
76 Kracauer 1995.
77 For more details, cf. Klein 2015c.
78 Cf. Klein 2015d.
79 Bausch/Weyrich 1979, broadcast again on ZDF Kultur on February 5, 2011.
80 The Pina Bausch Archive is currently (as of March 2020) still under development. The digital processing of the materials is underway, which means that it is still not possible to access them. The material used in this book is material that has either already been published or that I have generated myself during my research and in the interviews that I have conducted with dancers and rehearsal directors. Heavily abridged versions of two of these interviews, "Die Performanz des Rituals: Gabriele Klein im Gespräch mit Gitta Barthel" (The Performance of Ritual: Gabriele Klein in conversation with Gitta Barthel) and "Die Treue zur Form: Gabriele Klein im Gespräch mit Barbara Kaufmann" (Faithful to Form: Gabriele Klein in conversation with Barbara Kaufmann) can be found in Brandstetter/Klein 2015a.
81 Cf. Klein 2015d.
82 Cf. Brinkmann 2015, Klein 2015d.
83 Brinkmann 2015.
84 Brinkmann 2015.
85 Brinkmann 2015.
86 Klein 2015d: 173.
87 Klein 2015d: 170.
88 Klein 2015d: 171.
89 Derrida 2006: 68.
90 Cf. Derrida/Roudinesco 2004.
91 Derrida/Roudinesco 2004: 1-19.
92 The full name of the project is, "An Invitation from Pina: An Archive as a Workshop for the Future." The Pina Bausch Foundation began looking through Pina Bausch's legacy in 2010, working to secure it and make it accessible. Whenever possible, material has been digitized, and physical objects have been described, measured and photographed. Public events have taken place with names like, "Du und Pina: Teile deine Erinnerung an Pina Bausch. Ein Archiv als Erinnerungslabor" (You and Pina: Share your Memories of Pina Bausch. An Archive as Memory Lab) on September 27, 2014, and "Pina erinnern" (Remembering Pina; part II) on July 1, 2015, at the opera house in Wuppertal. The final publication *Tanz erben: Pina lädt ein* was edited by Marc Wagenbach and the Pina Bausch Foundation and published in 2014 by transcript-Verlag, Bielefeld.
93 The German society for musical performing and mechanical reproduction rights (GEMA) is a government-mandated collecting society and performance rights organization.
94 "These living archives claim that theirs is not a 'dusty[,]' 'locked' or inaccessible repository [...]. A Living Archive is often characterized as open,

95 collaborative and creative." Cf. Wagenbach/Pina Bausch Foundation 2014: 77.
95 Salomon Bausch, interviewed by Gabriele Klein, December 11, 2014, quoted in: Klein 2015e: 22.
96 Lutz Förster, interviewed by Gabriele Klein, December 10, 2014, quoted in: Klein 2015e: 22.
96 Klein 2015e: 23.
96 Cf. Ziemer 2016.
96 Derrida 2006: 18.

SOLO DANCE

1 Servos 1996b: 305. Unless otherwise noted, all translations are by E. Polzer.
2 Adolphe 2007: 36, translation by E. Polzer and L. J. White.
3 The work of refining the Feldpartitur software and the example analysis of dances and individual scenes took place within the framework of the research project "Gestures of Dance – Dance as Gesture: Cultural and Aesthetic Translation based on the International Coproductions of the Tanztheater Wuppertal" in collaboration with my research associates Elisabeth Leopold and Anna Wieczorek. For more on the application of the Feldpartitur software to dance analysis, cf. Klein/Leopold/Wieczorek 2018.
4 First, we chose the three pieces: the first and the last coproduction, as well as a piece from the second half of the 1990s, which lies in between the other two, was frequently on tour and thus constantly in the Tanztheater Wuppertal repertoire. After dramaturgically analyzing these pieces, we then selected these solos, as each plays a dramaturgically important role in the respective piece.
5 Cf. Rorty 1967.
6 Cf. Foster 1986.
7 Cf. Brandstetter 2015.
8 Cf. Austin 1975; Goffman 1959; Turner 1982, 1986; Klein/Göbel 2018a.
9 Cf. Butler 1990.
10 Cf. Bourdieu 2010; Garfinkel 1967; Goffman 1959, 1963, 1974; Schütz 1932.
11 Wortelkamp 2002: 598.
12 Cf. Wortelkamp 2002, 2006, 2012.
13 Cf. Adshead-Landsdale 1999.
14 Cf. Schneider 2016.
15 Cf. Jeschke 1983, 1999.
16 Cf. Moritz 2010, 2011. The name of the software literally means 'field notation.'
17 There is no standard, definitive translation of the original Jooss-Leeder terms into English. After reviewing the literature and consulting with Stephan Brinkmann, who teaches the Jooss-Leeder technique at the Folkwang Universität, the following translations are used in this book to describe different movement qualities (differing variations not used in this book are indicated in brackets): gliding, floating, shivering (dabbing), fluttering (flicking), thrusting (wringing), pressing, slashing (punching), pulling; furthermore: scooping and scattering (strewing). For swings: preparatory swing, upward swing, inverted swing, eight swing, pendulum swing, centrifugal swing. For the form: first (high/ low), second (narrow/wide) and third (forward /backward) dimension. For dynamics: strong/light, fast/slow, central/peripheral. For directions/design: droit, ouvert, rond, tortillé. For movement impulses: contraction, curve, inside fall, outside fall, rotation, twist. For inclination/tilt: fixed tilt, flexible tilt. For turns: stable turns, labile turns, transference of weight. For starting points and guidance: inside and outside guidance, little finger guidance, thumb guidance, fingertip guidance. Cf. Cébron 1990; Passow 2011; Winearls 1968.
18 Moritz 2014: 36, 37.
19 Winearls 1968: 64.
20 Cf. Wyss 2005.
21 Cf. "In the past, though, Bausch has pondered on plumpness (voluptuousness), as with Melanie Karen Lien, who featured largely in *Viktor* as the much abused, blowsy blonde" (Climenhaga 2013: 162). And: "A woman in a strapless dress (Melanie Karen Lien) becomes an object to be manipulated, placed into embraces that she hardly enjoys, with one man twisting her face into a kiss" (New York Times 2002: 2747).
22 The directions and positions (right and left) are described here and in the following from the camera's point of view and thus from the perspective of the audience.
23 Bausch 2016: 327.
24 The Jooss-Leeder method refers to an arch and/or a contraction as a 'curve.' A 'twist' is a rotation around the axis of the body. A 'tilt' is a flexible or stable inclination of the upper body.
25 Cf. Libonati 2014, 2017.
26 Stefan Brinkmann, interviewed by Gabriele Klein, May 2, 2013.
27 Newis 2016.
28 Dominique Mercy, interviewed by Gabriele Klein, November 14, 2013.
29 The other solos in this piece are generally 2 to 3 minutes long, some also 4 to 4.5 minutes, such as the solos of Nayoung Kim (3:58), Tsai-Chin Yu (4:17), Ditta Miranda Jasjfi (4:46) and Fernando Suels Mendoza (4:26).
30 Cf. Winearls 1968: 27
31 "Droit: direct and purposeful; Ouvert: balanced and simple; Tortillé: personal and complex; Rond: complete participation in physical action." Winearls 1968: 105.
32 Dominique Mercy, interviewed by Gabriele Klein, November 14, 2013.
33 Dominique Mercy, interviewed by Gabriele Klein, November 14, 2013.
34 Bausch 2016: 326.
35 Cf. Kolesch 2010.
36 Cf. Brandstetter/Klein 2015a.
37 Cf. Bohnsack 2009; Knoblauch/Schnettler 2012.
38 Cf. Charmaz 2006; Clarke 2005.
39 Cf. Forsythe 2009.
40 Cf. Forsythe 2010.
41 Barthes 2009: 177f.

RECEPTION

1 Bausch 2016: 332. Unless otherwise noted, all translations are by E. Polzer.
2 Geitel 2005: 175.
3 Ploebst 2001.
4 Geitel 2019: 286, 288.
5 This statement is based on an analysis of all German-language reviews of the international coproductions.
6 The term paratext (Greek *para* – 'next to,' 'toward,' 'beyond something') has its origins in intertextual research and designates either an additional interpretation by the author him- or herself or external proof of his or her intentions. It was applied to works of literature by the French literary scholar Gérard Genette, then transferred to

7. Heyn 1986.
8. Scheier 1986.
9. Töne 2007.
10. In large German theaters, there is a hierarchy between the three genres opera, drama/theater and dance (the latter mainly in form of ballet). This is called the *Dreispartensystem*.
11. Cf. Habermas 2008.
12. Haacke 1953: 296.
13. Cf. Thurner 2015a: 31-32.
14. Cf. Fischer 2012.
15. Boldt 2017.
16. Cf. Copeland/Cohen 1983.
17. US dance critic Marcia B. Siegel, cited in Copeland 1993: 29-30.
18. Copeland/Cohen 1983: 29-30; Thurner 2015a: 37-38.
19. Cf. Müller/Servos 1979.
20. Cf. Husemann 2009.
21. Cf. Husemann 2009; Klein/Kunst 2012.
22. Cf. Van Eikels 2013.
23. Cf. Agamben 2018.
24. Cf. Ziemer 2016.
25. Cf. Foucault 1985: 10.
26. Wendland 1978: 60.
27. Croce 1984.
28. Koegler 1979: 58.
29. Koegler 2009.
30. Robertson 1984: 12.
31. Birringer 1986: 85.
32. Thurner 2015a: 61, translation by E. Polzer and L. J. White.
33. I have analyzed a total of 94 reviews of the piece *Viktor*: 34 reviews of the premiere in Wuppertal in 1986, 60 reviews of restaged performances in Wuppertal in 1992 and 2007, and reviews of various performances on tour, e.g., in Rome 1986, New York 1988, Venice 1992, Tel Aviv 1995, Copenhagen 1996, Frankfurt 1997 and London 1999. Research assistants Elisabeth Leopold and Anna Wieczorek helped with the analysis.
34. Gilbert 1999.
35. Siegmund 1997.
36. Schmidt 1986.
37. Hirsch 1986.
38. Servos 1986: 44.
39. Regitz 1986.
40. Engler 1986.
41. Sowden 1995.
42. Hofmann 2017.
43. Esterházy 2001: 21. "Pina Bausch is one of those great artists. Through her, art acquires its reason for being; we are looking at the stage, her stage, deep in our heart (or some other internal organ), and then we see what art is for."
44. Brown 1999.
45. Schneider 1997.
46. Staude 1997.
47. Sowden 1995.
48. Schmidt 1999, translation by L. J. White.
49. Schmidt 2001.
50. Michaelis 1986, translation by L. J. White.
51. Newman 1999.
52. Heuer 1992.
53. Hirsch 1986.
54. Hirsch 1986.
55. Fischer 1986.
56. Pappenheim 1999.
57. Mölter 1990.
58. Cf. Schmidt 1979, 1983, 1996a, 1996b.
59. Schmidt 1998.
60. We pursued these questions on the basis of a data corpus encompassing 15 reviews written by Jochen Schmidt between 1986 and 2009 about each of the coproductions of the Tanztheater Wuppertal. We carried out this comparative analysis using the text analysis software MAXQDA as an inductive content analysis evaluation (as defined by Mayring 2015). For their help during the evaluation, I am indebted to my research assistants Elisabeth Leopold and Anna Wieczorek.
61. Schmidt 1996c.
62. Schmidt 2001, translation by L. J. White.
63. Schmidt 2000.
64. Schmidt 1994.
65. Schmidt 1999.
66. Schmidt 1986.
67. Cf. Brandstetter 2013; Schneider 2016; Wortelkamp 2006, 2012.
68. Thurner 2015a: 49.
69. Scurla 1986.
70. Scurla 1986.
71. Parry 1999.
72. Langer 1986.
73. Cf. Thurner 2015a.
74. Cf. Assmann 2013.
75. Servos 1996b: 304.
76. Lehmann 2008: 26.
77. Rancière 2011.
78. Cf. Deck/Sieburg 2008; Fischer-Lichte 1997; Rancière 2010; Sasse/Wenner 2002.
79. Seyfarth 2016: 125-126.
80. Bausch 2016: 332.
81. Cf. Lehmann 2005.
82. Cf. Carlson 2004; Fischer-Lichte 2004; Lehmann 2005; Schechner 2003.

other media by him and his successors. Cf. Genette 1997.

83 Cf. Dinkla/Leeker 2002; Fischer-Lichte u.a. 2001; Klein 2000; Leeker 2001; Leeker/Schipper/Beyes 2017; Schoenmakers u.a. 2015.
84 Cf. Fischer-Lichte 2007.
85 Cf. Boenisch 2002.
86 Cf. Fischer-Lichte 2004.
87 Cf. Rancière 2011.
88 Cf. Bourriaud 2002.
89 Cf. Fischer-Lichte 2004.
90 For critique of the concept of copresence: cf. Auslander 1999; Eiermann 2009; Siegmund 2006.
91 Cf. Becker 1982; Bourdieu 2014; Gerhards 1997; Silbermann 1986.
92 Cf. Husel 2014; Husemann 2009; Klein 2014a, 2015c.
93 Cf. Katz/Bumler/Gurevitch 1974.
94 Cf. Hall 2007.
95 Cf. Storey 2003.
96 Fischer-Lichte 2004: 24-25.
97 Fischer-Lichte 2004: 25.
98 Cf. Klein/Wagenbach 2019.
99 Cf. Böhme 2013.
100 On the concept of atmosphere, see also Schmitz 1969, especially the second part: "Der Gefühlsraum" (Emotional Space).
101 Böhme 2013: 96.
102 Böhme 2013: 33-34.
103 Rancière 2011: 15; also cf. Eiermann 2009: 311.
104 Cf. Fischer-Lichte 2007; Hiß 1993; Pavis 1988.
105 Husel 2014: 21.
106 Roselt 2008: 48.
107 Roselt 2008: 20-21.
108 Roselt 2004: 49-50.; also cf. Roselt/Weiler 2017: 81-97.
109 Husel 2014: 34.
110 Husel 2014: 21.
111 Brandl-Risi 2015: 234.
112 Cf. Breidenstein u.a. 2013; Klein/Göbel 2017b; Schäfer 2016a.
113 *Viktor* was the company's first coproduction. It was coproduced with the Teatro Argentina in Rome in 1986. *Masurca Fogo* was coproduced in 1998 with the Expo '98 Lisbon and the Goethe Institut Lisbon. *Rough Cut* was produced in 2005 in cooperation with the LG Arts Center and the Goethe Institut Seoul in Korea. The last piece "*…como el musquito en la piedra, ay si, si, si…*" from 2009 was produced in cooperation with the Festival Internacional de Teatro Santiago a Mil in Chile with the support of the Goethe-Institut in Chile. All four pieces were restaged in 2012 as part of the fringe program at the Olympic Games in London.
114 The audience surveys were conducted between 2013 and 2015: *Rough Cut* (February 3-4, 2013), *Viktor* (May 22- 23, 2014), "*…como el musquito en la piedra, ay si, si, si…*" (September 26-27, 2014), *Masurca Fogo* (March 26-27, 2015). Before the performances, the participants were first asked about their visual experience: "Are you seeing a piece by Pina Bausch for the first time tonight?" If they said no, then participants were asked concrete questions pertaining to the respective piece in order to inquire more deeply into their interest in the work of Pina Bausch and the Tanztheater Wuppertal: "What in particular interests you about the pieces of Pina Bausch?" and "What do you think is special about this dance theater ensemble?" Spectators who confirmed that they were seeing a piece by Pina Bausch for the first time were instead asked: (a) "What is your motivation for coming to see a piece by Pina Bausch?" (b) "What do you expect from the performance tonight?" and finally (c) "What do you know about Pina Bausch's artistic work?" After the performances, the questions were: (a) "What are your impressions of the piece? Could you please give me three keywords?" (b) "What do you think you will remember later?" and (c) "The piece is a coproduction with [here, the place and the country were mentioned]. What do you think you learned about the culture of the country or the city?" The audio recordings were transcribed and evaluated using qualitative content analysis methods supported by MAXQDA software. I carried out these evaluations together with my research associates Elisabeth Leopold and Anna Wieczorek.
115 Total number of people interviewed: *Rough Cut* 393 (278 before the performance, 115 after); *Viktor* 318 (228 before, 90 after); "*…como el musquito en la piedra, ay si, si, si…*" 426 (333 before, 93 after); *Masurca Fogo* 416 (296 before, 120 after). Detailed breakdown: Before the performance of *Viktor*: 228 over two performances, one on May 22, 2014: 104 (60 female/44 male), one on May 23, 2014: 124 (87 female/37 male). After the performance of *Viktor:* 90 over two performances, one on May 22, 2014: 42 (26 female/16 male) and one on May 23, 2014: 48 (32 female/16 male). Before the performance of *Rough Cut:* 278 over two performances, one on February 3, 2013: 147 (100 female/47 male), and one on February 4, 2013: 131 (83 female/47 male). After the performance of *Rough Cut:* 115 over two performances, one on February 3, 2013: 56 (40 female/16 male), and one on February 4, 2013: 59 (41 female/18 male). *Masurca Fogo* before the performance: 296 over two performances, one on March 26, 2015: 138 (92 female/46 male), and one on March 27, 2015: 158 (112 female/46 male). After the performance of *Masurca Fogo:* 120 over two performances, one on March 26, 2015: 59 (37 female/ 22 male), and one on March 27, 2015: 61 (37 female/15 male). Before the performance of "*…como el musquito en la piedra, ay si, si, si…*": 333 over two performances, one on September 26, 2014: 171 (113 female/58 male), and one on September 27, 2014: 162 (104 female/58 male). After the performance of "*…como el musquito en la piedra, ay si, si, si…*": 93 over two performances, one on September 26, 2014: 50 (34 female/16 male), and one on September 27, 2014: 43 (29 female/14 male).
116 Interview before *Masurca Fogo*, female, March 26, 2015.
117 Cf. Siegmund 2006.
118 Cf. Gumbrecht 2004, 2012.
119 Interview before *Masurca Fogo*, female, March 26, 2015.
120 Cf. Klein 2015c. The piece has since been adopted by various other companies as well (→ WORK PROCESS).
121 Alkemeyer/Schürmann/Volbers 2015: 41.
122 Interview before *Masurca Fogo*, male, March 27, 2015.
123 Interview before *Masurca Fogo*, male, March 27, 2015.
124 Interview before *Viktor*, female, May 22, 2014.
125 Interview before *Masurca Fogo*, female, March 27, 2015.
126 Interview after "*…como el musquito en la piedra, ay si, si, si…*", male, September 26, 2014.

127 Interview after *Rough Cut*, female, February 3, 2013.
128 Interview after *Masurca Fogo*, female, March 26, 2015.
129 Strecker 2019: 30.
130 Interview before *"...como el musguito en la piedra, ay si, si, si..."*, female, September 26, 2014.
131 Interview before *"...como el musguito en la piedra, ay si, si, si..."*, female, September 26, 2014.
132 Interview before *"...como el musguito en la piedra, ay si, si, si..."*, male, September 26, 2014.
133 Interview before *Viktor*, female, May 22, 2014.
134 Interview before *Masurca Fogo*, female, March 27, 2015.
135 Interview after *Rough Cut*, female, February 3, 2013, translation by L. J. White.
136 Interview before *Masurca Fogo*, female, March 27, 2015.
137 Interview after *Rough Cut*, female, February 4, 2013.
138 Interview after *Rough Cut*, female, February 4, 2013.
139 Interview after *Viktor*, female, May 22, 2014.
140 Interview after *"...como el musguito en la piedra, ay si, si, si..."*, female, September 26, 2014.
141 Interview after *Viktor*, male, May 23, 2014.
142 Interview after *Masurca Fogo*, female, March 26, 2015.
143 On April 9, 2016, Elisabeth Leopold and Anna Wieczorek gave a lecture on the connections examined in the context of this research project between aesthetic experience and linguistic translation while taking into account Bernhard Waldenfels' theories of perception. The lecture was entitled "'Betroffenheit Sprechen': Wie das Publikum über die Stücke von Pina Bausch spricht" ('Speaking about Being Moved': How the Audience Speaks about Pieces by Pina Bausch) and was given at the conference "'Das hat nicht aufgehört, mein Tanzen': Zu Aspekten von Rezeption und Tradierung in der Arbeit von Pina Bausch" ("It hasn't stopped, my dancing." Aspects of Reception and Tradition in the Work of Pina Bausch) in Munich.
144 Waldenfels 2002: 56, 59.
145 Interview after *Rough Cut*, female, February 3, 2013.
146 Interview after *Viktor*, female, May 23, 2014.
147 Interview after *Rough Cut*, female, February 3, 2013.
148 Interview after *Rough Cut*, female, February 3, 2013.
149 Interview after *Rough Cut*, male, February 3, 2013.
150 Interview after *Viktor*, female, May 22, 2014.
151 Interview after *Masurca Fogo*, female, March 26, 2015.
152 Cf. Rancière 2011.
153 Brandl-Risi 2015: 244

THEORY AND METHODOLOGY

1 Gibiec 2016: 214. Unless otherwise noted, all translations are by E. Polzer.
2 Cf. Bachmann-Medick 2006.
3 In the English version of this book, we have replaced the term 'appropriation' with the less controversial term 'adoption.' While in English-language debate, the term 'cultural appropriation' has negative connotations, above all against the backdrop of postcolonial critique, in the German-speaking context, 'appropriation' *(Aneignung)* is used among others in the field of subject theories, where it describes the capacity of the individual to habituate experience, i.e. to make experience relevant to its own lifeworld.
4 The verb 'authenticate' *(beglaubigen)* is used here in reference to Louis Althusser and Judith Butler to describe the validation of actions through performance. Althusser 2001; Butler 1990.
5 Cf. Braun/Gugerli 1993; Klein 1994.
6 Cf. Mersch 2013.
7 Hoghe/Weiss 2016: 81.
8 Seeba 2010: 62, translation by E. Polzer and L. J. White.
9 Benjamin 2012.
10 Benjamin 2012: 77-78.
11 Benjamin 2012: 78.
12 Benjamin 2012: 81.
13 Wetzel 2002: 162.
14 Cf. Benthien/Klein 2017b; Jäger/Stanitzek 2002; Jäger 2004a.
15 Jäger 2010: 304.
16 Jäger 2010: 312, translation by E. Polzer and L. J. White.
17 Jäger 2013: 79, translation by L. J. White.
18 Jäger 2010: 317.
19 Jäger 2004b: 65.
20 Jäger 2010: 317-318.

21 Bolter/Grusin 1999: 45.
22 Keazor/Liptay/ Marschall 2011: 7-12.
23 Bolter/Grusin 1999: 22, 30.
24 Bolter/Grusin 1999: 34.
25 Cf. Englhart 2008; Krämer 2004; Schoenmakers a.o. 2015.
26 Cf. Bachmann-Medick 2006a; Benthien/Klein 2017b; Klein 2009a: 24-26.
27 Cf. Bhabha 1994.
28 Cf. Bachmann-Medick 2006b; Bachmann-Medick 2008; Fuchs 2009.
29 See also the distinction that Reichert makes between "appropriative" and "assimilative" concepts of translation in: Reichert 2003.
30 Cf. Mersch 2013.
31 Cf. Debray 1997; Weber 1999.
32 Cf. Benjamin 2012; Davidson 1994; Derrida 1998; Düttmann 2001; Spivak 1988.
33 Bachmann-Medick 2011: 55.
34 Marinetti 2013: 32.
35 Basnett 2002: 6.
36 Cf. Bhabha 2007.
37 Bhabha 1994: 247.
38 Bhabha 1994: 321; see also Düttmann 2001.
39 Bhabha 1994: 326.
40 Bigliazzi/Koffler/ Ambrosi 2013: 1.
41 Longinovic 2002.
42 Project Profile Tanzfonds Erbe n.d.
43 Benjamin 2012:78.
44 Benjamin 2012: 82.
45 Bausch 2007.
46 Fischer 2004.
47 Düttmann 2001.
48 Fuhrig 2003: 14, translation by E. Polzer and L. J. White.
49 Bausch 2016: 331, 317, 318, 332.
50 Cf. Torop 2002.
51 Johnson 2003.
52 Cf. Jonathan 1990; Bhabha 1994; Soja 1996.
53 Cf. Spivak 1988.
54 Bhabha 2007.
55 Sloterdijk 1989.
56 Bauman 2004.
57 Müller-Funk 2012: 81.
58 Cf. Noeth 2019.
59 Waldenfels 1990: 39.
60 Derrida 1981:12.
61 Translator's note: the subheading of this chapter in the German edition of this book is *"Über-Setzung, Setzung, Durch-Setzung."* When *Setzung* is combined with the preposition *durch* (through), the German meaning shifts to 'asserting,' 'implementing' or 'enforcing.'
62 Mersch 2013.
63 Bausch 2016: 328.
64 Willemsen 2016: 188.
65 Cf. Assmann 2013.
66 Cf. Schlicher 1987, Huschka 2002.
67 Rancière 2004.
68 Belting/Buddensieg 2013: 61.
69 Mersch 2013.
70 Bhabha 2012: 13.
71 Meurer 2012: 24.
72 Wetzel 2002:166.
73 Meurer 2012: 39.
74 Cf. Hirschauer 2008; Reckwitz 2003; Schmidt 2012.
75 The research group "Translating and Framing: Practices of Medial Transformations" examined various media transformations with regard to the guiding concepts of text/image, dance/film, static image/moving image, written/oral. Cf. the website. For publications by the group see: Benthien/Klein 2017a; Knopf/Lembcke/Recklies 2018; Ott/Weber 2019; Schmid/Veits/Vorrath 2018.
76 Cf. Schatzki/Knorr-Cetina/Von Savigny 2001.
77 Marx 2008: 569.
78 Arendt 1958.
79 Dewey 1958.
80 Vgl. Klein/ Göbel 2017b.
81 Weber 1978: 4. Arendt 1958.
82 Cf. Hirschauer 2016.
83 Cf. Hirschauer 2016.
84 Shove/Pantzar/Watson 2012.
85 Reckwitz 2003.
86 Schatzki 1996.
87 Cf. Schmidt 2012.
88 Cf. Hirschauer 2016.
89 Reckwitz 2003.
90 Bourdieu 2010.
91 Foucault 1998, 2006.
92 Cf. Schäfer 2013.
93 Giddens 1979.
94 Bourdieu 1993.
95 Schäfer 2016b: 142.
96 Schatzki 2016: 32.
97 Cf. Alkemeyer 2014; Reckwitz 2006.
98 Hirschauer 2004.
99 Cf. Schindler 2011.
100 Cf. Krämer 2014.
101 Cf. Hirschauer 2016.
102 Garfinkel 1967.
103 Garfinkel/Sacks 1986.
104 Garfinkel 1988.
105 Vgl. Schatzki 1996; Hirschauer 2016.
106 Goffman 1959.
107 Goffman 1963.
108 Simmel 1896.
109 Cf. Gebauer/Schmidt 2013; Schmidt 2007.
110 Cf. Schäfer 2013.
111 Cf. Hirschauer 2016; Reckwitz 2008.
112 Cf. Huschka 2009.
113 Cf. Wirth 2002.
114 Cf. Van Eikels 2013.
115 Cf. Hirschauer 2004.
116 Vgl. Akrich/Latour 1992; Latour 1994.
117 Cf. Kalthoff/Hirschauer/ Lindemann 2008; Klein 2014a; Hirschauer 2004; Reckwitz 2003; Schatzki/Knorr-Cetina/ Von Savigny 2001; Schmidt 2012; Shove/Pantzar/ Watson 2012.
118 Cf. Beyer 2014; Kant 1914; Marx 1969; Müller 2015.
119 Reckwitz 2008:192.
120 Reckwitz 2004: 45, translation by E. Polzer and L. J. White.
121 Hirschauer 2004: 75, translation by E. Polzer and L. J. White.
122 Hirschauer 2004: 73, translation by E. Polzer and L. J. White.
123 Cf. Latour 2005.
124 Cf. Brandstetter/Klein 2015a.
125 Moritz 2014: 25-26.
126 Cf. Assmann A. 1999, 2013; Assmann A./Assmann J. 1983; Assmann J. 1988, 2013.
127 Cf. Klein 2014b; 2015a.
128 Reichertz 2014: 61.
129 Cf. Barthes 2009; Baudrillard 2017, 1994; Derrida 1984.
130 Klein 2014b.
131 Cf. Klein/Friedrich 2014.
132 Cf. Klein 2015a, 2015c, 2017.
133 For a more detailed discussion, cf. Klein 2014a.
134 Cf. Fischer-Lichte 2004; Fischer-Lichte/Risi/Roselt 2004.
135 Cf. Kelter/Skrandies 2016.
136 Geertz 2017.
137 Cf. Rosiny 2013.
138 Cf. Leeker 1995; 2002.
139 Cf. Diers 2015.
140 Cf. Jochim 2008.
141 Cf. Mersch 2015.
142 Cf. Mohn 2015.
143 Franco 1993.
144 Brandstetter 2013.
145 Cf. Schneider 2016.
146 Cf. Thurner 2015a; Wortelkamp 2006.
147 Cf Hiß 1993; Roselt/Weiler 2017.
148 Cf. Fischer-Lichte 2004; Fischer-Lichte/Risi/Roselt 2004; Roselt 2008; Thurner 2015b.
149 Cf. Foster 1986; Schellow 2016.
150 Cf. Klein/Haller 2006; Klein 2009b; Mohn 2015.
151 Cf. Dahms 2010; Haitzinger 2009; Manning 1993.
152 Cf. Brandstetter/Klein 2015b.
153 Cf. Jeschke 1999; Kennedy 2007, 2015; Kestenberg Amighi 1999.

154 Cf. Jeschke 1983; Wortelkamp 2006.
155 Klein 2015b.
156 Kennedy 2007; 2015.
157 Cf. Bender 2007; Eberhard-Kaechele 2007; Kestenberg Amighi 1999; Sossin 2007.
158 Jeschke 1999.
159 Cf. Camurri u.a. 2004; Naveda/Leman 2010; Shiratori/Nakazawa/Ikeuchi 2004; Wang/Hu/Tan 2003.
160 Moritz 2010; 2011; 2018.
161 Klein/Leopold/Wieczorek 2018.
162 For a more detailed discussion, cf. Klein/Göbel 2017b.
163 Cf. Badura u.a. 2015; Caduff/Siegenthaler/Wälchli 2010; Tröndle/Warmers 2011; Dombois u.a. 2012; Peters 2013; Busch 2015.
164 Cf. Butler 2015.
165 Burri u.a. 2014.
166 Cf. Bial 2016; Davis 2008; Schechner 2013.
167 Cf. Husemann 2009; Matzke 2014.
168 Cf. Hiß 1993; Roselt/Weiler 2017.
169 Bourdieu 1987.
170 Malzacher 2007.
171 Cf. Cvejic/Vujanovic 2012.
172 Cf. Alkemeyer/Schürmann/Volbers 2015.
173 Peters 2013.
174 Cf. Schindler 2016.
175 Cf. Schindler/Liegl 2013.
176 Cf. Kalthoff 2011.
177 Cf. Shove/Pantzar/Watson 2012.
178 Cf. Shove/Pantzar/Watson 2012.
179 Cf. Müller 2016.
180 Cf. Hirschauer 2001.
181 Cf. Law 2004.
182 Badura 2015: 23.
183 Cf. Schmidt 2016.
184 Bourdieu 2010.
185 Bourdieu 2005.
186 Cf. Habermas 1987.
187 Bourdieu/Wacquant 2006.
188 Cf. Hall 2018; Spivak 1988.
189 Cf. Waldenfels 1997.
190 Gugutzer 2016.

8 Belkin 2015.
9 Bourdieu 2014: 157.
10 Agamben 2011: 11, 13, 14.
11 Nietzsche 1997.
12 Cf. Zanetti 2011.
13 Zanetti 2011: 53, translation by E. Polzer and L. J. White.

TRANSLATING PRESENCE

1 Schlicher 1992: 229. Unless otherwise noted, all translations are by E. Polzer.
2 Voltaire 1961: 709.
3 Hölderlin 2019: 36.
4 Goethe 2012: 45.
5 Hölscher 2012.
6 Rebentisch 2013: 17.
7 Ritter 2008: 35.

Literature

1. PRINT MEDIA

Abraham, Anke (2016): "Sprechen." In: Robert Gugutzer/Gabriele Klein/Michael Meuser (eds.), *Handbuch Körpersoziologie, vol. 2: Forschungsfelder und methodische Zugänge*, Wiesbaden: Springer, pp. 457-470.

Adorno, Theodor W. (1983 [1967]): *Prisms*, translated by Samuel and Shierry Weber, Cambridge: The MIT Press.

Adorno, Theodor W. (1990): "Beitrag zur Ideologienlehre." In: Theodor W. Adorno, *Gesammelte Schriften, vol. 8: Soziologische Schriften I*, edited by Rolf Tiedemann, Frankfurt a.M.: Suhrkamp, pp. 457-477.

Adshead-Landsdale, Janet (1999): *Dancing Texts: Intertextuality in Interpretation*, Hampshire: Dance Books.

Agamben, Giorgio (2000 [1996]): "Notes on Gesture." In: Giorgio Agamben: *Means without End: Notes on Politics*, translated by Vincenzo Binetti and Cesare Casarino, Minneapolis: University of Minnesota Press, pp. 49-62.

Agamben, Giorgio (2011 [2009]): "What is the Contemporary?" In: Giorgio Agamben: *Nudities*, translated by David Kishik and Stefan Pedatella, Stanford: Stanford University Press, pp. 10-19.

Agamben, Giorgio (2018 [2007]): *The Adventure*, translated by Lorenzo Chiesa, Cambridge: MIT

Akrich, Madeleine/Latour, Bruno (1992): "A Summary of Convenient Vocabulary for the Semiotics of Human and Non-Human Assemblies." In: Wiebe E. Bijker/John Law (eds.), *Shaping Technology/Building Society: Studies in Sociotechnical Change*, Cambridge/Massachusetts: MIT Press, pp. 259-264.

Alkemeyer, Thomas (2014): "Warum die Praxistheorien ein Konzept der Subjektivierung benötigen." In: *Allgemeine Zeitschrift für Philosophie* 39/1, pp. 27-36.

Alkemeyer, Thomas (2017): "Significance in Action." In: European National Institutes for Culture and Institut für Auslandsbeziehungen e.V. (eds.), *Culture Report: EUNIC Yearbook 2016; A Global Game – Sport, Culture, Development and Foreign Policy*, Göttingen: Steidl, pp. 189-193.

Alkemeyer, Thomas/Boschert, Bernhard/Schmidt, Robert/Gebauer, Gunter (eds.) (2003): *Aufs Spiel gesetzte Körper: Aufführungen des Sozialen in Sport und populärer Kultur*, Konstanz: UVK.

Alkemeyer, Thomas/Schürmann, Volker/Volbers, Jörg (eds.) (2015): *Praxis denken: Konzepte und Kritik*, Wiesbaden: Springer.

Althusser, Louis (2001 [1977]): "Ideology and Ideological State Apparatus: Notes Towards an Investigation." In: Louis Althusser: *Lenin and Philosophy and ‚Other Essays*, translated by Ben Brewster, New York: Monthly Review Press.

Arendt, Hannah (1958): The *Human Condition*, Chicago: University of Chicago Press.

Arendt, Hannah (2006 [1963]): *Eichmann in Jerusalem: A Report on the Banality of Evil*, London: Penguin Classsics.

Assmann, Aleida (1999): *Erinnerungsräume: Formen und Wandlungen des kulturellen Gedächtnisses*, Munich: C.H. Beck.

Assmann, Aleida (2013): *Das neue Unbehagen an der Erinnerungskultur: Eine Intervention*, Munich: C.H. Beck.

Assmann, Jan (1988): "Kollektives Gedächtnis und kulturelle Identität." In: Jan Assmann/Tonio Hölscher (eds.), *Kultur und Gedächtnis*, Frankfurt a.M.: Suhrkamp, pp. 9-19.

Assmann, Jan (2013 [1992]): *Das kulturelle Gedächtnis: Schrift, Erinnerung und politische Identität in frühen Hochkulturen*, Munich: C.H. Beck.

Assmann, Aleida/Assmann, Jan (1983): "Schrift und Gedächtnis." In: Aleida Assmann/Jan Assmann/Christof Hartmeier (eds.), *Schrift und Gedächtnis: Archäologie der literarischen Kommunikation I*, Paderborn: Fink, pp. 265-284.

Augé, Marc (2008 [1992]): *Non-Places: An Introduction to Supermodernity*, translated by John Howe, London: Verso.

Auslander, Philip (1999): *Liveness: Performance in a Mediatized Culture*, London/New York: Routledge.

Austin, John L. (1975 [1962]): *How to Do Things with Words: The William James Lectures Delivered at Harvard University in 1955*, edited by James Opie Urmson and Marina Sbisà, Oxford: Clarendon Press.

Bachmann-Medick, Doris (2016a [2006]): *Cultural Turns: New Orientations in the Study of Culture*, translated by Adam Blauhut, Berlin: De Gruyter.

Bachmann-Medick, Doris (2016b [2006]): "Translational Turn." In: Doris Bachmann-Medick (ed.), *Cultural Turns: New Orientations in the Study of Culture*, translated by Adam Blauhut, Berlin: De Gruyter, pp. 175-210.

Bachmann-Medick, Doris (2008): "Übersetzung in der Weltgesellschaft: Impulse eines 'translational turn.'" In: Andreas Gipper/Susanne Klengel (eds.), *Kultur, Übersetzung, Lebenswelten: Beiträge zu aktuellen Paradigmen der Kulturwissenschaften*, Würzburg: Königshausen & Neumann, pp. 141-159.

Bachmann-Medick, Doris (2011): "Transnationale Kulturwissenschaften: Ein Übersetzungskonzept." In: René Dietrich/Daniel Smilovinski/Ansgar Nünning (eds.), *Lost or Found in Translation? Interkulturelle/Internationale Perspektiven der Geistes- und Kulturwissenschaften*, Trier: Wissenschaftlicher Verlag Trier, pp. 53-72.

Backoefer, Andreas/Haitzinger, Nicole/Jeschke, Claudia (eds.) (2009): *Tanz & Archiv 1: Reenactment*, Munich: epodium.

Badura, Jens (2015): "Forschen in den Künsten: Darstellende Kunst." In: Jens Badura/Selma Dubach/Anke Haarmann/Dieter Mersch/Anton Rey/Christoph Schenker/Germán Toro Pérez (eds.), *Künstlerische Forschung: Ein Handbuch*, Zurich: Diaphanes, pp. 23-25.

Badura, Jens/Dubach, Selma/Haarmann, Anke/Mersch, Dieter/Rey, Anton/Schenker, Christoph/Toro Pérez, Germán (eds.) (2015): *Künstlerische Forschung: Ein Handbuch*, Zurich: Diaphanes.

Bahr, Egon (2015): *Ostwärts und nichts vergessen! Politik zwischen Krieg und Verständigung*. Freiburg: Herder.

Barthes, Roland (2009 [1963]): "The Structuralist Activity." In: David Damrosch (ed.), *The Princeton Sourcebook in Comparative Literature*, Princeton: Princeton University Press, pp. 175-182.

Basnett, Susan (2002 [1980]): *Translation Studies*, London/New York: Routledge.

Baudrillard, Jean (2017 [1978]): *Simulacra and Simulation*, translated by Sheila Faria Glaser, Ann Arbor, MI: University of Michigan Press.

Bauman, Zygmunt (2004 [1999]): Liquid Modernity, Cambridge: Polity Press.

Becker, Howard S. (1982): *Arts Worlds*, Berkeley: University Press.

Belting, Hans/Buddensieg, Andrea (2013): "Zeitgenossenschaft als Axiom von Kunst im Zeitalter der Globalisierung." In: *Kunstforum International 220*, pp. 60-69.

Bender, Susanne (2007): "Einführung in das Kestenberg Movement Profile (KMP)." In: Susanne Bender/Sabine Koch (eds.), *Movement Analysis – The Legacy of Laban, Bartenieff, Lamb and Kestenberg*, Berlin: Logos, pp. 53-65.

Benjamin, Walter (2012 [1923]): "The Task of the Translator," translated by Steven Randell. In: Lawrence Venuti (ed.), *The Translation Studies Reader*, 3rd ed., New York: Routledge. pp. 75-84.

Benthien, Claudia/Klein, Gabriele (eds.) (2017a): *Übersetzen und Rahmen: Praktiken medialer Transformationen*, Paderborn: Fink.

Benthien, Claudia/Klein, Gabriele (2017b): "Praktiken des Übersetzens und Rahmens: Zur Einführung." In: Claudia Benthien/Gabriele Klein (eds.), *Übersetzen und Rahmen: Praktiken medialer Transformationen*, Paderborn: Fink, pp. 9-25.

Bentivoglio, Leonetta/Carbone, Francesco (2007): *Pina Bausch oder Die Kunst über Nelken zu tanzen*, translated by Unda Hörner, Frankfurt a.M.: Suhrkamp.

Betterton, Rosemary (1996): *An Intimate Distance: Women, Artists and the Body*, London/New York: Routledge.

Beyer, Wilhelm R. (2014): "Der Begriff der Praxis bei Hegel." In: *Deutsche Zeitschrift für Philosophie* 6/5, pp. 749-776.

Bial, Henry (ed.) (2016 [2004]): *The Performance Studies Reader*, 3rd ed., London/New York: Routledge.

Birringer, Johannes (1986): "Pina Bausch: Dancing Across Borders." In: *Drama Review* 30/2, pp. 85-97.

Bhabha, Homi K. (1994): *The Location of Culture*, London/New York: Routledge.

Bhabha, Homi K. (2012): *Über kulturelle Hybridität: Tradition und Übersetzung*, edited by Anna Babka and Gerald Posselt, translated by Kathrina Menke, Vienna: Turia + Kant.

Bigliazzi, Silvia/Koffler, Peter/Ambrosi, Paola (2013): "Introduction." In: Silvia Bigliazzi/Peter Koffler/Paola Ambrosi (eds.), *Theater Translation in Performance*, York/London: Routledge, pp. 1-26.

Bode, Sabine (2004): *Die vergessene Generation: Kriegskinder brechen ihr Schweigen*, Stuttgart: Klett-Cotta.

Boenisch, Peter M. (2002): *körPERformance 1.0: Theorie und Analyse von Körper- und Bewegungsdarstellungen im zeitgenössischen Theater*, Munich: ePodium.

Bonwetsch, Bernd (2009): *Kriegskindheit und Nachkriegsjugend in zwei Welten: Deutsche und Russen blicken zurück*, Essen: Klartext.

Böhme, Gernot (2013 [1995]): *Atmosphäre: Essays zur neuen Ästhetik*, Frankfurt a.M.: Suhrkamp.

Bohnsack, Ralf (2009): *Qualitative Bild- und Videointerpretation: Die dokumentarische Methode*, Opladen/Farmington Hills: Budrich.

Bolter, Jay David/Grusin, Richard (1999): *Remediation: Understanding New Media*, Cambridge/London: MIT Press.

Borzik, Rolf (2000): "Notizen." In: Tanztheater Wuppertal Pina Bausch (ed.), *Rolf Borzik und das Tanztheater*, Siegen: Bonn & Fries, p. 99.

Bourdieu, Pierre (2010 [1972]): *Outline of a Theory of Practice*, translated by Richard Nice, Cambridge: Cambridge University Press.

Bourdieu, Pierre (1990 [1980]): "Practical Logics." In: Pierre Bourdieu, *The Logic of Practice*, translated by Richard Nice, Cambridge: Polity Press, pp. 143-270.

Bourdieu, Pierre (2005 [1982]): *Language and Symbolic Power*, translated by Gino Raymond, Cambridge: Polity Press.
Bourdieu, Pierre (1993): "Narzißtische Reflexivität und wissenschaftliche Reflexivität." In: Eberhard Berg/Martin Fuchs (eds.), *Kultur, soziale Praxis, Text: Die Krise der ethnographischen Repräsentation*, Frankfurt a.M.: Suhrkamp, pp. 365-374.
Bourdieu, Pierre (2014 [1992]): *The Rules of Art: Genesis and Structure of the Literary Field*, translated by Susan Emanuel, Reprint, Cambridge: Polity Press.
Bourdieu, Pierre/Wacquant, Loïc J. D. (1992): *An Invitation to Reflexive Sociology*, Cambridge: Polity Press.
Bourriaud, Nicolas (2002 [1998]): *Relational Aesthetics*, translated by Simon Pleasance and Fronza Woods, Dijon: Les presses du réel.
Brandl-Risi, Bettina (2015): "Die Affekte des Publikums." In: Claudia Emmert/Jessica Ulrich/Kunstpalais Erlangen (eds.), *Affekte*, Berlin: Neofelis, pp. 232-245.
Brandstetter, Gabriele (2015 [1995]): *Poetics of Dance: Body, Image, and Space in the Historical Avant-Gardes*, translated by Elena Polzer and Mark Franco, Oxford University Press: Oxford.
Brandstetter, Gabriele (2002): "Figur und Inversion: Kartographie als Dispositiv von Bewegung." In: Gabriele Brandstetter/Sibylle Peters (eds.), de figura: Rhetorik – Bewegung – Gestalt, Munich: Fink, pp. 247-264.
Brandstetter, Gabriele (2006): "Tanztheater als 'Chronik der Gefühle': Fall-Geschichten von Pina Bausch und Christoph Marthaler." In: Margit Bischof/Claudia Feest/Claudia Rosiny (eds.), *e_motion: Jahrbuch der Gesellschaft für Tanzforschung* 16, Hamburg: LIT, pp. 17-34.
Brandstetter, Gabriele/Klein, Gabriele (eds.) (2013): *Dance [and] Theory*, Bielefeld: transcript.
Brandstetter, Gabriele/Klein, Gabriele (eds.) (2015a [2007]): *Methoden der Tanzwissenschaft: Modellanalysen zu Pina Bauschs "Le Sacre du Printemps/Das Frühlingsopfer,"* 2nd ed., Bielefeld: transcript.
Brandstetter, Gabriele/Klein, Gabriele (eds.) (2015b): "Bewegung in Übertragung: Methodische Überlegungen am Beispiel von Le Sacre du Printemps/Das Frühlingsopfer." In: Gabriele Brandstetter/Gabriele Klein (eds.), *Methoden der Tanzwissenschaft: Modellanalysen zu Pina Bauschs "Le Sacre du Printemps/Das Frühlingsopfer,"* Bielefeld: transcript, pp. 11-28.
Braun, Rudolf/Gugerli, David (1993): *Macht des Tanzes, Tanz der Mächtigen*, Munich: C.H. Beck.
Breidenstein, Georg/Hirschauer, Stefan/Kalthoff, Herbert/Nieswand, Boris (eds.) (2013): Ethnografie: *Die Praxis der Feldforschung*, Konstanz: UVK.
Brinkmann, Stephan (2013): *Bewegung erinnern: Gedächtnisformen im Tanz*, Bielefeld: transcript.
Brinkmann, Stephan (2015): "'Ihr seid die Musik!' Zur Einstudierung von Sacre aus tänzerischer Perspektive." In: Brandstetter, Gabriele/Klein, Gabriele (eds.), *Methoden der Tanzwissenschaft: Modellanalysen zu Pina Bauschs "Le Sacre du Printemps/Das Frühlingsopfer,"* Bielefeld: transcript, pp. 143-163.
Buikema, Rosemarie/Van der Tuin, Iris (eds.) (2009): *Doing Gender in Media, Art and Culture*, London/New York: Routledge.
Burri, Regula Valérie/Evert, Kerstin/Peters, Sybille/Pilkington, Esther /Ziemer, Gesa (eds.) (2014): *Versammlung und Teilhabe: Urbane Öffentlichkeiten und performative Künste*, Bielefeld: transcript.
Burkart, Günter (2018): "Liebe: historische Formen und theoretische Zugänge." In: Beate Kortendiek/Birgit Riegraf/Katja Sabisch (eds.), *Handbuch Interdisziplinäre Geschlechterforschung*, vol. 2, Wiesbaden: VS, pp. 1093-1102.
Burkert, Matthias (2019): "Das dumpfe Geräusch über die Steppe galoppierender Rinderherden/ The dull sound of cattle herds galloping across plains." In: Tanztheater Wuppertal Pina Bausch (ed.), *Spielzeit/Season 2019-2020*, Wuppertal, pp. 56-65.
Busch, Kathrin (ed.) (2015): *Anderes Wissen*, Paderborn: Fink.
Butler, Judith (1990): *Gender Trouble*, London/New York: Routledge.

Butler, Judith (2015): *Notes Toward a Performance Theory of Assembly,* Cambridge/London: Harvard University Press.

Caduff, Corina/Siegenthaler, Fiona/Wälchli, Tan (eds.) (2010): *Kunst und künstlerische Forschung,* Zurich: Züricher Jahrbuch der Künste.

Camurri, Antonio/Mazzarino, Barbara/Ricchetti, Matteo/Timmers, Renee/Volpe, Gualtiero (2004): "Multimodal Analysis of Expressive Gesture in Music and Dance Performances." In: Antonio Camurri/Gualtiero Volpe (eds.), *Gesture-Based Communication in Human-Computer Interaction: 5th International Gesture Workshop 2003,* Wiesbaden: Springer, pp. 20-39.

Carlson, Marvin (2004 [1996]): *Performance: A Critical Introduction,* 2nd ed., London/New York: Routledge.

Cébron, Jean (1990): "Das Wesen der Bewegung: Studienmaterial nach der Theorie von Rudolf von Laban." In: Urs Dietrich (ed.), *Eine Choreographie entsteht: Das kalte Gloria,* Essen: Die Blaue Eule, pp. 73-98.

Chabrier, Jean-Paul (2010): *Une Reine En Exil: Un tombeau de Philippine Bausch,* Arles Cedex: Actes Sud-Papiers.

Charmaz, Kathy (2006): *Constructing Grounded Theory: A Practical Guide Through Qualitative Analysis,* London/Los Angeles: Sage.

Clarke, Adele E. (2005): *Situational Analysis: Grounded Theory After the Postmodern Turn,* London/Los Angeles: Sage.

Climenhaga, Royd (2008): *Pina Bausch,* London: Routledge.

Climenhaga, Royd (ed.) (2012): *The Pina Bausch Sourcebook: The Making of Tanztheater,* London: Routledge.

Copeland, Roger (1993): "Dance Criticism and Descriptive Bias." In: *Dance Theatre Journal* 10/3, pp. 26-32.

Copeland, Roger/Cohen, Marshall (eds.) (1983): *What is Dance? Readings in Theory and Criticism,* Oxford: University Press.

Cramer, Franz Anton (2013): "Body, Archive." In: Gabriele Brandstetter/Gabriele Klein (eds.), *Dance [and] Theory,* Bielefeld: transcript, pp. 219-221.

Cvejic, Bojana/Vujanović, Ana (2012): *Public Sphere by Performance,* Berlin: b_books.

Dahms, Sybille (2010): *Der konservative Revolutionär: Jean Georges Noverre und die Ballettreformen des 18. Jahrhunderts,* Munich: epodium.

Dätsch, Christiane (ed.) (2018): *Kulturelle Übersetzer: Kunst und Kulturmanagement im transkulturellen Kontext,* Bielefeld: transcript.

Davidson, Donald (2001 [1984]): *Inquiries into Truth and Interpretation,* 2nd ed., Oxford: Clarendon Press.

Davis, Tracy C. (2008): *The Cambridge Companion to Performance Studies,* Cambridge/London: Cambridge University Press.

Debray, Régis (1997): *Transmettre,* Paris: Odile Jacob.

Deck, Jan/Sieburg, Angelika (eds.) (2008): *Paradoxien des Zuschauens: Die Rolle des Publikums im zeitgenössischen Theater,* Bielefeld: transcript.

Derrida, Jacques (1981 [1972]): *Positions,* translated by Alan Bass, London: Athlone Press.

Derrida, Jacques (1984): "Différance." In: ibid.: *Margins of Philosophy,* translated by Alan Bass, Chicago: University of Chicago Press, pp. 1-27.

Derrida, Jacques (1998 [1996]): *Monolingualism of the Other: or, The Prosthesis of Origin,* translated by Patrick Mensah, Stanford: Stanford University Press.

Derrida, Jacques (2006 [1993]): *Specters of Marx: The State of the Debt, the Work of Mourning and the New International,* translated by Peggy Kamuf, New York: Routledge.

Derrida, Jacques (2007 [1986]): *Schibbolet: Für Paul Celan,* 4th ed., translated by Wolfgang Sebastian Baur, Vienna: Passagen.

Derrida, Jacques/Roudinesco, Elisabeth (2004): *For What Tomorrow… A Dialogue,* translated by Jeff Fort, Stanford: Stanford University Press.

Dewey, John (1958 [1929]): *Experience and Nature,* 2nd ed., New York: Dover Publications.

Diers, Michael (2015): "Dis/tanzraum: Ein kunsthistorischer Versuch über die politische Ikonografie von Pina Bausch's Le Sacre du Printemps." In: Gabriele Brandstetter/Gabriele Klein (eds.), *Methoden der Tanzwissenschaft: Modellanalysen zu Pina Bauschs "Le Sacre du Printemps/Das Frühlingsopfer,"* Bielefeld: transcript, pp. 251-274.

Dinkla, Söke/Leeker, Martina (2002): *Tanz und Technologie/Dance and Technology: Auf dem Weg zu medialen Inszenierungen/Moving towards Media Production,* Berlin: Alexander.

Dombois, Florian/Bauer, Ute M./Mareis, Claudia/Schwab, Michael (eds.) (2012): *Intellectual Birdhouse: Artistic Practice as Research,* London: Koenig Books.

Düttmann, Alexander García (2001): "Von der Übersetzbarkeit." In: Hart Nibbrig, Christiaan Lucas (eds.), *Übersetzen: Walter Benjamin,* Frankfurt a.M.: Suhrkamp.

Eberhard-Kaechele, Marianne (2007): "Tabellarische Arbeitshilfen zur Diagnostik und Interventionsplanung mit dem KMP." In: Susanne Bender/Sabine Koch (eds.), *Movement Analysis – The Legacy of Laban, Bartenieff, Lamb and Kestenberg,* Berlin: Logos, pp. 65-87.

Eiermann, André (2009): *Postspektakuläres Theater: Die Alterität der Aufführung und die Entgrenzung der Künste,* Bielefeld: transcript.

Eikels, Kai van (2013): *Die Kunst des Kollektiven: Performance zwischen Theater, Politik und Sozio-Ökonomie,* Paderborn: Fink.

Endicott, Jo Ann (2007): "Die Heldin: Pina Bausch." In: *ballett tanz* 08/09, pp. 43-47.

Endicott, Jo Ann (2009): *Warten auf Pina: Aufzeichnungen einer Tänzerin,* Berlin: Henschel.

Engert, Kornelia/Krey, Björn (2013): "Das lesende Schreiben und das schreibende Lesen: Zur epistemischen Arbeit an und mit wissenschaftlichen Texten." In: *Zeitschrift für Soziologie* 42/5, pp. 366-384.

Englhart, Andreas (2008): *Das Theater des Anderen: Theorie und Mediengeschichte einer existenziellen Gestalt von 1800 bis heute,* Bielefeld: transcript.

Esterházy, Péter (2001): "Pourquoi Un Hommage à Pina Bausch." In: Théâtre de la Ville (ed.), *Viktor de Pina Bausch,* Paris: L'Arche Editeur, pp. 20-23.

Fischer-Lichte, Erika (1997): *Die Entdeckung des Zuschauers: Paradigmenwechsel auf dem Theater des 20. Jahrhunderts,* Tübingen/Basel: A. Franke.

Fischer-Lichte, Erika (2008 [2004]): *The Transformative Power of Performance: A New Aesthetics,* London/New York: Routledge.

Fischer-Lichte, Erika (2004): "Einleitende Thesen zum Aufführungsbegriff." In: Erika Fischer-Lichte/Clemens Risi/Jens Roselt: *Kunst der Aufführung – Aufführung der Kunst*, Berlin: Theater der Zeit, pp. 11-26.

Fischer-Lichte, Erika (2007 [1983]): *Semiotik des Theaters: Ein System der theatralischen Zeichen*, vol. 1, 5th ed., Tübingen: Günter Narr.

Fischer-Lichte, Erika/Horn, Christian/Umathum, Sandra/Warstat, Matthias (eds.) (2001): *Wahrnehmung und Medialität*, Tübingen/Basel: A. Francke.

Fischer-Lichte, Erika/Risi, Clemens/Roselt, Jens (2004b): *Kunst der Aufführung – Auf-führung der Kunst*, Berlin: Theater der Zeit.

Foster, Susan Leigh (1986): *Reading Dancing: Bodies and Subjects in Contemporary American Dance*, Berkeley/Los Angeles: University Press of California.

Foster, Susan Leigh (2019): *Valuing Dance: Commodities and Gifts in Motion*, Oxford: Oxford University Press.

Foucault, Michel (1985 [1984]): *The History of Sexuality, vol. 2: The Usage of Pleasure*, translated by Robert Hurley, London: Penguin Books.

Foucault, Michel (1984): "What is Enlightenment?" In: Paul Rabinow (ed.), *The Foucault Reader*, New York: Pantheon, pp. 32-50.

Foucault, Michel (2007 [1978]) "What is Critique?" In: Michel Foucault: *The Politics of Truth*, edited by Sylvère Lotringer, translated by Lysa Hochroth and Catherine Porter, Los Angeles: Semiotext(e).

Foucault, Michel (2003 [1994]): "Diskussion vom 20. Mai 1978." In: Michel Foucault: *Schriften in 4 Bänden: Dits et Ecrits IV*, edited by Daniel Defert and François Ewald, translated by Michael Bischoff, Ulrike Bokelmann, Horst Brühmann, Hans-Dieter Gondek, Hermann Kocyba und Jürgen Schröder, Frankfurt a.M.: Suhrkamp, pp. 25-43.

Foucault, Michel (2006 [2001]): *The Hermeneutics of the Subject: Lectures at the Collège de France, 1981-1982*, edited by Frédéric Gros, translated by Graham Burchell, New York: Picador.

Franco, Mark (1993): *Dance as Text: Ideologies of the Baroque Body*, Cambridge: Cambridge University Press.

Fränzel, Dieter E./Widmann, Rainer (2008 [2006]): *Sounds like Whoopataal: Wuppertal in der Welt des Jazz*, edited by JAZZ Age Wuppertal, Essen: Klartext.

Fraser, Andrea (2005): "From the Critique of Institutions to an Institution of Critique." In: *Artforum* 44/1, pp. 278-286.

Frei Gerlach, Franziska/Kreis-Schink, Annette/Opitz, Claudia/Ziegler, Béatrice (eds.) (2003): *Körperkonzepte/Concepts du corps: Interdisziplinäre Studien zur Geschlechterforschung/Contributions aux études genre interdisciplinaire*, Münster: Waxmann.

Fuchs, Martin (2009): "Reaching out; or, Nobody Exists in one Context only: Society as Translation." In: *Translation Studies* 2/1, pp. 21-40.

Fukuyama, Francis (1992): *The End of History and the Last Man*, New York: Free Press.

Garfinkel, Harold (1967): *Studies in Ethnomethodology*, New Jersey: Prentice-Hall.

Garfinkel, Harold (1988): "Evidence for Locally Produced, Naturally Accountable Phenomena of Order, Logic, Reason, Meaning, Method, etc. In and as of the Essential Quiddity of Immortal Ordinary Society (I of IV): An Announcement of Studies." In: *Sociological Theory* 6/1, pp. 10-39.

Garfinkel, Harold/Sacks, Harvey (1986): "On Formal Structures of Practical Actions." In: Harold Garfinkel (ed.), *Ethnomethodological Studies of Work*, London/New York: Routledge, pp. 160-193.

Gebauer, Gunter/Alkemeyer, Thomas/Boschert, Bernhard/Flick, Uwe/Schmidt, Robert (eds.) (2004): *Treue zum Stil: Die aufgeführte Gesellschaft*, Bielefeld: transcript.

Gebauer, Gunter/Schmidt, Robert (2013): "Aspekte des Performativen im Sport und der Arbeitswelt." In: Erika Fischer-Lichte (ed.), *Performing the Future: Die Zukunft der Performativitätsforschung*, Munich: Fink, pp. 191-202.

Geitel, Klaus (2005): *Zum Staunen geboren: Stationen eines Musikkritikers*, Henschel: Berlin.

Geitel, Klaus (2019): "Letzter Tango in Wuppertal: Pina Bausch choreografiert 'Herzog Blaubarts Burg.'" In: Klaus Geitel: *Tanzkritiken: Man ist kühn genug, um unmodern zu sein; 1959-1979*, Henschel: Berlin, pp. 286-288.

Geertz, Clifford (2017 [1973]): *The Interpretation of Cultures: Selected Essays*, New York: Basic Books.

Genette, Gérard (1997 [1987]): *Paratexts: Thresholds of Interpretation*, translated by Jane E. Lewin, Cambridge: Cambridge University Press.

Gerhards, Jürgen (ed.) (1997): *Soziologie der Kunst: Produzenten, Vermittler und Rezipienten*, Wiesbaden: Springer.

Giddens, Anthony (1979): *Central Problems in Social Theory: Action, Structure and Contradiction in Social Analysis*, Berkeley: University of California Press.

Göbel, Hanna Katharina (2016): "Artefakte." In: Robert Gugutzer/Gabriele Klein/Michael Meuser (eds.), *Handbuch Körpersoziologie*, vol. 2: Forschungsfelder und methodische Zugänge, Wiesbaden: Springer, pp. 29-42.

Goethe, Johann Wolfgang von (2012 [1792]): *Campaign in France*, translated by Robert Farie, edited by Ricardo Cunha Mattos Portella, Scotts Valley, CA: CreateSpace Independent Publishing Platform.

Goffman, Erving (1959): *The Presentation of Self in Everyday Life*, New York: Doubleday Anchor Books.

Goffman, Erving (1963): *Behavior in Public Places: Notes on the Social Organization of Gatherings*, New York: The Free Press.

Goffman, Erving (1974): *Frame Analysis: An Essay on the Organization of Experience*, Cambridge/Massachusetts: Harvard University Press.

Großmann, Mechthild (2000): "An Rolf zu denken ist schön, ihn zu beschreiben nicht möglich." In: Tanztheater Wuppertal Pina Bausch (ed.), *Rolf Borzik und das Tanztheater*, Siegen: Bonn & Fries, pp. 92-93.

Gumbrecht, Hans Ulrich (2004): *Production of Presence: What Meaning Cannot Convey*, Stanford: Stanford University Press.

Gumbrecht, Hans Ulrich (2012): *Präsenz*, Berlin: Suhrkamp.

Gugutzer, Robert (2016): "Leib und Körper als Erkenntnissubjekte." In: Robert Gugutzer/Gabriele Klein/Michael Meuser (eds.), *Handbuch Körpersoziologie*, vol. 2: Forschungsfelder und methodische Zugänge, Wiesbaden: Springer, pp. 381-394.

Haacke, Wilmont (1953): *Handbuch des Feuilletons*, Emsdetten: Lechte.

Habermas, Jürgen (2008 [1962]): *The Structural Transformation of the Public Sphere: An Inquiry into a Category of Bourgeois Society*, Cambridge: Polity Press.

Habermas, Jürgen (1987 [1968]): *Knowledge and Human Interests*, translated by Jeremy J. Shapiro, Cambridge: Polity Press.

Haitzinger, Nicole (2009): *Vergessene Traktate – Archive der Erinnerung: Zu Wirkungskonzepten im Tanz von der Renaissance bis Ende des 18. Jahrhunderts*, Munich: epodium.

Haitzinger, Nicole/Jeschke, Claudia (eds.) (2011): *Tanz & Archiv 3: Historiographie*, Munich: epodium.

Handke, Peter (2002 [1966]): "Offending the Audience." In: Margaret Herzfeld-Sander (ed.), *Contemporary German Plays II*, New York: Continuum, pp. 23-50.

Hall, Stuart (2018 [1994]): *Identity and Diaspora: Essential Essays, vol. 2*, Durham: Duke University Press.

Hall, Stuart (2007): "Encoding, Decoding." In: Simon During (ed.), *The Cultural Studies Reader*, London/New York: Routledge, pp. 477-487.

Hirschauer, Stefan (2001): "Ethnografisches Schreiben und die Schweigsamkeit des Sozialen: Zu einer Methodologie der Beschreibung." In: *Zeitschrift für Soziologie* 30/6, pp. 429-451.

Hirschauer, Stefan (2004): "Praktiken und ihre Körper: Über materielle Partizipanden des Tuns." In: Karl H. Hörning/Julia Reuter (eds.), *Doing Culture: Neue Positionen zum Verhältnis von Kultur und sozialer Praxis*, Bielefeld: transcript, pp. 73-91.

Hirschauer, Stefan (2008): "Körper macht Wissen – Für eine Somatisierung des Wissensbegriffs." In: Karl-Siegbert Rehberg (ed.), *Die Natur der Gesellschaft: Verhandlungen des 33. Kongresses der Deutschen Gesellschaft für Soziologie in Kassel*, Frankfurt a.M.: Campus.

Hirschauer, Stefan (2016): "Verhalten, Handeln, Interagieren: Zu den mikrosoziologischen Grundlagen der Praxistheorie." In: Hilmar Schäfer (ed.), *Praxistheorie: Ein Forschungsprogramm*, Bielefeld: transcript, pp. 45-67.

Hiß, Guido (1993): *Der theatralische Blick: Einführung in die Aufführungsanalyse*, Berlin: Reimer.

Hoghe, Raimund/Weiss, Ulli (2016 [1981]): *Bandoneon: Working with Pina Bausch*, translated by Penny Black, London: Oberon Books.

Hoghe, Raimund (1987): *Pina Bausch – Tanztheatergeschichten*, Frankfurt a.M.: Suhrkamp.

Hölderlin, Friedrich (2019 [1797/99]): *Hyperion, or the Hermit in Greece*, translated by Howard Gaskill, Cambridge: Open Book Publishers, pp. 34-36.

Howard, Patricia (2014): "A Voice for Orpheus: Expression and Technique in Mid-Eighteenth-Century Singing." In: MVSICES. 3, *Collana de Szudi Musicali Diretta da Roberto Carnevale e Marina Leonardi*, Palermo: NeoPoiesis Press, pp. 3-40.

Huschka, Sabine (2002): *Moderner Tanz: Konzepte – Stile – Utopien*, Reinbek bei Hamburg: Rowohlt.

Huschka, Sabine (ed.) (2009): *Wissenskultur Tanz: Historische und zeitgenössische Vermittlungsakte zwischen Praktiken und Diskursen*, Bielefeld: transcript.

Husemann, Pirkko (2009): *Choreografie als kritische Praxis: Arbeitsweisen bei Xavier Le Roy und Thomas Lehmen*, Bielefeld: transcript.

Husel, Stefanie (2014): *Grenzwerte im Spiel: Die Aufführungspraxis der britischen Kompanie "Forced Entertainment"; Eine Ethnografie*, Bielefeld: transcript.

Illies, Florian (2001): *Generation Golf: Eine Inspektion*, Frankfurt a.M.: Fischer.

Jäger, Ludwig (2004a): "Die Verfahren der Medien: Transkribieren – Adressieren – Lokalisieren." In: Jürgen Fohrmann/Erhard Schüttpelz (eds.), *Die Kommunikation der Medien*, Tübingen: Niemeyer, pp. 69-79.

Jäger, Ludwig (2004b): "Störung und Transparenz: Skizze zur performativen Logik des Medialen." In: Sybille Krämer (ed.), *Performativität und Medialität*, Munich: Fink, pp. 35-73.

Jäger, Ludwig (2010): "Intermedialität – Intramedialität – Transkriptivität." In: Arnulf Deppermann/Angelika Linke (eds.), *Sprache intermedial: Stimme und Schrift, Bild und Ton*, Berlin/New York: De Gruyter, pp. 301-324.

Jäger, Ludwig (2013): "Rahmenbrüche und ihre transkriptive Bearbeitung." In: Uwe Wirth (ed.), *Rahmenbrüche: Rahmenwechsel*, Berlin: Kadmos, pp. 77-94.

Jäger, Ludwig/Stanitzek, Georg (eds.) (2002): *Transkribieren – Medien/Lektüre*, Munich: Fink.

Janus, Ludwig (ed.) (2012 [2006]): *Geboren im Krieg: Kindheitserfahrungen im 2. Weltkrieg und ihre Auswirkungen*, 2nd ed., Gießen: Psychosozial.

Jeschke, Claudia (1983): *Tanzschriften: Ihre Geschichte und Methode; Die illustrierte Darstellung eines Phänomens von den Anfängen bis zur Gegenwart*, Bad Reichenhall: Schubert.

Jeschke, Claudia (1999): *Inventarisierung von Bewegung: Tanz als BewegungsText; Analysen zum Verhältnis von Tanztheater und Gesellschaftstanz (1910-1965)*, with Cary Rick, Tübingen: Niemeyer.

Jochim, Annamira (2008): *Meg Stuart: Bild in Bewegung und Choreographie*, Bielefeld: transcript.

Johnson, Barbara (2003): *Mother Tongues: Sexuality, Trials, Motherhood, Translation*, Cambridge, M.A.: Harvard University Press.

Jooss, Kurt (1957): "Gedanken über Stilfragen im Tanz." Lecture, September 23, 1957. In: Kurt Jooss: *Schrift 5*, Essen: Folkwang-Offizin der Folkwangschule für Gestaltung.

Jooss, Kurt (1993): "Tanztheater und Theatertanz." In: Hedwig Müller/Patricia Stöckemann (eds.), *"...jeder Mensch ist ein Tänzer": Ausdruckstanz in Deutschland zwischen 1900 und 1945*, Gießen: Anabas, pp. 76-77.

Kalthoff, Herbert (2011): "Beobachtung und Komplexität: Überlegungen zum Problem der Triangulation." In: *Sozialer Sinn* 11/2, pp. 353-365.

Kalthoff, Herbert/Hirschauer, Stefan/Lindemann, Gesa (eds.) (2008): *Theoretische Empirie: Zur Relevanz qualitativer Forschung*, Frankfurt a.M.: Suhrkamp.

Kant, Immanuel (1914): *Kants gesammelte Schriften, vol. 16: Handschriftlicher Nachlass 3: Logik;* edited by the Preußische Akademie der Wissenschaften, Berlin: Georg Reimer.

Kányádi, Sándor (1999): *Kikapcsolódás/Entspannung: Versek/Gedichte;* Zweisprachig ungarisch/deutsch, translated by Franz Hodjak, Bucharest: Kriterion.

Kastner, Jens (2010): "Zur Kritik der Kritik der Kunstkritik: Feld- und hegemonietheoretische Einwände." In: Stefan Nowotny/Garald Raunig (eds.), *Kunst der Kritik*, Vienna: Turia + Kant, pp. 125-147.

Katz, Elihu/Bumler, Jay G./Gurevitch, Michael (1974): "Utilization of Mass Communication by the Individual." In: Elihu Katz/Jay G. Bumler/ Michael Gurevitch (eds.), *The Uses of Mass Communications*, Beverly Hills: Sage, pp. 19-34.

Keazor, Henry/Liptay, Fabienne/Marschall, Susanne (2011): "Laokoon Reloaded: Vorwort." In: Henry Keazor/ Fabienne Liptay/Susanne Marschall (eds.), *Filmkunst: Studien an den Grenzen der Künste und Medien*, Marburg: Schüren, pp. 7-12.

Kelter, Katharina/Skrandies, Timo (2016): *Bewegungsmaterial: Produktion und Materialität in Tanz und Performance*, Bielefeld: transcript.

Kennedy, Antja (2007): "Laban Bewegungsanalyse: Eine Grundlage für Bewegung und Tanz." In: Susanne Bender/Sabine Koch (eds.), *Movement Analysis – The Legacy of Laban, Bartenieff, Lamb and Kestenberg*, Berlin: Logos, pp. 24-29.

Kennedy, Antja (2015): "Methoden der Bewegungsbeobachtung: Die Laban/Bartenieff Bewegungsstudien." In: Gabriele Brandstetter/Gabriele Klein (eds.), *Methoden der Tanzwissenschaft: Modellanalysen zu Pina Bauschs "Le Sacre du Printemps/Das Frühlingsopfer,"* Bielefeld: transcript, pp. 65-79.

Kestenberg Amighi, Janet (1999): *The Meaning of Movement: Developmental and Clinical Perspectives of the Kestenberg Movement Profile*, Amsterdam: Gordon and Breach.

Klein, Gabriele (1994): *FrauenKörperTanz: Eine Zivilisationsgeschichte des Tanzes*, Munich: Heyne.

Klein, Gabriele (ed.) (2003 [2000]): *Tanz, Bild, Medien*, 2nd ed., Münster: LIT.

Klein, Gabriele (2004): "Performing. Gender: Tanz Kunst Geschlecht." In: Krista Warnke/Berthild Lievenbrück (eds.), *Musik und Gender Studies*, Berlin: Weidler, pp. 123-134.

Klein, Gabriele (2009a): "Bodies in Translation: Tango als kulturelle Übersetzung." In: Gabriele Klein (ed.), *Tango in Translation: Tanz zwischen Medien, Kulturen, Kunst und Politik*, Bielefeld: transcript, pp.15-38.

Klein, Gabriele (ed.) (2009b): *Tango in Translation: Tanz zwischen Medien, Kulturen, Kunst und Politik*, Bielefeld: transcript.

Klein, Gabriele (2013): "Dance Theory as a Practice of Critique." In: Gabriele Brandstetter/Gabriele Klein (eds.), *Dance [and] Theory*, Bielefeld: transcript, pp. 137-150.

Klein, Gabriele (2014a): "Praktiken des Tanzens und des Forschens: Bruchstücke einer praxeologischen Tanzwissenschaft." In: Margrit Bischof/Regula Nyffeler (eds.), *Visionäre Bildungskonzepte im Tanz*, Zurich: Chronos, pp. 103-113.

Klein, Gabriele (2014b): "Praktiken des Übersetzens im Werk von Pina Bausch und dem Tanztheater Wuppertal." In: Marc Wagenbach/Pina Bausch Foundation (eds.), *Tanz erben: Pina lädt ein*, Bielefeld: transcript, pp. 23-33.

Klein, Gabriele (2015a): "Soziologie der Bewegung: Eine praxeologische Perspektive auf globalisierte Bewegungs-Kulturen." In: *Sport und Gesellschaft* 12/2, pp. 133-148.

Klein, Gabriele (2015b): "Die Logik der Praxis: Methodologische Aspekte einer praxeologischen Produktionsanalyse am Beispiel Das Frühlingsopfer von Pina Bausch." In: Gabriele Brandstetter/Gabriele Klein (eds.), *Methoden der Tanzwissenschaft: Modellanalysen zu Pina Bauschs "Le Sacre du Printemps/Das Frühlingsopfer,"* Bielefeld: transcript, pp. 123-141.

Klein, Gabriele (2015c): "'Die Treue zur Form': Gabriele Klein im Gespräch mit Barbara Kaufmann." In: Gabriele Brandstetter/Gabriele Klein (eds.), *Methoden der Tanzwissenschaft: Modellanalysen zu Pina Bauschs "Le Sacre du Printemps/Das Frühlingsopfer,"* Bielefeld: transcript, pp. 165-175.

Klein, Gabriele (2015d): "Ein Tanz-Erbe wählen: Über Verantwortung im Umgang mit dem Werk von Pina Bausch." *In: Theater der Zeit 3*, pp. 20-25.

Klein, Gabriele (2015e): "Künstlerische Praktiken des Ver(un)sicherns: Produktionsprozesse am Beispiel des Tanztheater Wuppertal Pina Bausch." In: *Paragrana: Internationale Zeitschrift für Historische Anthropologie* 24/1, pp. 201-208.

Klein, Gabriele (2017): "Tanz weitergeben: Tradierung und Übersetzung der Choreografien von Pina Bausch." In: Gabriele Klein/Hanna Katharina Göbel (eds.), *Performance und Praxis: Praxeologische Erkundungen in Tanz, Theater, Sport und Alltag*, Bielefeld: transcript, pp. 63-87.

Klein, Gabriele (2019a [2015]): "Zeitgenössische Choreografie." In: Gabriele Klein (ed.), *Choreografischer Baukasten: Das Buch*, 2nd ed., Bielefeld: transcript, pp. 17-49.

Klein, Gabriele (2019b [2015]): "Einleitung." In: Gabriele Klein (ed.), *Choreografischer Baukasten: Das Buch*, 2nd ed., Bielefeld: transcript, pp. 11-16.

Klein, Gabriele/Haller, Melanie (2006): "Bewegung, Bewegtheit und Beweglichkeit: Subjektivität im Tango Argentino." In: Margrit Bischof/Claudia Feest/Claudia Rosiny (eds.), *e_motion: Jahrbuch der Gesellschaft für Tanzforschung* 16, Münster: LIT, pp. 157-172.

Klein, Gabriele/Kunst, Bojana (eds.) (2012): *On Labour & Performance, Performance Research* 17/6.

Klein, Gabriele/Friedrich, Malte (2014 [2003]): *Is this real? Die Kultur des HipHop*, 5th ed., Berlin: Suhrkamp.

Klein, Gabriele/Göbel, Hanna Katharina (eds.) (2017a): Performance und Praxis: Praxeologische Erkundungen in Tanz, Theater, Sport und Alltag, Bielefeld: transcript,

Klein, Gabriele/Göbel, Hanna Katharina (2017b): "Performance und Praxis: Ein Dialog." In: Gabriele Klein/Hanna Katharina Göbel (eds.), *Performance und Praxis: Praxeologische Erkundungen in Tanz, Theater, Sport und Alltag*, Bielefeld: transcript, pp. 7-42.

Klein, Gabriele/Leopold, Elisabeth/Wieczorek, Anna (2018): "Tanz – Film – Schrift: Methodologische Herausforderungen und praktische Übersetzungen in der Tanzanalyse." In: Christine Moritz/Michael Corsten (eds.), *Handbuch Qualitative Videoanalyse*, Wiesbaden: Springer, pp. 235-258.

Klein, Gabriele/Wagenbach, Marc (2019): "'And so you see ....' On the Situatedness of Translating Audience Perceptions." In: Michaela Ott/Thomas Weber (eds.), *Situated in Translations: Cultural Communities and Media Practices*, Bielefeld: transcript. pp. 191-213.

Kleinschmidt, Katarina (2018): *Artistic Research als Wissensgefüge: Eine Praxeologie des Probens im zeitgenössischen Tanz*, Munich: epodium.

Kleihues, Alexander/Naumann, Barbara/Pankow, Edgar (eds.) (2010): *Intermedien: Zur kulturellen und artistischen Dynamik*, Zurich: Chronos.

Klementz, Constanze (2007): "Kritik versus kritische Praxis? Über die Möglichkeit einer zeitgenössischen Tanzkritik." In: Sabine Gehm/Pirkko Husemann/Katharina von Wilcke (eds.), *Wissen in Bewegung: Perspektiven der künstlerischen und wissenschaftlichen Forschung im Tanz*, Bielefeld: transcript, pp. 263-269.

Knoblauch, Hubert/Schnettler, Bernt (2012): "Videography: Analysing Video Data as a 'Focused' Ethnographic and Hermeneutical Exercise." In: *Qualitative Research* 12/3, pp. 334-356.

Knopf, Eva/Lembcke, Sophie/Recklies, Mara (eds.) (2018): *Archive dekolonialisieren: Mediale und epistemische Transformationen in Kunst, Design und Film*, Bielefeld: transcript.

Koegler, Horst (1979): "Tanztheater Wuppertal." In: *Dance Magazin* 2, pp. 51-58.

Koldehoff, Stefan/Pina Bausch Foundation (eds.) (2016): *O-Ton Pina Bausch: Interviews und Reden*, Wädenswil: Nimbus.

Kolesch, Doris (2010): "Die Geste der Berührung." In: Christoph Wulf/Erika Fischer-Lichte (eds.), *Gesten: Inszenierung, Aufführung, Praxis*, Munich: Fink, pp. 225-241.

Kracauer, Siegfried (1995 [1963]): *The Mass Ornament: Weimar Essays*, translated by Thomas Y. Levin, Cambridge, MA/London: Harvard University Press.

Krämer, Hannes (2014): *Die Praxis der Kreativität: Eine Ethno-grafie kreativer Arbeit*, Bielefeld: transcript.

Krämer, Sybille (ed.) (2004): *Performativität und Medialität*, Munich: Fink.

Krämer, Sybille (2008): *Medium. Bote. Übertragung: Kleine Metaphysik der Medialität*, Frankfurt a.M.: Suhrkamp.

Latour, Bruno (1994): "On Technical Mediation – Philosophy, Sociology, Genealogy." In: *Common Knowledge* 3/2, pp. 29-64.

Latour, Bruno (2005): *Reassembling the Social: An introduction to Actor-Network-Theory*, Oxford: Oxford University Press.

Law, John (2004): *After Method: Mess in Social Science Research*, London/New York: Routledge.

Leeker, Martina (1995): *Mime, Mimes und Technologie*, Paderborn: Fink.

Leeker, Martina (2001): *Maschinen, Medien, Performances: Theater an der Schnittstelle zu digitalen Welten*, Berlin: Alexander.

Leeker, Martina/Schipper, Imanuel/Beyes, Timon (eds.) (2017): *Performing the Digital: Performativity and Performance Studies in Digital Cultures*, Bielefeld: transcript.

Legewie, Heiner (1987): "Interpretation und Validierung biographischer Interviews." In: Gerd Jüttemann/Hans Thomae (eds.), *Biographie und Psychologie*, Berlin: Springer, pp. 138-150.

Lehmann, Hans-Thies (2006 [1999]): *Postdramatic Theatre*, translated by Karen Jürs-Munby, New York: Routledge.

Lehmann, Hans-Thies (2008): "Vom Zuschauer." In: Jan Deck/Angelika Sieburg (eds.), *Paradoxien des Zuschauens: Die Rolle des Publikums im zeitgenössischen Theater*, Bielefeld: transcript, pp. 21-26.

Lepecki, André (2006): *Exhausting Dance: Performance and the Politics of Movement*, New York/London: Routledge Taylor & Francis Group.

Libonati, Beatrice (2014): *Den Hang hinauf/Su per l'erta: Gedichte und Skizzen/Poesie e Schizzi*, Wuppertal: NordPark.

Libonati, Beatrice (2017): *Kleine himmlische Oden*, Wuppertal: NordPark.

Linsel, Anne (2013): *Pina Bausch: Bilder eines Lebens*, Hamburg: Edel Books.

Longinovic, Tomislaw (2002): "Fearful Asymmetries: A Manifesto of Cultural Translation. In: *The Journal of the Midwest Modern Language Association*, vol. 35, no. 2 (2002), pp. 5–12.

Luhmann, Niklas (1995 [1984]): *Social Systems*, translated by John Bednarz, Stanford: Stanford University Press.

Luhmann, Niklas (2009 [1993]): *Law as a Social System*, translated by Klaus A. Ziegert, Oxford: Oxford University Press.

Malzacher, Florian (2007): "Dramaturgien der Fürsorge und der Verunsicherung: Die Geschichte von Rimini Protokoll." In: Miriam Dreysse/Florian Malzacher (eds.), *Experten des Alltags: Das Theater von Rimini Protokoll*, Berlin: Alexander, pp. 14-43.

Manning, Susan (1993): *Ecstasy and the Demon: The Dances of Mary Wigman*, Minnesota: University Press.

Marinetti, Christina (2013): "Transnational, Multilingual and Post-Dramatic: Rethinking the Location of Translation in Contemporary Theater." In: Silvia Bigliazzi/Peter Koffler/Paola Ambrosi (eds.), *Theater Translation in Performance*, New York/London: Routledge, pp. 27-37.

Marx, Karl (2008 [1845]): "Theses on Feuerbach." In: *Karl Marx/Friedrich Engels, The German Ideology: Including "Theses on Feuerbach" and "Introduction to the Critique of Political Economy,"* Amherst, NY: Prometheus.

Matzke, Annemarie (2014): *Arbeit am Theater: Eine Diskursgeschichte der Probe*, Bielefeld: transcript.

Mayring, Philipp (2015): *Qualitative Inhaltsanalyse: Grundlagen und Techniken*, 12th ed., Weinheim: Beltz.

Menke, Christoph (2008): "Die ästhetische Kritik des Urteils." In: *Glänta Eurozine* 4, pp. 30-34.

Mersch, Dieter (2010a): "Intransitivität – Un/Übersetzbarkeiten." In: Alexander Kleihues/Barbara Naumann/Edgar Pankow (eds.), *Intermedien: Zur kulturellen und artistischen Dynamik*, Zurich: Chronos, pp. 299-312.

Mersch, Dieter (2010b): "Meta/Dia: Zwei unterschiedliche Zugänge zum Medialen." In: *Zeitschrift für Medien- und Kulturforschung 2,* pp. 185-208.

Mersch, Dieter (2013): "Transferre/Perferre: Übersetzen als Praxis." Unpublished lecture, Universität Hamburg, January, 23, 2013. Microsoft Word File.

Mersch, Dieter (2015): "Medien des Tanzes – Tanz der Medien: Unterwegs zu einer dance literacy." In: Gabriele Brandstetter/Gabriele Klein (eds.), *Methoden der Tanzwissenschaft: Modellanalysen zu Pina Bauschs "Le Sacre du Printemps/Das Frühlingsopfer,"* Bielefeld: transcript, pp. 317-335.

Meurer, Ulrich (2012): "Gemeinsame Sequenzen: Einige Vorworte zu Übersetzung und Film." In: Ulrich Meurer (ed.), *Übersetzung und Film: Das Kino als Translationsmedium,* Bielefeld: transcript, pp. 9-44.

Meyer, Marion (2012): *Pina Bausch: Tanz kann fast alles sein,* Remscheid: Bergischer Verlag.

Meyer, Marion (2018 [2012]): *Pina Bausch: The Biography,* translated by Penny Black, London: Oberon Books Ltd.

Millet, Kate (2016 [1969]): *Sexual Politics,* New York: Columbia University Press.

Mohn, Bina Elisabeth (2015): "Kamera-Ethnografie: Vom Blickentwurf zur Denkbewegung." In: Gabriele Brandstetter/Gabriele Klein (eds.), *Methoden der Tanzwissenschaft: Modellanalysen zu Pina Bauschs "Le Sacre du Printemps/Das Frühlingsopfer,"* Bielefeld: transcript, pp. 209-230.

Mittag, Detlef R. (ed.) (1995): *Kriegskinder: Kindheit und Jugend um 1945: Zehn Überlebensgeschichten,* Berlin: Internationale Liga für Menschenrechte.

Moritz, Christine (2010): "Die Feldpartitur: Ein System zur mikroprozessualen Analyse von Videodaten." In: Michael Corsten/Melanie Krug/ibid. (eds.), *Videographie praktizieren: Herangehensweisen, Möglichkeiten und Grenzen,* Wiesbaden: Springer, pp. 163-193.

Moritz, Christine (2011): *Die Feldpartitur: Multikodale Transkription von Videodaten in der qualitativen Sozialforschung,* Wiesbaden: Springer.

Moritz, Christine (2014): "Vor, hinter, für und mit der Kamera: Viergliedriger Analyserahmen in der Qualitativen Sozialforschung." In: Christine Moritz (ed.), *Transkription von Video- und Filmdaten in der Qualitativen Sozialforschung: Multidisziplinäre Annäherungen an einen komplexen Datentypus,* Wiesbaden: Springer, pp. 17-54.

Moritz, Christine/Corsten, Michael (eds.) (2018): *Handbuch Qualitative Videoanalyse,* Wiesbaden: Springer.

Müller-Funk, Wolfgang (2012): "Transgression und dritte Räume: ein Versuch, Homi Bhabha zu lesen." In: Homi K. Bhabha, *Über kulturelle Hybridität: Tradition und Übersetzung,* edited by Anna Babka and Gerald Posselt, Vienna: Turia + Kant.

Müller, Hedwig/Servos, Norbert (1979): *Pina Bausch – Wuppertaler Tanztheater: Von Frühlingsopfer bis Kontakthof,* Cologne: Ballett-Bühnen.

Müller, Horst (2015): *Das Konzept PRAXIS im 21. Jahrhundert: Karl Marx und die Praxisdenker, das Praxiskonzept in der Übergangsperiode und die latent existierende Systemalternative,* Norderstedt: BoD.

Müller, Sophie M. (2016): *Körperliche Unfertigkeiten: Ballett als unendliche Perfektion,* Weilerswist: Velbrück.

Naveda, Luiz/Leman, Marc (2010): "The Spatiotemporal Representation of Dance and Music Gestures using Topological Gesture Analysis (TGA)." In: *Music Perceptio: An Interdisciplinary Journal* 28/1, pp. 93-111.

New York Times (ed.) (2002): *The New York Times Guide to the Arts of the 20th Century, vol. 4, 1900-1929,* Chicago: Fitzroy Dearborn Publisher.

Nietzsche, Friedrich (1997 [1874]): *Untimely Meditations,* translated by R. J. Hollingdale, Cambridge: Cambridge University Press.

Noeth, Sandra (2019): *Resilient Bodies, Residual Effects,* Bielefeld: transcript.

Ott, Michaela/Weber, Thomas (eds.) (2019): *Situated in Translations: Cultural Communities and Media Practices,* Bielefeld: transcript.

Pabst, Peter (2019): "Peter über Pina/Peter on Pina." In: *Tanztheater Wuppertal Pina Bausch (ed.), Spielzeit/Season 2019-2020,* Wuppertal, pp. 18-25.

Passow, Barbara (2011): "Jooss-Leeder Technik." In: Ingo Diehl/Frederike Lampert (eds.), *Tanztechniken 2010: Tanzplan Deutschland,* Leipzig: Henschel, pp. 96-132.

Pavis, Patrice (1988): *Semiotik der Theaterrezeption,* Tübingen: Narr.

Peters, Sibylle (ed.) (2013): *Das Forschen aller: Artistic Research als Wissensproduktion zwischen Kunst, Wissenschaft und Gesellschaft,* Bielefeld: transcript.

Rancière, Jacques (2004): *The Politics of Aesthetics: The Distribution of the Sensible,* London/New York: Continuum Inter.

Rancière, Jacques (2011 [2008]): *The Emancipated Spectator,* translated by Gregory Elliot, London/New York: Verso.

Rebentisch, Juliane (2013): *Theorien der Gegenwartskunst,* Hamburg: Junius.

Reckwitz, Andreas (2003): "Grundelemente einer Theorie sozialer Praktiken: Eine sozialtheoretische Perspektive." In: *Zeitschrift für Soziologie* 32/4, pp. 282-301.

Reckwitz, Andreas (2004): "Die Reproduktion und die Subversion sozialer Praktiken: Zugleich ein Kommentar zu Pierre Bourdieu und Judith Butler." In: Karl H. Hörning/Julia Reuter (eds.), *Doing Culture: Neue Positionen zum Verhältnis von Kultur und sozialer Praxis,* Bielefeld: transcript, pp. 40-54.

Reckwitz, Andreas (2006): *Das hybride Subjekt: Eine Theorie der Subjektkulturen von der bürgerlichen Moderne zur Postmoderne,* Weilerswist: Velbrück.

Reckwitz, Andreas (2008): "Praktiken und Diskurse: Eine sozialtheoretische und methodologische Relation." In: Herbert Kalthoff/Stefan Hirschauer/Gesa Lindemann (eds.), *Theoretische Empirie: Zur Relevanz qualitativer Forschung,* Frankfurt a.M.: Suhrkamp, pp. 188-209.

Reichert, Klaus (2003): *Die unendliche Aufgabe: Zum Übersetzen,* Munich: Carl Hanser.

Reichertz, Jo (2014): "Das vertextete Bild: Überlegungen zur Gültigkeit von Videoanalysen." In: Christine Moritz (ed.), *Transkription von Video- und Filmdaten in der Qualitativen Sozialforschung: Multidisziplinäre Annäherungen an einen komplexen Datentypus*, Wiesbaden: Springer, pp. 55-72.

Rettich, Herbert (2000): "Eine Nacht bei den Krokodilen." In: *Tanztheater Wuppertal Pina Bausch (ed.), Rolf Borzik und das Tanztheater*, Siegen: Bonn & Fries, pp. 88-89.

Ritter, Henning (2008): "Der Imperativ der Zeitgenossenschaft." In: Gabriele Mackert/Viktor Kittlausz/Winfried Pauleit/GAK Gesellschaft für aktuelle Kunst Bremen (eds.), *Blind Date: Zeitgenossschaft als Herausforderung*, Nuremberg: Verlag für moderne Kunst Nuremberg, pp. 34-43.

Robertson, Allen (1984): "Close Encounter: Pina Bausch's Radical Tanztheater is a World where Art and Life are Inextricably Interwoven." In: *Ballet News*, pp. 10-14.

Rogge, Ralf/Schulte, Armin (2003): *Solingen im Bombenhagel: Deutsche Städte im Bombenkrieg*, edited by Stadtarchiv Solingen, Gudensberg-Gleichen: Wartburg.

Rorty, Richard M. (1967): *The Lingusitic Turn: Essays in Philosophical Method*, Chicago: University Press.

Roselt, Jens (2004): "Kreatives Zuschauen – Zur Phänomenologie von Erfahrungen im Theater." In: *Der Deutschunterricht 2*, pp. 46-56.

Roselt, Jens (2008): *Phänomenologie des Theaters*, Paderborn: Fink.

Roselt, Jens/Weiler, Christel (2017): *Aufführungsanalyse: Eine Einführung*, Stuttgart: UTB.

Rosiny, Claudia (2013): *Tanz Film: Intermediale Beziehungen zwischen Mediengeschichte und moderner Tanzästhetik*, Bielefeld: transcript.

Rutherford, Jonathan (1990): "The Third Space: Interview with Homi K. Bhabha." In: Jonathan Rutherford (ed.), *Identity: Community, Culture, Difference*, London: Lawrence & Wishart, pp. 207-211.

Sasse, Sylvia/Wenner, Stefanie (eds.) (2002): *Kollektivkörper: Kunst und Politik von Verbindung*, Bielefeld: transcript.

Schäfer, Hilmar (2013): *Die Instabilität der Praxis: Reproduktion und Transformation des Sozialen in der Praxistheorie*, Weilerswist: Velbrück.

Schäfer, Hilmar (ed.) (2016a): *Praxistheorie: Ein soziologisches Forschungsprogramm*, Bielefeld: transcript.

Schäfer, Hilmar (2016b): "Praxis als Wiederholung: Das Denken der Iterabilität und seine Konsequenzen für eine Methodologie praxeologischer Forschung." In: Hilmar Schäfer (ed.), *Praxistheorie: Ein soziologisches Forschungsprogramm*, Bielefeld: transcript, pp. 137-162.

Schäfer, Hilmar/Schindler, Larissa (2016): "Schreiben." In: Robert Gugutzer/Gabriele Klein/Michael Meuser (eds.), *Handbuch Körpersoziologie, vol. 2: Forschungsfelder und methodische Zugänge*, Wiesbaden: Springer, pp. 471-486.

Schatzki, Theodore R. (1996): *Social Practices: A Wittgensteinian Approach to Human Activity and the Social*, Cambridge/London: Cambridge University Press.

Schatzki, Theodore R. (2016): "Practice Theory as Flat Ontology." In: Gert Spaargaren/Don Weenink/Machiel Lamers (eds.), *Practice Theory and Research: Exploring the Dynamics of Social Life*, London/New York: Routledge, pp. 28-42.

Schatzki, Theodore R./Knorr-Cetina, Karin D./Savigny, Eike von (eds.) (2001): *The Practice Turn in Contemporary Theory*, London/New York: Routledge.

Schechner, Richard (2003 [1988]): *Performance Theory*, 3rd ed., London/New York: Routledge.

Schechner, Richard (2013 [2003]): *Performance Studies: An Introduction*, 3rd ed., London/New York: Routledge.

Schellow, Constanze (2016): *Diskurs – Choreographien: Zur Produktivität des „Nicht" für die zeitgenössische Tanzwissenschaft*, Munich: epodium.

Schindler, Larissa (2011): *Kampffertigkeiten: Eine Soziologie praktischen Wissens*, Stuttgart: Lucius und Lucius.

Schindler, Larissa (2016): "Beobachten." In: Robert Gugutzer/Gabriele Klein/Michael Meuser (eds.), *Handbuch Körpersoziologie, vol. 2: Forschungsfelder und methodische Zugänge*, Wiesbaden: Springer, pp. 395-408.

Schindler, Larissa/Liegl, Michael (2013): "Praxisgeschulte Sehfertigkeit: Zur Fundierung audiovisueller Verfahren in der visuellen Soziologie." In: *Soziale Welt* 64/1-2, pp. 51-67.

Schlicher, Susanne (1992 [1987]): *TanzTheater: Traditionen und Freiheiten*, 2nd ed., Reinbek bei Hamburg: Rowohlt.

Schmid, Johannes C. P./Veits, Andreas/Vorrath, Wiebke (eds.) (2018): *Praktiken medialer Transformationen: Übersetzungen in und aus dem digitalen Raum*, Bielefeld: transcript.

Schmidt, Jochen (1998): *Pina Bausch: Tanzen gegen die Angst*, Munich: Econ.

Schmidt, Robert (2007): "Die Verheißungen eines sauberen Kragens: Zur materiellen und symbolischen Ordnung des Büros." In: Eva Heisler/Elke Koch/Thomas Scheffer (eds.), *Drohung und Verheißung: Mikroprozesse in Verhältnissen von Macht und Subjekt*, Freiburg:R ombach, pp. 111-135.

Schmidt, Robert (2012): Soziologie der Praktiken: Konzeptionelle Studien und empirische Analysen, Berlin: Suhrkamp.

Schmidt, Robert (2016): "Theoretisieren: Fragen und Überlegungen zu einem konzeptionellen und empirischen Desiderat der Soziologie der Praktiken." In: Hilmar Schäfer (ed.), *Praxistheorie: Ein soziologisches Forschungsprogramm*, Bielefeld: transcript, pp. 245-263.

Schmidt, Robert/Volbers, Jörg (2011): "Sitting Praxeology: The Methodological Significance of 'Public' in Theories of Social Practices." In: *Journal for the Theory of Social Behaviour* 41/4, pp. 419-440.

Schmitt, Michael/Klanke, David (2014): "Tanzt, tanzt, sonst werden wir vergessen: Pädagogik, Theatralität und Tanztheater im Spannungsfeld von Leib/Körper, Bildung und Gedächtnis." In: Andrea Bartl/Nils Ebert (eds.), *Der andere Blick der Literatur: Perspektiven auf die literarische Wahrnehmung der Wirklichkeit*, Würzburg: Königshausen & Neumann, pp. 121-139.

Schmitz, Hermann (1969): *System der Philosophie*, vol. 3, Bonn: Bouvier.

Schneider, Katja (2016): *Tanz und Text: Zu Figurationen von Bewegung und Sprache*, Munich: Kieser.

Schoenmakers, Henri/Bläske, Stefan/Kirchmann, Kay/Ruchatz, Jens (eds.) (2015): *Theater und Medien/Theatre and the Media: Grundlagen – Analysen – Perspektiven; Eine Bestandsaufnahme*, Bielefeld: transcript.

Schulze-Reuber, Rika (2008): *Das Tanztheater Pina Bausch: Spiegel der Gesellschaft*, 2nd ed., Frankfurt a.M.: Fischer.

Schulze, Gerhard (2000 [1992]): *Erlebnisgesellschaft: Kultursoziologie der Gegenwart*, 8th ed., Frankfurt a.M.: Campus.

Schulze, Janine (ed.) (2010): *Are 100 Objects Enough to Represent the Dance? Zur Archivierbarkeit im Tanz*, Munich: epodium.

Schütz, Alfred (1932): *Der sinnhafte Aufbau der sozialen Welt: Eine Einleitung in die verstehende Soziologie*, Vienna: Springer.

Seeba, Hinrich C. (2010): "'Lost in Translation': Übersetzung als Bewältigung des Unverständlichen." In: *Zeitschrift für interkulturelle Germanistik* 1/1, pp. 59-74.

Servos, Norbert (1986): "Der schöne Bastard: Ein Essay zur grenzgängerischen und notwendigen Autonomie des Tanztheaters." In: *Theater Heute*, pp. 42-51.

Servos, Norbert (1996): *Pina Bausch – Wuppertaler Tanztheater oder Die Kunst einen Goldfisch zu dressieren*, Seelze-Velber: Kallmeyer.

Servos, Norbert (2008 [2003]): *Pina Bausch: Tanztheater*, 2nd ed., Munich: K. Kieser.

Shiratori, Takaaki/Nakazawa, Atsushi/Ikeuchi, Katsushi (2004): "Detecting Dance Motion Structure through Music Analysis." In: *Automatic Face and Gesture Recognition: Proceedings;* Sixth IEEE International Conference, pp. 857-862.

Shove, Elisabeth/Pantzar, Mika/Watson, Matt (2012): *The Dynamics of Social Practice: Everyday Life and How it Changes*, Los Angeles: Sage.

Siegmund, Gerald (2006): *Abwesenheit: Eine performative Ästhetik des Tanzes*, Bielefeld: transcript.

Siegmund, Gerald (2017): "Rehearsing In-Difference: The Politics of Aesthetics in the Performances of Pina Bausch and Jérôme Bel." In: Rebekah J. Kowal/ibid./Randy Martin (eds.), *The Oxford Handbook of Dance and Politics*, Oxford: University Press, pp. 181-198.

Siegmund, Gerald (2018): "Doing the Contemporary: Pina Bausch as a Conceptual Artist." In: *Dance Research Journal*, 50/2, pp.15-30.

Simmel, Georg (1896): "Soziologische Aesthetik." In: *Die Zukunft* 17/5, pp. 204-216.

Silbermann, Alphons (1986): *Empirische Kunstsoziologie: Eine Einführung*, Wiesbaden: Springer.

Sloterdijk, Peter (1989): *Eurotaoismus: Zur Kritik der politischen Kinetik*, Frankfurt a.M.: Suhrkamp.

Sossin, Mark (2007): "History and Future of the Kestenberg Movement Profile." In: Susanne Bender/Sabine Koch (eds.), *Movement Analysis – The Legacy of Laban, Bartenieff, Lamb and Kestenberg*, Berlin: Logos, pp. 103-119.

Soja, Edward W. (1996): *Thirdspace*, Oxford: Blackwell.

Spivak, Gayatri Chakravorty (1988): *Can the Subaltern Speak?* In: Cary Nelson/Lawrence Grossberg (eds.), Marxism and the Interpretation of Culture, Urbana, IL: University of Illinois Press, pp. 271-313.

Steckelings, KH.W. (2014): *backstage*, edited by Stefan Koldehoffin Cooperation with the Pina Bausch Foundation, Wädenswil: Nimbus.

Storey, John (2003): *Cultural Studies and the Study of Popular Culture*, Edinburgh: Edinburgh University Press.

Tankard, Meryl (2000): "'He said he'd love to set me on fire.'" In: *Tanztheater Wuppertal Pina Bausch (ed.), Rolf Borzik und das Tanztheater*, Siegen: Bonn & Fries, pp. 87-88.

Tanztheater Wuppertal Pina Bausch (ed.) (2010): *Peter für Pina: Die Bühnenbilder von Peter Pabst für Stücke von Pina Bausch*, Dortmund: Kettler.

Tanztheater Wuppertal Pina Bausch (ed.) (2014): *Schönheit wagen: Tanzkleider von Marion Cito 1980-2009*, Dortmund: Kettler.

Thurner, Christina (2010): "Tänzerinnen-Traumgesichter: Das Archiv als historiografische Vision." In: Nicole Haitzinger (ed.), *Tanz & Archiv 2: Biografik*, Munich: epodium, pp. 12-21.

Thurner, Christina (2013): "Leaving and Pursuing Traces: 'Archive' and 'Archiving' in a Dance Context." In: Gabriele Brandstetter/Gabriele Klein (eds.), *Dance [and] Theory*, Bielefeld: transcript, pp. 241-245.

Thurner, Christina (2015a): *Tanzkritik: Materialien (1997-2004)*, Zurich: Chronos.

Thurner, Christina (2015b): "Prekäre physische Zone: Reflexionen zur Aufführungsanalyse von Pina Bauschs Le Sacre du printemps." In: Gabriele Brandstetter/Gabriele Klein (eds.), *Methoden der Tanzwissenschaft: Modellanalysen zu Pina Bauschs "Le Sacre du Printemps/Das Frühlingsopfer,"* Bielefeld: transcript, pp. 53-64.

Thurner, Christina/Wehren, Julia (eds.) (2010): *Original und Revival: Geschichts-Schreibung im Tanz*, Zurich: Chronos.

Torop, Peeter (2002): "Translation as Translating Culture." In: *Sign Systems Studies* 30/2, pp. 594-605.

Tröndle, Martin/Warmers, Julia (eds.) (2011): *Kunstforschung als ästhetische Wissenschaft: Beiträge zur transdisziplinären Hybridisierung von Kunst und Wissenschaft*, Bielefeld: transcript.

Turner, Victor (1982): *From Ritual to Theatre: The Human Seriousness of Play*, New York: PAJ Publications.

Turner, Victor (1986): *The Anthropology of Performance*, New York: PAJ Publications.

Vogel, Manfred (2000): "Für Rolf, den Herren der sieben Meere…" In: *Tanztheater Wuppertal Pina Bausch (ed.), Rolf Borzik und das Tanztheater*, Siegen: Bonn & Fries, pp. 84-86.

Vogel, Walter (2000): *Pina*, Munich: Quadriga.

Voltaire, François-Marie (1961 [1764]): "Conformez-vous aux temps." In: François-Marie Voltaire: *Mélanges*, edited by Jacques van den Heuvel, Paris: Gallimard, pp. 709-712.

Wagenbach, Marc/Pina Bausch Foundation (eds.) (2014): *Inheriting Dance: An Invitation from Pina*, Bielefeld: transcript.

Waldenfels, Bernhard (1990 [1987]): *Der Stachel des Fremden*, 5th ed., Frankfurt a.M.: Suhrkamp.

Waldenfels, Bernhard (1997): *Topographie des Fremden: Studien zur Phänomenologie des Fremden 1*, Frankfurt a.M.: Suhrkamp.

Waldenfels, Bernhard (2002): *Bruchlinien der Erfahrung*, Frankfurt a.M.: Suhrkamp.

Wang, Liang/Hu, Weiming/Tan, Tieniu (2003): "Recent Developments in Human Motion Analysis." In: *Pattern Recognition* 36/3, pp. 585-601.

Weber, Max (1978 [1922]): *Economy and Society, vol. 1*, edited by Guenther Roth and Claus Wittich, Berkeley: University of California Press.

Weber, Thomas (1999): "Nachwort: Zur mediologischen Konzeption von Jenseits der Bilder." In: Régis Debray (ed.), *Jenseits der Bilder: Eine Geschichte der Bildbetrachtung im Abendland*, Rodenbach: Avinus, pp. 403-411.

Wehren, Julia (2016): *Körper als Archiv in Bewegung: Choreografie als historiographische Praxis*, Bielefeld: transcript.

Weir, Lucy (2018): *Pina Bausch's Dance Theatre: Tracing the Evolution of Tanztheater*, Edinburgh: Edinburgh University Press.

Wendland, Jens (1978): "Pina Bauschs Operette 'Renate wandert aus' in Wuppertal." In: *Das Tanzarchiv: Deutsche Zeitschrift für Tanzkunst und Folklore* 2, pp. 60-61.

West, Candace/Zimmerman, Don H. (1987): "Doing Gender." In: *Gender & Society* 1, pp. 125-151.

Wetzel, Michael (2002): "Unter Sprachen – Unter Kulturen: Walter Benjamins 'Interlinearversion' des Übersetzens als Inframedialität." In: Claudia Liebrand/Irmela Schneider (eds.), *Medien in Medien*, Cologne: DuMont, pp. 154-178.

Winearls, Jane (1968 [1958]): *Modern Dance: The Jooss-Leeder Method*, 2nd ed., London: Adam & Charles Black.

Winterberg, Sonya/Winterberg, Yury (2009): *Kriegskinder: Erinnerungen einer Generation*, Berlin: Rotbuch.

Wirth, Uwe (ed.) (2002): *Performanz: Zwischen Sprachphilosophie und Kulturwissenschaften*, Frankfurt a.M.: Suhrkamp.

Wortelkamp, Isa (2002): "Flüchtige Schrift/Bleibende Erinnerung." In: Gabriele Klein/Christa Zipprich (eds.), *Tanz Theorie Text*, Münster: LIT, pp. 597-609.

Wortelkamp, Isa (2006): *Sehen mit dem Stift in der Hand: Die Aufführung im Schriftzug der Aufzeichnung*, Freiburg: Rombach.

Wortelkamp, Isa (2012): *Bewegung Lesen: Bewegung Scheiben*, Berlin: Revolver.

Wyss, Christine (2005): "Anne Martin." In: Andreas Kotte (ed.), *Theaterlexikon der Schweiz*, vol. 2, Zurich: Chronos, pp. 1189-1190.

Zanetti, Sandro (2011): "Poetische Zeitgenossenschaft." In: *Variations: Literaturzeitschrift der Universität Zürich* 19/2011, pp. 39-54.

Ziemer, Gesa (2016): Complicity: *New Perspectives on Collectivity*, transcript: Bielefeld.

2. DIGITAL PUBLICATIONS

Belkin, Ljudmila (2015): "Fremde Zeitgenossenschaften." Faust Kultur, June 5. http://faustkultur.de/2294-0-Belkin-Fremde-Zeitgenossenschaften.html#.VhuV6qKFfm3.

Boldt, Esther (2017): "Die Lust am Tanz-Text." Goethe-Institut. https://www.goethe.de/de/kul/tut/gen/tan/20894672.html.

Butler, Judith (2001): "What is Critique? An Essay on Foucault's Virtue." eipcp – european institute for progressive cultural politics, May. https://transversal.at/transversal/0806/butler/en.

Casati, Rebecca (2015): "Zig-a-zigah: Spice Girls, Kurt Cobain und Stüssy; Die neunziger Jahre waren zu allem bereit." Zeit Magazin, July 9. https://www.zeit.de/zeit-magazin/2015/28/90er-jahre-stil-kurt-cobain.

Cramer, Franz Anton (2009): "Verlorenes Wissen – Tanz als Archiv." map. media archiv performance. http://www.perfomap.de/map1/i.-bewegung-plus-archiv/verlorenes-wissen-2013-tanz-und-archiv.

Cramer, Franz Anton (2014): "Was vermag das Archiv? Artefakt und Bewegung." *map.media archiv performance*. http://www.perfomap.de/map5/instabile-ordnung-en/was-vermag-das-archiv-artefakt-und-bewegung.

Fischer, Eva-Elisabeth (2012): "Wie die Ballettkritik zur Tanzkritik wurde." Goethe-Institut, August. https://www.goethe.de/de/kul/tut/gen/tan/20364450.html.

Forsythe, William (2009): Synchronous Objects. http://synchronousobjects.osu.edu.

Forsythe, William (2010): Motion Bank. http://motionbank.org.

Hofmann, Isabella (2017): "Ein Fest der Sinne: Tanztheater Wuppertal mit 'Viktor' auf Kampnagel." Kulturport.de, February 2. https://www.kultur-port.de/index.php/blog/theater-tanz/13998-tanztheater-wuppertal-viktor-kampnagel.html.

Hölscher, Lucian (2012): "Der Zeitgenosse – eine geschichtstheoretische Begriffsbetrachtung." Ruhr-Universität Bochum. http://www.ruhr-uni-bochum.de/lehrstuhl-ng3/publikationen/hoelscher/DerZeitgenosse.pdf.

Ibacache, Javier (2010): "Was für Pina Bausch Chiles zerbrochene Liebe war," translated by Ulrike Prinz. Humboldt: Eine Publikation des Goethe Instituts, accessed March 11, 2019. http://www.goethe.de/wis/bib/prj/hmb/the/154/de6568384.html.

Kluge, Alexander (2010): "100 Heilige Abende." Welt Online, December 24. https://www.welt.de/print/die_welt/vermischtes/article11810988/100-Heilige-Abende.html.

Koegler, Horst (2009): "With a Whiff of Nostalgia: 'Uraufführung 2009' – Pina Bausch and her Tanztheater Wuppertal after their return from Chile." tanznetz, June 25. https://www.tanznetz.de/blog/15091/with-a-whiff-of-nostalgia.

Krug, Hartmut (2008): "Das Theater der 68er." Deutschlandfunk Kultur, April 9. https://www.deutschlandfunkkultur.de/johann-kresnik-theater-der-68-er-hat-viel-bewirkt.954.de.html?dram:article_id=143331.

Linsel, Anne (2009): "Die Liebe nach dem Tod." kultur.west, September 1. https://www.kulturwest.de/inhalt/die-liebe-nach-dem-tod/.

Meyer, Frank (2008): "Johann Kresnik: Das Theater der 68-er hat viel bewirkt." Deutschlandfunk Kultur, April 9. https://www.deutschlandfunkkultur.de/johann-kresnik-theater-der-68-er-hat-viel-bewirkt.1013.de.html?dram:article_id=167821.

Newis, Philippa (2016): "Como el musguito is a giddy roller coaster and well worth the ride." Bachtrack, February 13. https://bachtrack.com/de_DE/review-como-el-musguito-tanztheater-wuppertal-pina-bausch-sadlers-wells-february-2015.

Parra, Violeta (2015 [1980]): "To Be Seventeen Again (Volver a los diecisiete)," translated by Gabriela Durand. Cantos Cautivos, September 1. https://www.cantoscautivos.org/en/testimony.php?query=10738.

Pina Bausch Foundation (n.d.a): "An Invitation from Pina." Pina Bausch Foundation, accessed April 12, 2019. http://www.pina-bausch.org/en/projects/page-58.

Pina Bausch Foundation (n.d.b): "Nelken-Line: Your Videos." Pina Bausch Foundation, accessed February 8, 2019. http://www.pinabausch.org/de/projekte/dance-the-nelken-line-eure-videos.

Ploebst, Helmut (2001): "Writing about dance performance." Sarma: Laboratory for discursive practices and expanded publication, November 5. http://sarma.be/docs/977.

Pritzlaff, Dietmar Wolfgang (2007): "Die Reise nach Indien." Read-me-Net, May 22. http://diwopd.vs120040.hl-users.com/seiten_extra_redaktion/01_seiten/06_bamboo_blues.html.

Probst, Carsten (2015): "Happening in Wuppertal: Die letzte Sternstunde der Fluxusidee." Deutschlandradio Kultur, June 5. https://www.deutschlandfunkkultur.de/happening-in-wuppertal-die-letzte-sternstunde-der-fluxus idee.932.de.html?dram:article_id=321707.c

Rauterberg, Hanno (2004): "Die Feigheit der Kritiker ruiniert die Kunst." Zeit Online, January 22. https://www.zeit.de/2004/05/Kunstkritik.

Schmöe, Stefan (2013): "Himmel und Erde." Omm: Veranstaltungen & Kritiken Musiktheater. http://www.omm.de/veranstaltungen/musiktheater20132014/W-bamboo-blues-sweet-mambo.html.

Serwer, Andy (2009): "The '00s: Goodbye (at Last) to the Decade from Hell." Time Magazine, November 24. http://content.time.com/time/magazine/article/0,9171,1942973,00.html.

Siefer, Werner (2009): "Die Jahre, in denen die Welt den Turbo einlegte." Focus Magazin 50, December 7. https://www.focus.de/magazin/archiv/tid-16599/das-jahrzehnt-2000-2009-die-jahre-in-denen-die-welt-den-turbo-einlegte_aid_460506.html.

Spivak, Gayatri Chakravorty (2008): "More Thoughts on Cultural Translation." eipcp – european institute for progressive cultural politics, April. *https://transversal.at/transversal/0608/spivak/en*.

Tanzfonds Erbe (n.d.): "Förderung von künstlerischen Projekten zum Tanz im 20. Jahrhundert." Tanzfonds Erbe, accessed March 25, 2019. *https://tanzfonds.de/ueber-uns*.

3. NEWSPAPER ARTICLES AND RADIO BROADCASTS

Brown, Ismene (1999): "Entranced by the mistress of misery." In: *The Daily Telegraph*, JANUARY 29.

Croce, Arlene (1984): "Bausch's Theatre of Dejection." In: *The New Yorker*, JULY 16.

Engler, Günter (1986): "Pina Bauschs Tanztheater begeistert die Römer." In: *Westdeutsche Allgemeine Zeitung (WAZ)*, OCTOBER 13.

Fischer, Ulrich (1986): "Getanzte Kritik am traditionellen Ballett." In: *Kieler Nachrichten*, MAY 21.

Gilbert, Jenny (1999): "A legend in her own company." In: *The Critics*, JANUARY 31.

Gopnik, Blake (2007): "What is Feminist Art?" In: *The Washington Post*, APRIL 22.

Heuer, Otto (1992): "Rückkehr in die Wüste." In: *Rheinische Post*, APRIL 21.

Heyn, Ursula (1986): "Pinas zerquälte Weltsicht: Tanztheater-Revolution unter der Schwebebahn." In: *Westfalenpost*, MAY 16.

Hirsch, Waldemar (1986): "Der neue Tanzabend von Pina Bausch: Kommerz darf sein – aber die Dosierung muss stimmen." In: *Bergische Morgenpost*, MAY 24.

Keil, Klaus (2009): "Überraschendes Stück von Pina Bausch." In: *Colognische Rundschau*, JUNE 14.

Kramer, Rüdiger (1986): "Tanzabend II." In: *Ortszeit Ruhr*, JUNE.

Kuckart, Judith (1986): "Wuppertal: 'Viktor' (Pina Bausch)." *Sender Freies Berlin*, TRANSCRIPT OF RADIO BROADCAST FROM MAY 11 AT 11:45 A.M.

Kuckart, Judith (2018): "Als Pina Bausch mich durchschaute." *Neue Zürcher Zeitung*, JUNE 6. *https://www.nzz.ch/feuilleton/ja-ich-erinnere-mich-ld.1391790*.

Langer, Roland (1986): "Kompaktes Tanztheater." In: *Frankfurter Rundschau*, MAY 21.

Makrell, Judith (1999): "The agony and the ecstasy." In: *The Guardian*, JANUARY 21.

Michaelis, Rolf (1986): "Tanz bis ins Grab." In: *Die Zeit* (22), MAY 23.

Michaelis, Rolf (1992): "Todesreigen." *Zeit Online*, JANUARY 10. *https://www.zeit.de/1992/03/todesreigen*.

Newmann, Barbara (1999). "Dance: Tanztheater Wuppertal's images stay in the memory." In: *Country Life*, FEBRUARY 11.

Pappenheim, Mark (1999): "Viktor: Tanztheater Wuppertal at Sadler's Wells, London." In: *The Express*, JANUARY 30.

Parry, Jann (1999): "Did the earth move for you?" In: *The Observer Review*, JANUARY 31.

Pfeiffer, Rolf (2009): "Altes Thema mit neuen Motiven." In: *Westfälische Rundschau*, JUNE 16.

Rauterberg, Hanno (2004): "Die Feigheit der Kritiker ruiniert die Kunst." *Zeit Online*, JANUARY 22. *https://www.zeit.de/2004/05/Kunstkritik*.

Regitz, Hartmut (1986): "Einsamkeit zu zweit." In: *Rheinische Post*, MAY 16.

Rosenbaum, Wilhelm (2014): "Pina Bausch: Solingens 'schwierige' Tochter." *Solinger Tageblatt*, SEPTEMBER 28, 2014. *solinger-tageblatt.de/solingen/pina-bausch-solingens-schwierige-tochter-3984447.html*.

Scheier, Helmut (1986): "Verschlüsselte Realität." In: *Nürnberger Nachrichten*, MAY 16.

Schmidt, Jochen (1986): "Die beschädigte Welt: Pina Bauschs neues Tanzstück 'Viktor' in Wuppertal." In: *Frankfurter Allgemeine Zeitung (FAZ)*, MAY 23.

Schmidt, Jochen (1994): "Winterreise auf schwarzem Eis." In: *FAZ*, FEBRUARY 15.

Schmidt, Jochen (1996c): "Da schweigen die Mammutbäume im Walde." In: *Baseler Zeitung*, MAY 14.

Schmidt, Jochen (1999): "Wir küssen einfach zu wenig." In: *FAZ*, APRIL 12.

Schmidt, Jochen (2000): "Es qualmt, aber das Feuer ist erloschen." In: *FAZ*, MAY 8.

Schmidt, Jochen (2001): "Pina Colada am Barmer Ersatzstrand." In: *FAZ*, May 14.

Schneider, Katja (1997): "Ins Torfgrab tanzen." In: *Süddeutsche Zeitung (SZ)*, JUNE 4.

Scurla, Frank (1986): "Von einer aus den Fugen geratenen Welt." In: *WAZ*, MAY 16.

Siegmund, Gerald (1997): "Fertig zur Fleischbeschau." In: *FAZ*, MAY 31.

Sowden, Dora (1995): "Pina Bausch emerges as the 'Viktor.'" In: *The Jerusalem Post*, NOVEMBER 28.

Staude, Sylvia (1997): "Rituale in der Tiefe des Grabs." In: *Frankfurter Rundschau*, MAY 31.

Stiftet, Ralf (1998): "Das Huhn und der Blütentanz." In: *Westfälischer Anzeiger*, JUNE 6.

Strecker, Nicole (2010): "'Peter für Pina': Ein Bildband dokumentiert die Arbeit des Bühnenbildners Peter Pabst." In: *WDR 3 Mosaik*, MANUSCRIPT OF BROADCAST FROM DECEMBER 21.

Töne, Martina (2007): "Tanztheater zwischen Altar und Grab: 'Viktor' ist zurück – und ewig grüßt der Tod." In: *Westdeutsche Zeitung*, MARCH 13.

Wilink, Andreas (2014): "Lebendige Kleider." *Die Welt*, AUGUST 24. https://www.welt.de/print/wams/nrw/article131531272/Lebende-Kleider.html.

4. INTERVIEWS AND SPEECHES

Adolphe, Jean-Marc (2007): "Man weiß gar nicht, wo die Phantasie einen hintreibt," interview with Pina Bausch, March 1, 2006. In: Guy Delahaye (ed.), *Pina Bausch*, Heidelberg: Wachter, pp. 25-39.

Bausch, Pina (2007): "What Moves Me," speech on the occasion of the award of the Kyoto Prize in Kyoto on November 11. Pina Bausch Foundation. http://www.pinabausch.org/en/pina/what-moves-me.

Bausch, Pina (2016): "Etwas finden, was keiner Frage bedarf," speech at the 2007 Kyoto Prize Workshop in Arts and Philosophy. In: Stefan Koldehoff/Pina Bausch Foundation (eds.), *O-Ton Pina Bausch: Interviews und Reden*, Wädenswil: Nimbus, pp. 317-332.

Berghaus, Ruth (2016): "Wenn wir anfangen, gibt es gar nichts außer uns," interview with Pina Bausch at the Akademie der Künste der DDR, Berlin (Ost), May 29, 1987. In: Stefan Koldehoff/Pina Bausch Foundation (eds.), *O-Ton Pina Bausch: Interviews und Reden*, Wädenswil: Nimbus, pp. 91-121.

Fischer, Eva-Elisabeth (2004): "Pina Bausch über Lust," interview with Pina Bausch. In: *Süddeutsche Zeitung*, September 25/26.

Fuhrig, Dirk (2003): "Ganz außergewöhnlich wunderbar," interview with Pina Bausch. In: *ballett-tanz* 8/9, pp. 14.

Gibiec, Christiane (2016): "Wir sind uns mit unserem Körper am nächsten," interview with Pina Bausch, October 17, 1998. In: Stefan Koldehoff/Pina Bausch Foundation (eds.), *O-Ton Pina Bausch: Interviews und Reden*, Wädenswil: Nimbus, pp. 210-219.

Gleede, Edmund (2016): "5 Fragen an Pina Bausch zu ihrer Inszenierung von Glucks Orpheus und Eurydike," interview with Pina Bausch, season 1975/76. In: Stefan Koldehoff/Pina Bausch Foundation (eds.), *O-Ton Pina Bausch: Interviews und Reden*, Wädenswil: Nimbus, pp. 29-33.

Gliewe, Gert (1992): "Meine Seele weiß genau, was ich will," interview with Pina Bausch. In: *Abendzeitung*, MAY 22.

Heynkes, Jörg (2016): "Mit dem Theater wollte ich eigentlich nie etwas zu tun haben," interview with Pina Bausch, MARCH 1, 1980. In: Stefan Koldehoff/Pina Bausch Foundation (eds.), *O-Ton Pina Bausch: Interviews und Reden*, Wädenswil: Nimbus, pp. 61-65.

Koegler, Horst (ed.) (1973): "Was wollen die neuen Ballettchefs?," interview with Pina Bausch and Alfonso Catá. In: *Jahrbuch Ballett 1973: Chronik und Bilanz des Ballettjahres*, Seelze-Velber: Kallmeyer, pp. 40-41.

Michaelsen, Sven (2015): "'Ich vergesse meinen Körper sehr oft.' Der Tänzer und Choreograf Raimund Hoghe erklärt, wann er seinen Buckel schön findet – und warum er nie in den Urlaub fährt," interview with Raimund Hoghe. In: *Süddeutsche Zeitung Magazin* 21, MAY 29.

Mölter, Veit (1990): "Alle meine Informationen entstammen dem Gefühl," interview with Pina Bausch January 4, 1990. In: *Westfälische Rundschau*, JANUARY 4.

Meyer, Marion (2008): "Ich liebe und bewundere sie," interview with Peter Pabst. In: *Westdeutsche Zeitung*, NOVEMBER 11.

Panadero, Nazareth (2016): "Marta, Mia und ich: Über die Probenarbeit in München." In: Bayerisches Staatsballett (ed.), *Für die Kinder von gestern, heute und morgen: Ein Stück von Pina Bausch*, program booklet, pp. 31.

Schmidt-Mühlisch, Lothar (2000): "Der Anfang bin ich," interview with Pina Bausch. In: *Die Welt*, MAY 5.

Schmidt, Jochen (1979): "Nicht wie sich die Menschen bewegen, sondern was sie bewegt," interview with Pina Bausch, November 9, 1978. In: Hedwig Müller/Norbert Servos (eds.), *Pina Bausch – Wuppertaler Tanztheater: Von Frühlingsopfer bis Kontakthof*, Cologne: Ballett-Bühnen, pp. 5-8.

Schmidt, Jochen (1983): "Meine Stücke wachsen von innen nach außen," interview mit Pina Bausch, November 26, 1982. In: *Ballett International* 2, pp. 8-15.

Schmidt, Jochen (1996a): "Die Dinge, die wir für uns selbst entdecken, sind das Wichtigste," interview with Pina Bausch, April 21, 1982. In: Norbert Servos: *Pina Bausch – Wuppertaler Tanztheater oder Die Kunst einen Goldfisch zu dressieren*, Seelze-Velber: Kallmeyer, pp. 295-296.

Schmidt, Jochen (1996b): "Ich bin immer noch neugierig," interview with Pina Bausch, December 23, 1983. In: Norbert Servos: *Pina Bausch – Wuppertaler Tanztheater oder Die Kunst einen Goldfisch zu dressieren*, Seelze-Velber: Kallmeyer, pp. 302-303.

Schwarzer, Alice (1987): "Tanz: Besuch bei Pina Bausch," interview with Pina Bausch. In: *emma*, JULY 1. https://www.emma.de/artikel/tanztheater-pina-bausch-264046.

Schwarzer, Alice (2010): "Ein Stück für Pina Bausch," interview with Mechthild Großmann. In: *emma*, JANUARY 1. https://www.emma.de/node/264664.

Servos, Norbert (1995): "Man muss ganz wach, sensibel und empfindsam sein," interview with Pina Bausch, September 30. In: *Ballett international/tanz aktuell* 12, pp. 37-39.

Servos, Norbert (1996b): "Tanz ist die einzig wirkliche Sprache," interview with Pina Bausch, February 16, 1990. In: N.S.: *Pina Bausch – Wuppertaler Tanztheater oder Die Kunst einen Goldfisch zu dressieren,* Seelze-Velber: Kallmeyer, pp. 304-306.

Seyfarth, Ingrid (2016): "Ich bin das Publikum," interview with Pina Bausch, June 28, 1987. In: Stefan Koldehoff/Pina Bausch Foundation (eds.), *O-Ton Pina Bausch: Interviews und Reden,* Wädenswil: Nimbus, pp. 123-127.

Strecker, Nicole (2019): "Eine besondere Art von Hommage," interview with Bettina Wagner-Bergelt and Jo Ann Endicott. In: *kultur.west* 5/19, pp. 30-31.

Wenders, Wim (2009): "Wim Wenders on 9/4/09 for Pina, at the memorial ceremony." Tanztheater Wuppertal Pina Bausch. http://www.pina-bausch.de/en/pina/speeches/.

Wendland, Jens (1975): "Das Experiment ist noch nicht zu Ende," interview with Gerhard Bohner and Marion Cito. In: *Die Zeit,* February 14, 1975. https://www.zeit.de/1975/08/das-experiment-ist-noch-nicht-zu-ende.

Willemsen, Roger (2016): "Wenn ich mir ganz genau zuhöre, macht sich das Stück selber," interview with Pina Bausch, April 24, 1998. In: Stefan Koldehoff/Pina Bausch Foundation (eds.), *O-Ton Pina Bausch: Interviews und Reden,* Wädenswil: Nimbus, pp. 185-195.

Fischer, Eva-Elisabeth/Käsmann, Frieder (1994): "Das hat nicht aufgehört, mein Tanzen…": Pina Bausch im Gespräch mit Eva-Elisabeth Fischer, Munich: Bayerischer Rundfunk.

Forsythe, William (1999): *Improvisation Technologies: A Tool for the Analytical Dance Eye,* Ostfildern: Hatje Cantz. DVD.

Gsovsky, Tatjana (1985): Ein Leben für den Tanz. Die Wanderungen der Tatjana Gsovsky, Cologne: Westdeutscher Rundfunk. Documentary.

Linsel, Anne (1985): *Ein unheimlich starker Tänzer: Der Pina-Bausch-Tänzer Jan Minarik,* Cologne: Westdeutscher Rundfunk. TV documentary.

Linsel, Anne (1994): *Nelken in Indien: Pina Bausch und ihr Tanztheater Wuppertal in Indien,* Straßburg: ARTE. VT documentary.

Linsel, Anne (2006): *Pina Bausch,* Cologne: ARD und Westdeutscher Rundfunk. TV documentary.

Linsel, Anne/Hoffmann, Rainer (2010): *Tanzträume: Jugendliche tanzen Kontakthof von Pina Bausch,* DVD, Cologne: Real Fiction.

Wenders, Wim (2011): *PINA – dance, dance, otherwise we are lost,* Berlin: Neue Road Movies. DVD.

Wildenhahn, Klaus (1982): *Was tun Pina Bausch und ihre Tänzer in Wuppertal?,* Cologne/Hamburg: Norddeutscher und Westdeutscher Rundfunk. TV documentary.

6. VIDEOS/DVDS

Akerman, Chantal (1983): *One Day Pina Asked …* New York: Icarus Films. DVD.

Bausch, Pina (1990): *Die Klage der Kaiserin/La Plainte de l'Impératrice/The Plaint of the Empress,* Paris: L'Arche Édition. DVD and book.

Bausch, Pina (2013): *Probe Sacre/Une répétition du sacre/Sacre rehearsal,* Paris: L'Arche Édition. DVD and book.

Bausch, Pina/Weyrich, Pit (1979): *Le Sacre du Printemps / Das Frühlingsopfer (choreography: Pina Bausch),* Hamburg: ZDF Produktion. Dance performance documentary.

Images

PIECES

1. *Vollmond,* Wuppertal, 2006. Photo: Laurent Philippe.
2. Protest against the German Emergency Acts in Munich, 1968. © interPhoto/ Friedrich Rauch.
3. *Kontakthof,* Wuppertal, 2013. Photo: Laurent Philippe.
4. Pina Bausch in *Im Wind der Zeit,* Essen, 1969. The piece was awarded first prize at the Choreographischer Wettbewerb (a choreographic competition) in Cologne 1969. Photo: Rolf Borzik. © Pina Bausch Foundation.
5. Penelope Slinger, *Wedding Invitation,* 1973. © Penelope Slinger. All rights reserved, dacs. 2019.
6. *Fritz,* Wuppertal, 1974. Photo: Rolf Borzik. © Pina Bausch Foundation.
7. Prisoner of the National Front for the Liberation of South Vietnam, Thuong Duc, Vietnam, 1967. Photo: pfc David Epstein. Public Domain. National Archives Identifier (NAID) 531447.
8. Niki de Saint-Phalle, *She – A Cathedral,* Stockholm, 1966. © AFP via Getty Images
9. *Bluebeard: While Listening to a Taped Recording of Béla Bartók's "Duke Bluebeard's Castle,"* Venice, 1985. Photo: G. Arici/M. Smith for the Gran Teatro La Fenice di Venezia.
10. Graffiti after the nuclear disaster of Chernobyl, Eppertshausen near Frankfurt a.M., Germany, May 5, 1986. Photo: AP Photo/ Frank Rumpenhorst. © picture alliance/AP Images.
11. *Ahnen,* Wuppertal, 2014. © Oliver Look.
12. Wuppertaler Bühnen poster, 1989. Photo: Uwe Stratmann. Poster courtesy of the Wuppertaler Bühnen and singer Claudia Visca.
13. *Ahnen,* Wuppertal, 1987. Photo: Ulli Weiss. © Pina Bausch Foundation.
14. After the fall of the wall, Berlin, November 11, 1989. Section of the Berlin wall near Potsdamer Platz. Photo: John Tlumacki. © The Boston Globe via Getty Images.
15. Love Parade. Approx. 350,000 ravers near the Gedächtniskirche, Berlin, 1995. Photo: Reinhard H. Franzen.
16. *The Window Washer,* Wuppertal, 1997. Photo: Maarten Vanden Abeele.
17. *"...como el musguito en la piedra, ay si, si, si...",* Sankt Pölten, 2015. Photo: Laurent Philippe.
18. *Wiesenland,* Wuppertal, 2012. Photo: Jochen Viehoff.
19. Pina Bausch in *Danzón,* Wuppertal, 1995. Photo: Maarten Vanden Abeele.
20. US soldiers and Iraqi demonstrators in Baghdad, near Fallujah, Iraq, April 8, 2004. Photo: Ali Haider/EPA/ Shutterstock.
21. *Orpheus und Eurydike,* Wuppertal, 1975. Photo: Ulli Weiss. © Pina Bausch Foundation.
22. *Água,* Wuppertal, 2004. Photo: Gert Weigelt.

COMPANY

1. Rehearsals for *He Takes Her By The Hand And Leads Her Into The Castle, The Others Follow,* Bochum, 1978. Photo: Ulli Weiss. © Pina Bausch Foundation.
2. Pina Bausch during the filming of *The Plaint of the Empress,* Wuppertal, 1988. Photo: Detlef Erler.
3. Former Café Müller building, Solingen. Photo: Atamari. CC BY-SA 3.0.
4. Costumes made by Marion Cito for *Água.* Photos: Joachim Schmitz und Sala Seddiki.
5. Costumes made by Marion Cito for *Two Cigarettes in the Dark.* Photo: Laurent Philippe.
6. Costumes made by Marion Cito for *Água.* Photo: Laurent Philippe.
7. Set design by Peter Pabst for *The Window Washer,* November 8, 2006. Photo: Ulli Weiss. © Pina Bausch Foundation.
8. Bukhansan National Park, Seoul. Research trip for *Rough Cut,* Korea, 2004. Photo: Robert Sturm.
9. Stage by Peter Pabst for *1980 – A Piece by Pina Bausch,* Wuppertal, 1980. Photo: BPK/Walter Vogel.

10 *Rough Cut*, Wuppertal 2005. Photo: Ulli Weiss. © Pina Bausch Foundation.
11 Protagonists at the Next Wave Festival, Brooklyn Academy of Music, New York, 1997. From right to left, back to front: Andrew Ginzel, Bill T. Jones, Bob Telson, Howard Gilman, John Kelly, Joseph V. Melillo, Susan Marshall, Joanne Akalaitis, Lou Reed, Ping Chong, Pina Bausch, Jene Highstein, Kristen Jones, Merce Cunningham, Mark Morris, Harvey Lichtenstein. Photo: Joanne Savio. www.joannesavio.com.
12 Pina Bausch at her desk during a rehearsal, 1987. Photo: Bettina Filtner.
13 *Nefés*, Wuppertal, 2011. Photo: Jochen Viehoff.
14 Research trip for *"…como el musguito en la piedra, ay si, si, si…"*, Chiloé Island, Chile, 2009. Pictured: Dominique Mercy, Rainer Behr, Silvia Farias, Eddie Martinez. Photo: Robert Sturm.

WORK PROCESS

1 Frozen tuna at the old Tsukiji fish market in Tokyo. Research trip for Ten Chi, Japan. 2003. Photo: Robert Sturm.
2 Rehearsals for *I'll Do You In,* Wuppertal, 1974. Photo: KH.W. Steckelings.
3 Examples of 'questions' posed by Pina Bausch. From the exhibit *Vorsichtshalber vorsichtig: Installationen von Peter Pabst anlässlich Jubiläumsspielzeit PINA40* (Precautionary as a Precaution: Installations by Peter Pabst for the Anniversary Season PINA40), January 18 - March 14, 2014, Sculpture Park Waldfrieden, Wuppertal.
4 Stephan Brinkmann's notebook for *Wiesenland*. © Stephan Brinkmann.
5 Stephan Brinkmann's notebook for *Wiesenland*. © Stephan Brinkmann.
6 Description of the work process by Matthias Burkert, Wuppertal, 2019. From: "Das dumpfe Geräusch über die Steppe galoppierender Rinderherden." In: Tanztheater Wuppertal Pina Bausch (ed.), Spielzeit 2019-2020, Wuppertal: 2019, p. 57.
7 Unknown lady in Chichibu. Research trip for *Ten Chi,* Japan, 2003. Photo: Robert Sturm.
8 Visit to Nyírbátor, Home of the Kék Láng ensemble (Blue Flame). Research trip for *Wiesenland,* Hungary, 1999. Photo: Stephan Brinkmann.
9 Pina Bausch and the company during a concert by the Kék Láng ensemble. Research trip for *Wiesenland,* Hungary, 1999. Photo: Stephan Brinkmann.
10 Dance class under a bridge in Gokseong, Research trip for *Rough Cut,* Korea, 2004. Pictured: Michael Strecker, Melanie Maurin, Rainer Behr, Daphnis Kokkinos. Photo: Robert Sturm.
11 Members of the Tanztheater Wuppertal at Villa Grimaldi in Santiago de Chile. Research trip for *"…como el musguito en la piedra, ay si, si, si…",* Chile, 2009. Photo: Robert Sturm.
12 Pina Bausch in Kolkata. Research trip for *Bamboo Blues,* India, 2006. Photo: Martin Wälde.
13 Pina Bausch's worktable, Wuppertal, approx. 1983. Photo: BPK/Walter Vogel.
14 Prompt book for *The Window Washer,* compiled by assistant Irene Martinez-Rios. © Pina Bausch Foundation.
15 Prompt book for *Masurca Fogo,* compiled by assistant Irene Martinez-Rios. Notes penciled in by Robert Sturm after the piece was passed on. © Pina Bausch Foundation.
16 Stephan Brinkmann's notebook for *Wiesenland*. © Stephan Brinkmann.

SOLO DANCE

1 Rainer Behr in *Nefés,* Madrid, 2006. Photo: Jong-Duk Woo.
2 Camera movements, spatial paths and levels. Excerpt from the Feldpartitur digital notation software, compiled on the basis of video excerpts from the premiere of *Masurca Fogo,* April 4, 1998, Schauspielhaus Wuppertal. Solo by Beatrice Libonati. © Score: Gabriele Klein. © Videos: Pina Bausch Foundation.
3 Excerpt from the Feldpartitur digital notation software, compiled on the basis of video excerpts from the premiere of *Viktor,* May 14, 1986, Schauspielhaus Wuppertal. Solo by Anne Martin. © Score: Gabriele Klein. © Videos: Pina Bausch Foundation. Parts, repetition, variation, structure. Excerpt from the Feldpartitur digital notation software, compiled on the basis of video excerpts from the premiere of *"…como el musguito en la piedra, ay si, si, si…",* June 12, 2009, Opernhaus, Wuppertal. Solo by Dominique Mercy. © Score: Gabriele Klein. © Videos: Pina Bausch Foundation.
5 Body parts. Excerpt from the score, solo by Dominique Mercy (→4).
6 Movements of the hands and touching the body. Screenshot of the score, solo by Anne Martin (→3).
7 Show/offer. Screenshot of the score, solo by Anne Martin (→3).
8 Wipe/rub. Screenshot of the score, solo by Anne Martin (→3).
9 Drop. Screenshot of the score, solo by Anne Martin (→3).
10 Stop. Screenshot of the score, solo by Anne Martin (→3).
11 Fluttering. Screenshot of the score, solo by Anne Martin (→3).
12 Psst. Screenshot of the score, solo by Anne Martin (→3).
13 Face circle. Screenshot of the score, solo by Anne Martin (→3).
14 Measure. Screenshot of the score, solo by Anne Martin (→3).
15 Wave. Screenshot of the score, solo by Anne Martin (→3).
16 Arm movements and torso. Excerpt from the score, solo by Beatrice Libonati (→2).
17 Transferring weight. Excerpt from the score, solo by Beatrice Libonati (→2).
18 Hand movements. Excerpt from the score, solo by Beatrice Libonati (→2).
19 Hand movement and fist. Screenshot of the score, solo by Beatrice Libonati (→2).
20 Finger touch. Screenshot of the score, solo by Beatrice Libonati (→2).
21 Touching palms-body. Screenshot of the score, solo by Beatrice Libonati (→2).
22 Touching hand-foot. Screenshot of the score, solo by Beatrice Libonati (→2).
23 Head movements. Screenshot

of the score, solo by Beatrice Libonati (→2).
24 Arm movements. Screenshot of the score, solo by Dominique Mercy (→4).
25 Scooping movement. Screenshot of the score, solo by Dominique Mercy (→4).

RECEPTION

1 Public broadcast of Pina Bausch's memorial service, Wuppertal, 2009. Photo: DDP images/Lennart Preiss.
2 Pina Bausch, press conference in Düsseldorf, June 6, 2008. Photo: Michael Kneffel/Alamy Stock Photo.
3 Raimund Hoghe, *Cantatas*, Brussels 2013. © Rosa-Frank.com.
4 *Viktor*, Lyon, 1994. Photo: Guy Delahaye.
5 Program booklet, restaging of *Água*, 2005. © Pina Bausch Foundation.
6 *Palermo Palermo*, Tokyo, 2008. Photo: Jong-Duk Woo.
7 Advertisement for *Nefés*, Istanbul, 2003. Photo: Robert Sturm.

THEORY AND METHODOLOGY

1 Premiere of the film *pina* by Wim Wenders, Berlinale, Berlin, February 13, 2011. Pictured: President of Germany Christian Wulff, Donata Wenders, Wim Wenders, German Chancellor Angela Merkel. Photo: Federal Government of Germany/Guido Bergmann.
2 Advertisement for *Masurca Fogo*. Grand Theatre of the Hong Kong Cultural Center, 2001. © Leisure and Cultural Services Department (LCSD), Hong Kong.
3 Special issue stamp commemorating Pina Bausch's 75th birthday, first edition, July 1, 2015. Design: Dieter Ziegenfeuter. Photo: Wilfried Krüger. Issued by the German Ministry of Finance (BMF).
4 Advertisement for *Bamboo Blues*, Spoleto, Italy, 2009. Robert Sturm standing beside the poster photo that he shot during the research trip to Kolkata. Photo: Robert Sturm.
5 Rainer Behr in *Nefés*, Madrid, 2006. Photo: Jong-Duk Woo.
6 Pina Bausch with Texas cowboy Lonnie Rodriguez and journalist Billy Porterfield during the research trip for *Only You*, USA, 1996. Photo: Robert Pandya, courtesy of Texas Performing Arts, College of Fine Arts, University of Texas in Austin.
7 Filming *The Plaint of the Empress*, Wuppertal, 1988. Pictured: Pina Bausch, Titus Köhler and Mechthild Großmann. Photo: Detlef Erler.
8 Pina Bausch in Genoa, Italy, 1994. Photo: Joanne Savio. www.joannesavio.com.

TRANSLATING (INTO) THE PRESENT: DOING CONTEMPORANEITY

1 Pina Bausch during rehearsals for *Ahnen*, Wuppertal, 1987. Screenshot of the DVD *Pina Bausch: AHNEN ahnen; Fragments de répétition* – Rehearsal Fragments. © 2014, L'Arche Editeur, Paris.
2 Program booklet for *"...como el musguito en la piedra, ay si, si, si..."*, 2009. © Pina Bausch Foundation.
3 Reproduction of the Lichtburg, the Tanztheater Wuppertal's rehearsal space. From the exhibit *Pina Bausch and the Tanztheater*, Bonn, 2016. Photo: Jirka Jansch. © Kunst- und Ausstellungshalle der Bundesrepublik Deutschland (Art and Exhibition Hall of the Federal Republic of Germany).

Chronology of Works

Below is a list of Pina Bausch's pieces with the Tanztheater Wuppertal including the place and date of each premiere. The Pina Bausch Foundation is responsible for assigning the pieces with their official titles. In the chronology of works below, the foundation has used the titles assigned for international performances as they were chosen by Pina Bausch, even if some of them include orthographic inconsistencies.
As the titles of the pieces and their orthography are an essential part of Pina Bausch's artistic signature and because such practices of translation form a genuine component of this book, we, too, have decided to use the titles originally chosen by Pina Bausch. For more detailed information about the pieces, please consult the website of the Tanztheater Wuppertal Pina Bausch: *pina-bausch.de/en/works/*.

Fritz
January 5, 1974,
Wuppertal, Opernhaus

Iphigenie auf Tauris
April 21, 1974,
Wuppertal, Opernhaus

*Adagio – Five Songs
by Gustav Mahler*
December 8, 1974,
Wuppertal, Opernhaus

I'll Do You In
December 8, 1974,
Wuppertal, Opernhaus

Orpheus und Eurydike
May 23, 1975,
Wuppertal, Opernhaus

The Rite of Spring
December 3, 1975,
Wuppertal, Opernhaus

The Seven Deadly Sins
June 15, 1976,
Wuppertal, Opernhaus

Bluebeard. While Listening to a Taped Recording of Béla Bartók's "Duke Bluebeard's Castle"
January 8, 1977,
Wuppertal, Opernhaus

Come dance with me
May 26, 1977,
Wuppertal, Opernhaus

Renate Emigrates
December 30, 1977,
Wuppertal, Opernhaus

He Takes Her By the Hand And Leads Her Into The Castle, The Others Follow
April 22, 1978, Bochum, Schauspielhaus

Café Müller
May 20, 1978,
Wuppertal, Opernhaus

Kontakthof
December 9, 1978,
Wuppertal, Opernhaus

Arien
May 12, 1979,
Wuppertal, Opernhaus

Legend of Chastity
December 4, 1979,
Wuppertal, Opernhaus

*1980 – A Piece
by Pina Bausch*
May 18, 1980, Wuppertal, Schauspielhaus

Bandoneon
December 21, 1980,
Wuppertal, Opernhaus

Walzer
June 17, 1982, Amsterdam, Theater Carré

Nelken (Carnations)
December 30, 1982,
Wuppertal, Opernhaus

*On the Mountain
a Cry was Heard*
May 13, 1984, Wuppertal, Schauspielhaus

*Two Cigarettes
in the Dark*
March 31, 1985, Wuppertal, Schauspielhaus

Viktor
May 14, 1986, Wuppertal, Schauspielhaus

Ahnen
March 21, 1987, Wuppertal, Schauspielhaus

Palermo Palermo
December 17, 1989, Wuppertal, Opernhaus

Tanzabend II
April 27, 1991, Wuppertal, Schauspielhaus

The Piece with the Ship
January 16, 1993, Wuppertal, Opernhaus

Ein Trauerspiel
February 12, 1994, Wuppertal, Schauspielhaus

Danzón
May 13, 1995, Wuppertal, Schauspielhaus

Only You
May 11, 1996, Wuppertal, Schauspielhaus

The Window Washer
February 12, 1997, Wuppertal, Opernhaus

Masurca Fogo
April 4, 1998, Wuppertal, Schauspielhaus

O Dido
April 10, 1999, Wuppertal, Opernhaus

Kontakthof with Seniors
February 25, 2000, Wuppertal, Schauspielhaus

Wiesenland
May 5, 2000, Wuppertal, Schauspielhaus

Água
May 12, 2001, Wuppertal, Opernhaus

For the Children of yesterday, today and tomorrow
April 25, 2002, Wuppertal, Schauspielhaus

Nefés
March 21, 2003, Wuppertal, Opernhaus

Ten Chi
May 8, 2004, Wuppertal, Schauspielhaus

Rough Cut
April 15, 2005, Wuppertal, Schauspielhaus

Vollmond (Full Moon)
May 11, 2006, Wuppertal, Schauspielhaus

Bamboo Blues
May 18, 2007, Wuppertal, Schauspielhaus

Kontakthof with Teenagers
November 7, 2008, Wuppertal, Schauspielhaus

'Sweet Mambo'
May 30, 2008, Wuppertal, Schauspielhaus

"... como el musguito en la piedra, ay si, si, si..."
(Like Moss on the Stone)
June 12, 2009, Wuppertal, Opernhaus